Martin Guggenheim is Clinical Professor of Law and Director of the Juvenile Rights Clinic at the New York University School of Law. Previously, Mr. Guggenheim served as staff attorney and acting Director of the Juvenile Rights Project of the American Civil Liberties Union and as staff attorney for the Juvenile Rights Division of the New York City Legal Aid Society. Mr. Guggenheim has litigated many important cases concerning juvenile justice and children's rights. He is the co-author of *Standards Relating to Abuse and Neglect* and, along with Alan Sussman, of *The Rights of Parents*. He is also the author of numerous legal articles on juvenile law.

Alan N. Sussman is an attorney practicing law in Kingston, New York, with the firm of Ricken, Goldman, Sussman and Blythe. Additionally, he is Adjunct Associate Professor at the New York University School of Law where he teaches a course on juvenile justice. Previously, Mr. Sussman served as staff attorney for the Juvenile Rights Division of the New York City Legal Aid Society and as "Ombudsman" for the children in institutions under the authority of the New York State Division for Youth. He is the author of the First Edition of *The Rights of Young People*, co-author, along with Mr. Guggenheim, of *The Rights of Parents*, co-author of *Reporting Child Abuse and Neglect: Guidelines for Legislation*, and served as editor of the monthly ACLU publication, *Children's Rights Report*.

AN AMERICAN CIVIL LIBERTIES UNION HANDBOOK

THE RIGHTS OF YOUNG PEOPLE

Martin Guggenheim
and
Alan Sussman

General Editor of this series:
Norman Dorsen, President ACLU

BANTAM BOOKS
TORONTO • NEW YORK • LONDON • SYDNEY • AUCKLAND

THE RIGHTS OF YOUNG PEOPLE

A Bantam Book / published by arrangement with the American Civil Liberties Union

Bantam edition / April 1985

ISBN 0-553-24818-9

Published simultaneously in the United States and Canada

Bantam Books are published by Bantam Books, Inc. Its trademark, consisting of the words "Bantam Books" and the portrayal of a rooster, is Registered in U.S. Patent and Trademark Office and in other countries. Marca Registrada. Bantam Books, Inc., 666 Fifth Avenue, New York, New York 10103.

PRINTED IN THE UNITED STATES OF AMERICA

O 0 9 8 7 6 5 4 3 2 1

To Denise Guggenheim
and
Emily Dava Sussman

Acknowledgments for the First Edition

I would like to thank those who helped in the preparation of this work: Marilyn Allen, Rhonda Avidon, and Victoria Jung-Blythe for typing the manuscript; Lydia Tugendrajch, Jane Barrett, and Joseph Adams for research resulting in the charts of state laws that appear in the appendixes; Wayne Mucci and Barbara Flicker for opening the offices of the Juvenile Justice Standards Project for my perusal of reports; Peter D. Garlock for his initial input; Harriet Pilpel for her review of chapter II; and Marty Guggenheim of the American Civil Liberties Union, Peter B. Sandmann of the Youth Law Center, and David J. Lansner of the Legal Aid Society for their valuable criticisms and comments.

I am indebted to the authors of the previously published books on the rights of juveniles listed in the bibliography; especially the works of Samuel M. Davis, Sanford J. Fox, and the National Juvenile Law Center.

Finally, I express appreciation for the understanding and support of Melinda Brown.

Acknowledgments for the Second Edition

I would like to thank those who helped in the preparation of this work. Special thanks go to Jim Burns, for assistance in the research and editing of the entire book; Jane Hutta and Dan Parker for research resulting in the charts on state laws; Jim Morrissey and Janet Calvo for reviewing chapter VIII, "Medical Care, Contraception, Abortion, and Pregnancy" and for providing ideas and helpful suggestions; and Karen Stember, Jean Macnab, and Channabel Latham for seeing to it that the manuscript was typed with speed and accuracy.

A book of this breadth would be immeasurably more difficult to produce if existing works could not be relied upon. In preparing this book, all of the works listed in the bibliography were referred to. I am especially indebted to Professor Samuel M. Davis and his up-to-date, complete text on juvenile delinquency.

A special acknowledgment is due the New York University Law Center Foundation Faculty Research Program for its generous support.

Finally, I would like to thank my wife, Denise Guggenheim, for her patience and understanding.

MARTIN GUGGENHEIM

Contents

Preface

This guide sets forth your rights under the present law, and offers suggestions on how they can be protected. It is one of a continuing series of handbooks published in cooperation with the American Civil Liberties Union (ACLU).

Surrounding these publications is the hope that Americans, informed of their rights, will be encouraged to exercise them. Through their exercise, rights are given life. If they are rarely used, they may be forgotten and violations may become routine.

This guide offers no assurances that your rights will be respected. The laws may change and, in some of the subjects covered in these pages, they change quite rapidly. An effort has been made to note those parts of the law where movement is taking place, but it is not always possible to predict accurately when the law *will* change.

Even if the laws remain the same, their interpretations by courts and administrative officials often vary. In a federal system such as ours, there is a built-in problem of state and federal law, not to speak of the confusion between states. In addition, there are wide variations in the ways in which particular courts and administrative officials will interpret the same law at any given moment.

If you encounter what you consider to be a specific abuse of your rights, you should seek legal assistance. There are a number of agencies that may help you, among them, ACLU affiliate offices, but bear in mind that the ACLU is a limited-purpose organization. In many communities, there are federally funded legal service offices that provide assistance to persons who cannot afford the costs of legal representation. In general, the rights that the ACLU defends are freedom of inquiry and expression; due process of law; equal protection of the laws;

and privacy. The authors in this series have discussed other rights (even though they sometimes fall outside the ACLU's usual concern) in order to provide as much guidance as possible.

These books have been planned as guides for the people directly affected; therefore, the question and answer format. (In some areas there are more detailed works available for "experts.") These guides seek to raise the major issues and inform the nonspecialist of the basic law on the subject. The authors of these books are themselves specialists who understand the need for information at "street level."

If you encounter a specific legal problem in an area discussed in one of these handbooks, show the book to your attorney. Of course, he will not be able to rely exclusively on the handbook to provide you with adequate representation. But if your attorney hasn't had a great deal of experience in the specific area, the handbook can provide helpful suggestions on how to proceed.

NORMAN DORSEN, President
American Civil Liberties Union

The principal purpose of this handbook, as well as others in this series, is to inform individuals of their legal rights. The authors from time to time suggest what the law should be, but their personal views are not necessarily those of the ACLU. For the ACLU's position on the issues discussed in this handbook, the reader should write to Librarian, ACLU, 132 W. 43rd St., NY, NY 10036.

Introduction

The title of this book can be misleading, in part because the category "young people" is too broad. The subject matter incorporates the age range of infants to eighteen-year-olds. The problem presented by this sizable group concerns the term *rights*, which has vastly different meanings depending on the context.

Ordinarily when we speak of "rights," such as the right to vote, speak, travel, work and marry, we refer to laws that free individuals from external authority by granting them more control over their own destiny. These rights are guarantees that individuals who choose to engage in any of these activities will not be punished. On the other hand, laws that restrict choice by enjoining behavior are criminal or penal laws.

As applied to young people, ordinary language can be misleading. For obvious reasons, it is not possible to provide freedom of choice to infants and to the very young. Some of the laws that apply to very young children, although frequently called children's rights, enjoin adult behavior (child protection laws), while others impose affirmative duties on adults (child support laws). Many are actually *restrictive;* compulsory education laws, for instance, give children the "right" to go to school; but if they don't exercise this right, they may be punished.

Laws that make decisions for very young children are justified out of necessity, since they cannot make decisions for themselves. At some point as children grow up, however, these kinds of rights can become disabilities. The Supreme Court recently observed that "[c]onstitutional rights do not mature and come into being magically only when one attains the state-defined age of majority." This is because children do not become "persons" magically. As children develop, they gradually are able to make decisions for themselves. It is not easy to persuade a 17-year-old who wants to work that it is his "right" to be prohibited from taking a particular job, or a 16-year-old who wants to quit school that it is his right to be forced to attend daily, or a 17-year-old who wants to marry that it is his right not to be able to. In any event, this book covers all of these situations and could accurately be entitled *Young People and the Law*.

Two further observations may be helpful to the reader. Young people have disabilities imposed on them by their parents and by the state; they also have *rights* (in the adult sense of the word) which protect them from arbitrary actions by their parents and by the state. Yet, this book is not divided on this basis. Division by subject matter is preferable. But the reader should remember that this distinction permeates the book.

On the other hand, the disparate impact of laws on very young children and on adolescents has been recognized. Implicitly or explicitly, some laws affect only adolescents (abortion or contraceptive use rights, emancipation, and, generally, incorrigibility laws). Others, such as juvenile delinquency or child protection laws, affect all children. These distinctions are imperfect and there are unavoidable overlaps. Nonetheless, chapters I–VI affect all people under eighteen, while chapters VII–XI affect adolescents exclusively or to a disproportionate degree.

Writing a book of this genre is a challenging endeavor. Laws relating to children have changed dramatically in the past twenty years. The three prominent subject areas of this book—juvenile delinquency, child abuse and neglect, and adolescents' rights to medical treatment—reflect unparalleled legislative activity. Juvenile delinquency laws, for example, have undergone, and continue to undergo, radical reconsideration in each state capital. Since the landmark 1967 Supreme Court decision, *In re Gault*—with its stinging condemnation of many practices of juvenile courts—politicians and scholars have complained alternatively that juvenile justice is either too harsh or too lenient. Actually, what is under attack are the very premises of juvenile justice: that young people who commit crimes are "sick" and in need of rehabilitation, and that the state's only appropriate response to young law violators is treatment, not punishment. As a result, for the first time since their creation, many juvenile delinquency laws now frankly embrace punishment as their purpose and include determinate sentences.

In the area of child protection, the explanation for change is found in medical, social, and legal terms. Medically, the "discovery" of the battered-child syndrome occurred relatively recently (1962) and fostered a major rewriting of child-protection legislation in every state during the following decade. Socially, as children have been recognized as independent of their parents, laws relating to foster care, adoption, and termination of parental rights have been revised and expanded to account for current thinking. Legally, the combination of a wealth of legal scholarship in the 1970s, and a cadre of legal services lawyers representing parents and children, forced appellate courts for the first time, to consider the appropriateness and legality of many laws authorizing coercive state intervention into the family.

In the area of sex-related medical care, it was only twelve years ago that the Supreme Court first ruled that adult women have a constitutionally protected right to obtain an abortion. Since that time, the degree to which this right is applicable to sexually active, postpubescent women under age eighteen has been a controversial judicial issue. This has resulted in many important decisions that have broad implications for the rights of all adolescents, male and female.

As popular thinking about parents, families, and young people change, it should not be surprising to find laws changing as well. The rights, limitations, privileges, and disabilities that laws impose on young people, and the degree to which the state may intervene in the family and impose minimum conditions of care in the upbringing of children, are quintessential examples of the use of law as social experimentation. The debate over some of these issues has been waged at such a pitch in the past few years that, without predicting the direction, continued change should be anticipated. At present, if this book does its job, the reader will obtain a reasonable understanding of the complex laws currently affecting young people.

MARTIN GUGGENHEIM
New York, New York

THE RIGHTS OF YOUNG PEOPLE

I

Police and Pretrial Procedures

Arrest

On what grounds may police officers lawfully arrest a young person?

Young people may be arrested for virtually all the reasons that would justify the arrest of an adult, plus a variety of additional grounds as well.[1] Most states permit policemen to arrest a young person if they have reasonable grounds to believe that (1) he has committed a delinquent act; (2) he has run away from home; or (3) he or she is in need of supervision, or pursuant to a court order. In some states the latitude of grounds for arrest is even wider; for example, when a young person's surroundings "endanger his health or welfare."[2]

It should be noted that in the clear majority of states, the word *arrest* is not used in reference to juveniles; the phrase "taking into custody" is employed instead. This differentiates the juvenile court process, which is theoretically protective in nature, from the adult criminal system, which is penal. But even when states do not use the term *arrest*, the constitutional limits on policemen who take children into custody are much the same as those governing the arrest of adults.[3] (In this chapter, the terms *arrest* and *taken into custody* will be used interchangeably.)

Does a young person have the right to be arrested only on "probable cause"?

It depends on the activity for which the young person is arrested.

If the activity is one that would constitute a crime if

committed by an adult, it might be argued that a child has the right to be taken into custody only on those grounds that would permit police officers to arrest adults.[4] This would include the right to be free from arrests not supported by a warrant issued by an impartial magistrate, and those not supported by probable cause.[5] Most statutory schemes, however, permit police to arrest juveniles on grounds somewhat less strict than probable cause, such as "reasonable cause" or "when it appears. . . ." The pertinent California statute reads:

> A peace officer may, without a warrant, take into temporary custody a minor: (a) Who is under the age of 18 years when such officer has reasonable cause for believing that such minor is a person described in Section . . . 601 or 602, or (b) Who is a ward . . . of the juvenile court or concerning whom an order has been made under Section 636 or 702, when such officer has reasonable cause for believing that person has violated an order of the juvenile court or has escaped from any commitment ordered by the juvenile court, or (c) Who is under the age of 18 years and who is found in any street or public place suffering from any sickness or injury which requires care, medical treatment, hospitalization or other remedial care. . . .[6]

If a young person is arrested for being "in need of supervision," it is unlikely that the police have probable cause to believe that a "crime" was committed; nevertheless, an arrest for such activity is legal.[7]

In fact, most states grant police officers rather unlimited authority to take juveniles into custody in situations involving noncriminal conduct, under circumstances in which they are "endangered."[8] Although New York, for example, restricts the power of the police to arrest juveniles accused of crime to circumstances in which the police are empowered to arrest adults,[9] police officers in New York may pick up any child "who has run away from home or who in the reasonable opinion of the peace officer, appears to have run away from home."[10]

How does one know if an arrest has been made?

One may be arrested without being told. An arrest

occurs when someone has been taken into custody by the police, or otherwise deprived of freedom of action in any significant way.[11] If a young person is taken to a police station he is clearly under arrest, but one may also be under arrest if placed in a police car. Sometimes an arrest occurs when a person is only told to stop and to comply with a police officer's order. Usually, a police officer will say, "You are under arrest." If a young person doesn't know—and it is often unclear—he should simply ask the policeman, "Am I under arrest?"

Some courts have adopted a "reasonable belief" test to determine whether or not an arrest took place. Under this analysis the question is whether the individual stopped by the police reasonably believes he has been deprived of his or her freedom.[12] When this test is invoked, a juvenile may have *greater* reason than an adult to think that he or she has been arrested, and therefore greater justification to claim all the rights of arrested suspects, because a child's lack of maturity may cause the young person to believe that he or she is under greater compulsion to obey figures of authority.

Must a young person identify himself when asked to do so by a police officer?

It depends. Some states make it a crime if any person refuses to identify himself upon request by a police officer.[13] The Supreme Court has ruled, however, that a person may not be convicted for failing to tell a police officer his name and address, if there are no circumstances justifying a "reasonable suspicion" that the person was involved in criminal conduct.[14]

What are the rights of a young person if arrested?

First, one has the right *not* to answer any questions, except to supply one's name, age, address, and the name of one's parents, even if the police use force or intimidation which is illegal. Judges may not infer that a person is guilty because he has invoked the right not to answer questions; remaining silent does not imply guilt.

Second, the arrestee has the right to call his or her parents or a lawyer or both. If he does not have a lawyer, he has the right to ask for one.

Third, the arrestee has the right to stop answering

questions at any time, or to wait until his or her lawyer arrives before continuing.

Fourth, the arrestee must be informed that if he or she does answer any questions, anything said may be used against him or her in court.

These four rights, often called *Miranda* rights,[15] are warnings that the police are supposed to give to an arrested person before any interrogation takes place. If these rights have been violated, however, typically the only sanction imposed on the police will be that no information given to them may be used at the trial to convict the arrestee. However, if the arrestee pleads guilty, thereby avoiding a trial, no penalty will be imposed upon the police if *Miranda* rights have been violated.

Custody

Once arrested and taken into custody, does a child have the right to have his parents notified?

Yes. It is generally not enough to inform a child of the right to notify his or her parents; in most states the police must notify the parents themselves.[16]

After being arrested and taken into custody, does a young person have the right to be released in the custody of his parents?

The answer is a qualified yes. This does not mean that in every case an arrested child *will* be released to his or her parents; it means that the prevalent policy of most states is to release a child rather than placing him in a secure detention facility or a jail. In California, this choice is given legislative preference, and the California Supreme Court has determined that detention should be the *exception* rather than the rule, to be used only upon a showing of "immediate and urgent necessity."[17]

After an arrest, a police officer has a great deal of discretion as to the immediate disposition of the child. In most states there are usually no clearly delineated legal criteria set forth to guide police officers in making such decisions.[18] An officer may simply release the child in the custody of his parents, as permitted in thirty-six states. In some states, if the child is not released to his parents, he is turned over to a probation officer who must make this decision.[19] In Massachusetts, for example, the probation officer or arresting officer work in conjunction with the court that issued the arrest warrant,[20] in order to arrive at a final determination.

Confessions

Once arrested, if a young person is not given his *Miranda* warnings, may a confession be used against him?

No. Although the Supreme Court has not ruled on the applicability of *Miranda* to juvenile proceedings,[21] most state and federal courts that have considered the question have ruled that *Miranda* is fully applicable to these proceedings.[22] In addition, many states have passed laws that stipulate that *Miranda* warnings be read to juveniles when questioned by police officers, either directly, by incorporating the *Miranda* warnings[23] or indirectly, by restricting the admissibility of a juvenile's confession to circumstances where it is admissible for an adult.[24]

If the *Miranda* warnings are given and if a child subsequently confesses to an offense, does that mean that his subsequent confession will be used against him?

Not necessarily. *Miranda* warnings are only the minimum requirement for the admission of a confession. Confessions under *all* circumstances must be voluntary even when the *Miranda* warnings are properly given. If confessions are given under physical or psychological pressure or under coercive conditions, they may violate a suspect's Fifth- and Sixth-Amendment rights.[25] In such cases they may be declared inadmissible into evidence, even if *Miranda* warnings are given.

The confessions of young people are often given extrajudicial scrutiny to determine if they were voluntary, since juveniles may be more susceptible to coercion or intimidation than adults.[26] In overturning the conviction of a young person based on an involuntary confession, the United States Supreme Court stated, in a case decided before *Miranda:*

> [W]hen, as here, a mere child—an easy victim of the law—is before us, special care in scrutinizing the record must be used. . . . No friend stood at the

> side of this 15-year-old boy as the police, working in relays, questioned him hour after hour, from midnight until dawn. No lawyer stood guard to make sure that the police went so far and no farther, to see to it that they stopped short of the point where he became the victim of coercion. No counsel or friend was called during the critical hours of questioning.[27]

Ordinarily, once an adult is given the *Miranda* warnings, he has the privilege of *waiving* his rights; that is, he may decide to confess immediately, even after being told that he has a right to remain silent.[28] A young person, however, may not waive his rights so easily. His age, lack of understanding, and fear of authority may render his confession invalid or inadmissible even if he was read the *Miranda* warnings.[29] As stated by the Supreme Court:

> [W]e cannot believe that a lad of tender years is a match for the police in such a contest. He needs counsel and support if he is not to become first the victim of fear, then of panic.[30]

The burden of showing that the accused understood his rights before waiving them is on the prosecutor. No statement is admissible unless the prosecution can show that the accused knowingly and intelligently waived his rights.[31]

If a young person confesses to the police without first consulting with an interested adult, is the confession valid?

Not in many states. Although the United States Supreme Court does not require an adult's presence as a matter of federal law, states are free to establish their own rules. In Pennsylvania, for example, the lack of opportunity to confer with an interested adult renders a juvenile's confession inadmissible at trial.[32] Proof of guilt is necessary by means other than the juvenile's own statement.

A number of states have passed laws that render inadmissible a child's confession if it was not made in the presence of an interested adult, usually an attorney or relative.[33] This rule is based on the assumption that young people may not fully understand the import of the *Miranda* warnings and that the presence of an adult, interested in protecting the child's welfare, is necessary before an intelligent waiver can be made.

The majority of jurisdictions, however, reject the rule that confessions made without the presence of counsel or parents are per se inadmissible.[34] These states adopt the "totality of circumstances" doctrine that holds that whether or not a juvenile's post-*Miranda* confession is valid depends on a number of factors considered *together:* (1) whether or not an attorney or parents are present; (2) the age, education *and* maturity of the child; (3) his prior experience with the police process; and (4) the length of time he was detained before confessing.[35] Even under this doctrine, if the child is too young to understand the meaning of the *Miranda* warnings, or if he was detained for a long time before the confession is obtained, a child's waiver may be found to be involuntary and the confession may be suppressed.[36]

The Supreme Court recently decided a case from California in which a young person, after being given his *Miranda* warnings, refused to talk until he could see his probation officer.[37] The police denied his request and the child's subsequent confession was entered on the record at his trial and he was convicted. The Supreme Court ruled that the confession could be used against him and that its entry into evidence was proper. The Court reasoned that a request to see a probation officer was not the same as a request to see an attorney, since the former is not in a position to provide the type of legal assistance necessary to protect the constitutional rights of an accused. Thus, on the basis of the circumstances before the Court, it concluded that the child (who was over sixteen years old) voluntarily and knowingly consented to interrogation by the police after he had been properly forewarned that statements he made might be used against him.

By this decision, the Supreme Court has ruled that any statements made before a request for a lawyer is granted are inadmissible. When the *Miranda* warnings are properly given, however, and no request for counsel has been made, the Court will utilize the "totality of circumstances" rule to judge whether the statements made were voluntary. This is consistent with the rule for adults. The Supreme Court has held, for example, that an accused adult cannot be subjected to further interrogation before requested counsel is provided, unless the accused initiates communication with the police.[38]

Must the *Miranda* warnings be given in precise terms?

No. The Supreme Court recently held that the *Miranda* warnings need not be given in rigid or precise terms. If the essential meaning of *Miranda* is conveyed, a suspect's willingness to talk will be construed as a waiver of the right to remain silent. Thus, informing a juvenile in the presence of his parents that he has (1) the right to remain silent; (2) the right to talk to a lawyer; and (3) the right to have a lawyer appointed without cost to himself, may well be sufficient even if the police fail to inform him that free counsel will be appointed before any further questioning can take place.[39]

If a young person requests the presence of his parents instead of an attorney, may an admission made before their arrival be used against him?

Not in most states. The growing trend is to require police compliance with a juvenile's request to meet with his parents before any interrogation may continue.[40]

If a confession is taken illegally, are there any circumstances in which it still may be introduced at trial?

Yes. If the accused testifies at his own trial and his version of the facts differs from what he told the police, he may be asked in cross-examination to explain this discrepancy, and the confession—even though not prefaced with *Miranda* warnings—may be read to the judge or jury.[41]

Does the geographical place in which a young person's confession is taken affect its admissibility at trial?

Yes, in a few states. In these states there are rules or statutes directing the police to take a young person to a certain location (usually the juvenile court or special detention facilities) immediately after the arrest has been made. Confessions made by a young person at any other place (typically the police station) may be declared inadmissible on the grounds that they were gained in violation of the rule or statute.[42]

In some cases, however, if the *Miranda* warnings are given and if other circumstances indicate a voluntary atmosphere, a confession may be deemed admissible even if taken at an improper location.[43]

If an invalid confession of a young person leads the

police to further evidence, does he have the right to have the latter-acquired evidence suppressed?

Yes. The "fruits" of an invalid confession uttered by a young person are excludable from evidence, as is the confession itself.[44]

Bail

Do juveniles who are arrested and placed in detention have the right to be released on bail?

It depends on the state. Juveniles have the right to be released from detention by posting bail, as do adults, in Alabama, Arkansas, the District of Columbia, Georgia, Louisiana, Massachusetts, Oklahoma, South Dakota, and West Virginia.

There is no right to be released on bail, however, in California, Colorado, Connecticut, Florida, Hawaii, New Jersey, New York, Ohio, Oregon, Rhode Island, Texas, and Washington.

Decisions regarding bail are a matter of judicial discretion in Maine, Minnesota, Nebraska, South Carolina, Tennessee, Vermont, and Virginia.

California's highest court has held that juveniles have no right to be released on bail because the imposition of bail may result in a *loss* of liberty.[45] That is to say, if bail is required, a child's lack of financial resources may do more to insure that he remains in detention than permit his freedom. Instead, California law contains a preference for the release of children to the custody of their parents. Other courts have ruled that the release of a child to his parents is an accepted equivalent to bail.[46] In a New York case, a court found no law that permitted bail and it reiterated the statutory mandate that an arrested child either be detained in a juvenile center or released in the custody of his parents.[47] The New York court reasoned that fixing bail would unfairly make a child's detention or release dependent upon the financial circumstances of his parents.

If the right to be released on bail exists, are young people guaranteed the right to be free from excessive bail?

Yes. There is no reason why the Eighth Amendment's prohibition of excessive bail, and similar prohibitions in most state constitutions, do not apply to children as well as adults.[48] It is likely that the right to be free from excessive bail would be even more strictly applied to children, since they usually have little or no income or assets.

Detention Hearings

Is a child who has been placed in pretrial detention entitled to a detention hearing as soon as possible?

Yes, in most states. In a number of jurisdictions, a child's right to a hearing to challenge the detention is required by statute.[49] In other states a detention hearing has been established as a constitutional right by federal or state courts.[50]

In a few states, however, a child's detention may be legitimized solely by a court *order*, in which case he may not be entitled to a full detention hearing, though this is probably unconstitutional.[51]

How soon after a child is detained must a detention hearing be held?

The time limit varies by state.

In states that require hearings to be held within a certain period of time, the usual limit is within 48 or 96 hours of detention.[52] Some states merely require them to be held "promptly." In California, a detention hearing must be held within one judicial day after detention,[53] and in New York, it must be held within 72 hours.[54]

Pursuant to the Federal Juvenile Delinquency Act, an arrested child may not be detained "for longer than a reasonable period of time before brought before a magistrate." In one case, an 80-hour delay between an arrest and presentation before a magistrate was found to violate this provision[55] (and statements of the accused taken during this time were therefore ordered suppressed).

In practice, however, many children are held in confinement without hearings, since they are often detained by police over weekends when court is not in session, and then released.

If a child in detention is denied or not afforded a prompt detention hearing, does that constitute grounds for challenging his detention?

Yes. In such circumstances a child may file for a writ of habeas corpus or other appropriate remedy to secure a hearing or his release.[56]

If a detention hearing is held, what must the state prove in order to continue the detention of a child?

Recent cases indicate that it is not constitutional for the state merely to sustain allegations that a child is a danger to himself or others or that he is likely to flee the jurisdiction or that there are no parents or guardians willing to take custody of the child. According to these decisions, the state must prove that an offense was committed and that there is reasonable or probable cause to believe that the detained child committed the offense.[57] A number of states require by statute that probable cause be shown.[58]

Moreover, once probable cause is found a child may not be detained or remain in detention unless the state *also* proves that there is an immediate and urgent necessity for the protection of the minor or others or that he is likely to flee the jurisdiction of the court.[59]

Is preventive detention of juveniles permitted?

Yes, in almost every state, *preventive detention* (detaining an accused before trial to *prevent* anticipated, future criminal behavior) is permitted.[60] In 1984 the Supreme Court upheld the constitutionality of preventive detention of juveniles.[61]

If a detention hearing is held, may probable cause or other proof be sustained on the basis of hearsay evidence?

It depends on the state. Generally, hearsay evidence in detention hearings may sustain a finding of probable cause.[62] In some states, however, hearsay evidence alone is insufficient.[63]

Does a child have the right to be represented by an attorney at a detention hearing?

While a number of states have determined that such a right exists, it is not required by the Constitution.

An Alaska court recently upheld the right of a child to be represented by counsel at detention hearings by stating, "[D]ue process safeguards are necessary not only at the adjudicative hearing, but at any stage which may result in deprivation of the child's liberty."[64] New York and California also require representation by counsel.[65]

Nevertheless, the United States Supreme Court recently held that a probable cause hearing was not a "critical stage" of the criminal process (for adults),[66] thereby permitting states to determine pretrial probable cause without an adversary hearing at which counsel must be present.

What determination may a judge make at the end of a detention hearing?

A judge may order that the child (1) remain in secure detention; (2) be removed to a nonsecure setting such as a community-based group facility or a temporary foster home; or (3) be transferred to a shelter care or a psychiatric clinic if appropriate and necessary.

Of course, if the criteria for detention are not met, the judge must release the child pending the outcome of the *adjudicatory* (fact-finding) hearing.

Jail and Detention

What rights do young people have when held in a juvenile detention facility?

A person detained before trial is presumed innocent.[67] As such, a child who is detained has the right to be free of almost every restriction except those related to the purpose of insuring his presence at trial,[68] and his right to treatment[69] (see chapter IV).

A child in a detention facility has the right to—

1. adequate and sanitary physical conditions;
2. proper educational facilities and opportunities;
3. adequate recreational exercise periods;
4. sufficient illumination and air circulation;
5. access to competent medical and psychological care;
6. freedom from overcrowding;
7. proper clothing and bedding;
8. regular laundering;
9. necessary toilet and hygienic supplies;
10. regular visiting opportunities;
11. access to a library and reading matter.[70]

Like adults, children may not be punished while in pretrial detention[71] and children may be placed in isolation or solitary confinement only if certain strict and rigorous standards and procedures are adhered to by the institution.[72]

A child is also entitled to a place of detention that meets his individual or special needs.[73]

Do young people have the right not to be detained in an adult jail while awaiting trial?

Yes, in most states. Federal law prohibits states, as a condition of receiving federal moneys, from *regularly* confining accused delinquents with incarcerated adults.[74] As a result, a number of states prohibit the pretrial confinement of juveniles with adults.[75] Many states continue to permit children to be sent to adult jails under certain circumstances.

A number of states provide for the jailing of children with a court order,[76] but most permit it without a court order if the child is above a certain age or if he or she is a "menace" while in a juvenile detention facility. Some states permit the detention of young people in adult jails if no juvenile detention homes are available, with the condition that they be housed separately from the adult population.[77] In some cases, ironically, compliance with this rule results in children being placed in segregation or solitary confinement because few adult jails have facilities for juveniles apart from the general population.

Some children detained at jails with no separate facilities have successfully sued for release or for a change in conditions,[78] and at least one court found a young person's confinement with the general jail population without a probable cause hearing to constitute cruel and unusual punishment.[79]

It is common practice for young people to be detained in adult jails when local or regional juvenile detention facilities are filled to capacity. This practice was prohibited by an Arizona court that found that lack of space in a juvenile detention facility was not sufficient reason for placement in an adult jail, even when juveniles were given their own cells.[80]

Searches and Seizures

The Fourth Amendment guarantees citizens the right to be free from unreasonable searches and seizures. This right was held applicable to states by the Supreme Court in 1961,[81] and requires the suppression of all illegally obtained evidence.

Judicial interpretations of the Fourth Amendment have also led to limitations placed on warrantless searches incident to an arrest[82] and standards for obtaining search warrants.[83]

Does the Fourth-Amendment prohibition against unreasonable searches and seizures apply to juveniles?

Yes. No court considering the question has held the Fourth Amendment to be inapplicable to juvenile proceedings. This means that evidence taken from, or used against, a child, gained as a result of an unreasonable search and seizure, may not be introduced as evidence in a juvenile court hearing; a child is entitled to ask for its suppression.[84] In order to give this rule the full force of law, some state laws require that evidence admissible in juvenile court must be held to the same standards of admissibility as required in adult criminal trials.[85]

As in adult proceedings, however, there are many situations in which searches and seizures are legal. Limited searches that are conducted incident to lawful arrests, for example, are permitted,[86] as are searches conducted pursuant to lawfully issued search warrants and searches conducted with the consent of the individual.[87] On the other hand, if the arrest of a youth is unlawful or if a warrant does not provide a reliable description of the premises or is untimely executed, searches conducted thereto may be invalid.[88]

Does a minor have the legal capacity to consent to a search?

Like the matter of waiving one's *Miranda* rights, there is no clear answer to this question. Whether or not a child can be said to have consented to a search depends on a number of circumstances, such as the age and intelligence of the child as well as his knowledge at the time of the consent that he or she is waiving a constitutional right. Generally, courts favor the notion that a child is not aware of his rights and thus lacks the knowledge and capacity to waive them. Under this interpretation, even if a child consents to an improper search, evidence seized thereby may still not be admissible, especially if a child's "consent" was made under duress or coercion.[89]

Similarly, if consent is given as a result of misrepresentation or trickery on the part of the police, the consent cannot be said to be knowing. In a California case, for example, a child's consent was held invalid since entry into his apartment was gained by a policeman who posed as a "friend" of the landlord.[90]

If an individual's consent may legalize a search, can a parent or another adult provide the consent necessary for the lawful search of a child or a child's room?

Ordinarily, one person may not consent to the search of another, but most cases hold that a parent may legitimize the search of a home in which evidence is found and used against a child in juvenile court.[91] Under this interpretation, a child's protest or failure to consent to a search may be of no value whatsoever if his parents give law enforcement officials permission to conduct a search of the child's room or the entire home. This legal theory is based on the ground that a parent has a proprietary interest or immediate control of the area search.[92] A child, on the other hand, does not have the legal capacity to provide unilateral consent on his or her parent's behalf.[93]

There have been some qualifications of this rule. A Michigan court has held that parental consent is valid only so long as the search is limited to an area in the home commonly accessible to all members of the family, such as the basement.[94] This was followed by a second case in which a Michigan court found the search of a child's room invalid. The court stated that one's consent to search is a personal right (belonging to the child only, in this case) which cannot be waived by a parent who has "no punishable involvement in the crime suspected or charged."[95] In similar cases, a California court held that a sister of the suspect lacked the authority to consent to a search of the bedroom,[96] and a second court ruled that a father may not consent to a police search of his son's toolbox.[97]

Are searches of school lockers legal?

It depends on who conducts the search. The Fourth Amendment protects individuals from unreasonable searches conducted by law enforcement officers. Searches conducted by private individuals are not covered. Ironically, then, unreasonable searches of student lockers made by police officers, acting alone, may be illegal, and contraband seized may not be introduced into evidence at a trial, but searches by school principals or other ("private") school officials under certain circumstances may be legal and contraband found may be turned over to the police.[98] However, a few court rulings suggest that students may be protected from unreasonable searches conducted by some school officials as well as policemen.[99]

In addition to the "private" search rationale, cases justifying school official searches of student lockers have relied on theories (1) that the school has a duty to maintain the discipline, order, and protection of all pupils;[100] (2) that the school, acting *in loco parentis,* has the authority to consent to a search of a student's locker;[101] and (3) that since a student does not own his locker, he cannot protest its search.[102] A California case held that school officials may search student lockers, since they stand *in loco parentis,* if the search is within the school's duties and if the search is reasonable under the facts and circumstances. In this case the prevention of marijuana use was held to be within the duties of school officials and the search of a student's locker where marijuana was found was determined reasonable.[103]

What about body and clothing searches in school? Do children have a right to challenge them?

It depends on the state. The New York Court of Appeals has ruled that searches of *students* themselves (as distinguished from student *lockers*) are within the purview of the Fourth Amendment.[104] Significantly, the court found students to be protected from unreasonable searches by employees of the state, "whether they be police officers *or schoolteachers*."[105] The court set forth factors that would determine the reasonableness of the search. These include the age, history, and record of the student, the prevalence and seriousness of the problem in the school to which the search is directed, and the need to make the search without delay.[106] The case was distinguished from the school locker situation on the ground that a student has no reasonable expectation of privacy in a locker over which the school authorities have exclusive control, whereas a student has an expectation of privacy in his or her clothing and body.

In another New York case, the search of a student's coat pocket was held to come under the Fourth Amendment's prohibition against unreasonable searches and seizures since it was carried out by a uniformed high school security guard.[107] The guard, who was employed by the Board of Education, and *not* technically a peace officer, was held by the court to the same constitutional standards as a peace officer since he was acting as an agent of the government cloaked with police powers while safeguarding a municipal facility. The court determined that the security guard had no probable cause to suspect that the student possessed contraband, and the illegally seized evidence (a packet of marijuana) was not admitted into evidence.

In Illinois, on the other hand, a court upheld the legality of a search of a student's clothing by a school official because it constituted, in the words of the court, a "private search" that is not protected by the Fourth Amendment. All that is needed to justify a search in a school setting, the court concluded, is "reasonable suspicion" of illegal activity.[108] But even in Illinois, when the school official acts in concert with law enforcement officers in conducting the search, the search loses its private characterization and becomes an official search subject to the protections of the Fourth Amendment.[109]

Can trained dogs be used to sniff students' lockers and cars for drugs without a search warrant?

Yes. Courts that have decided this question have permitted school officials to bring dogs onto school premises that are trained to detect the odor of drugs in lockers.[110] It should be noted that these decisions do not reflect a diminution of the privacy rights of children. Instead, they conform with Fourth-Amendment cases affecting adults in which courts have adopted a doctrine of "public smell" (analogous to the exclusion from the Fourth-Amendment protection of things exposed to "public view"). Since dogs are being used only to smell odors that can otherwise be smelled in public, the use of dogs near school lockers is lawful.

Can trained dogs be used to sniff students themselves for drugs without a warrant?

Probably not. A federal court of appeals recently ruled that the interest in the integrity of one's person prohibits the use of dogs that sniff children since it is too intrusive a search violating an individual's expectation of privacy.[111] Such a use of dogs is lawful only when there is an individualized suspicion of illegal conduct.[111a]

Are police officers allowed to "stop and frisk" minors?

Yes. If the police officer reasonably suspects that the

person stopped has committed or is committing a crime and the officer suspects that he is in danger, a warrantless stop and frisk for weapons is permissible.[112]

Generally, however, stopping and frisking young people without resonable suspicion of a particular crime is illegal and evidence found pursuant to illegal frisks must be suppressed.[113]

On the other hand, it could be reasoned that "In Need of Supervision" statutes authorize police officers to arrest young people on a probable cause of truancy or if they suspect that they are runaways. Once legally arrested, a search of the person and a limited search of his immediate surroundings is authorized.[114]

Fingerprints and Photographs

Once arrested, does a young person have the right not to be fingerprinted and photographed?

It depends on the state. In about half of the states there are laws that limit the power of police (and juvenile courts) to fingerprint or photograph young persons after an arrest. The scope of the limitation, however, varies.

In some states the police are prohibited from taking fingerprints or photographs of young persons without the consent of a juvenile court judge.[115]

In others, fingerprints and photographs may be taken only if there exists a strong suspicion that the child has committed a serious or felonious offense,[116] or if juveniles above a certain age are arrested for serious felonies.[117]

In a few states there are restrictions on police practices of filing and disseminating fingerprints and photographs. The law, for example, may require that fingerprints and photographs of young people be kept separate and apart from those of adults or that copies may not be forwarded to the Federal Bureau of Investigation or both.[118]

Do children have the right to have records of fingerprints and photographs destroyed or returned?

Some state laws permit the destruction or return of lawfully taken fingerprints and photographs when certain conditions are met. All copies of prints and photos taken of children under 16 in New Jersey, for example, must be forwarded to the juvenile court for destruction when the court determines that the purpose for which they were permitted (comparison and identification) have been fulfilled.[119] In New York, if a child is not found to be delinquent or is found to have committed an offense constituting a crime less severe than a felony, all fingerprints, palmprints, and photographs taken must be destroyed.[120] Even if the child is adjudicated delinquent for a felony, all copies of fingerprints and photographs must be destroyed when the young person reaches the age of 21 if there is no record of criminal convictions after age 16.[121] In Georgia, photographs and fingerprints will be destroyed if the case against a child is not filed or is dismissed. In all other cases, the records will be destroyed when the child reaches the age of 21, as long as he has no criminal record beyond the age of 16.[122]

When fingerprints and photographs are *unlawfully* taken, it is likely that a juvenile court has the power to order their destruction;[123] but when they are taken lawfully, and when there is no statutory mechanism to provide for their destruction or expungement, there is considerable controversy over whether a juvenile court has the authority to order the police to destroy or expunge their records.

In Indiana, copies of fingerprints and photographs must be destroyed or returned to the child if charges were not filed or were subsequently dismissed by juvenile court, so long as the youth has no record of prior arrests nor additional charges pending.[124]

Identification and Lineups

Do juvenile suspects have the right to be protected against improper identification at lineups?

Yes. In 1967, the United States Supreme Court rendered three important decisions outlining the rights of adults in police lineups that protected them from improper identification. In *U.S. v. Wade* the Supreme Court held that the Sixth Amendment requires the presence of counsel at a lineup when a defendant is later identified in court as a result of that lineup.[125] In *Gilbert v. California* the Court ruled that testimony as to the identity of a defendant made at such a lineup could not be admitted into evidence,[126] and in *Stovall v.*

Denno it held that any identification procedure that is unfairly suggestive or conducive to mistake violates a defendant's Fourteenth-Amendment right to due process.[127]

The Supreme Court has not ruled on the application of these cases to juvenile court proceedings. It is reasonable, however, to assume that the philosophy established in *In re Gault* and its progeny,[128] extending the rule of fundamental fairness and due process to juvenile court proceedings, establishes the right to be free from improper identification.

At least five state courts, in fact, have so ruled. In California, a witness's identification of a child at a confrontation arranged by the police, wherein the juvenile defendant was the only suspect present, was held to be improper.[129] A Rhode Island court overturned the conviction of a youth who was improperly identified by a witness at a police lineup where he was not represented by counsel.[130] New York, Pennsylvania, and Washington, D.C., courts have also looked suspiciously at similarly tainted identifications of juveniles.[131]

NOTES

1. *See, e.g.*, WELF. & INST. CODE §625 (Supp. 1982): *In re Daniel R.*, 274 Cal. App. 2d 749, 79 Cal. Rptr. 247 (1969).
2. *See, e.g.*, *In re James L.*, 194 N.E.2d 797 (Ohio Juv. Ct. 1963).
3. *See, e.g.*, GA. CODE ANN. §24A–1301 (1982); TENN. CODE ANN. §37–213(b) (Supp. 1982); OHIO REV. CODE ANN. §2151.31 (Supp. 1981).
4. *See, e.g.*, N.Y. FAM. CT. ACT §§305.2(1), (2) (1983).
5. *Michigan v. Summers*, 452 U.S. 692 (1981); *U.S. v. Mendenhall*, 446 U.S. 544 (1980); *Ybarra v. Illinois*, 444 U.S. 85 (1979); *Michigan v. DeFillippo*, 443 U.S. 31 (1979); *Dunaway v. New York*, 442 U.S. 200 (1979); *Spinelli v. U.S.*, 393 U.S. 410 (1969); *Beck v. Ohio*, 379 U.S. 89 (1964).
6. CAL. WELF. & INST. CODE §625 (Supp. 1982).
7. *See, e.g.*, WELF. & INST. CODE §601 (S. 1982): OHIO REV. CODE ANN. §2151.31(c) (Supp. 1981): *In re Daniel R.*, 274 Cal. App. 2d 749, 79 Cal. Rptr. 247 (1969).
8. MINN. STAT. ANN. §260.165(1)(c)(2) (1982); OHIO REV. CODE ANN. §2151.31(c) (Supp. 1981).
9. N.Y. FAM. CT. ACT §§305.2(1), (2) (1983).
10. *Id.* at §718(b) (1983).
11. *Dunaway v. New York*, *supra* note 6; *Miranda v. Arizona*, 384 U.S. 436, 444 (1966).
12. *Seals v. U.S.*, 325 F.2d 1006 (D.C. Cir. 1963); *Kelly v. U.S.*, 298 F.2d

310 (D.C. Cir. 1961); *In re Appeal in Pima Co.*, 110 Ariz. 98, 515 P.2d 600 (1973).

13. Tex. Penal Code Ann. tit. 8, §38.02(a) (1974).
14. *Brown v. Texas*, 443 U.S. 47 (1979).
15. *Miranda v. Arizona*, *supra* note 11, held applicable in juvenile cases: *People v. Horton*, 261 N.E.2d 693 (Ill. App. 1970); *In re Creek*, 243 A.2d 49 (D.C. Ct. App. 1968); *In re Aaron D.*, 30 A.D.2d 183, 290 N.Y.S.2d 935 (1st Dept. 1968); *Leach v. State*, 428 S.W.2d 817 (Tex. Civ. App. 1968). *See also* Cal. Welf. & Inst. Code §625 (Supp. 1982).
16. *See, e.g.*, Wis. Stat. Ann. §48.19(2) (Supp. 1982); N.Y. Fam. Ct. Act §305.2(3) (1983); *Cox v. Turley*, 506 F.2d 1347 (6th Cir. 1974). *See* contra, *In re Fletcher*, 251 Md. 520, 248 A.2d 364 (1968), *cert. denied*, 396 U.S. 852 (1969).
17. Cal. Welf. & Inst. Code §635 (Supp. 1982); *In re William M.*, 3 Cal. 3d 16, 473 P.2d 737, 89 Cal. Rptr. 33 (1970).
18. *But see* Ky. Rev. Stat. Ann. §208.120 (1977); N.M. Stat. Ann. §32–1–24 (1981); N.Y. Fam. Ct. Act §§305.2, 307.3 (1983); Wis. Stat. Ann. §48.205(1) (1979 & Supp. 1982).
19. *See, e.g.*, Ill. Ann. Stat. ch. 37 §§703–2, 703–4 (Supp. 1982); Tex. Fam. Code Ann. §52.02 (1975).
20. Mass. Gen. Laws Ann. ch. 119 §67 (Supp. 1982).
21. *Fare v. Michael C.*, 442 U.S. 707, 717 n.4 (1979).
22. *See, e.g.*, *In re Meyers*, 25 N.C. App. 555, 214 S.E.2d 268 (1975); *In re Rust*, 53 Misc. 2d 51, 278 N.Y.S.2d 333 (1967); *In re Creek*, 243 A.2d 49 (D.C. Ct. App. 1968); *Leach v. State*, 428 S.W.2d 817 (Tex. Civ. App. 1968). *But see* special circumstances permitting the admissibility of confessions in the absence of *Miranda* warnings; i.e., *In re Orr*, 38 Ill. 2d 417, 231 N.E.2d 242, *cert. denied*, 391 U.S. 924, (1967).
23. *See, e.g.*, Cal. Welf. & Inst. Code §§625, 627.5 (1972 & Supp. 1982); Colo. Rev. Stat. Ann. §19–2–102(3)(c)(I) (1978); Okla. Stat. Ann. tit. 10, §1109(a) (Supp. 1981).
24. *See, e.g.*, Ga. Code Ann. §24A–200(z) (1982); Tenn. Code Ann. §37–227(b) (1977).
25. *See, e.g.*, *Sims v. Georgia*, 385 U.S. 538 (1967); *Escobedo v. Illinois*, 378 U.S. 478 (1964); *Brown v. Mississippi*, 297 U.S. 278 (1936).
26. *See, e.g.*, *Haley v. Ohio*, 332 U.S. 596 (1948); *Gallegos v. Colorado*, 370 U.S. 49 (1962); *Husk v. State*, 305 So.2d 19 (Fla. Dist. Ct. App. 1974), *aff'd*, 332 So.2d 699 (Fla. Dist. Ct. App. 1976).
27. *Haley v. Ohio*, *supra* note 26, at 599–600.
28. *See, e.g.*, *Johnson v. Zerbst*, 304 U.S. 458 (1938).
29. *In re Gault*, 387 U.S. 1, 55 (1967).
30. *Haley v. Ohio*, *supra* note 26, at 599–600.
31. *Tague v. Louisiana*, 444 U.S. 469 (1980).
32. *Commonwealth v. Henderson*, 437 A.2d 387 (Pa. 1981). *See also*, *People v. Rivera*, 78 A.D.2d 556, 431 N.Y.S.2d 1015 (2d Dept. 1980); *In re K.W.B.*, 500 S.W.2d 275 (Mo. Ct. App. 1973); *In re Aaron D.*, 30 A.D.2d 183, 290 N.Y.S.2d 935 (1st Dept. 1968).

33. Colo. Rev. Stat. §19–2–102, §3(c)(I) (1978); Conn. Gen. Stat. Ann. §466–137 (Supp. 1982); Okla. Stat. Ann. tit. 10, §1109(a) (Supp. 1981); Tex. Fam. Code Ann. §51.09 (Supp. 1982). *But see People v. L.A.*, 609 P.2d 116 (Colo. 1980).
34. *See, e.g., State v. Jackson*, 118 Ariz. 270, 576 P.2d 129 (1978); *Harris v. Commonwealth*, 217 Va. 715, 232 S.E.2d 751 (1977); *In re Thompson*, 241 N.W.2d 2 (Iowa 1976).
35. *See, e.g., West v. U.S.*, 399 F.2d 467 (5th Cir. 1968); *In re Welfare of Deane*, 619 P.2d 1002 (Wash. Ct. App. 1980); *State ex rel. T.S.V.*, 607 P.2d 827 (Utah 1980); *Edwards v. State*, 227 Kan. 723, 608 P.2d 1006 (1980); *In re S.W.T.*, 279 N.W.2d 507 (Minn. 1979); *People v. Lara*, 67 Cal. 2d 365, 432 P.2d 202, 62 Cal. Rptr. 586, (1967), *cert. denied*, 392 U.S. 945 (1968).
36. *Gallegos v. Colorado, supra* note 26. *See, e.g., State ex rel. Holifield*, 319 So.2d 471 (La. Ct. App. 1975); *Walker v. State*, 12 Md. App. 684, 280 A.2d 260 (1971); *In re Rambeau*, 266 Cal. App. 2d 1, 72 Cal. Rptr. 171 (1968).
37. *Fare v. Michael C., supra* note 21. *See also People v. Maes*, 194 Colo. 235, 571 P.2d 305 (1977).
38. *Edwards v. Arizona*, 451 U.S. 471 (1981). *See also Rhode Island v. Innis*, 446 U.S. 291 (1980); *People v. Taylor*, 61 Ill. App. 3d 37, 377 N.E.2d 838 (1978), *aff'd*, 76 Ill. 2d 289, 391 N.E.2d 366 (1979).
39. *California v. Prysock*, 453 U.S. 355 (1981).
40. *See, e.g., In re Patrick Stephen W.*, 163 Cal. Rptr. 848 (Ct. App. 1980); *Dowst v. State*, 336 So.2d 375 (Fla. Dist. Ct. App.), *cert. denied*, 339 So.2d 1172 (1976) *State ex rel. Dino*, 359 So.2d 586 (La.) *cert. denied*, 439 U.S. 1047 (1978); and cases cited in *supra* note 32. Cf. *U.S. ex rel. Riley v. Franzen*, 653 F.2d 1153 (7th Cir. 1981).
41. *Harris v. New York*, 401 U.S. 222 (1971).
42. *See, e.g., U.S. v. Binet*, 442 F.2d 296 (2nd Cir. 1971); *In re L.R.S.*, 573 S.W.2d 888 (Tex. Civ. App. 1978); *In re Schirner*, 264 Pa. Super. 1185, 399 A.2d 728 (1979); *State v. Shaw*, 93 Ariz. 40 378 P.2d 487 (1963); *State v. Arbeiter*, 408 S.W.2d 26 (Mo. 1966); *People v. Wolff*, 23 Mich. App. 550, 179 N.W.2d 206 (1970); *In re A.J.A.*, 248 So.2d 690 (Fla. App. 1971).
43. *See, e.g., State v. Hogan*, 297 Minn. 430, 212 N.W.2d 664 (1973); *In re Turner*, 56 Misc. 2d 638, 289 N.Y.S.2d 652 (1968). *See also Emilio M. v. City of New York*, 37 N.Y.2d 173, 332 N.E.2d 874, 371 N.Y.S.2d 697 (1975); *People v. Zepeda*, 116 Ill. App. 2d 246, 253 N.E.2d 598 (1969).
44. *Davis v. Mississippi*, 394 U.S. 721 (1969); *Lynumn v. Illinois*, 372 U.S. 528 (1963).
45. *In re William M.*, 3 Cal. 3d 16, 473 P.2d 737, 89 Cal. Rptr. 33 (1970) (citing Cal. Welf. & Inst. Code §635). *See also L.O.W. v. District Ct.*, 623 P.2d 1253 (Colo. 1981).
46. *Baldwin v. Lewis*, 300 F. Supp. 1220 (E.D. Wis. 1969), *rev'd on other grounds*, 442 F.2d 29 (7th Cir. 1971); *In re Castro*, 243 Cal. App.2d 402, 52 Cal. Rptr. 469 (1966).

47. *People ex rel Wayburn v. Schupf,* 47 A.D.2d 79, 365 N.Y.S.2d 235 (2nd Dept. 1975). *See also Aubry v. Gadbois,* 50 Cal. App.3d 470, 123 Cal. Rptr. 365 (1975). *But see In re Donald D.,* 96 Misc. 2d 870, 410 N.Y.S.2d 36 (Fam. Ct. 1978).
48. *See, e.g., Ex parte Osborne,* 75 S.W.2d 265 (Tex. Crim. App. 1934).
49. *See, e.g.,* CAL. WELF. & INST. CODE §632 (Supp. 1982); ME. REV. STAT. ANN. tit. 15, 3203 (1980 & Supp. 1982); N.Y. FAM. CT. ACT §307.4 (1983).
50. *Baldwin v. Lewis, supra* note 46; *Cox v. Turley,* 506 F.2d 1347 (6th Cir. 1974); *Cooley v. Stone,* 414 F.2d 1213 (D.C. Cir. 1969); *T.K. v. State,* 126 Ga. App. 269, 190 S.E.2d 588 (1972); *State ex rel. Morrow v. Lewis,* 55 Wis. 502, 200 N.W.2d 193 (1972); *Doe v. State,* 487 P.2d 47 (Alaska 1971); *In re Colar,* 9 Cal. App. 3d 613, 88 Cal. Rptr. 651 (1970).
51. *See Grannis v. Ordean,* 234 U.S. 385, 394 (1914); *Armstrong v. Manzo,* 380 U.S. 545, 552 (1965). *But see State v. Banks,* 271 Ark. 331, 609 S.W. 2d 10 (1981).
52. *See, e.g.,* IND. CODE §31–6–4–5 (f) (Supp. 1982).
53. CAL. WELF. & INST. CODE §632 (Supp. 1982).
54. N.Y. FAM. CT. ACT §307.4 (1983).
55. 18 U.S.C. §5033 (1976); *U.S. v. DeMarce,* 513 F.2d 755 (8th Cir. 1975).
56. *See, e.g., T.K. v. State, supra* note 50; *State ex rel. Morrow v. Lewis,* 55 Wis. 2d 502, 200 N.W.2d 193 (Wis. 1972); *Fullwood v. Stone,* 394 F.2d 939 (D.C. Cir. 1967); cases cited in *supra* note 50.
57. *Moss v. Weaver,* 525 F.2d 1258 (5th Cir. 1976); *Cooley v. Stone, supra* note 34; *Baldwin v. Lewis, supra* note 30; *Roberts v. Mills,* 290 Or. 441, 622 P.2d 1094 (1981); *Bell v. Superior Court,* 117 Ariz. 551, 574 P.2d 39 (Ct. App. 1977); *State ex rel. Joshua,* 327 S.2d 429 (La. Ct. App.), *cert. denied,* 329 So. 2d 450 (La. 1976); *Cox v. Turley,* 506 F.2d 1347 (6th Cir. 1974); *Black Bonnet v. State,* 357 F. Supp. 889 (D.S.D. 1973); *People ex rel. Guggenheim v. Mucci,* 32 N.Y. 2d 307, 298 N.E. 2d 109, 344 N.Y.S.2d 944 (1973). Contra, *Morris v. D'Amario,* 416 A.2d 137 (R.I. 1980).
58. *See, e.g.,* ALASKA STAT. §47.10.140(c) (1979); D.C. CODE §16–2312 (Supp. 1982); ILL. ANN. STAT. ch. 37, §703–6 (Supp. 1982); ME. REV. STAT. ANN. tit. 15, §3203 (5) (D) (1980); N.Y. FAM. CT. ACT §§325.1-325.3 (1983).
59. *See e.g., Doe v. State,* 478 P.2d 47 (Alaska 1971); *In re William M.,* 3 Cal. 3d 16, 89 Cal. Rptr. 33, 473 P.2d 737 (1970); *Commonwealth ex rel. Sprowal v. Hendricks,* 438 Pa. 435, 265 A.2d 348 (1970).
60. *See e.g.,* ALASKA STAT. §47.10.140 (1979); CAL. WELF. & INST. CODE §§628, 635 (Supp. 1982); COLO. REV. STAT. §19–2–103 (1978 & Supp. 1981); D.C. CODE §16–2310 (Supp. 1978); FLA. STAT. §39.03 (Supp. 1981), GA. CODE ANN. §24A–1401 (1981); HAW. REV. STAT. §571–32 (Supp. 1981); ILL. REV. STAT. ch 37, §703–4 (Supp. 1982); IND. CODE §31–6–4–5 (1979 & Supp. 1982); IOWA CODE ANN. §232.22 (Supp. 1982); KAN. STAT. ANN. §38–815b(c) (Supp. 1981);

Ky. Rev. Stat. §208.110 (1977); La. Rev. Stat. Ann. §13:1577 (Supp. 1982); Md. Cts. & Jud. Proc. Code Ann. §3–815 (1980 & Supp. 1982); Mich. Comp. Laws §712A.15 (Supp. 1982); Minn. Stat. §260.171 (1982); Miss. Code Ann. §43–23–11 (1981); N.J. Stat. Ann. §2A:4–56 (Supp. 1977); N.M. Stat. Ann. §32–1–24 (1981); N.Y. Fam. Ct. Act §320.5(3)(b) (1983); N.D. Cent. Code §27–20–14 (1974); Ohio Rev. Code Ann. §2151.31 (Supp. 1981); Oreg. Rev. Stat. §419.573 (1981); Pa. Stat. Ann. tit. 42, §6325 (1978); Tenn. Code Ann. §37-214 (Supp. 1982); Utah Code Ann. §78–3a–30 (1977); Vt. Stat. Ann. tit. 33, §§643 (1981); Va. Code §16.1.248 (1982); Wyo. Stat. §14–6–206 (1978). There are 5 states in which preventive detention is prohibited (Arkansas and Massachusetts.)

61. *Schall v. Martin*, ____ U.S. ____ (1984).
62. *Gerstein v. Pugh*, 420 U.S. 103 (1975); *Moss v. Weaver, supra* note 57; Cal. Rules of Court R. 1323(c) (1980).
63. *See, e.g., People ex rel. Guggenheim v. Mucci*, 46 A.D.2d 683, 360 N.Y.S.2d 71 (2nd Dept. 1974); N.Y. Fam. Ct. Act §325.2(3) (1983).
64. *Doe v. State supra* note 50. *See also T.K. v. State, supra* note 50.
65. N.Y. Fam. Ct. Act §307.4(2) (1983), *People ex rel. Lauring v. Mucci*, 44 A.D.2d 479, 355 N.Y.S.2d 786 (1st Dept. 1974); Cal. Welf. & Inst. Code §633 (1971).
66. *Gerstein v. Pugh, supra* note 62, modifying *Coleman v. Alabama*, 399 U.S. 1 (1970).
67. *Bell v. Wolfish*, 441 U.S. 520 (1979); *Swansey v. Elrod*, 386 F. Supp. 138 (N.D. Ill. 1975); *Jones v. Wittenberg*, 323 F. Supp. 93 (N.D. Ohio 1971), *aff'd Jones v. Metzger*, 456 F.2d 854 (6th Cir. 1972).
68. *Bell v. Wolfish, supra* note 67; *Covington v. Harris*, 419 F.2d 617 (D.C. Cir. 1969).
69. *Martarella v. Kelly*, 349 F. Supp. 575 (S.D.N.Y. 1972); 359 F. Supp. 478 (S.D.N.Y. 1973).
70. *Swansey v. Elrod, supra* note 67; *Martarella v. Kelly, supra* note 69; *Fulwood v. Stone*, 394 F.2d 939 (D.C. Cir. 1967); *Creek v. Stone*, 379 F.2d 106 (D.C. Cir. 1967); *Tommy P. v. Board of County Commissioners*, 97 Wash. 2d 385 645 P.2d 697 (1982); *In re L.*, 24 Or App. 257, 546 P.2d 153 (1975).
71. *Bell v. Wolfish, supra* note 67; *Baker v. Hamilton*, 345 F. Supp. 345 (W.D. Ky. 1972); *Anonymous v. State*, 517 P.2d 183 (Nev. 1973); cases cited in *supra* note 70.
72. *Baker v. Hamilton, supra* note 71.
73. *In re Harris*, 2 Crim. L. Rptr. 2412 (Ill. Juv. Ct. 1967); *In re Savoy*, 98 Wash. L. Rptr. 1236 (D.C. Juv. Ct. 1970).
74. The Juvenile Justice and Delinquency Prevention Act of 1974, 42 U.S.C. §5633(13) (Supp. 1980).
75. *See, e.g.*, Pa. Stat. Ann. tit. 42, §6327 (1982); *State ex rel. R.C.F. v. Wilt*, 252 S.E.2d 168 (W. Va. 1978).
76. *See, e.g., C.C.C. v. District Court*, 188 Colo. 437, 535 P.2d 1117 (1975).
77. *See, e.g.*, Ohio Rev. Code Ann. tit. 21 §2151.312 (1976).

78. *Miller v. Carson*, 392 F. Supp. 515 (M.D. Fla. 1975); *Baker v. Hamilton*, *supra* note 71; *White v. Reid*, 125 F. Supp. 647 (D.D.C. 1954).
79. *Cox v. Turley*, *supra* note 50.
80. *Anonymous Juvenile in Pima County v. Collins*, 21 Ariz. 140 517 P.2d 98 (1973). *See also Swansey v. Elrod*, *supra* note 67; *Miller v. Carson*, *supra* note 78; *Osorio v. Rios*, 429 F. Supp. 570 (D.P.R. 1976).
81. *Mapp v. Ohio*, 367 U.S. 643 (1961).
82. *See, e.g.*, *New York v. Belton*, 453 U.S. 454 (1981); *Michigan v. DeFillippo*, *supra* note 6; *Chimel v. California*, 395 U.S. 752 (1969).
83. *See, e.g.*, *Franks v. Delaware*, 438 U.S. 154 (1978); *U.S. v. Harris*, 403 U.S. 573 (1971); *Spinelli v. U.S.*, *supra* note 6; *Aguilar v. Texas*, 378 U.S. 108 (1964).
84. *See, e.g.*, *Brown v. Fauntleroy*, 442 F.2d 838 (D.C. Cir. 1971); *State v. Gordon*, 219 Kan. 643, 549 P.2d 886 (1976); *J.M.A. v. State*, 542 P.2d 170 (Alaska 1975); *Nelson v. State*, 319 So. 2d 154 (Fla. Dist. Ct. App. 1975); *Dixon v. State*, 23 Md. App. 19, 327 A.2d 516 (1974); *In re Harvey*, 222 Pa. Super. 222, 295 A.2d 93 (1972); *In re Marsh*, 40 Ill. 2d 53, 237 N.E. 2d 529 (1968); *State v. Lowry*, 95 N.J. Super. 307, 230 A. 2d 907 (1967).
85. Cal. Welf. & Inst. Code §70 (Supp. 1982); GA. CODE ANN. §24A–2002 (1982); ILL. ANN. STAT. ch. 37, §704–6 (Supp. 1982); MISS. CODE ANN. §§43–21–203(4), 43–21–559(1) (1981); TEX. FAM. CODE ANN. §54.03 (3) (1982).
86. *See, e.g.*, *Hardy v. Cunningham*, 167 N.W.2d 508 (N.D. 1969); *State in Interest of L.B.*, 99 N.J. Super. 589, 240 A.2d 709 (1968).
87. *See generally U.S. v. Mendenhall*, *supra* note 6; *Schneckloth v. Bustamonte*, 412 U.S. 218 (1973); *Bumper v. North Carolina*, 391 U.S. 543 (1968); *State v. Johnson*, 68 N.J. 349, 346 A.2d 66 (1975).
88. *Dunaway v. New York*, *supra* note 6; Davis v. Mississippi, 394 U.S. 721 (1969); *State v. Bishop*, 46 Or. App. 607, 612 P.2d 744 (1980); *Kwok T. v. Mauriello*, 43 N.Y.2d 213, 371 N.E.2d 814, 401 N.Y.S. 2d 52 (1977); *Ciulla v. State*, 434 S.W.2d 943 (Tex. Civ. App. 1968).
89. *See, e.g.*, *In re Williams*, 49 Misc.2d 154, 267 N.Y.S.2d 91 (Fam. Ct. 1966). *See contra In re Ronny*, 40 Misc. 2d 194, 242 N.Y.S.2d 844 (Fam. Ct., 1963).
90. *In re Robert T.*, 8 Cal. App. 3d 990, 88 Cal. Rptr. 37 (1970).
91. *Grant v. State*, 267 Ark. 60, 589 S.W.2d 11 (1979); *People v. Mortimer*, 46 A.D.2d 275, 361 N.Y.S.2d 955 (1974); *Urbasek v. People*, 76 Ill. App.2d 375, 222 N.E.2d 233 (1966); *State v. Carder*, 9 Ohio St. 2d 1, 222 N.E.2d 620 (1966).
92. *Chapman v. U.S.*, 365 U.S. 610 (1961); *U.S. v. Stone*, 401 F.2d 32 (7th Cir. 1968); *Tolbert v. State*, 224 Ga. 291, 161 S.E.2d 279, *cert. denied*, 393 U.S. 1005, (1968).
93. *May v. State*, 199 So.2d 635 (Miss. 1967). *But see In re Robert H.*, 78 Cal. App. 3d 894, 144 Cal. Rptr. 565 (1978).
94. *People v. Bunker*, 22 Mich. App. 396, 177 N.W.2d 644 (1970).

95. *People v. Flowers*, 23 Mich. App. 523, 179 N.W.2d 56 (1970), relying on *Stoner v. California*, 376 U.S. 483 (1964).
96. *Beach v. Superior Court*, 11 Cal. App. 3d 10o32, 90 Cal. Rptr. 200 (1970).
97. *In re Scott K.*, 24 Cal. 3d 395, 595 P.2d 105, 155 Cal. Rptr. 671 (1979).
98. *People v. Overton*, 20 N.Y.2d 360, 283 N.Y.S.2d 22, 229 N.E.2d 596 (1967); *reconsidered*, 24 N.Y.2d 522, 301 N.Y.S.2d 479, 249 N.E.2d 366 (1969); *In re Donaldson*, 75 Cal. Rptr. 220, 269 Cal. App.2d 220 (1969); *In re Boykin*, 39 Ill. 2d 617, 237 N.E.2d 460 (1968).
99. *See, e.g., People v. Scott D.*, 34 N.Y.2d 483, 358 N.Y.S.2d 403, 315 N.E.2d 266 (1974); *People v. Bowers*, 72 Misc. 2d 800, 339 N.Y.S.2d 783 (Crim. Ct. 1973); *State v. Baccino*, 282 A.2d 869 (Del. Super. Ct. 1971); *Waters v. U.S.*, 311 A.2d 835 (D.C. 1973).
100. *Commonwealth v. Dingfelt*, 322 A.2d 145 (Pa. 1974).
101. *People v. Overton*, *supra* note 98; *In re Donaldson*, *supra* note 75.
102. *People v. Overton*, *supra* note 98.
103. *In re W.*, 29 Cal. App. 3d 777, 105 Cal. Rptr. 775 (1973).
104. *People v. Scott D.*, *supra* note 99.
105. *Id.* at 485 (emphasis added). *See also State v. Mora*, 307 So.2d 317 (La.); *vacated and remanded, sub nom. Louisiana v. Mora*, 423 U.S. 809 (1975); 330 So.2d 900 (La.), *cert. denied*, 429 U.S. 1004 (1976); *State v. Young*, 234 Ga. 438, 216 S.E.2d 586, *cert. denied*, 423 U.S. 1039 (1975); *In re L.L.*, 90 Wis. 2d 585, 280 N.W.2d 343 (1979).
106. *People v. Scott D.*, *supra* note 99, at 489.
107. *People v. Bowers*, *supra* note 99.
108. *In re J.A.*, 85 Ill. App. 3d 567, 406 N.E.2d 958 (1980). *See also State v. Baccino*, 282 A.2d 869 (Del. Super. Ct. 1971).
109. *Picha v. Wielgos*, 410 F. Supp. 1214 (N.D. Ill. 1976).
110. *See, e.g., Horton v. Goose Creek Independent School Dist.*, 690 F.2d 470, (5th Cir. 1982); *Zamora v. Pomeroy*, 639 F.2d 662 (10th Cir. 1981); *Doe v. Renfrow*, 631 F.2d 91 (7th Cir. 1981); *cert. denied*, 451 U.S. 1022 (1981). *But see Jones v. Latexo Independent School Dist.*, 499 F. Supp. 2232 (E.D. Tex. 1980).
111. *See Horton v. Goose Creek Independent School Dist.*, *supra* note 110.
111a. *See Bellnier v. Land*, 438 F. Supp. 47 (N.D.N.Y. 1977).
112. *See, e.g., U.S. v. Mendenhall*, *supra*, note 6; *Ybarra v. Illinois*, *supra* note 6; *Dunaway v. New York*, *supra* note 6; *Terry v. Ohio*, 392 U.S. 1 (1968); *Sibron v. New York*, 392 U.S. 40 (1968); *In re Lang*, 44 Misc. 2d 900, 255 N.Y.S.2d 987 (Fam. Ct. N.Y. Co. 1965).
113. *In re Herman S.*, 79 Misc. 2d 519, 359 N.Y.S.2d 645 (Fam. Ct. 1974).
114. *New York v. Belton*, *supra* note 82; *Rawlings v. Kentucky*, 448 U.S. 98 (1980); *Chimel v. California*, *supra* note 82.
115. *See, e.g.*, KAN. STAT. ANN. §38–805–c (1981); MINN. JUV. CODE §260.161(3) (1982); MO. STAT. ANN. §211.151 (1961); N.J. STAT. ANN. 2A:4–66 (Supp. 1974); N.M. STAT. 832–1–27(I) (1981).

116. *See, e.g.*, GA. CODE ANN. §24A–3503 (a) (1981).
117. N.Y. FAM. CT. ACT §§306.1(1)(a), (b) (1983).
118. *See, e.g.*, COLO. REV. STAT. §19–2–102(6) (Supp. 1981); GA. CODE ANN. §24A–3503(b) (1981); ILL. STAT. ANN. ch. 37 §702–8(2) (1972); N.Y. FAM. CT. ACT. §306.1(4) (1983).
119. N.J. STAT. ANN. §2A:4–66 (Supp. 1974).
120. N.Y. FAM. CT. ACT. §354.1(2) (1983).
121. *Id*. at §354.1(7) (1983). *See also Matter of Todd H*., 49 N.Y.2d 1022, 406 N.E.2d 1338, 429 N.Y.S.2d 401 (1980).
122. GA. CODE ANN. §24A–3503 (1981).
123. *See, e.g., Oberg v. Dept. of Law & Public Safety,* 41 N.J. Super. 256, 124 A.2d 618 (1956).
124. IND. STAT. ANN. §31–6–8–1.5(d) (1980).
125. 388 U.S. 218 (1967).
126. *Id*. at 263 (1967).
127. *Id*. at 293 (1967). *But see Watkins v. Sowders*, 449 U.S. 341 (1981); *Manson v. Braithwaite*, 432 U.S. 98 (1977).
128. 387 U.S. (1967); *In re Winship*, 397 U.S. 358 (1970).
129. *In re Carl T.,* 1 Cal. App. 3d 344, 81 Cal. Rptr. 655.
130. *In re Holley,* 107 R.I. 615, 268 A.2d 723 (1970).
131. *In re James H*., 34 N.Y. 2d 814, 316 N.E.2d 334, 359 N.Y.S.2d 814 (1974); *In re Stoutzenberger,* 235 Pa. Super. 500, 344 A.2d 668 (1975); *In re McKelvin*, 258 A.2d 452 (D.C. Ct. App. 1969).

II

Courts and Fact-Finding Procedures

A young person may be brought to court after an arrest or merely if a parent or teacher files a petition that alleges illegal conduct or behavior evidencing a need for supervision. Like adults, children are presumed innocent until proven guilty, and guilt can only be established in a court of law, after certain strict procedures have been followed. Unlike adults, however, children are not tried in criminal courts but in special tribunals where many of the procedures are similar to those in adult courts. Children have been granted some—but not all—of the rights possessed by criminal defendants.

Jurisdiction of Juvenile and Adult Courts

What courts hold hearings and makes decisions regarding young people charged with delinquency or status offenses?

Virtually every state has a juvenile court (sometimes called a family court, domestic relations court, children's court, or even probate court) to which matters regarding the offenses of children are referred. In most states the juvenile courts are separate and distinct from other civil and criminal courts and in large cities they may even be housed in separate facilities. In smaller communities juvenile cases may be heard periodically at a "juvenile term" of another court of general jurisdiction.

The level of the juvenile court within the judicial system varies by state.

1. In California, the juvenile court is a division of the superior court.

2. In the District of Columbia, cases involving young people are heard by the Family Division of the superior court.

3. In Florida and Illinois the juvenile courts are part of the circuit court.

4. In Massachusetts, there are four special juvenile courts—in Boston, Springfield, Worcester, and Bristol County—but elsewhere it is held as a separate session of the district court.

5. In New Jersey there is a juvenile and domestic relations court.

6. In New York there is a family court in every county.

7. Pennsylvania directs juvenile matters to the court of common pleas, family court, or juvenile court, depending on the location.

What is the maximum age jurisdiction of juvenile court?

It depends on the state. The majority of states set 18 as the age *below* which a child is subject to the juvenile court jurisdiction; in these states, young people 18 or older will be prosecuted as adults in adult criminal courts. In a few states, (including New York) juvenile court jurisdiction extends only to young people below the age of 16. (A complete list will be found in Appendix A.)

In several states there is an age range (often between 16 and 18) over which *both* juvenile and adult courts have jurisdiction. In these states a young person who is within the age limit of the juvenile court jurisdiction may voluntarily give up his right to be tried as a juvenile or be involuntarily transferred to adult court if certain conditions are found to exist.

In a few states a young person must also be a *minimum* age in order to be subjected to juvenile court jurisdiction. The theory (adopted from common law) is that a child below a certain age is incapable of forming the *intent* to commit a criminal act. These states are Massachusetts and New York, which require a child to be at least 7 years of age,[1] and Colorado, Mississippi, Vermont, and Texas, which set the minimum age at 10.[2] In California, the adult penal law states that children under the age of 14 are not capable of forming the intent to commit a crime, unless there is proof of their knowledge of the wrongfulness of the act. This led one California juvenile court to find a 9-year-old incapable of intending to commit a crime.[3] On the other hand, an Illinois court has suggested that the minimum age beneath which "intent" is deemed impossible is virtually irrelevant since the presentation of a child in juvenile court is never criminal and focuses on rehabilitation rather than punishment.[4]

In any event, the burden is on the prosecution—not on the accused—to prove that the child's age is within the range of the juvenile court's jurisdiction.[5]

When is a child's age computed for the purpose of establishing juvenile court jurisdiction?

In a majority of states jurisdiction is determined by the age of the child at the time the offense was allegedly committed.[6] In a few states the age of the young person at the time of arrest or trial determines whether he or she will be tried in juvenile or adult court.[7] In the former group of states, it may be possible for a child to be tried as a juvenile even after passing beyond the maximum jurisdictional age, as long as the offense was committed when the individual was a juvenile.

Approximately ten states solve the problem by requiring that a young person be under a certain age at the time of the alleged offense, *and* that he be under another (older) age at the time of the judicial proceedings.[8]

With regard to status offenders (PINS, CINS, and so forth, discussed in chapter X), the problem of establishing the time of the offense is difficult. At what point in time for example, could it be said that a child *habitually* disobeyed parents? And what happens to a child who runs away from home but is not taken into custody or returned until he or she has already turned eighteen? (In many cases, as a practical matter, children who have passed beyond the age of jurisdiction at the time of their arrest or at the time of trial are not prosecuted at all.)

May a state establish different ages of juvenile court jurisdiction for boys and girls?

No. Legislation establishing a longer period of time during which females may be subject to the jurisdiction of the juvenile court has been declared unconstitutional in Illinois, New York, and Oklahoma.[9] In all three cases the courts found no rational bases for distinguishing between the two sexes and held that such distinctions violate the Fourteenth Amendment's guarantee to equal protection of the laws.

Can a state set different ages at which a young person is subject to the jurisdiction of a juvenile court depending on the location of the offense or the court?

No. This is also unconstitutional since it denies all young people in one state, regardless of their location, equal protection of the laws.[10]

What is a "juvenile delinquent"?

In most states, a juvenile delinquent is a person under the age of eighteen who commits an offense or violation against a law of the state.[11] As will be discussed in the chapter on noncriminal misbehavior, a minority of states still include status offenses in their definition of *delinquency*. In many states, however, delinquency does not include the entire range of criminal offenses. A number of states, for example, limit delinquency to all crimes except the most serious.[12] In such states when young people are accused of committing certain crimes, such as murder or rape, they are prosecuted as adults in adult criminal courts. In still other states, minor criminal offenses, such as disorderly conduct or traffic offenses,[13] or acts for which adults are not subject to incarceration,[14] are not within the jurisdiction of the juvenile court. In these states, young people may be able to commit one or two minor offenses without any risk of penalty. However, a *series* of such offenses may be the basis of a charge of incorrigibility (for example, PINS and CINS).

Transfer to Adult Courts

Can a young person ever be tried as an adult in a criminal court?

Yes. All states have a mechanism that allows some young people to be tried not as juveniles in juvenile court but as adults in criminal court. This mechanism is usually called the transfer or waiver of juvenile court jurisdiction.

Generally, the trials of young people may be transferred to adult criminal courts only if certain conditions are met; for instance, if a very serious crime was committed by a juvenile, or if a young person has a lengthy juvenile court history.[15] In some states, the age of the child alone, without regard to the offense constitutes grounds for transfer to adult court;[16] other states authorize transfer on the basis of the charge, regardless of age.[17]

The conditions under which transfer may occur differ in each state. In Connecticut, for example, a juvenile may be transferred to adult court for trial if he or she is 14 years of age or older and is charged with murder or some other serious felony and if he or she has been previously convicted of a serious felony.[18] In Michigan, a 15-year-old may be transferred if he or she is charged with a felony.[19] In Illinois, a child must be over 13 and a juvenile court judge must decide that it is not in the best interest of the child or the public to proceed in juvenile court before he or she may be transferred for trial in an adult court.[20]

If a young person is tried in juvenile court, can he later be transferred to criminal court for trial on the same charge?

No. The United States Supreme Court has ruled that young people are protected against double jeopardy by the Fifth Amendment.[21] Therefore, if a child is tried as a juvenile in a juvenile court, he cannot be tried again in adult court on the same charge.

How is it decided whether a young person's case should be transferred?

The United States Supreme Court, in *Kent v. U.S.*,[22] strongly suggested that the matter be determined by a juvenile court, which is the case in most states today.

In a few states, however, the decision rests with the prosecutor who may select the court in which a child will be tried by charging him or her with a crime in either juvenile or adult court.[23] In some states (including Florida and New Jersey) the child him or herself may request to be transferred.[24] In a few others (including New York) the matter is decided by an adult criminal court judge who decides whether a case of a fourteen- or fifteen-year-old originally brought to criminal court because of the seriousness of the offense should remain there or be transferred *down* to the family court.

If the determination to transfer is made by a juvenile court, does a young person have the right to a hearing before the transfer takes place?

Yes. In the *Kent* case, the Supreme Court held that

before a court decides to transfer a case, it must hold a due process hearing. Moreover, the child has the right to be represented by an attorney who must be given access to the child's social records and reports, and, if the court decides to transfer the case, it must state its reasons in writing and supply the statement to the child.[25] This does not mean, however, that all states require hearings before young people are prosecuted as adults. In cases where the decision to transfer rests with the prosecutor, no hearings need be held.

At a transfer hearing, what factors are considered by the court?

In *Kent*, the Supreme Court suggested eight factors that should be considered when a juvenile court conducts a hearing to determine whether a juvenile case should be transferred to criminal court. These include—

1. the seriousness of the offense (whether it was committed in a violent or willful manner, and whether it resulted in damage to property or injury to persons);
2. the amount of evidence supporting the allegation;
3. the desirability of trying the case in an adult court when the juvenile's accomplices are also adults;
4. the sophistication and maturity of the juvenile;
5. the likelihood of rehabilitation if treated as a juvenile offender.[26]

Presently, most states have their own requirements listed in statutes.[27] About half of the states that prescribe conditions for transfer require a finding of probable cause that the juvenile committed the alleged offense,[28] and two thirds require an inquiry into the amenability of the child to treatment services provided by the juvenile court and its ancillary agencies.[29]

It is important to note that while a transfer hearing may involve questions about the seriousness of the offense and the strength of evidence against the child, the guilt or innocence of the accused is *not* the purpose of the hearing; it is solely to decide whether the forthcoming trial (at which guilt or innocence *will* be determined) should be held in a juvenile or adult court.

In Illinois, for example, the juvenile court, in making its decision, must consider (1) the age and previous history of the child; (2) the sufficiency of evidence against him including the aggressiveness of the alleged offense; (3) whether there are facilities available to the juvenile court for the treatment and rehabilitation of the minor; and (4) whether the security of the public may require that the child remain in custody for a period beyond his minority.[30]

In New York, the court considers—

1. the seriousness of the crime charged;
2. any injuries to the victim;
3. the child's age, maturity, and prior contacts with the law;
4. the weight of evidence against him or her;
5. the scope of punishment available to a family court;
6. the likelihood of a child's rehabilitation given the range of services available to a family court;
7. the public protection if the child were not prosecuted as an adult.[31]

The Minnesota Supreme Court has ruled that the age of the child and the seriousness of his or her alleged crime *alone* are insufficient to justify transfer in the absence of a state law that says otherwise. According to the highest court in Minnesota the hearing is required to consider the child's suitability (or lack thereof) to treatment as a juvenile and the question of the safety of the public if the child is not prosecuted as an adult. In one case the court ruled that since there was no evidence of the child's psychological status or social history, his prior transfer to adult court was found invalid.[32] In a later case, however, the same court approved a transfer order by a lower court where the only findings were that the juvenile was over sixteen and was charged with first-degree murder.[33] In that case the statute provided that age plus the charge of murder was sufficient by itself to show that the juvenile was not amenable to treatment as a delinquent.[34] Although sufficient, the juvenile may introduce evidence to establish that he *is* amenable to treatment. In the absence of such evidence, however, the two facts of age and the seriousness of the charge may be enough.

Upon whom is the burden of proof placed in a transfer hearing?

The prosecution. If the court must make certain findings before transferring a case from juvenile to adult court, the burden of showing that transfer is appropriate is upon the prosecution. It may meet this burden by different *standards* of proof, depending on the jurisdiction. These standards range from a "preponderance of evidence,"[35] to "clear and convincing" proof.[36] However, this answer is somewhat misleading in states where the prosecution must only prove that the juvenile is over a certain age and is charged with a particular crime. In these states, the prosecution will meet its burden at a transfer hearing merely by introducing a birth certificate and a copy of the charge itself. Having met its burden, the burden then shifts to the juvenile to show why the transfer should not take place.

In addition, some states *require* transfer when a young person is charged with a serious offense, *unless* the young person can show that he is amenable to treatment as a juvenile. In such cases, the burden of proof is on the accused.[37]

If the conditions for transfer are met, does that make the transfer automatic?

Not necessarily. The criteria for transfer, even though they are different in each state, generally *permit* transfers; they do not *require* them. Oklahoma, for example, enacted legislation a few years ago that stipulated that any 16- or 17-year-old who was charged with any of 11 serious crimes was to have his case transferred to adult court.[38] But a state appellate court ruled that this law was unconstitutional because the assumption that *all* such children are competent to stand trial as adults could not be legally justified.[39]

Do young people have the right to appeal decisions to transfer their cases to criminal courts?

Yes, but there is no uniform rule whether the appeal may be taken immediately after a decision to transfer or whether it must await a final disposition of the case itself.

In California,[40] Hawaii,[41] and Idaho,[42] for example, young people are permitted to appeal a court's decision to transfer their case, but the appeal must be made before the case goes to trial in adult court. In Colorado[43] and Iowa,[44] on the other hand, the original transfer decision is not appealable until a final judgment of guilt is made by the adult court. In Illinois (to illustrate how complicated this issue may become), a child may appeal the transfer decision only after his or her conviction in adult court, but the state may appeal a court's decision *not* to transfer the case as soon as the no-transfer decision itself is made.[45] In Oklahoma, the state may not appeal the decision of an adult court to transfer a case *down* to the juvenile court.[46]

Can a confession made during or before a transfer hearing be used against a child at a subsequent fact-finding hearing in juvenile or criminal court?

The general rule is no.[47] This is based on the theory that a transfer hearing is less formal than a fact-finding hearing and is calculated to foster candor and cooperation among all parties. Thus, a young person's knowledge that statements made there could be used against him later would serve to destroy the purpose of such hearing.[48]

In a transfer hearing, is hearsay testimony admissible into evidence? Are admissions made without *Miranda* warnings admissible?

Probably. Since, as just mentioned, the purpose of a transfer hearing is not to determine the guilt of a child, but simply to determine in what court he should be prosecuted, hearsay testimony would most likely *not* be excluded even though it might be excluded from evidence at the trial itself.[49]

For the same reason, statements made by a child to the police without having been first afforded his *Miranda* warnings may well be admissible in a transfer hearing even though they might not be at the trial itself.[50]

Intake and Diversion

What is "Intake"?

Intake is an informal screening process conducted by court officials or probation officers who decide if a complaint against a child should be referred to the juvenile court for a formal hearing or handled in some other way.

Most experts estimate that about half of the complaints received by juvenile courts are disposed at Intake; that is, they do not result in the filing of formal petitions. Cases disposed at Intake may result in outright dismissal, in referral to a public or private community agency where services will be provided, or in some type of informal supervision by probation officers.[51] In some states there exists a form of nonjudicial disposition called *diversion* (diversion away from the judicial process) which is determined by Intake officials.

What factors determine the decisions of Intake officials?

Few states or counties have written guidelines, but Intake officials generally consider a number of factors including—

1. the previous offenses of the child;
2. the seriousness of the present allegations;
3. the child's family situation;
4. the child's school record;
5. estimates of the child's future course of conduct.[52]

Generally, the child's "attitude" has a great impact on the decisions of Intake officials.

Does a young person against whom a complaint has been lodged have the right to have his case considered at Intake before a formal hearing takes place?

Yes, in many states. There has been no declaration of a constitutional right, but in many states some form of Intake is mandatory. In some states it is called by a different name, such as a preliminary investigation or informal adjustment.

Does a child have the right to remain silent at Intake?

Yes. In fact, a child does not have to participate in Intake proceedings at all if he does not want to.[53]

Are statements made by young people at Intake proceedings excluded from evidence at juvenile court fact-finding hearings?

Usually.[54] But statements made during Intake interviews are often used against a child at *dispositional* hearings, held after a finding of delinquency or "in need of supervision" has been made.

Does a young person have the right to be represented by counsel at Intake?

No. Intake proceedings are considered informal, personalized conferences, separate in form and purpose from structured adjudicatory hearings where counsel is guaranteed. The purpose of an Intake proceeding is to seek an adjustment of the case, hopefully with the consent of all parties, not to determine guilt or innocence. For this reason, a child's request for counsel is almost always denied.[55]

While it may be argued that counsel is required by the Constitution since adults are granted the right to counsel at arraignments,[56] only one state—Colorado—statutorily permits counsel for the child to be present at the Intake stage.[57]

What is "diversion"?

Diversion is a term used to describe the rerouting of a child out of the juvenile court process into a noncriminal or nonjudicial disposition. Diversion usually takes place after a proceeding has commenced (often at Intake) but before its formal completion. A child "diverted" from the court process may be sent to a youth agency or a "youth services bureau" that will provide direct services or coordinate the provision of existing community and governmental services.

Youth services bureaus themselves are community-based agencies that are normally independent of the juvenile court and the public child welfare system. Depending on the individual youth service bureau, diversion may entail—

1. group, family, and individual counseling;
2. placement in foster homes;
3. work;
4. educational and recreational programs;
5. employment aid;
6. referral to other agencies.

Most bureaus also work with children who are not referred from the courts.

Of course, not every juvenile court provides for diversion and not every county or locality has a youth service bureau. Diversion itself is a relatively novel concept, still in an experimental stage in many communities.

A few examples of diversion programs are the Bronx Diversion Project, the Cambridge Youth Resources Bureau, the Pacifica (California) Youth Service Bureau, the Sacramento 601 Diversion Project, the East Palo Alto Community Youth Responsibility Program, the Wayne County Juvenile Facility Network Program, and the San Antonio Youth Service Project.

In localities where diversion programs have been instituted, they usually operate with the consent and cooperation of juvenile court judges, probation officers, and county or district attorneys. In addition, most programs rely on the *voluntary* participation of young people diverted to them from the courts.

In Washington, a first offender charged with a less serious crime than a felony has a statutory right to be referred to an advisory unit. The unit, however, is not obliged to divert the case.[58]

Notice of Charges and the Plea

Do minors have the right to be notified of the charges against them before a juvenile court hearing is held?

Yes. Any action against or involving a child must be commenced with the filing of a petition. Each state has its own requirements for the exact contents of a petition, but it must notify the child (and his parents) that proceedings have been commenced and it must contain the *specific* charges against the child.

The United States Supreme Court explained this requirement in the following words:

> Notice, to comply with due process requirements, must be given sufficiently in advance of scheduled court proceedings so that reasonable opportunity to prepare will be afforded, and it must "set forth the alleged misconduct with particularity." . . . (T)he requirements (are) that the child and his parents or guardian be notified, in writing, of the specific charge or factual allegations to be considered at the hearing, and that such written notice be given at the earliest practicable time, and in any event sufficiently in advance of the hearing to permit preparation.[59]

Following this decision, the Mississippi Supreme Court held that juvenile court petitions must recite factual allegations so as to apprise the juvenile and his parents of particular acts of misconduct, and that if a delinquency charge is based upon a violation of criminal law, the petition must contain the same particularity as an adult criminal indictment.[60]

Notice similar to that extended to adult defendants also has been required by case law in Georgia, Indiana, Illinois, New York, Pennsylvania, and Washington as well.[61] This usually means that it is not sufficient merely to repeat general words of the statute *(habitually violated penal ordinances,* or *was delinquent)* in the petition, but that the facts and circumstances of particular acts of misconduct must be alleged with some specificity.[62] This also means that if a petition charges one offense, a young person may not be found guilty of another, wholly unrelated charge.[63] In some states, failure to also advise the accused juvenile of the possible consequences of a finding of guilty prior to the commencement of the trial may result in a reversal, if the child is convicted.[64]

Who must receive notice of the charges—the young person or his parents?

Usually both.[65] Failure to serve timely notice on the child and his parents may constitute grounds for reversal, if the child is later convicted.[66] Normally, notice is given by service of a summons or petition on the juvenile and his parents.

Does a young person have the right to plead "not guilty" to the charges against him?

Yes. Juveniles have the right to plead "not guilty" and thereby demand a trial (hearing) on the allegations.

Does a young person have the right to plead "guilty" to the charges against him?

Yes. When a guilty plea (admission) is entered, the juvenile admits the truth of the allegations made against him, waives other constitutional rights to which he is entitled and loses his right to a hearing. After a plea of guilty, therefore, the only issue before the juvenile court is what sentence or disposition to impose.

Since a plea of guilty has such serious consequences for an accused juvenile, most courts will not permit a child to plead unless he is fully aware of what he is doing. This usually means that the child must be told the significance of the charge and the possible consequences he or she faces as a result of admitting guilt.[67] Unless the accused is so advised, most courts will not accept a guilty plea, and in many states, if a guilty plea is accepted without these prior admonitions, the subsequent conviction may be reversed.[68]

Does a child have a right to "plea-bargain" in juvenile court?

Almost no law exists on this subject, but plea bargaining is a commonplace activity in juvenile as well as adult courts.[69] Generally, this means that the prosecution or the court will accept a plea of guilty to a less serious offense than the one charged, or a plea of guilty to one of two or more charges if the accused and his attorney agree not to invoke his right to a trial on the original charge(s). In some respects, plea bargaining has less value for juveniles than adults, because if they are found guilty, they are usually convicted of "delinquency" rather than a specific offense. But because judges, prosecutors, and institutional personnel usually look behind the label of delinquency to ascertain the exact offense committed, especially if the juvenile comes to court for a second time, lawyers for certain juveniles may believe that it is in a child's interest to seek a "plea bargain," if possible.

Speedy Trial

Do juveniles have the right to a speedy trial?

Yes. The right to a speedy trial is guaranteed all persons facing *criminal* prosecutions by the Sixth Amendment and this right must be upheld by all the states.[70] A juvenile court proceeding is considered criminal if it may lead to the commitment of a child or the loss of liberty.[71]

A number of state courts have specifically ruled that the right to a speedy trial is enforceable in juvenile courts.[72] In Illinois, an adjudicatory hearing must be set within 30 days of the filing of a delinquency petition, unless the child is in detention, in which case the adjudicatory hearing must be set within 10 judicial days from the date the court ordered detention.[73] In California, a hearing must be held within 30 days of the filing of the petition, except in cases where a minor is in detention. If this is the case, the hearing must be held within 15 judicial days from the date of the order of the court directing such detention.[74]

In New York, for most offenses charged, a fact-finding

hearing must commence within 3 days after the filing of a petition if the young person is in detention. If the charge would constitute a serious felony, however, the hearing must commence within 14 days, and if the charge is homicide or an assault in which the victim is incapacitated, the hearing must be held within a "reasonable length of time."[75]

Under the Federal Juvenile Delinquency Act, a person must be tried within 30 days after being taken into custody.[76]

As with other issues involving procedural rights for juveniles, courts often disagree on whether or not standards governing adult criminal trials ought to be extended to juvenile proceedings as well. With regard to the issue of speedy trials, it appears as though most appellate courts are willing to grant young people the same protection as adults, even though the rather "special" nature and goals of juvenile court hearings are always duly noted.[77] Thus, some courts have ruled that if a delay beyond the statutory time limit is for a short period only, if the reasons for the delay are justifiable, and if no prejudice to the juvenile has resulted, the delay will not necessarily result in a dismissal of the charges against a child.[78]

If a case is transferred from one tribunal to another, when does the time for a speedy trial begin to run?

Generally, the time commences from the moment of arrest. Under this doctrine, a child whose case has been transferred from a juvenile to an adult criminal court would be entitled to a speedy trial pursuant to time limits set by rules of criminal procedure, and the time would begin to run on the date of the child's arrest, not upon the later transfer date.[79]

Discovery and Impartiality

Does a young person appearing in juvenile court have the right to make pretrial motions, including motions for discovery?

Yes and no. Motions to suppress illegally obtained evidence, confessions, and identification may be made by a young person's attorney before trial. However, motions to require the disclosure of pertinent facts or information held by the police or prosecuting attorney (referred to as discovery), which may aid in the defense of the child, are permitted only in some jurisdictions.

In a number of states (including Alaska, California, Colorado, Minnesota, and New Jersey) discovery is permitted only at the discretion of the court.[80] In the District of Columbia, North Dakota, Ohio, Tennessee, and Texas, the law is fairly explicit in requiring discovery, if requested.[81] In New York, a recently enacted law requires disclosure to the accused upon demand of grand jury minutes, autopsy reports, scientific reports, photographs, and, prior to the commencement of the hearing, written statements of witnesses.[82] In many adult criminal trials, the defendant is entitled to be informed of the identity of witnesses who are known by the state to have information in favor of the accused.[83]

Regardless of the presence or absence of a statute, children and their attorneys have a constitutional right to obtain copies of police records that will be considered by the juvenile court as well as evidence *essential* to the preparation of their defense, including exculpatory (favorable) material possessed by the state.[84]

Beyond this, however, the right to discovery is unclear. In the adult sphere, discovery is more liberal in civil than in criminal cases. Juvenile courts are civil in nature, but delinquency proceedings are often referred to as quasi-criminal, containing both civil and criminal qualities. In many states, therefore, some but not all of the rules of civil discovery are applied in juvenile courts.[85]

Does a young person have the right to be tried by an impartial judge?

Yes. The right to an impartial arbiter of the facts is an essential part of due process of law.[86] A judge who is a close friend of the child's parents—especially if the parents are the petitioners—or who has learned of the facts of the case before trial should not sit in determination of the matter at a hearing or trial.[87]

Similarly, a juvenile may not be tried by a probation officer or by a judge who also acts as a prosecutor.[88]

Right to an Attorney

Does a young person have the right to be represented by an attorney at a delinquency or supervision hearing?

Yes. The United States Supreme Court has held that juveniles are entitled to be represented by a lawyer at any delinquency or status offense hearing at which the child is subject to a loss of liberty.[89] This right is guaranteed under the due process clause of the Fourteenth Amendment.

If a child or his parents cannot afford to hire an attorney, will one be provided for free?

Yes,[90] but some state laws require parents to repay the state for the state-supplied attorney if they are financially able to hire counsel and refuse to do so.[91]

Does a young person have the right to consult with his lawyer before the hearing, in order to discuss the facts of the case?

Yes. If the attorney has not consulted with the young person, the case should not proceed to a hearing.[92]

Does a young person have the right to make his lawyer represent his own views and wishes?

Yes, but attorneys will not always do what a child wants.

The role of an attorney is to protect the legal interests of the young person and express his wishes in court, but some attorneys—and many courts—feel that a child is not mature enough to make intelligent decisions, even when they concern his own life.[93]

A lawyer should advise the young person as to what he thinks is the most beneficial course of action, but, after offering advice, he has a duty to represent the wishes of his client.[94] If a child wishes to plead "not guilty" to a charge of delinquency, for example, his attorney should not enter a "guilty" plea against the expressed choice of the client.[95]

This statement suggests that the attorney must play an *adversary* role in court if the child wishes to contest the charge against him. The Supreme Court as much as agreed when it quoted a National Crime Commission Report in *In re Gault*.

> The juvenile courts deal in cases in which facts are disputed and in which, therefore, rules of evidence, confrontations of witnesses and other adversary procedures are called for. . . . And in all cases children

need advocates to speak for them and guard their interests. . . .[96]

A year earlier the same Court stated:

> We do not agree . . . that counsel's role is limited to presenting "to the court anything on behalf of the child which might help the court in arriving at a decision; it is not to denigrate the staff's submissions and recommendation." On the contrary, if the staff's submissions include materials which are susceptible to challenge and impeachment, it is precisely the role of counsel to "denigrate" such matter.[97]

It is often the case that lawyers chosen and paid by a child's parents tend to represent the wishes of the parents rather than those of the child. Of course, if the viewpoints of the parents and the child are the same, this presents no problem. But if the young person has wishes contrary to those of his parents or feels that the attorney is not adequately representing *his own* position, for whatever reason, he should inform the lawyer and the judge and ask that a new attorney be appointed. It could thus be said that a child has the right to "fire" his attorney, even if the lawyer was hired by his parents or appointed by the court free of charge.

Can a young person give up his right to counsel?

Yes, but like giving up (waiving) the right to remain silent when questioned by the police (see chapter I), waiving the right to counsel is a complex issue.[98] This is because a person can only give up a constitutional right if he does it *knowingly* and *intelligently*. In this regard a court will often consider the "totality of the circumstances" to determine if the waiver was legal.[99]

Generally, a knowing and intelligent waiver can be made only (1) if the accused has a full appreciation of the charges against him; (2) if he has been advised of the range of possible punishments to which he is liable; and (3) if he is made aware of the fact that an attorney may assist him in pursuing possible defenses to the charges and circumstances in mitigation to the offense.[100] Courts are often reluctant to accept a child's waiver of counsel, since children are assumed unable to make knowledgable legal decisions without an attorney.[101] Pursuant to these standards, a Maryland appellate court held that a child did not knowingly and intelligently waive his right to counsel when he and his mother merely signed a form.[102]

Counsel plays such an important role in protecting the rights of juveniles that a number of states prohibit any waiver of counsel unless counsel is already present and has consulted with the juvenile about waiver,[103] and, in at least one state, the right to counsel may not be given up at all.[104]

If a *parent* waives his child's right to counsel, it is likely that the waiver will not be valid.[105] Similarly, if a parent can afford an attorney but gives up his child's right to counsel because he does not want to pay for one, the waiver may not be considered binding.[106]

Other Procedural Rights

Does a juvenile have the right to a trial from which the public and the press are excluded?

There is no clear answer to this question. The Supreme Court has never ruled that the press or public has a constitutional right to attend juvenile delinquency proceedings and, in many states, the juvenile justice system is predicated on the premise of anonymity for juvenile offenders. But recent changes make this question difficult to answer.

A few years ago, it could be said that juveniles had the right to exclude the press and public from their trials. This was because children were considered to be in need of protection from public exposure that might adversely affect their potential for rehabilitation. Today, however, juvenile courts are more hesitant to keep the courtroom doors closed. The right of juveniles to exclude the public and press from trials is much less secure, in part because of recent judicial victories gained by advocates of press freedom, and in part because some states are beginning to de-emphasize the rehabilitative function of juvenile justice.

In a recent opinion, the United States Supreme Court ruled that unless it can be demonstrated that closing a courtroom is required to protect a defendant's right to a fair trial, the exclusion of the press and public from a trial violates the First Amendment.[107] Although the Court's decision involved an *adult* criminal case, and although most state laws still grant some authority for judges to limit (to some degree) the public from trials of juveniles,[108] the trend is toward public access to all judicial proceedings.

Even more recently, the Supreme Court ruled that a Massachusetts law that excluded the press and public from sex-offense trials during the testimony of a minor *victim* violated the First Amendment.[109] The purpose of the law was to protect victims against public exposure. While the Court recognized the legitimacy of such a state purpose, the Massachusetts law prohibited access in *all* cases. The Court did not rule out the possibility that barring access would be constitutional in certain cases, requiring a case-by-case determination of whether the state's legitimate concern for a minor victim's protection justifies closing court proceedings. The result reached by the Court in the Massachusetts case led the dissenters to observe that the present state of the law ironically permits states to assure the anonymity of juvenile *offenders* while it prohibits the automatic protection of minor *victims*.[110]

A number of state courts have recently broadened the power of the press to gain access to juvenile proceedings. A New York family court, for example, ruled that the competing rights of the press and the child may be resolved by "selective" exclusion of the press and public from juvenile delinquency proceedings, meaning that each case in which the press requests admission will be dealt with on its own terms, with regard to—

1. the risk of disruption of the orderly administration of justice;
2. the possibility of any unwarranted stigma and facilitation of the rehabilitation of the youth;
3. the need to preserve a sense of privacy;
4. the age of the child;
5. the particular vulnerability of the juvenile and his family;
6. the sensitivity of the issues involved.[111]

And the Supreme Court of Oregon made a more sweeping decision by ruling that an Oregon statute, which granted judges the power to exclude anyone from the court, was unconstitutional.[112]

About fifteen states (including California, Illinois, and

Pennsylvania) have laws that permit the press and public to attend juvenile court proceedings so long as they do not disclose the name of the accused child,[113] but even this prohibition may be unconstitutional.

In a few other states (including Maine, Montana, and Utah) a child is guaranteed a private trial *unless* the crime he is being charged with would be a felony if it were in adult court.[114]

On the other hand, in virtually every state, accused juveniles have the right to have their parents attend their trial, and in a few states they have the right to insist that the trial be open to the public.[115]

Can the press be prosecuted for reporting the identity of a young person accused of being delinquent?

In most cases, no. In two important rulings by the United States Supreme Court, the press was vindicated when challenged for publishing the names of accused delinquents. In one case, an Oklahoma law required closure of juvenile detention hearings unless the presiding judge opened them.[116] Though no order was made in this case, the media were present at the juvenile's detention hearing and learned the minor's name. Film footage of the arrested juvenile was shown on local television and his name was published in three Oklahoma newspapers. Following prior precedents,[117] the Supreme Court held that the First Amendment prohibited states from preventing the publication of widely disseminated information at court proceedings that were in fact open to the public. In the second case, two West Virginia newspapers reported the identity of a junior high school student who was accused of murdering a classmate.[118] The newspapers were prosecuted under a state law prohibiting newspapers from publishing the name of any youth charged as a juvenile offender without the written approval of the juvenile court. The Supreme Court held that the statute violated the First-Amendment rights of the newspapers. The Court ruled that imposing criminal penalties for the publication of truthful information is unconstitutional where the only purpose of the law is to protect the anonymity of a juvenile offender.

Similarly, in South Carolina, a statute prohibiting media use of the name or photograph of a child under the jurisdiction of the family court was held invalid by that state's highest court. Following the reasoning of the United States Supreme

Court, the court held that the statute was "unconstitutional insofar as [it] prevent(s) the truthful publication by the media of information lawfully obtained concerning a juvenile charged with a crime."[119] Therefore, as applied to a newspaper that lawfully had in its possession the photograph of a juvenile charged with homicide, the statute violated the First Amendment. Such a statute is constitutional as applied to restriction on the *gathering* of certain information, for example, by barring access to court proceedings. But once information is already in the press's possession, restricting dissemination will be permitted only in rare, "compelling" cases.

Do young people have the right to be tried by a jury in juvenile court?

Generally not. The United States Supreme Court has ruled that the constitutional guarantee of a trial by jury extends to every adult who faces possible imprisonment,[120] but in 1971, the Supreme Court ruled in *McKeiver v. Pennsylvania*,[121] that states have no constitutional obligation to grant this right to juveniles.

A number of state courts have also ruled that a child has no right to a trial by jury,[122] even among states that have recently "toughened up" their juvenile court statutes by making sentences more punitive than rehabilitative.[123] The *McKeiver* decision has been held applicable to trials taking place under the Federal Juvenile Delinquency Act as well.[124]

Nevertheless, while the Supreme Court held that states do not have to grant jury trials to juveniles, the *McKeiver* decision does not *prohibit* states from extending juveniles that right if they desire. Accordingly, approximately fifteen states grant jury trials in some form, either by statute or by judicial decree. These states include Alaska, Colorado, Kansas, Iowa, Massachusetts, Michigan, Montana, New Mexico, Oklahoma, South Dakota, Tennessee, Texas, West Virginia, Wisconsin, and Wyoming.[125]

Even when jury trials are granted, the right is often qualified. In South Dakota, for example, the right is granted only at the discretion of the judge.[126]

Does a child have the right to have juvenile court hearings transcribed?

Yes. The United States Supreme Court has not ruled on this issue, but it has critized juvenile courts that do not transcribe their proceedings.[127] As early as 1958, an Oklahoma court ruled that the absence of a formal transcription denied a child-defendant due process.[128] Recently, appellate courts in Louisiana and California have held that the lack of a transcript of a juvenile court proceeding constitutes grounds for setting aside an adjudication of delinquency.[129]

The presence of a juvenile court reporter has the positive effect of promoting fairness, especially since juvenile court proceedings are conducted in private. The existence of a transcript, of course, also provides a record from which an appeal may be taken. In the words of a National Crime Commission Report, cited by the Supreme Court, "[R]ecords make possible appeals which, even if they do not occur, impart by their possibility a healthy atmosphere of accountability."[130]

The trend in recent juvenile court legislation is to require word-by-word records of hearings.[131] Today more than half the states require a transcript of all hearings either if requested by a party or ordered by the court.

What standard of proof must the state bear to sustain a finding of delinquency against a child in juvenile court?

In 1970, the United States Supreme Court held, in *In re Winship*, that the state must prove a child's guilt "beyond a reasonable doubt" in all delinquency hearings. The Court stated that proof beyond a reasonable doubt is among the essentials of due process and fair treatment required when a juvenile is charged with an act that would constitute a crime if committed by an adult.[132] The *Winship* decision rendered unconstitutional the customary lower standard of "preponderance of the evidence," which is allowed in most civil trials.

The *Winship* rule is applicable only to delinquency proceedings. In almost all states the standard of proof in nondelinquency trials, such as in PINS or status offense cases (see chapter X), is still set at either a preponderance of the evidence or clear and convincing evidence.[133]

Some states provide that proof beyond a reasonable doubt is applicable to delinquency *and* noncriminal cases when they are codified under the single term of *delinquency.*[134]

Does a young person have the right to be free from self-incrimination?

Yes. The protection of the Fifth Amendment was extended to juveniles by the United States Supreme Court in 1967.[135] This means that the state cannot force a young person to testify on his or her own behalf; the accused also has the right *not* to deny the allegations.

Moreover, if a child decides to exercise his or her Fifth-Amendment right and not "take the stand," a judge may not comment on this fact or use it against the child, even if there is no jury; otherwise, it may constitute reversible error.[136]

Of course, a young person has the right to testify if he so desires. However, if he testifies on his own behalf, he thereby makes himself available for cross-examination by the state.[137]

Do young people have the right to present evidence and witnesses on their own behalf?

Yes.[138] There is no requirement to do so, but a court may not prevent an accused from presenting evidence.

Do young people have the right to have expert witnesses testify on their behalf, even if they have no money to pay for them?

Yes. Young people have the right to a full defense of the charges against them, including witness fees paid to experts, if reasonable and necessary.

The Supreme Court has ruled that in criminal trials a state can no more discriminate against defendants on account of poverty than on account of religion, race, or color.[139] One federal circuit court took this rule to mean that an indigent defendant is entitled to have a psychiatrist testify on his behalf[140] and another circuit court held that the Supreme Court ruling was applicable to juvenile as well as adult trials.[141]

This series of cases, plus the *Gault* doctrine that stipulates that a young person has the right to counsel, *and* to be provided counsel for free if he cannot afford to pay,[142] would appear to establish the right of juveniles to have expert witnesses testify on their behalf and to have the state pay their expenses, if necessary.

Do young people have the right to cross-examine their accusers and those who testify against them?

Yes.[143] This is one of the most basic rights of an accused.

Do young people have the right to exclude hearsay testimony at a fact-finding hearing?

Yes.[144] This right guarantees that the witness testifying knows the facts from his own personal knowledge.

Can a young person be convicted solely on the evidence of his own confession or the confession of an accomplice?

It depends on the state. A number of states (including Georgia, Maryland, New Jersey, New York, Pennsylvania, and Texas) provide that a child's out-of-court confession is insufficient to support a conviction unless it is corroborated by other evidence.[145] (This rule does not apply, of course, to confessions made by juvenile defendants themselves while under oath in court.)

States are also divided on whether or not a child may be convicted upon the uncorroborated testimony of an accomplice. Such testimony may be sufficient to support a conviction in Louisiana, Ohio, and in some California courts.[146] Uncorroborated testimony of an accomplice is *not* sufficient in other states (including Nevada, New York, Oklahoma, Oregon, and Texas), where such evidence must be supported by other, independent proof of guilt.[147]

Of course, a young person cannot be found delinquent in the absence of *any* sworn testimony,[148] and evidence must always reach the level of "beyond a reasonable doubt" to support a finding of delinquency, regardless of the rules of a particular state with respect to uncorroborated statements or testimony.[149]

Does a young person have the right to have his or her social report excluded from the fact-finding hearing?

Almost always. The sole purpose of the adjudicatory hearing is to determine the guilt or innocence of the young person with regard to the charges alleged in the petition. Social reports, which ordinarily contain a history of the child, his family setting, performance in school, and even psychological profiles, have no bearing on the issue of whether or not a young person is guilty of the acts alleged and may not be put into evidence.[150]

However, social reports may be considered by the judge before and during the dispositional hearing, in which the court determines the form of treatment the young person is to receive after he has been found guilty.[151] (Dispositional hearings will be discussed at greater length in chapter III.)

Does a young person have the right to claim insanity as a defense to the charge against him?

This is by no means clear. Since the goal of juvenile proceedings is the treatment of wrongdoers, rather than their punishment, an argument could be made that a child's insanity should have no bearing on the course of the fact-finding phase of the trial itself, but should only be raised upon disposition. Such is the rule in some states (including the District of Columbia).[152]

Insanity is a valid defense to the charge of delinquency in other states (including Arizona, California, Louisiana, New Jersey, New York, Oregon, and Wisconsin).[153] The child who claims insanity as a defense must prove that at the time of the commission of the act, he was laboring under a defect of reason or disease of the mind such that he did not understand the nature or the quality of the act, or that if he did understand it, he did not know that what he was doing was wrong.[154]

If a young person is incompetent, does he have to stand trial?

Probably not. Any person who is unable to understand the nature of the charges against him and is unable to assist in his own defense may be declared incompetent and as a result, may not be forced or permitted to proceed to trial. In adult criminal proceedings, the failure of a trial court to conduct a hearing on competency, if necessary, may result in a denial of due process.[155]

The issue of competency is directed toward whether or not the accused has the mental ability to proceed with a trial. It should not be confused with the term *insanity*, which pertains to the mental state of the defendant at the time he committed the act. In the case of juveniles it is likely that the issue of competency would be dealt with during Intake screening, but a formal competency hearing might be granted.[156]

Are young people granted the right to be free from double jeopardy?

Yes. The Fifth Amendment protects citizens from double jeopardy which, simply stated, means that people may not be prosecuted or punished twice for the same offense.

In 1975, in *Breed v. Jones*,[157] the Supreme Court settled the issue in favor of children. In that case a seventeen-year-old was tried in juvenile court and a finding of delinquency was made. Later, he was found unamenable to treatment and was transferred to adult criminal court where he was tried and found guilty of the same offense. The Supreme Court found the second trial unconstitutional since it put the child in jeopardy a second time.

The fact that a child faces possible *treatment* rather than *punishment* as a consequence of a juvenile court proceeding is of no bearing, the Court held, since the double-jeopardy clause was intended to protect individuals from the risk of trial and conviction, not punishment. This finding laid to rest the argument that since the juvenile court hearings are *civil* in nature, a child is not entitled to claim the right to be free from double jeopardy.[158] The *Breed* decision determined that jeopardy attaches at the time the juvenile court begins to take evidence.

In some states, a juvenile court trial is preceded by what is known as a Master's Hearing or Referee's Hearing, at which evidence is presented to a hearing officer who makes recommendations to the juvenile court judge. The question as to whether a referee's dismissal and a subsequent request by the prosecution to the juvenile court for a new hearing, is violative of the prohibition against double jeopardy has received considerable attention in recent years. Such a scheme constitutes double jeopardy only if the juvenile is exposed to two different trials. In 1978, the United States Supreme Court held that a Maryland scheme did not offend the prohibition against double jeopardy, even when a Master's recommendation of dismissal was overturned by the juvenile court judge.[159] Because in Maryland the juvenile court may not conduct a new hearing but is empowered only to review the Master's findings and accept or reject them on the basis of the evidence presented to the Master, Maryland's scheme was found to be constitutional.

In contrast, the California Supreme Court held that the reversal by a juvenile court judge of a Referee's dismissal of charges unlawfully subjects a child to two separate trials.[160] As a result, if a Referee dismisses a delinquency petition in California, the charges cannot be heard again by a judge in a delinquency hearing.

Since jeopardy is said to attach at the time evidence is first presented at a juvenile court hearing, a child may be placed in double jeopardy if he or she is tried again in juvenile court on the same charge of delinquency after the original hearing was interrupted and declared a mistrial.[161]

In Arizona, the state supreme court found that jeopardy attached to a child who was committed to a state mental hospital in lieu of criminal prosecution, thereby barring a later trial for the same offense even though there was no adjudication of delinquency.[162]

In Illinois, an appellate court ruled that if a child was charged with a status offense (for example, PINS or CINS) and if the charges were subsequently dismissed, he or she could not later be charged with delinquency for the same alleged offense.[163]

Does a young person have the right to appeal a juvenile court finding?

Yes, in most states. But in the absence of statutory authorization, the right is not always clear. The Constitution does not grant adult or juvenile defendants the right to appeal, but virtually every state has laws that permit *adults* to appeal cases and convictions. In *In re Gault*, the Supreme Court did not rule on whether *juveniles* have the right to appeal, and a number of lower courts have held that there is no denial of due process if state law does not provide for the right of young people to appeal decisions of juvenile courts.[164] Generally, then, the right to appeal is at the discretion of state legislatures. A great number of state laws do provide for the right to appeal. These include California, Connecticut, the District of Columbia, Florida, Massachusetts, New York, and Texas, among others.[165] Moreover, the trend is clearly in the direction of legislatively or judicially declaring the right of appeal where no right has existed before.[166]

An appeal, of course, is only one method by which a postconviction remedy may be pursued. Even when no right to appeal exists, review by other procedures such as writs of habeas corpus are available to all individuals including juveniles.[167] At least one federal court held that a child who has been deprived of his liberty has a right to appeal his conviction, even in the absence of statutory authorization.[168]

If a juvenile decides to appeal, does he have a right to be provided with an attorney?

Probably. The right to appeal does not make much sense without a corollary right to the assistance of counsel.[169] This would include the right to counsel *free of charge* if the juvenile or his parents are without funds to pay.[170] Moreover, a number of juvenile court acts provide for the assistance of counsel at every stage of the proceeding,[171] which might well include the appellate process.

If a juvenile decides to appeal, does he have a right to be furnished with a free transcript of the proceedings?

The Supreme Court ruled in 1956, that if an indigent adult criminal files an appeal of his conviction, he must be furnished with a free transcript of his trial.[172] It would therefore stand to reason that juveniles are entitled to the same right. Indeed, this position has been upheld by a number of state courts and established by a number of state statutes.[173]

If the parents of a child charged with delinquency or in need of supervision refuse to cooperate or attend the hearing, does a child have the right to have the petition substituted with a neglect petition?

Perhaps. If the court has reason to believe that a young person is delinquent because he is neglected and that he may receive better treatment if found to be a neglected child, the court may withdraw a delinquency petition and file one alleging parental neglect in its place.[174] (There are certain dangers involved with this procedure, however, not the least of which is that if found to be neglected, a child may be placed in a child-caring institution for his protection.)

Can a young person be held for contempt of a juvenile or family court?

Yes. If a young person shows contempt for a juvenile court by acting disrespectfully or by disrupting the proceedings, he may be held in contempt by a juvenile court judge.[175]

Can a young person be held for contempt of an adult court?

Yes. This constitutes the one major exception to the exclusive jurisdiction of juvenile courts over the criminal conduct of young people. If a young person disobeys an order of an adult court or shows disrespect for it, a judge may hold him in contempt without referring the matter to juvenile court.[176]

May juveniles be forced to testify before adult grand juries?

Probably, so long as they are properly served with a subpoena to testify. At least one court, however, has given juveniles greater protection than adults who are called to appear before grand juries. The Supreme Court of Louisiana recently held that juveniles, but not adults, were entitled to be accompanied by an attorney to assist them in invoking proper constitutional protections.[177]

The Effect of Juvenile Court Findings and the Confidentiality of Records

If a young person is found by a juvenile court to be delinquent or in need of supervision, is he then considered a criminal? Does he lose any of his civil rights?

No. Juvenile court proceedings are noncriminal in nature and their dispositions are not penal in character.[178] While certain procedural rights have been granted juveniles on the theory that the proceedings are quasi-criminal, the effect of an adjudication remains noncriminal.

In many states, statutes expressly state that no adjudication of the juvenile court may operate to impose the civil disabilities imposed by adult convictions, that no child is to be deemed a criminal, and that his adjudication is not to be considered a conviction of a crime.[179]

Are juvenile court records confidential?

Yes, in most states. The vast majority of states make court records confidential and limit public access to them.[180] The purpose of confidentiality is to enhance the rehabilitative prospects of young people by eliminating or reducing disclosure to schools, to future employers, to governmental agencies, and to the community at large. This policy complements the theory that juvenile court procedures are not criminal in nature and are not meant to subject a child to future civil disabilities.

The confidentiality of records also serves the general protective purpose of juvenile court proceedings. In this regard the United States Supreme Court stated,

> There is no reason why, consistently with due process, a state cannot continue, if it deems it appropriate, to provide and to improve provisions for the confidentiality of records of police contacts and court action relating to juveniles.[181]

However, there is a slowly developing trend to opening records to public inspection. At least six states allow legal records of juvenile offenders to be inspected by the public.[182] Maine permits unfettered public access to court proceedings involving juveniles charged with serious offenses.[183] New Mexico[184] allows public inspection of the juvenile records of repeat offenders and Alaska[185] permits inspection of police records by the public.

What does "confidential" mean?

Unfortunately, there is no clear or commonly accepted definition of this word. First, there is confusion as to which records are intended to be confidential. Does the category include, for example, police records, probation reports, or *copies* of records sent to other agencies? Second, few states describe the select group of people entitled to gain access to confidential records, or those (all others) to whom information is to be denied. Third, there is a wide range of practices employed to keep records physically confidential. Some states, for example, permit the *destruction* of juvenile court records, others *seal* them, and still others merely mark them "confidential." (Generally, sealed records are kept in locked files or otherwise rendered inaccessible without extraordinary effort. Expungement or destruction, on the other hand, involves the erasure, inking out, or obliteration of records or parts of them. Records neither sealed nor expunged or destroyed are often stored in a manner similar to all other records.) Finally, in many states there is no agreement as to what confidentiality means with regard to a juvenile or a former delinquent who is asked whether or not he has a juvenile record.

Do young people have the right to have their juvenile court records sealed?

A number of states provide for the sealing of records under certain conditions. California permits an individual to petition the juvenile court for sealing 5 years after the court's jurisdiction over the child has elapsed, or when he reaches age 18;[186] Massachusetts provides that a person may petition 3 years after court jurisdiction has concluded,[187] and in other states the time period is 2 years.[188] Many states also require that, if records are to be sealed, the juvenile must not be convicted of a subsequent offense. Very few states, however, actually create procedures for the *notification* of a young person that he has the right to have his record sealed.

Does a young person have the right to have his juvenile court record expunged or destroyed?

Only in a minority of states, and the circumstances permitting destruction vary. In California, for example, the law permits courts to destroy previously sealed records.[189] Washington allows the court to destroy juvenile records routinely after the individual's twenty-third birthday.[190] In Connecticut, records must be erased immediately if the young person is not found delinquent, and if a child is found delinquent all references to the case must be removed from records if he is not charged with another offense for two years thereafter.[191]

In a few states where the right to have one's court records expunged does not exist by statute, a court may still order expungement if it is convinced that this course of action will serve the ends of justice. In New York, for example, where court records are kept from public access but not destroyed, that state's highest court ruled that judges have the power to order its own records expunged since even "nominally sealed records . . . may have unfortunate and undeserved consequences for the future of the individual concerned."[192]

Who is permitted to inspect the juvenile court records?

Even though juvenile court records are confidential, a number of people are entitled to gain access to them. This is often equally true when they are "sealed." In a number of states records are open for inspection to the juvenile him or herself, to any health or child care agency caring for the child, other juvenile court personnel, such as probation officers, and persons engaged in research projects.[193] Some states grant access to any person provided they have the permission of the court, and some have no defined procedures at all. In the latter case, total discretion is exercised by file clerks, who often permit inspection by prospective employers, officials of federal and state investigatory agencies, and representatives of the armed forces.

Even when rules governing access are clearly defined, few states provide criminal or even civil penalties for those who improperly disclose the contents of juvenile court records.[194]

Are police arrest records confidential?

Not usually. Most state laws that make juvenile court records confidential do not extend to records maintained by the police.[195] Those who justify this practice refer to the fact that police records are simply outside the scope and power of juvenile court laws and that an available record of one's prior involvement with the law assists juvenile court judges and law enforcement officers.[196]

The more states that permit juvenile records to become permanent, however, through such devices as photographing, fingerprinting, and palmprinting upon arrest, the more likely it is that mechanisms will be created to authorize destruction of these records.

Only in recent years, for example, has New York permitted certain juveniles to be fingerprinted. In recognition of the unfairness of keeping unreliable records, New York passed for the first time a law authorizing the destruction of records in either of two specified cases. First, unless a juvenile is adjudicated delinquent for committing what would be a felony, all fingerprints, palmprints, and photographs taken *must* be destroyed immediately upon dismissal of the proceedings.[197] Second, if, however, he is adjudicated delinquent, all such records must be destroyed when he reaches twenty-one or has been discharged from placement for three years, whichever occurs later, as long as he has had no subsequent criminal convictions or pending charges.[198] New York's highest court has broadly interpreted this law to empower family court judges to order the destruction of police records in all appropriate cases and not merely when juveniles had been fingerprinted first.[199] Before this decision, New York courts had consistently ruled that the family court was without the power to order the destruction of any records other than its own court records, regardless of the circumstances justifying destruction.[200]

Since juvenile court records are confidential, and in some states sealed or expunged as well, does a young person who has been taken to juvenile court have the right to deny the fact that he has a record?

Yes, in a growing number of states. In Alabama, California, Colorado, Connecticut, District of Columbia, Georgia, Idaho, Indiana, Kansas, Kentucky, Louisiana, Minnesota, Nevada, New Mexico, Ohio, Texas, Utah, Vermont, Virginia, Washington, West Virginia, and Wyoming, laws provide that once a record is sealed the proceedings shall be deemed "never to have occurred." In some states this means that the court may respond to an outside inquiry that no records exist. In others, it entitles the child himself to reply in the negative. California, for example, provides that after sealing, "the proceedings in such case shall be deemed never to have occurred, and the person may properly reply accordingly to any inquiry about the events, records of which are ordered sealed."[201]

In other states, however, a child who has been the subject of a juvenile court proceeding is placed in an extremely difficult position when he is later asked by a prospective employer if he has a juvenile court record. It would appear that statutes protecting the confidentiality of juvenile court records and those rendering delinquents free from criminal and civil disabilities are meant to keep information regarding a young person's previous misbehavior from public scrutiny. Nevertheless, if a child tells the truth about his record, he may be denied employment, and if he lies about prior court contacts he may be subjecting himself to conclusions of dishonesty if it should be discovered that a record exists. The young person's dilemma is created by laws that pretend to insure confidentiality and promote rehabilitation but fail to provide a mechanism whereby a young person may escape his past.

Moreover, very few states prevent employers from denying jobs to prospective employees based on the existence of a juvenile court record,[202] and applications for government-related jobs often require a sworn statement that all information supplied is true.

Courts are becoming sympathetic to the problem of protecting a young person from his previous court involvement. In a recent federal case, for example, a juvenile pleaded guilty to a narcotics charge and was confined under the Youth Corrections Act.[203] After serving his sentence the conviction was "set aside" pursuant to the federal statute that reads:

> Upon the unconditional discharge by the division of a committed youth offender before the expiration of the maximum sentence imposed upon him, the conviction shall be automatically set aside and the division shall issue to the youth offender a certificate to that effect.
>
> Where a youth offender has been placed on probation by the court, the court may thereafter, in its discretion, unconditionally discharge such youth offender from probation prior to the expiration of the maximum period of probation theretofore fixed by the court, which discharge shall automatically set aside the conviction, and the court shall issue to the youth offender a certificate to that effect.[204]

In ordering all records expunged, the court directed that "the government and its agents will be required to respond in the negative to any and all inquiries concerning the set-aside conviction and arrest records." In addition, the court announced that the juvenile may legally reply in the negative whether he was ever arrested or convicted.[205]

If a young person testifies as a witness in an adult criminal proceeding, must he answer questions about his juvenile court record, if asked?

Yes. The United States Supreme Court has held that a juvenile witness against an adult criminal defendant could be cross-examined about his own prior delinquency and his current probationary status. The Court based its ruling on the theory that a criminal defendant's right to test the credibility of testimony against him and seek the truth is greater than the state's desire to protect the records of children.[206]

Can juvenile records be used to impeach a witness in juvenile court?

Yes.[207] A witness's prior records generally may be used at trial.

May juvenile records be used against a former juvenile delinquent who is later an accused in an adult criminal case?

Generally, no. In most states an accused adult cannot be impeached on cross-examination on the basis of previous "conviction" or "crimes" for which he was adjudicated a delinquent, since under state law these acts are not "crimes." However, many states permit the use of juvenile records for consideration in determining the sentence to impose on an already convicted adult.[208]

May juvenile records be used for other purposes in other courts?

Perhaps. Courts will consider, on a case-by-case basis, whether otherwise confidential records may be used for specific purposes. A Louisiana court, for example, recently allowed disclosure of a juvenile delinquent's records in order to allow a victim the chance to sue the juvenile and his parents for monetary damages caused by alleged delinquent acts. The court found the victim's interest in bringing suit to constitute good cause to authorize disclosure.[209]

NOTES

1. MASS. GEN. LAWS ANN. ch. 119 §52 (1969); N.Y. Fam. Ct. Act. §301.2 (1983).
2. *See, e.g.*, COLO. REV. STAT. ANN. §19–1–103(3) (9)(a) (1978); TEX. FAM. CODE ANN. §51.02(1)(A) (1975).
3. *Michael B. v. Kirkpatrick*, 44 Cal. App. 3d 443, 118 Cal. Rptr. 685 (1975). *See also In re Gladys R.*, 1 Cal. 3d 855, 464 P.2d 127, 83 Cal. Rptr. 671 (1970); *Commonwealth v. Durham*, 255 Pa. Super. 539, 389 A.2d 108 (1978).
4. *In re Dow,* 75 Ill. App. 3d 1002, 393 N.E.2d 1346 (1979). *See also In re Michael*, 423 A.2d 1180 (R.I. 1981); *In re Skinner,* 249 S.E.2d 746 (S.C. 1978); *K.M.S. v. State*, 129 Ga. App. 683, 200 S.E.2d 916 (1973).
5. *See, e.g.*, N.Y. FAM. CT. ACT. §§301.2, 302.1(1), 302.1(2) (1983); *In re Kalvin*, 99 Misc.2d 996, 417 N.Y.S.1d 826 (Fam. Ct. 1979); *In re Roger W.*, 61 A.D.2d 884, 402 N.Y.S.2d 874 (4th Dept. 1978); *In re J.T.*, 526 S.W.2d 646 (Tex. Civ. App. 1975); *Miguel v. State*, 500 S.W.2d 680 (Tex. Civ. App. 1973).
6. At least 30 states follow this approach. *See, e.g.*, CAL. WELF. & INST. CODE §§602, 604(a) (Supp. 1982); MASS. GEN. LAWS ANN. ch. 119, §72A (Supp. 1982); 42 PA. CONS. STAT. ANN. §6302 (1982); TEX. FAM. CODE ANN. §51.02(1) (1975).
7. *See, e.g.*, OR. REV. STAT. §419.478 (1981).
8. *See, e.g.*, N.H. REV. STAT. ANN. §169–B;4 (Supp. 1981).
9. *Lamb v. Brown*, 456 F.2d 18 (10th Cir. 1972), *People v. Ellis*, 57 Ill.

2d 127, 311 N.E.2d 98 (1974); *In re Patricia A.*, 31 N.Y.2d 83, 286 N.E.2d 432,335 N.Y.S.2d 33 (1972).

10. *Long v. Robinson*, 316 F. Supp. 22 (D. Md. 1970), *aff'd*. 436 F.2d 1116 (4th Cir. 1971).
11. *See, e.g.*, MASS. GEN. LAWS ANN. ch. 119, §52 (1969).
12. *See, e.g.*, ILL. ANN. STAT. ch. 37, §702–7 (Supp. 1982); WIS. STAT. ANN. §48.18(1) (1979).
13. *See, e.g.*, N.Y. FAM. CT. ACT §301.2 (1983); *In re B.L.*, 301 N.W.2d 387 (N.D. 1981); *In re A.A.*, 36 A.D.2d 1001, 321 N.Y.S.2d 59 (3d Dept. 1971); *In re John M.*, 65 Misc.2d 609, 318 N.Y.S.2d 904 (Fam. Ct. 1971). *See also* R.I. Gen. Laws §14–1–3 (f) (1981).
14. *See, e.g.*, TEX. FAM CODE §51.03(a)(1) (Supp. 1982).
15. *See, e.g.*, KY. REV. STAT. ANN. §208.170 (1977); MASS. GEN. LAWS ANN. ch. 119, §61 (Supp. 1982); OHIO REV. CODE ANN. §2151.26 (A) (Supp. 1981).
16. *See, e.g.*, FLA. STAT. ANN. §39.02(5)(a)(b) (Supp. 1981); ILL. ANN. STAT. ch. 37, §702.7 (Supp. 1982); WIS. STAT. ANN. §48.18(1) (1979).
17. *See, e.g.*, ME. REV. STAT. ANN. tit. 15, §3101(4)(A) (1980); N.H. REV. STAT. ANN. §169–B:24 (Supp. 1981); S.C. Code §43–17–60 (1977).
18. CONN. GEN. STAT. ANN. §§46b–126, 46b–127 (Supp. 1982).
19. MICH. COMP. LAWS ANN. §712A.4(1) (Supp. 1982).
20. ILL. ANN. STAT. ch. 37, §702–7 (Supp. 1982).
21. *Breed v. Jones*, 421 U.S. 519 (1975).
22. 383 U.S. 541 (1966). *See also People v. Rahn*, 59 Ill. 2d 302, 319 N.E.2d 787 (1974).
23. *See, e.g., U.S. v. Bland*, 472 F.2d 1329 (D.C. Cir. 1972), *cert. denied*, 412 U.S. 909 (1973); *State v. Grayer*, 191 Neb. 523, 215 N.W.2d 859 (1974); ARK. STAT. ANN. §45–418 (Supp. 1979); UTAH CODE ANN. §78–3a–25(7) (Supp. 1981). *But see* 18 U.S.C. §5031–5032 (1976); *State ex rel. Coats v. Johnson*, 597 P.2d 328 (Okla. Crim. App. 1979).
24. *See, e.g.*, FLA. STAT. ANN. §§39.02(5) & 39.02(2) (Supp. 1981); N.J. STAT. ANN. §§2A:4–48, 2A:4–49 (Supp. 1982).
25. *Kent v. U.S. supra* note 22. *See also* COLO. REV. STAT. ANN. §19–1–106, 19–3–108 (1978 & Supp. 1981); MONT. CODE ANN. §41–5–511 (1981); *State v. Doe*, 6 Hawaii 561, 606 P.2d 1326 (1980); *Inge v. Slayton*, 395 F. Supp. 560 (E.D. Va. 1975); *Kempler v. Maryland*, 428 F.2d 169 (4th Cir. 1970); *Lewis v. State*, 86 Nev. 889, 478 P.2d 168 (1970).
26. 383 U.S. 541 at 566–67. *See also* similar standards codified in D.C. CODE ANN. §16–2307 (1966); ILL. ANN. STAT. ch. 37, §702–7(3)(a) (Supp. 1982).
27. Among the exceptions are Nevada and Rhode Island.
28. *See, e.g.*, N.C. GEN. STAT. §§7A–608, 7A–609, 7A–610 (1981); TEX. FAM. CODE §54.02(f) (1975); VA. CODE ANN. §16.1–269(A)(3)(a) (Supp. 1979); *Davis v. State*, 297 So.2d 289 (Fla. 1974). *See* contra *U.S. ex. rel. Bombacino v. Bensinger*, 498 F.2d 875 (7th Cir.), *cert. denied*, 419 U.S. 1019 (1974).
29. *See, e.g.*, GA. CODE ANN. 24A–2501 (a)(3) (1981). This does *not* mean

that if suitable rehabilitative facilities to treat a child are unavailable, he is to be considered unamenable to treatment. *See, e.g., In re J.E.C.*, 302 Minn. 387, 225 N.W.2d 245 (1975).

30. 37 ILL. STAT. ANN. ch. 37, (3)(a) (Supp. 1982).
31. N.Y. C.P.L. §180.75(4); *People v. Martinez*, 97 Misc. 2d 598, 412 N.Y.S.2d 276 (1978); *People v. Russell*, in 7 Fam. L. Rptr. 2001 (Sup. Ct. 1980).
32. *In re Dahl*, 278 N.W.2d 316 (Minn. 1979). *See also Commonwealth v. Greiner*, 479 Pa. 364, 388 A.2d 698 (1978); *J.G.B. v. State*, 136 Ga. App. 75, 220 S.E.2d 79 (1975).
33. *In re Givens*, 307 N.W.2d 489 (Minn. 1981).
34. MINN. STAT. ANN. §260.125(3) (1982).
35. *See, e.g., In re Randolph T.*, 292 Md. 97, 437 A.2d 230 (1981), *cert. denied*, 455 U.S. 993 (1982).
36. *See, e.g.*, MASS. GEN. LAWS ANN. ch. 119, §61 (Supp. 1982); MINN. STAT. §260.125(2)(d)(2) (1982).
37. *See, e.g.*, CAL. WELF. & INST. CODE §707 (Supp. 1982).
38. Okla. Stat. Ann. tit. 10, §§1104.2, 1112(b) (1982).
39. *State ex rel. Coats v. Johnson, supra* note 23.
40. *People v. Chi Wo Wong*, 18 Cal.3d 698, 135 Cal. Rptr. 392, 557 P.2d 976 (1976).
41. *State V. Stanley*, 60 Haw. 527, 592 P.2d 422, *cert. denied*, 444 U.S. 871 (1979).
42. *State v. Harwood*, 98 Idaho 793, 572 P.2d 1228 (1977).
43. *D. H. v. People*, 192 Colo. 542, 561 P.2d 5 (1977).
44. *In re Clay*, 246, N.W.2d 263 (Iowa 1976).
45. *People v. Jiles*, 43 Ill. 2d 145, 251 N.E.2d 529 (1969); *People v. Martin*, 67 Ill. 2d 462, 367 N.E.2d 1329 (1977).
46. *J.G.J. v. State ex rel. Lamm*, 609 P.2d 787 (Okla. Crim. App. 1980).
47. *Clemmons v. State*, 162 Ind. App. 50, 317 N.E.2d 859 (1974), *cert. denied*, 423 U.S. 859 (1975). See *contra, State ex rel. Arbeiter v. Reagan*, 427 S.W.2d 371 (Mo. 1968).
48. *See* the adult parallel in *Simmons v. U.S.*, 390 U.S. 377 (1968).
49. *See, e.g., In re T.D.S.*, 289 N.W.2d 137 (Minn. 1980); *People v. Taylor*, 76 Ill. 2d 289, 391 N.E.2d 366 (1979); *People v. Hamilton*, 80 Ill. App. 3d 794, 400 N.E.2d 599 (1980); *People v. Martinez*, 97 Misc.2d 598, 412 N.Y.S.2d 276 (1978).
50. *See, e.g., In re D.E.D.*, 101 Wis.2d 193, 304 N.W.2d 133 (Ct. App. 1981); *Winstead v. State*, 371 So.2d 418 (Ala. 1979); *Marvin v. State*, 95 Nev. 836, 603 P.2d 1056 (1979); *In re B.T.*, 145 N.J. Super. 268, 367 A.2d 887 (1976), *cert. denied*, 37 N.J. 49, 372 A.2d 314 (1977).
51. *See, e.g.*, IDAHO CODE. ANN. §16–1801 (1979); ILL. ANN. STAT. ch. 37 §703–8 (1972); N.Y. FAM. CT. ACT §308.1 (1983).
52. *See, e.g.*, New York City Fam. Ct. Intake, Office of Probation, Directive F–50–26; D.C. Sup. Ct. Rules, Nos. 102–103 (1971); Fla. Intake Manual 17 (undated); Md. Dept. of Juv. Services, Intake Criteria.

53. *See, e.g.*, COLO. REV. STAT. ANN. §19–3–101 (1978). *See also In re Gault*, 387 U.S. 1, 55 (1967).
54. *See, e.g.*, ILL. REV. STAT. ch. 37, §703–8(5) (1972); N.Y. FAM. CT. ACT §308.1 (7) (1983); *In re Wayne H.*, 24 Cal. 3d 595, 596 P.2d 1, 156 Cal. Rptr. 344 (1979).
55. *In re S.*, 73 Misc.2d 187, 341 N.Y.S.2d 11 (Fam. Ct. 1973); *In re H.*, 71 Misc.2d 1042, 337 N.Y.S.2d 118 (Fam. Ct. 1972).
56. *White v. Maryland*, 373 U.S. 59 (1963). *See also Coleman v. Alabama*, 399 U.S. 1 (1970); *Hamilton v. Alabama*, 368 U.S. 52 (1961).
57. COLO. REV. STAT. ANN. §19–3–101(2)(c)(I) (1978).
58. *See, e.g., State v. Chatham*, 28 Wash. App. 580, 624 P.2d 1180 (1981); WASH. REV. CODE ANN. §13.40.070 (Supp. 1982).
59. *In re Gault, supra* note 53, at 33.
60. *In re Dennis*, 291 So.2d 731 (Miss. 1974).
61. *T.L.T. v. State*, 133 Ga. App. 895, 212 S.E.2d 650 (1975); *In re Bryant*, 18 Ill. App.3d 887, 310 N.E.2d 713 (1974); *Davies v. State*, 171 Ind. App. 487, 357 N.E.2d 914 (1976); *In re Walsh*, 59 Misc.2d 917, 300 N.Y.S.2d 859 (Fam. Ct. 1969); *In re Wilson*, 438 Pa. 425, 264 A.2d 614 (1970); *In re Richard*, 75 Wash.2d 208, 449 P.2d 809 (1969).
62. *Johnson v. State*, 401 S.W.2d 298 (Tex. Civ. App. 1966); *In re Long*, 184 So.2d 861 (Miss. 1966).
63. *See, e.g., In re J.*, 26 Cal. App. 3d 768, 103 Cal. Rptr. 21 (1972); *In re Maricopa County Juv. Action*, 21 Ariz. App. 542, 521 P.2d 641, *vacated and remanded*, 523 P.2d 1034 (1974); *In re Howard*, 515 P.2d 1399 (Okl. 1973).
64. *D.J.M. v. State*, 598 S.W.d 726 (Tex. Civ. App. 1980); Tex. Code Ann. §54.03(b) (1975).
65. *See, e.g.*, CAL. WELF. & INST. CODE §658 (Supp. 1982); MINN. STAT. ANN. §§260.135, 260.141 (1982); TEX. FAM. CODE ANN. §§53.6, 53.07 (1975).
66. *R.L.R. v. State*, 487 P.2d 27 (Alaska 1971); *Commonwealth v. Superintendent of State Correctional Institution*, 212 Pa. Super. 422, 242 A.2d 903 (1968). *But see U.S. v. Watts*, 513 F.2d 5 (10th Cir. 1975).
67. *See, e.g., In re Chatman*, 36 Ill. App. 3d 227, 343 N.E.2d 569 (1976); *People v. Simpson*, 35 Mich. App. 1, 192 N.W.2d 118 (1971); *R.L.R. v. State, supra* note 67; *In re Lawrence S.*, 29 N.Y.2d 206, 275 N.E.2d 577, 325 N.Y.S.2d 921 (1971). The leading adult case in this area, *Boykin v. Alabama*, 395 U.S. 238 (1969) was extended to juvenile court proceedings in California by *In re M.*, 11 Cal. App. 3d 741, 96 Cal. Rptr. 887 (1970), and in Arizona by *In re Maricopa County Juvenile Action No. J–86715*, 122 Ariz. 300, 594 P.2d 554 (1979).
68. *See, e.g., In re Myacutta A.*, 75 A.D.2d 774, 428 N.Y.S.2d 231 (1st Dept. 1980); *Robinson v. Leahy*, 401 F. Supp. 1027 (N.D. Ill. 1975); *In re James K.*, 47 A. D.2d 946, 367 N.Y.S.2d 312 (2d Dept. 1975); *In re Francis W.*, 42 Cal. App. 3d 892, 117 Cal. Rptr. 277 (1974). For

a slightly different result, *see In re R.B.*, 81 Ill. App. 3D 462, 401 N.E.2d 568 (1980).

69. *See, e.g., In re Ray O.*, 97 Cal. App. 3d 136, 158 Cal. Rptr. 550 (1979); *People v. Arbuckle*, 22 Cal. 3d 749, 587 P.2d 220, 150 Cal. Rptr. 778 (1978).
70. *Klopfer v. North Carolina*, 386 U.S. 213 (1967); *In re Russell C.*, 120 N.H. 260, 414 A.2d 934 (1980).
71. *In re Gault, supra* note 53, at 40–50.
72. *See, e.g., P.V. v. District Court*, 609 P.2d 110 (Colo. 1980); *In re Russell C., supra* note 71; *In re Anthony P.*, 104 Misc.2d 1024, 430 N.Y.S.2d 479 (Fam. Ct. 1980); *Piland v. Clark Co. Juv. Ct.*, 85 Nev. 489, 457 P.2d 523 (1969); *State v. Henry*, 78 N.M. 573, 434 P.2d 692 (1967).
73. ILL. ANN. STAT. ch. 37, §704–2 (Supp. 1982).
74. CAL. WELF. & INST. CODE §675 (1972).
75. N.Y. FAM. CT. ACT, §§340.1, 340.1(3) (1983).
76. 18. U.S.C. §5036 (1976).
77. *See, e.g., U.S. v. Furey*, 500 F.2d 338 (2d Cir. 1974); *In re G.T.*, 304 A.2d 865 (D.C. App. 1973).
78. *See, e.g., In re C.B.*, 173 N.J. Super. 424, 414 A.2d 572 (1980); *In re Armour*, 59 Ill. 2d 102, 319 N.E.2d 496 (1974).
79. *U.S. v. Furey, Supra* note 78; *Benton v. State*, 307 So.2d 198 (Fla. Dist. Ct. App. 1975), *aff'd*, 337 So. 2d 797 (1976). Contra *State v. White*, 223 N.W.2d 173 (Iowa 1974).
80. *See, e.g., Z. v. Superior Court*, 3 Cal. App. 3d 797, 91 Cal. Rptr. 594, 478 P.2d 26 (1970); *In re Hitzeman*, 281 Minn. 275, 161 N.W.2d 542 (1968); *Ames v. Ames*, 89 N.J. Super. 267, 214 A.2d 544 (1965).
81. *See* D.C. CODE §16–2333 (Supp. 1981); LA. CODE JUV. PROC. ANN. art 59 (1982); N.D. CENT. CODE §27–20–52 (1974); Ohio R. Juv. Proc. 25–25 (1976); TEX. FAM. CODE ANN. §51.14 (1975). *See also T.P.S. v. State*, 590 S.W.2d 946 (Tex. Civ. App. 1979).
82. N.Y. FAM. CT. ACT. §331.2, 331.4 (1983).
83. *See, e.g., Jackson v. Wainwright*, 390 F.2d 288 (5th Cir. 1968).
84. *Brady v. Maryland*, 373 U.S. 83 (1963).
85. *See, e.g., People ex. rel Hanrahan v. Felt*, 48 Ill.2d 171, 269 N.E.2d 1 (1971); *Z. v. superior Court, supra* note 81; *Matter of Edwin R., supra* note 83.
86. *Chapman v. California*, 386 U.S. 18, 23 (1967); *In re Gault, supra* note 53, at 25–26.
87. *See, e.g., State ex rel. Duffy v. Lake Juvenile Court*, 238 Ind. 404, 151 N.E.2d 293 (1958); *Anonymous v. Superior Court, County of Pima*, 14 Ariz. App. 502, 484 P.2d 655 (1971); *In re James H.*, 41 A.D.2d 667, 34 N.Y.S.2d 92 (2nd Dept. 1973), *rev'd on other grounds*, 34 N.Y.2d 814, 359 N.Y.S.2d 48 (1974). It is also reasonable that a juvenile court judge should be disqualified after hearing the facts at Intake. *See In re Reis*, 7 Cr. L. Rptr. 2151 (R.I. Fam. Ct. April 14,1970).

88. *In re Ruth H.*, 26 Cal. App. 3d 77, 102 Cal. Rptr. 534 (1972); *Lois R. v. Superior Court, County of Los Angeles*, 19 Cal. App.3d 895, 97 Cal. Rptr. 158 (1971); *Gloria M. v. Superior Court, County of Los Angeles*, 21 Cal. App.3d 525, 98 Cal. Rptr. 604 (1971).
89. *In re Gault*, supra note 54, at 36, incorporating *Gideon v. Wainwright*, 372 U.S. 335 (1963). *See also* CAL. WELF. & INST. CODE §679 (Supp. 1982); N.Y. FAM. CT. ACT §249 (Supp. 1981); D.C. CODE ANN. §16–2304(a) (1973) (Supp. 1978).
90. *In re Gault, supra* note 53, at 41.
91. *County of York v. Johnson*, 206 Neb. 200, 292 N.W.2d 31 (Neb. 1980).
92. *In re Gary T.*, 29 A.D.2d 980, 289 N.Y.S.2d 790 (2nd Dept. 1968); *In re Orcutt*, 173 N.W.2d 66 (Iowa 1969).
93. *See, e.g., Miller v. Quantose*, 332 F. Supp. 1269, 1275 (E.D. Wis. 1971). *See also* Issacs, "The Role of the Lawyer Representing Minors in the New Family Court," 12 *Buff. L. Rev.* 501 (1963).
94. Canon 7 of the American Bar Association Code of Professional Responsibility (1970) states, "A lawyer should represent a client zealously within the bounds of the law," but the association's commentary offers little explanation concerning the role of counsel in representing minors. Ethical Consideration (E.C.) 7–3 states, "A lawyer may serve simultaneously as both advocate and advisor, but the two roles are essentially different . . . while serving as advocate, a lawyer should resolve in favor of his client. . . ." E.C. 7–11 states, "The responsibilities of a lawyer may vary according to the intelligence, experience, mental condition or age of client. . . ."
95. *See, e.g., In re M.G.S.*, 267 Cal. App.2d 239, 72 Cal. Rptr. 808 (1968); *Haziel v. U.S.*, 404 F.2d 1275 (1968); *See also In re F.*, 11 Cal. 3d 249, 520 P.2d 986, 113 Cal. Rptr. 170 (1974).
96. 387 U.S. 1 at 39, n. 65 (1966).
97. *Kent v. U.S.*, 386 U.S. 541 at 563 (1966). *See also* Wizner, "The Child and the State: Adversaries in the Juvenile Justice System," 4 *Colum. Human Rts. L. Rev.* 389 (1972).
98. An adult defendant has the right to elect to proceed without counsel in a criminal case when the election is made knowingly and intelligently. *Faretta v. California*, 422 U.S. 806 (1975).
99. *See, e.g., In re R.M.*, 105 N.J. Super. 372, 252 A.2d 237 (1969); *People v. Lara*, 67 Cal.2d 365, 432 P.2d 202, 62 Cal. Rptr. 586 (1967), *cert. denied*, 392 U.S. 945 (1968); *In re Francis W.*, 42 Cal. App.3d 892, 117 Cal. Rptr. 277 (1974).
100. *Von Moltke v. Gillies*, 332 U.S. 708, 724 (1948); *In re S.*, *supra* note 68; *In re Butterfield*, 253 Cal. App. 2d 794, 61 Cal. Rptr. 874 (1967).
101. *See, e.g., R.L.R. v. State, supra* note 66.
102. *In re Appeal from Civil Court, Cecil County*, 25 Md. App. 26, 332 A.2d 680 (1975). *See also* TEX. FAM. CODE ANN. §§51.09, 51.10 (1975 & Supp. 1982).

103. *See, e.g., State ex rel. J.M. v. Taylor,* 276 S.E.2d 199 (W.Va. 1981); *Matter of Dominick F.,* 74 A.D.2d 485, 428 N.Y.S.2d 113 (4th Dept. 1980); N.Y. FAM. CT. ACT §249–a (Supp. 1981). *See also Commonwealth v. Juvenile,* 389 Mass. 128, 449 N.E.2d 634 (1983).
104. TEX. FAM. CODE ANN. §§51.09(a), 51.10(b) (1975 & Supp. 1982).
105. *In re Gault, supra* note 54, at 41; *In re Matter of Celli,* 27 A.D.2d 702, 276 N.Y.S.2d 967 (4th Dept. 1967); *In re L.G.T.,* 216 So.2d 54 (Fla. App. 1968); *McBride v. Jacobs,* 247 F.2d 595 (1957).
106. *In re H.,* 2 Cal. 3d 513, 468 P.2d 204, 86 Cal. Rptr. 76 (1970). *But see* contra *In re Blaylock v. DeFoor,* 255 Ga. 688, 171 S.E.2d 146 (1969).
107. *Richmond Newspapers, Inc. v. Virginia,* 448 U.S. 555 (980).
108. *Smith v. Daily Mail Publishing Co.,* 443 U.S. 97, 105 (1979).
109. *Globe Newspaper Co. v. Superior Court,* 457 U.S. 596 (1982).
110. 457 U.S. at 612 (Burger, C.J., dissenting).
111. *In re Robert M.,* 109 Misc. 2d 427, 439 N.Y.S.2d 986 (1981).
112. *State ex rel Oregonian Pub. Co. v. Seiz,* 613 P.2d 23 (Ore. 1980). *See also Seattle Times Co. v. County of Benton,* 661 P.2d 964 (Wash. 1983); *R.L.K. v. State,* 269 N.W.2d 367 (Minn. 1978); *In re L.,* 24 Or. App. 257, 546 P.2d 153 (1976); *State ex rel E.R. v. Flynn,* 88 Wash. 2d 37, 276 N.W.2d 313 (1979). Compare *Brian W. v. Superior Court,* 20 Cal. 3d 618, 574 P.2d 788, 143 Cal. Rptr. 717 (1978).
113. CAL. WELF. & INST CODE §676 (Supp. 1982); Cal. Jur. Ct. R. 1311(e) (1980); ILL. ANN. STAT. ch. 37, §§701–20(6), 702–10.1 (Supp. 1982); 42 PA. CONS. STAT. ANN. §6336(d) (1982). *See also* D. Mirell and D. Fainer, Jr., "Delinquency Hearings and the First Amendment," *Juv. & Fam. Ct. J.,* p. 17 (Nov. 1980).
114. ME. REV. STAT. ANN. tit. 15 §3307(2) (Supp. 1982); MONT. CODE ANN. §41–5.60 (1981); UTAH CODE ANN. §78–3a–33 (1977).
115. *See, e.g.,* CAL. WELF. & INST. CODE §676 (Supp. 1982); *R.L.R. v. State, supra* note 67.
116. *Oklahoma Publishing Co. v. District Court,* 430 U.S. 308 (1977).
117. *See, e.g., Nebraska Press Assn. v. Stuart,* 427 U.S. 539 (1976).
118. *Smith v. Daily Mail Publishing Co., supra* note 109.
119. *State ex rel. v. The Times & Democrat,* 276 S.C. 26 274 S.E.2d 910 (1981).
120. *Duncan v. Louisiana,* 391 U.S. 145 (1968); *Baldwin v. New York,* 399 U.S. 66 (1970).
121. 403 U.S. 528 (1971).
122. *In re S.,* 44 A.D.2d 352, 355 N.Y.S.2d 143 (1st Dept. 1974); *Richard M. v. Superior Court,* 4 Cal.3d 370, 93 Cal. Rptr. 752, 482 P.2d 664 (1971).
123. *See, e.g., U.S. ex rel Murray v. Owens,* 465 F.2d 289 (2nd Cir.), *cert. denied.* 409 U.S. 1117 (1972); *Matter of Wick,* 644 P.2d 630 (Or. App. 1982); *State v. Lawley,* 91 Wash. 2d 654, 591 P.2d 772 (1979); *People v. Young,* 99 Misc. 2d 328, 416 N.Y.S.2d 171 (Fam.

Ct. 1979); *In re William M.*, 90 Misc. 2d 173, 393 N.Y.S.2d 535 (Fam. Ct. 1977). Contra *In re Felder,* 93 Misc.2d 369, 402 N.Y.S.2d 528 (Fam. Ct. 1978).

124. *U.S. v. Doe*, 385 F. Supp. 902 (D. Ariz. 1974); *U.S. v. Torres*, 500 F.2d 944 (2nd Cir. 1974).
125. *See, e.g., R.L.R. v. State, supra* note 66; COLO. REV. STAT. ANN. §19–1–106(4) (1978); MASS. GEN. LAWS ANN. ch. 119, §55A (Supp. 1982); MICH. COMP. LAWS ANN. §712A.17(2) (Supp. 1982); TEX. FAM. CODE ANN. §54.03(c) (Supp. 1980); WIS. STAT. ANN. §48.31(2) (Supp. 1982).
126. S.D. COMPL. LAWS ANN. §26–8–31 (1977).
127. *In re Gault, supra* note 53, at 58.
128. *In re Smith*, 326 P.2d 835 (Okl. 1958).
129. *State in Interest of Collins*, 288 So.2d 918 (La. 1973); *Dan J. v. Superior Court*, 4 Cal. 3d 836, 94 Cal. Rptr. 619, 484 P.2d 595 (1971).
130. *In re Gault, supra* note 53, at 58, note 102. *See also In re Gonzalez*, 139 Mont. 592, 336 P.2d 718 (1961).
131. *See, e.g.*, COLO. REV. STAT. §19–1–107(3) (1978).
132. *In re Winship*, 397 U.S. 358 (1970).
133. *See, e.g.*, CAL. WELF. & INST. CODE §701 (Supp 1982); ILL. ANN. STAT. ch. 37 §704–6 (Supp. 1982).
134. *See, e.g.*, 42 PA. CONS. STAT. ANN. §6341 (1982).
135. *In re Gault, supra* note 53, at 55.
136. *State in Interest of D.A.M.* 132 N.J. Super. 192, 333 A.2d 270 (1975).
137. *Harris v. New York*, 401 U.S. 222 (1971). To see whether a juvenile defendant must testify about a prior conviction as a juvenile, see *In re K.P.,* 167 N.J. Super. 290, 400 A.2d 840 (1979).
138. *In re Gault, supra* note 53, at 55.
139. *Griffin v. Illinois*, 351 U.S. 12, 17 (1956).
140. *Jacobs v. U.S.*, 350 F.2d 571 (4th Cir. 1965).
141. *Reed v. Duter,* 416 F.2d 744 (7th Cir. 1969).
142. 387 U.S. 1 at 36 (1967).
143. *In re Gault, supra* note 53, at 56 incorporating *Pointer v. Texas*, 380 U.S. 400 (1965).
144. *In re Gault, supra* note 53, at 56.
145. *See, e.g.*, GA. CODE ANN. §15–11–31(b) (1982); *In re Appeal* No. 544, 25 Md. App. 26, 332 A.2d 680 (1975); *In re W.J.*, 116 N.J. Super. 462, 282 A.2d 770 (1971); N.Y. FAM. CT. ACT §344.2 (1983); PA. STAT. ANN. tit. 42, §6338(b) (1982); TEX. FAM. CODE ANN. §54.03(e) (Supp. 1982).
146. *See, e.g., State ex rel Williams*, 325 So.2d 854 (La.Ct. App. 1976); *In re Collins*, 20 Ohio App. 2d 319, 253 N.E.2d 824 (1969); *In re Mitchel K.*, 22 Cal. 3d 946, 587 P.2d 1144, 151 Cal. Rptr. 330 (1978), *cert. denied*, 444 U.S. 845 (1979). *In re R.C.*, 39 Cal. App.3d 887, 114 Cal. Rptr. 735 (1974).
147. *See, e.g., A Minor v. Juvenile Dept; Fourth Jud. Dist.*, 96 Nev. 332,

608 P.2d 509 (1980); *In re Arthur M.*, 34 A.D.2d 761, 310 N.Y.S.2d 399 (1st Dept. 1970); *Smith v. State*, 525 P.2d 1251 (Okla. Crim. App. 1974); *State v. Smith*, 1 Ore. App. 583, 465 P.2d 247 (1970); TEX. FAM. CODE ANN. §54.03(e) (Supp. 1982).

148. *Landry v. State*, 504 S.W.2d 580 (Tex. Civ. App. 1973), *cert. denied*, 420 U.S. 945 (1975).
149. *In re Winship*, *supra* note 132.
150. *See, e.g.*, N.Y. FAM. CT. ACT §308.1(7) (1983); *In re Gladys R.*, 1 Cal.3d 855, 83 Cal. Rptr. 671, 464 P.2d 127 (1970); *In re Alexander*, 16 Md. App. 416, 297 A.2d 301 (1972).
151. *See, e.g.*, N.Y. FAM. CT. ACT §350.3 (1983).
152. D.C. CODE §16–2315(d) (Supp. 1978); *In re C.W.M.*, 407 A.2d 617 (D.C. App. 1979).
153. *See, e.g.*, *State ex rel Dandoy v. Superior Court*, 127 Ariz. 184, 619 P.2d 12 (1980); *In re M.G.S.*, 167 Cal. App.2d 329, 72 Cal. Rptr. 808 (1969); *State ex rel Causey*, 363 So.2d 472 (La. 1978); N.J. STATE ANN. §2A:4–60 (Supp. 1982); N.Y. FAM. CT. ACT §322.2 (1983); *In re L.J.*, 26 Or. App. 461, 552 P.2d 1322 (1976); *Winburn v. State*, 32 Wis.2d 152, 145 N.W.2d 178 (1966).
154. *In re H.C.*, 106 N.J. Super. 583, 256 A.2d 322 (Juv. & Dom. Rel. Ct. 1969).
155. *Pate v. Robinson*, 383 U.S. 375 (1966).
156. *See, e.g.*, D.C. CODE §16–2315(a) (Supp. 1978); ME. REV. STAT. ANN. tit. 15, §§3310(3), 3318 (1980); N.Y. FAM. CT. ACT §322.2 (1983).
157. 421 U.S. 519 (1975).
158. *See McCarver v. State*, 379 So.2d 979 (Fla. Dist. Ct. App. 1980).
159. *Swisher v. Brady*, 438 U.S. 204 (1978).
160. *Jesse W. v. Superior Court*, 26 Cal.3d 41, 603 P.2d 1296, 160 Cal. Rptr. 700 (1979). *See also State ex rel. Anglin v. Mitchell*, 596 S.W.2d 779 (Tenn. 1980); *In re Perrone C.*, 26 Cal.3d 49, 603 P.2d 1300, 160 Cal. Rptr. 704 (1979).
161. *See, e.g.*, *District of Columbia v. I.P.* 335 A.2d 224 (D.C. Ct. App. 1975).
162. *Coleman v. Superior Court in & for County of Pima*, 110 Ariz. 386, 519 P.2d 851 (Ariz. 1974).
163. *In re R.L.K.*, 67 Ill. App. 3d 451, 384 N.E.2d 531 (1978). *See also Garrison v. Jennings*, 529 P.2d 536 (Okla. Crim. App. 1974).
164. *See, e.g.*, *In re Waterman*, 212 Kan. 826, 516 P.2d 466 (1973); *Adoptive Parents v. Superior Court*, 105 Ariz. 438, 466 P.2d 732 (1970).
165. *See, e.g.*, CAL. WELF. & INST. CODE §800 (Supp. 1982). *See also In re N.*, 36 Cal. App.3d 935, 112 Cal. Rptr. 89 (1974); CONN. GEN. STATE. §46b–142 (Supp. 1982); D.C. CODE ANN. 11–741 (1966).
166. *See, e.g.*, *In re Brown*, 439 F. 2d 47 (3rd Cir. 1971).
167. *See, e.g.*, *Creek v. Stone*, 379 F.2d 106 (D.C. Cir. 1967); *State v. Raegan*, 427 S.W.2d 371 (Mo. 1968); *State v. Wade*, 39 Wash. 2d 744, 238 P.2d 914 (1951).

168. *In re Brown*, 439 F.2d 47 (3rd Cir. 1971).
169. *Douglas v. California*, 372 U.S. 353 (1963); *Anders v. California*, 386 U.S. 738 (1967).
170. *Reed v. Duter, supra* note 142; *In re L.G.T.*, 216 So.2d 54 (Fla. App. 1968); *In re Chambers*, 261 Iowa 31, 152 N.W.2d 818 (1969).
171. *See, e.g.*, N.Y. Fam. Ct. Act §249 (Supp. 1981); Cal. Welf. & Inst. Code §633 (1972).
172. *Griffin v. Illinois, supra* note 140.
173. *See, e.g., State ex rel. S.M.O. v. Resheske*, 329 N.W.2d 275 (Wis. App. 1982); *Agnew v. Superior Court*, 118 Cal. App. 2d 230, 257 P.2d 661 (1953); *Commonwealth v. Juvenile*, 280 N.E.2d 144 (Mass. 1972); *In re Boykin*, 39 Ill. 2d 617, 237 N.E.2d 460 (1968); Cal. Welf. & Inst. Code §800 (Supp. 1982).
174. *See, e.g.*, N.Y. Fam. Ct. Act §311.4 (1983); *In re Richard C.*, 43 A.D.2d 862, 352 N.Y.S.2d 15 (2nd Dept. 1974).
175. *People ex rel. Wayburn v. Schupf*, 47 A.D.2d 79, 365 N.Y.S.2d 235 (2nd Dept. 1975).
176. *See, e.g., In re Williams*, 306 F. Supp. 617 (D. D.C. 1969); *Thomas v. State*, 21 Md. App. 572, 320 A.2d 538 (1974); *Application of Balucan*, 44 Haw. 271, 353 P.2d 631 (1960).
177. *In re Grand Jury Subpoenas Issued to Graham*, 387 So.2d 1140 (La. 1980).
178. *Pee v. U.S.*, 274 F.2d 556 (1959); *White v. Reid*, 125 F. Supp. 647 (D.C. 1954); *In re Holmes Appeal*, 379 Pa. 599, 109 A.2d 523 (1954).
179. *See, e.g.*, Minn. Stat. Ann. §260.211 (1982); N.Y. Fam. Ct. Act §380.1 (1983).
180. *See, e.g.*, Minn. Stat. Ann. §260.161 (1982).
181. *In re Gault, supra* note 53, at 25.
182. Arkansas, Idaho, Iowa, Louisiana, Mississippi, and Rhode Island.
183. Me. Rev. Stat. Ann. §§3307, 3308 (1980 & Supp. 1982).
184. N.M. State. Ann. §32–1–45 (1981).
185. A.S. §09.25.120 (1978).
186. Cal. Welf. & Inst. Code §781 (Supp. 1982).
187. Mass. Gen. Laws Ann. ch. 276, §100B (1972).
188. *See, e.g.*, Conn. Gen. Stat. Ann. §46b–146 (Supp. 1982); Ohio Code Ann. §2151.358 (Supp. 1982).
189. Cal. Welf. & Inst. Code §§826, 826.5 (Supp. 1982).
190. Wash. Rev. Code §13.50–050(23)(a) (Supp. 1982).
191. Conn. Gen. Stat. Ann. §46b–146 (Supp 1982).
192. *Dorothy D. v. New York City Probation Dept.*, 49 N.Y.2d 212, 400 N.E.2d 1432, 424 N.Y.S.2d 890 (1980). *See also, St. Louis v. Drolet*, 67 Ill. 2d 43, 364 N.E.2d 61 (1977).
193. *See, e.g.*, N.M. Stat. Ann. §32–1–45 (1981).
194. Those providing penalties include Alaska, Colorado, Maine, New Mexico, South Carolina, and Vermont.
195. *See, e.g., Aetna Casualty & Surety Co. v. Barnard*, 393 Mich. 597, 227 N.W.2d 551 (1975).

196. *See, e.g., Monroe v. Tielsch*, 84 Wash. 2d 217, 525 P.2d 250 (1974).
197. N.Y. Fam. Ct. Act §354.1 (1983).
198. *Id.* at (4).
199. *Matter of Todd H.*, 49 N.Y.2d 1022, 406 N.E.2d 1338, 429 N.Y.S.2d 401 (1980).
200. *See, e.g., Matter of Antonio P.*, 40 N.Y.2d 960, 390 N.Y.S.2d 919, 359 N.E.2d 427 (1976); *Matter of Richard S. v. City of New York*, 32 N.Y.2d 592, 347 N.Y.S.2d 54, 300 N.E.2d 426 (1973); *Matter of Donald J.*, 37 A.D.2d 717, 325 N.Y.S.2d 235 (2d Dept. 1971).
201. Cal. Welf. & Inst. Code §781(a) (Supp. 1982).
202. *See, e.g.*, Mass. Gen. Laws ch. 119 §60 (Supp. 1982).
203. 18 U.S.C. §5010.
204. *Id.* at §§5021(a) & (b).
205. *U.S. v. Doe*, 495 F. Supp. 650 (D.R.I. 1980).
206. *Davis. v. Alaska*, 415 U.S. 308 (1974). *See also State v. Brown*, 135 N.J. Super. 584 334 A.2d 392 (1975); *State v. Interest of A.S.*, 130 N.J. Super, 308, 327 A.2d 260 (N.J. Juv. & Dom. Rel. Ct. 1974).
207. *In re C.D.L.*, 306 N.W.2d 819 (Minn. 1981).
208. *See, e.g., State v. McClendon*, 611 P.2d 728 (Utah 1980).
209. *Thibodeaux v. Judge, Juvenile Division of 14th Judicial Dist.*, 377 So.2d 508 (La. App. 1979).

III

Post-trial Dispositions: Probation, Parole, Training Schools, and Other Institutions

The purpose of the fact-finding hearing or trial is to determine whether allegations contained in the petition actually occurred. If the court decides that the facts were proven, it will enter a "finding" that is similar to a *conviction* (although in neglect and abuse matters this term loses some of its meaning). If no finding is made, the matter will in all probability be dropped, although voluntary services may be recommended. If a finding is made, the court must decide what should be done next. This decision, called a disposition, is made at a dispositional hearing.

Dispositional hearings are usually held a few days or weeks after the fact-finding hearing. There may be some instances when the dispositional hearing is held immediately after a finding has been made, but generally the court will schedule it for a later date to allow probationary, psychological, or school-related reports concerning the child to be prepared and presented to the court.

Dispositional Hearings

Does a young person have the right to a dispositional hearing?

Generally, yes. Pursuant to most interpretations of the Supreme Court's ruling in *Kent v. U.S.*,[1] a child has a constitutional right to have dispositional decisions preceded by a hearing. This has been established subsequently by numerous state statutes and court rulings.[2]

How soon after a finding has been made, must a dispositional proceeding take place?

There is no clear time limit, other than a reasonable amount of time necessary to gather social reports, mental examinations, or whatever other evidence may be required.[3] One court in Illinois, however, declared that a delay of 9 months awaiting a social report could not be permitted.[4] In New York, by statute, a dispositional hearing must be held within 2 months of the fact-finding hearing, but if the juvenile is in detention, the hearing must be held within 20 days for most delinquency cases and 60 days for very serious felony cases.[5] Although dispositional hearings occasionally are held immediately upon the completion of the fact-finding hearing,[6] a strong argument can be made that due process of law requires that the juvenile and his counsel be given an opportunity to prepare for the hearing in advance.

Is a young person entitled to be represented by counsel at a dispositional hearing?

Yes. Even though the *Gault* case required counsel at fact-finding hearings only (see chapter II), almost every state requires an attorney to represent a child at dispositional proceedings as well.[7]

What type of evidence may be considered in a dispositional proceeding?

Unlike fact-finding hearings, in which only relevant, material, and competent evidence may be admitted, a juvenile court may hear almost any evidence it considers helpful in reaching an informed decision in dispositional proceedings. Generally, this means all relevant and material evidence, but it may include incompetent (hearsay) evidence as well.[8]

Does an attorney for a juvenile have the right to examine social reports and cross-examine their authors and contributors during the dispositional proceeding?

It depends upon the state. Clearly, young people have *fewer* due process rights at the dispositional phase of the hearing than during the fact-finding phase, where cross-examination is guaranteed (see chapter II). This has led some courts to deny attorneys the right to review social reports and to cross-examine probation officers, social workers, and psychologists who contributed to, or prepared, the reports.[9]

Other courts have held that the ability to cross-examine the authors of reports that comprise part of the record is part of the child's constitutional right to due process of law.[10]

The Minnesota Supreme Court recently[11] ruled that juveniles in that state are entitled to a limited right to cross-examine witnesses in dispositional hearings even though the statute at issue does not mention dispositional hearings or distinguish them from adjudicatory hearings.[12]

At what age does the continuing jurisdiction of the juvenile court end?

Once a child comes under the jurisdiction of a juvenile court, he may be sentenced, committed, or placed on probation or parole beyond the date of the birthday that would have placed him beyond the reach of the juvenile court in the first place. (See appendix A for the ages of original jurisdiction.) The power to control the lives of children beyond that age is called the continuing jurisdiction of the court.

In most states (including California and Illinois) the juvenile court is granted continuing jurisdiction until the age of 21.[13] In a number of states, this jurisdiction ends at age 18.[14] In New York, jurisdiction ends at age 18 for most juvenile delinquents,[15] but may last up to age 21 for serious felony offenders.[16]

If the upper age limit has passed during a period of probation or parole, it is likely that the juvenile court loses its jurisdiction to revoke probation or parole.[17] Similarly, if a case is reversed on appeal during which time the child has meanwhile passed the age of original jurisdiction, the case will likely be dismissed rather than remanded to juvenile court for further consideration.[18]

Do juvenile courts have the power to sentence offenders to longer periods of incarceration than adults for identical conduct?

Yes. In a number of jurisdictions juveniles may be committed to an institution until the age of twenty-one, regardless of the age at which they are placed.[19] Court challenges to juvenile schemes that effectively deprived children of liberty for longer periods than adults, have generally been rejected on the theory that children are not being punished but rehabilitated and that rehabilitation frequently takes a long time to accomplish.[20] A few states, however, have recently recognized the unfairness of punishing juveniles more severely than adults for identical conduct and have restricted the power to do so.[21]

Under California law, a juvenile may not be sentenced to a longer sentence than an adult for the same crime.[22] In a recent case, however, the California Supreme Court rejected an equal protection claim by a juvenile who was sentenced to the maximum without a showing of certain aggravating circumstances that are required before an adult could receive the same sentence.[23] In 1976, the same court declared unconstitutional a statute that allowed young offenders who were convicted of misdemeanors in adult courts to serve longer sentences than adults.[24]

Can a juvenile be sentenced to death for a capital offense?

No state authorizes capital punishment or life imprisonment for delinquents *adjudicated in juvenile court*. However, if the juvenile is transferred to adult court, it is possible that he may be sentenced to death if convicted of a crime punishable by death, since most states make no distinction on the basis of age in the type of sentence that may be imposed. No person under the age of 18 has been executed in this country for decades.

The United States Supreme Court recently considered whether juveniles can be capitally punished.[25] The Court did not specifically answer the question. It did, however, reverse a death sentence for a 21-year-old man who was age 16 when he killed a police officer. In reversing, the Supreme Court held that sentencing courts must carefully consider the youth of an offender and all mitigating factors that may justify imposition of a less severe sentence. Although the Court recognized that "the normal 16-year-old customarily lacks the maturity of an adult,"[26] it did not foreclose the possibility of the death penalty being imposed on minors who commit capital offenses.

The California Supreme Court ruled in 1983, that under California law a person under 18 at the time the crime was committed may not be sentenced to life imprisonment without the possibility of parole.[27]

Probation and Parole

Do juvenile courts have the power to place a young person on probation?

Yes. Probation is a disposition designed to keep a child under some form of control by the juvenile court without actually sending him to a training school or institution. Probation usually involves the imposition of certain restrictions on the liberty or freedom of the child.

A young person placed on probation may have to be at home by a certain hour of the night or he may have to attend school and maintain passing grades. In some cases, the restrictions may be vague, such as "obeying all laws" or "staying out of trouble." In many cases, juveniles on probation must remain within the state and report to a probation officer on a regular basis.

If a child violates the terms or conditions of probation, he may have his probation revoked and be subject to placement in a training school or some other institution.

For how long a period of time may a young person be placed on probation?

It depends on the state. Some states have two-year limits, while others permit courts to place a child on probation for as long as the court has jurisdiction over the child (usually until he is twenty-one). Recently, a few states have instituted periodic reviews of young people on probation. Judges always have the discretion to discharge a person from probationary status if they see fit.

Does a young person have the right to be free from unreasonable restrictions and conditions while on probation?

Yes. Most terms of probations are up to the judge; very few are spelled out by statute.[28] But even with wide discretion, the conditions of probation should be consistent with the purpose of rehabilitation and treatment and may not violate a young person's constitutional rights (other than the right of liberty).

In New York, for example, a probation restriction that prohibited an adult from entering another county without permission was found unconstitutional.[29] In Virginia, a probation condition that required two delinquent boys to attend church every Sunday for one year was found to violate the constitutional guarantee of freedom of religion.[30]

Conditions requiring some form of treatment are generally permissible. If a child is ordered to undergo psychiatric counseling or treatment, however, it should first be demonstrated to the court that there is *need* for such treatment.

If a young person is accused of violating probation, is he entitled to a hearing before probation may be revoked?

Yes. Adults have been granted the right to a hearing when the state attempts to revoke probation.[31] Most states now extend this right to children as well.[32]

What this means is that a probation officer does not have the absolute power to revoke probation; it can only be revoked by a juvenile court after a hearng.[33]

Is a young person entitled to be represented by counsel at a probation revocation hearing?

Yes, in many states.[34] The United States Supreme Court has ruled that adults are not absolutely guaranteed the right to counsel at probation revocation hearings, but that the right depends on the "peculiarities of particular cases."[35] The Court stated that an important factor to be considered in such cases is "whether the probationer appears to be capable of speaking effectively for himself."[36] According to this test, it may be argued that juveniles have an absolute right to counsel at such hearings since they are not as capable of speaking for themselves as adults.[37] Moreover, when states grant the right of counsel to adults in probation revocation hearings, juveniles may be entitled to counsel in those states as well, based on the constitutional principle of equal protection of the laws.[38]

What does the state have to prove in order to revoke a child's probation?

The state must prove that the person on probation violated one or more of the conditions of probation previously set by the judge or probation department. The state must also show that such violations were committed "without just cause."[39] Therefore, a child may be able to win if he can demonstrate that he had a good excuse for what he did or that the violation was insubstantial.

A Texas court, for example, ruled that slight, technical

violations of terms of probation do not justify revocation. In that case, a child stopped attending school because his custodian moved outside the district. The court concluded that the child's conduct did not amount to a violation of a "reasonable and lawful" order of the court.[40] In California, a court found no violation of probation when a child was never told that he had to obey certain probation orders in the first place.[41] And in Oregon, a court required consideration of the parolee's overall conduct, not merely a focus on whether there was a violation, before revocation would be permitted.[42] And the Supreme Court of Wisconsin recently held that probation may not be revoked for the violation of a condition of which the juvenile was unaware. The court ruled that due process of law requires adequate notice and fair warning to the probationer of acts that may lead to a loss of liberty.[43]

If the state alleges that a young person violated probation by committing an act that would be a crime if committed by an adult, it must prove the charge "beyond a reasonable doubt."[44] If, however, the charge is that the young person violated a condition that does not constitute a crime, the state may only have to prove its case by a "preponderance of the evidence"[45] (see chapter X).

Can juvenile courts place a young person on probation for a longer period of time than an adult would receive for identical conduct?

Yes. As with the power to incarcerate for a longer period of time, courts generally permit lengthier probationary periods for juveniles on the theory that they need more attention and help than adults.[46] In a recent California case, a court upheld the power of the juvenile court to place a delinquent on probation for possession of marijuana, even though an adult convicted of the same crime could only be fined as a maximum sentence. The court reasoned that a juvenile's greater potential for rehabilitation justified the differential treatment.[47]

What is "parole"?

Parole is a conditional release from an institution before the end of the original period of placement. Freedom on parole, like probation, is subject to certain terms or conditions. Unlike probation, however, the decision to release a child on parole is not made by the judge but by the institution itself or the agency that runs the institution.

If a child on parole is found to have violated one or more of the conditions, he may have his parole revoked and may be returned to the same or another institution.

Does a young person have the right to a hearing and the right to be represented by counsel when faced with a revocation of parole?

Generally, the same rights that attend to the revocation of probation are equally applicable to the revocation of parole.[48] However, in a few states, parole revocation hearings and the assistance of counsel are not required.[49]

Institutional Commitments

Are juvenile court sentences based solely on the nature of the offense committed?

Generally, no.[50] This question touches upon the aspect of juvenile court that distinguishes it from adult criminal court. Sentencing that is imposed because of the crime committed is the essence of the "punitive" model of criminal justice, which is imployed in the adult system. A punitive model includes at least three aspects: (1) "deterrence" (imposing sanctions on an offender to deter others from breaking the law); (2) "incapacitation" (locking up the offender to prevent him from committing more crimes); and (3) "retribution" (paying back an offender by imposing a punishment or sanction that appropriately corresponds to the offense, an eye for an eye). The hallmark of the punitive model is "proportional justice" (sometimes referred to as just desserts, whereby the offender receives as a punishment what is "deserved" by the offending conduct.) Virtually no juvenile justice scheme in the United States is based upon the punitive model.

In contrast, the juvenile justice system is "rehabilitative"; its major purpose is to help the offender with whatever problems he may have that motivated him to break the law in the first place. Instead of proportional sentencing, sentences are unrelated to the acts that the offender committed. Instead of being fixed, sentences are indeterminate and carried out until the offender becomes "better."

For most of this century the rehabilitative model has

been the only one used by juvenile courts. In the last decade, however, both conservatives and liberals have complained that his model is unwise.

Liberals have emphasized the unfairness of a system that permits the incarceration of petty offenders and murderers for the same length of time with no distinction made on the basis of the degree of wrongdoing. Conservatives have emphasized the leniency too often shown to serious offenders (with such phrases as "getting away with murder").

As a result, a trend is developing in the United States by which punishment—in addition to rehabilitation—is becoming a stated purpose in juvenile court. Until 1980, in Minnesota, for example, the only stated purposes of its juvenile justice system was to rehabilitate offenders.[51] Now, while those purposes remain intact for neglected children, for youths charged with crime,

> . . . [T]he purpose of the laws relating to children alleged or adjudicated to be delinquent is to promote the public safety and reduce juvenile delinquency by maintaining the integrity of the substantive law prohibiting certain behavior and by developing individual responsibility for lawful behavior.[52]

This shift in purpose is likewise resulting in laws that impose definite sentences for certain juvenile offenders and longer sentences for more serious offenses.[53]

Can a juvenile court take into account protection of the community when committing a juvenile?

In a growing number of states, yes. As just stated, legislatures are more willing to recognize a punitive purpose in juvenile delinquency laws. A large number of states still do not do so, but juvenile court judges rarely ignore protection of the community when sentencing a juvenile. A number of states have placed themselves in hopelessly ambiguous territory between the child's best interests and society's need for protection. In these states, judges have virtually no guidelines to assist them in making decisions whether to commit juveniles. In Indiana, for example, a juvenile delinquent has a statutory right to a disposition that (1) least interferes with family autonomy; (2) is least disruptive of family life; (3) imposes the least restraint on his and his family's freedom;

and (4) provides a reasonable opportunity for participation by his family. However, these rights are qualified by the words, "[w]hen consistent with the safety of the community and the welfare of the child."[54]

Can juvenile courts impose mandatory sentences on juveniles adjudicated delinquent for certain offenses?

Generally, no. But a number of states now provide for mandatory sentences. In New York, for example, 14- or 15-year-old juveniles who are adjudicated delinquent for inflicting serious physical injury upon a person age 62 or older are subject to mandatory sentences of up to 3 years in restrictive placement, including a minimum of an initial period of 6 months to 1 year in a secure facility.[55] In Delaware, the authority to sentence a juvenile to a mandatory commitment for multiple offenders was upheld by that state's highest court.[56] Since 1977, juvenile court judges in Colorado are required to sentence a juvenile 15 or older who has committed any of several serious felonies or a child of any age who has committed a second felony offense to an out-of-home placement for not less than 1 year.[57]

Can a juvenile court order the exact place of commitment of a child?

Generally, no. Even though it can prescribe the form of treatment a child must receive, in most states if a court determines that a child must be committed, it may only place the child in the control of a state youth agency that has the discretion to commit the child to a facility that it thinks best.[58]

If a young person is committed to a juvenile institution, how long does he have to remain there?

Almost every state practices "indeterminate sentencing," which means that a child may be sentenced for a maximum period of time no matter how insignificant or serious the conduct. Before the expiration of the maximum amount of time, however, he may be released at the discretion of the agency that operates the institution.

The maximum periods of commitment vary among the states. In Texas, all dispositions terminate when a young person reaches his eighteenth birthday.[59] In Connecticut, the maximum period of initial commitment is 2 years. In Illinois and Massachusetts, a child may be committed until the age of 21.[60] In New York, for most offenses, a child may be placed initially for 18 months and extended yearly until he reaches 18.[61] For serious felony offenders, or repeat felony offenders, the initial placement may be for 5 years and extended yearly until the child reaches 21.[62]

Are indeterminate sentences constitutional?

Yes. Courts have consistently upheld laws that permit young people to be committed for an undetermined length of time.[63]

Can a juvenile court order a child placed in an institution for a specified minimum length of time?

Again, the answer is generally no. In most states the state agency charged with delivering and supervising the child's treatment determines how long the juvenile remains in a facility. Most courts have the power to place a child for an indeterminate length of time, with a maximum number of months or years permitted. However, commitments for specific periods of time are usually considered punitive, and outside the proper scope of juvenile courts.[64]

As just explained, there is a trend developing that permits specific sentences of delinquents. In New York, juveniles aged 13, 14, or 15 who are adjudicated delinquent for committing serious felonies, and who are found by the court to require "restrictive placement" after a dispositional hearing, may be placed for mandatory minimum periods ranging from 6 months to 1 year in a maximum security juvenile facility and an additional 6 months to 1 year in a "residential facility" as a fixed minimum sentence before release is possible.[65]

Can a young person be committed by a juvenile court to a mental hospital?

It depends on the state. In states that conduct hearings and findings of mental disability that are separate from juvenile jurisdiction, a child may not be committed by a juvenile court or a probation officer in the absence of the separate due process rights afforded by the applicable mental health law.[66]

In some states, moreover, a child cannot be committed for treatment in a mental hospital if he is held with adults rather than with adolescents or children in a special unit. In one case a juvenile court held that mingling children with adults in a locked hospital ward was irrational and illegal when, in the same state, the confinement of a delinquent in jail with adults was prohibited.[67]

Does a child who has been found delinquent have the right not to be committed to adult correctional institutions?

Generally, yes. The Juvenile Justice and Delinquency Prevention Act of 1974, provides that, as a condition for receipt of federal moneys, states must not confine juveniles in institutions in which they have regular contact with adults who have been convicted of a crime or who are awaiting trial on criminal charges.[68] In most states, if a child is to be incarcerated, he must be sent to a facility primarily designed to treat juveniles separate and apart from adult correctional institutions.[69] A few states still permit delinquents adjudicated in juvenile court to be sent to adult correctional facilities.[70]

It may be said that children committed to adult institutions have been deprived of their freedom without due process of law, since they receive less procedural guarantees than adults similarly committed, and none of the care and treatment they are promised as juveniles.[71] Nevertheless, this argument has been rejected by a number of courts.[72]

Do young people committed to juvenile institutions have the right to be free from transfers to adult correctional facilities?

Yes, in most states.[73] Constitutionally, there is a strong case against such transfers, since the juvenile court process is founded upon the notion that children are to be rehabilitated rather than punished. Transfers to penal institutions, of course, contradict this basic premise.[74] In reviewing the transfer of a juvenile to an adult penal institution, a Vermont court stated:

> The validity of the whole juvenile system is dependent on its adherence to its protective, rather than its penal aspects. . . . (T)he noncriminal aspect "is the legal backbone of the constitutionality of all American juvenile court legislation. If, after such juvenile proceedings, the juvenile can, by the discretionary act of an executive officer, be transferred to a place of penal servitude, the entire claim of 'parens

> patriae' becomes a hypocritical mockery. . . ." Such action confines a person in a penal institution without having been found guilty of a crime.[75]

In the District of Columbia, a federal court held that overcrowding at a juvenile institution could not serve as a rational basis for transferring a child to an adult correctional facility.[76]

In a few states, however, young people may be transferred to adult prisons. Courts have upheld the legality of such transfers on the grounds that (1) they are necessary to maintain security; (2) they are not necessarily incompatible with the rehabilitative ideal; or (3) transfers to penal institutions are valid as long as juveniles are segregated from adults.[77]

If transfers are allowed, juveniles are entitled to a due process hearing to determine if the proposed transfer is justified.[78]

Can a juvenile receive credit for time served in custody awaiting sentence?

In most jurisdictions, no. Since the final sentence is supposed to be for treatment, most states do not credit time spent in facilities other than in the treatment facility to which the juvenile is finally sent. Even in states that give credit to adults awaiting sentence, courts have refused to credit detention time for juveniles and have rejected equal protection claims.[79] Where a juvenile is transferred to adult court and sentenced as an adult, however, the time spent awaiting trail and sentence has been credited to the sentence given the young offender as an adult.[80] In California, juveniles who are sentenced by juvenile court must be given credit toward the total time that the sentenced juvenile may spend incarcerated, but only when the total time incarcerated for pre- and postsentence would be greater than the total sentence an adult could receive.[81]

Right to Treatment

Does a young person placed in a training school have the right to receive treatment?

Yes. The right to treatment is the cornerstone of the

juvenile justice system and extends to children in any institution as a result of a juvenile court placement, not just training schools.[82] It may be said that juvenile court procedures are invoked *only because* treatment will be provided to those found to have committed certain offenses and to be in need of treatment.[83]

The right to treatment is often seen as the justification for the denial of many due process rights in juvenile court procedures. In this sense, when treatment is *not* given a young person in an institution it can be argued that his liberty is being denied in violation of due process and equal protection of the laws.[84]

What does the "right to treatment" mean?

It means more than mere custodial or even kind and considerate care. It has recently been interpreted to mean affirmative and positive programs provided by the institution or agency to help rehabilitate, counsel, and meet the needs of children and individuals.

One case in which the right to treatment recieved its most eloquent description dealt with civilly committed mental patients.

> [T]he purpose of involuntary hospitalization . . . is *treatment* and not mere custodial care or punishment. This is the only justification from a constitutional standpoint . . . that allows civil commitments to mental institutions. . . .
>
> To deprive any citizen of his or her liberty upon the altruistic theory that the confinement is for humane therapeutic reasons and then fail to provide adequate treatment violates the very fundamentals of due process.[85]

The same philosophy has been held applicable to juvenile institutions as well.[86]

In some cases courts have ordered child-caring institutions to maintain a certain staff-child ratio, educational and training requirements for staff working with children, and to deliver certain therapeutic, rehabilitative, recreational, and educational services.[87]

Often the right to treatment is interpreted to mean that

in addition to offering affirmative rehabilitative programs, institutions may not maintain inadequate physical facilities or engage in unregulated or excessive punitive measures.

Does the right to treatment mean that a child has the right to individualized care and treatment?

Probably. A number of courts have held that a child's right to treatment includes the right to individualized care and treatment.[88] Since children have different needs, the rehabilitative program delivered must reflect each child's individual needs.

Does a juvenile court have the power to order specific treatment for a child or the right to require certain conditions in a child-caring program or institution?

Recent cases indicate that a juvenile court has this power. The legal problem involved is that most institutions and social welfare programs are administered by the executive branch of the state or local government and the constitutional separation of powers often makes it difficult for the judicial branch to tell the executive what to do. In all but a few states, however, juvenile courts *retain* jurisdiction (authority) over children for a certain length of time after the dispositional hearing has ended. The usual period of time is until the child's twenty-first birthday. This sometimes makes it possible for juvenile courts to follow up dispositional orders and to provide relief for children who are not obtaining the treatment for which they were committed in the first place.

In New York, for example, a number of judicial opinions have indirectly established the power of family courts to order and carry out specific treatment plans. One appellate court determined that a family court had the power to order treatment for a child in need of supervision who demonstrated severe learning problems and emotional retardation.[89] Another appellate court found that it was an abuse of discretion for a family court to commit a child to a training school with a qualification that therapy be rendered, when evidence indicated that therapy was not available there.[90] Finally, a family court vacated a child's placement in a training school that refused to treat the child who was earlier found to be in need of psychiatric care by the same court.[91]

In a Minnesota case a juvenile court made a survey of

available institutions for children and found them all incapable of providing the security and rehabilitation necessary for the treatment of children referred by the court. As a result, the court, on its own accord, listed the offenses for which a child's liberty could be deprived and created a screening board to recommend appropriate treatment.[92]

Does a young person have the right to be afforded the "least restrictive alternative" to confinement?

Not necessarily, but this appears to be a growing trend in state and federal court interpretations of juvenile court laws.

Most statutes provide language that permits courts to interpret legislative intent to require the least restrictive placement necessary for an adjudicated delinquent. Thus, in a line of cases that still appears to be effective in New York, courts have ruled that, where the juvenile court has discretion to sentence an offender, an adjudicated delinquent's placement in a training school could be ordered only as a last resort, after other alternatives had been exhausted.[93] Other courts have held that commitments to secure institutions may not stand if there is evidence that it is antithetical to the needs of the child or not the most helpful form of care and treatment. The California Supreme Court held that a juvenile court judge could not commit a child to the Youth Authority unless he was fully satisfied that it is probable that the juvenile would benefit. In that case, a Youth Authority commitment based on the ground that suitable alternatives did not exist was struck down, in light of expert testimony that the child was not an appropriate subject and would not benefit from commitment.[94] A Maryland court found that a child should be placed in a wholesome family environment whenever possible and that he should be separated from his parents only when necessary for his welfare or in the interest of public safety. In so holding, the court ordered that the evidence did not justify a child's separation from his parents or placement in a training center or other juvenile institution.[95] In concluding that placement in a training school could be harmful for a child "in need of supervision," a New York court placed her in the custody of the commissioner of social services instead.[96]

An Indiana court recently acknowledged that commitment to training schools should be resorted to only if less drastic dispositions are inadequate, but observed that there are times when such a commitment is in the best interests of society and the juvenile.[97]

The North Carolina Supreme Court recently voided an out-of-state placement of a juvenile on the grounds that the statute required use of "community-based" programs.[98] The statute stated:

> The purpose of dispositions in juvenile actions is to design an appropriate plan to meet the needs of the juvenile and to achieve the objectives of the State in exercising jurisdiction. If possible, the initial approach should involve working with the juvenile and his family in their own home so that the appropriate community resources may be involved in care, supervision, and treatment according to the needs of the juvenile. Thus, the judge should arrange for appropriate community-level services to be provided to the juvenile and his family in order to strengthen the home situation.[99]

New York's highest court, however, recently rejected the claim that "in the postadjudicative stage, therapeutic treatment in the least restrictive setting is the cornerstone for an adjudication of juvenile delinquency."[100] That ruling was in the context of a statutorily mandated sentence of incarceration.

The Rights of Young People in Training Schools and Institutions

Do young people have the right to challenge the legality of their confinement?

Yes. If a child is placed or committed to an institution by a court, he has an absolute right to challenge the legality of his confinement on four grounds: (1) that a legal irregularity occurred prior to confinement; (2) that he was placed in an inappropriate facility; (3) that the purpose for which he was committed—treatment—is not being fulfilled; and (4) that the conditions of his confinement are unconstitutional.

The confinement may be challenged by direct appeal, by a writ of habeas corpus, or by a civil rights action in a federal court.[101]

Does an inmate of a juvenile institution have the right to sue an institution or institutional personnel for monetary damages?

Yes. Since no loss of civil rights results from a juvenile court adjudication (see chapter II), a child in an institution does not lose the right to maintain a civil suit against his keepers. Children also possess the right to sue for monetary damages incurred at the institution as a result of negligence, intentional injury, or cruel and unusual punishment.[102] Civil suits may have to be brought by a parent, next friend, or guardian who stands in the place of the child (see chapter VI).

Does a child in a juvenile institution have the right to retain a lawyer in order to protect his rights?

Yes, but it is unlikely that a young person in an institution has the right to have an attorney appointed to represent him, free of charge.

Adult prisoners have been guaranteed the right of access to the courts and attorneys for some time[103] and at least one court has held that the refusal of an institution to permit a child to confer privately with an attorney is unconstitutional.[104]

Do young people committed to training schools or other institutions have the right to be free from cruel and unusual punishment?

Yes. Cruel and unusual punishment, though difficult to interpret, is that which "offends contemporary concepts of decency and human dignity and precepts of civilization which we profess to possess."[105] It has also been established that the concept of cruel and inhuman punishment "is not fastened to the obsolete, but may require meaning as public opinion becomes enlightened by a human justice."[106]

In addition to finding that beatings, excessive solitary confinement, and unnecessary psychological medication constitute cruel and unusual punishment, courts have found that other severe forms of discipline in juvenile institutions are unconstitutional as well.

In Illinois, for example, a federal court held that two mentally retarded youths in a state hospital were denied their constitutional rights when they were bound to their beds in spread-eagle fashion for more than three days and forced to scrub walls for over ten hours while only half-clothed.[107]

Do young people in institutions have the right to be free from corporeal punishment?

Not necessarily, but they have a right to be free from *excessive* corporeal punishment. The United States Supreme Court has upheld the power of schoolteachers to spank misbehaving students, reasoning, in part, that such spanking did not offend the constitutional prohibition against cruel and unusual punishment since the prohibition applied only to those convicted of committing crimes.[108] Ironically, the ban against cruel and unusual punishment has been held fully applicable to delinquents confined in facilities. Thus, schoolchildren who have never broken the law are less protected against corporeal punishment imposed by teachers than are delinquents.[109]

Beatings and paddlings in training schools have been severely criticized. Citing a previously established ban on the use of a strap in adult prisons, a federal court found that the use of a thick board as a paddle violates a child's right to be free from cruel and unusual punishment.[110] Another federal court found that kicking, stomping, and beating children with fists and sticks constitutes cruel and unusual punishment.[111]

While in a training school, does a young person have the right not to be placed in solitary confinement for extended periods of time?

Yes. Most courts that have considered this issue have determined that solitary confinement (sometimes called room confinement or segregation) should be used only under extreme or emergency conditions. Confinement for routine purposes of punishment or for prolonged periods of time may constitute cruel and unusual punishment in violation of a child's rights guaranteed by the Eighth Amendment.[112]

In New York, solitary confinement may not be employed for more than twenty-four hours without approval from the state director of the Division of Youth. The places of confinement (cells) must be furnished, heated, ventilated and lit the same as any other living area in the institution. Solitary confinement in New York may not be used for purposes of punishment. It may be lawfully used only in cases when a child constitutes a serious and evident danger to himself or others.[113]

In Indiana, a federal court set forth standards for solitary confinement that require the institution to provide a hearing before a child may be committed. The child must be notified of the charges against him, and at the hearing he has the right to confront his accusers and present evidence and witnesses on his own behalf.[114]

In Rhode Island, minimal conditions of confinement in all rooms of training schools (including isolation cells) must include sufficient light, personal hygienic supplies, clean and adequate clothing and bedding, writing and reading materials, daily showers, and access to medical care facilities.[115]

In Texas, a federal court ruled that confinement in solitary or secure cells may be utilized only to prevent imminent physical harm to the inmate or others, or to prevent the imminent and substantial destruction of property. Even then the court ruled that solitary confinement may constitute cruel and unusual punishment when the decision to place a child is totally discretionary and when there are no limits on the duration of confinement.[116]

In Mississippi, a federal court ruled that confinement in an Intensive Treatment Unit is permissible only if the inmate (1) constitutes an immediate threat to the physical well-being of himself or others; (2) is kept confined for no more than twenty-four hours; (3) is visited by staff every three hours; (4) is placed in a cell with transparent window, lights, mattresses, bed clothes, and personal hygiene articles, such as toothbrushes; and (5) is given reading and writing materials.[117]

Do young persons confined in training schools have the right to be free from psychological medication, administered for disciplinary purposes?

Yes. In some institutions children are either injected with, or forced to swallow, powerful tranquilizing drugs. Psychological medication is often administered without proper medical supervision, as punishment or for merely maintaining order by controlling behavior. This practice has been declared unconstitutional as cruel and unusual punishment.[118]

In New York State training schools, regulations prohibit the administration of medication used to restrain children unless a child is so uncontrollable that no other means of restraint can prevent the child from harming *himself*, and even then, such medication can only be authorized by a physician.[119]

Do young people in training schools have the right to send and receive unopened and uncensored mail?

It depends on the school. It is not uncommon for training school officials to open, read and censor mail in the name of "treating" the child or promoting his "best interest."

In adult prisons this practice is slowly coming under control[120] and a few jurisdictions have put an end to unrestricted interference with a child's mail as well. In New York[121] and Texas,[122] regulations permit training school inmates to send and receive uncensored and unread mail; however, if the institution suspects that a child is receiving contraband, it may require the child to open incoming letters in the presence of a staff member.

In Indiana, another federal court prohibited the training school from opening outgoing mail and from limiting letters to and from those named on a "correspondence list." The only restriction on correspondence the court allowed was to permit institutional personnel to open incoming letters and packages that reasonably appeared as though they may contain contraband.[123]

In most states, an institutionalized child has the right to send and receive unread and uncensored mail between him and his attorney.[124]

Do young people in training schools have the right to free expression?

In 1969, the Supreme Court ruled that students do not lose their First-Amendment rights when they go to school.[125] In that case, the Supreme Court upheld the right of students to protest the Vietnam War by wearing black armbands as a form of (symbolic) free speech. No case of similar magnitude has addressed the issue of free expression among training school inmates.

But in New York, training school residents *are* granted certain rights of free expression, including the right to wear personal (noninstitutional) clothing; the right to wear watches and jewelry; and the right to choose their own length and style of hair, beards, and mustaches.[126] And in Texas, a federal court declared that juveniles have a constitutional right to

> the liberty to exercise freedom of choice in areas such as dress, hairstyle, choice of friends and other personal matters [and the right to] an environment that permits the juvenile to express, either verbally

> or non-verbally, the emotions, such as anger, affection or unhappiness that he may feel, unless the expression is harmful or destructive.[127]

The same court even declared that young inmates have the constitutional right to a coeducational living environment (except in the case of very small facilities for one sex only), which "must provide frequent and regular contacts with members of the opposite sex in a variety of settings."[128]

Do inmates of juvenile institutions have the right to be informed of institutional rules and regulations?

Yes. It is a fundamental precept of American law that citizens have the right to receive written notice of the laws, rules, and regulations to which they are held accountable, and for which violations may result in a fine or deprivation of liberty.[129] It is quite common, however, that children in institutions are not provided with a list of rules, thereby leaving them with no certain knowledge of what types of behavior are expected or prohibited.

Do inmates in juvenile institutions have the right to present grievances to an ombudsman or some other impartial agency?

No, but some states and courts have created ombudsman and grievance mechanisms at training schools and at other juvenile institutions.

An ombudsman is a person to whom inmates have access to express complaints and who, in turn, has the duty or discretion to relate these complaints to officials of the institutions, the state, or a court. The ombudsman is, in theory, not part of the bureaucratic structure of any institution or agency. This insures independence and impartiality and permits him to intervene at any level of the administrative hierarchy. Grievance procedures or committees, on the other hand, are institutionalized complaint bureaus which, depending on the form, have the capacity to settle disputes between inmates and staff or administration.

The New York State Division for Youth voluntarily placed ombudsmen-attorneys in training schools and in other institutions under its jurisdiction in 1972. Since then, the ombudsman idea has grown and at least two other states (Minnesota and Iowa) have experimented with similar programs. Moreover, two courts have ordered that ombudsmen be placed in juvenile institutions to receive complaints of individual residents and monitor institutional compliance with court-ordered changes and standards.[130]

Recently the Kentucky Department of Child Welfare, the California Youth Authority, and the Illinois Department of Corrections have created grievance review boards or similar grievance procedures for inmates and residents of juvenile institutions in these states.[131]

Are children who are committed to juvenile facilities and training schools entitled to periodic reviews of their placement?

Not necessarily. A small number of states, including Alaska and Minnesota),[132] require an annual review of all court orders, but most states allow a placement to continue for as long as initially ordered with no further review of any kind. In nearly all states, orders of the court may be changed from time to time upon a showing of altered circumstances.[133] Whenever a court *modifies* a placement or seeks to *extend* a placement that is due to expire, a powerful argument exists that the juvenile has the constitutional right to a hearing with counsel and an opportunity to confront and cross-examine witnesses.[134]

Does a child in a juvenile institution have the right to be free from arbitrary transfers to a more secure juvenile institution?

The answer to this is unclear. After originally being placed in minimum-security training schools or other facilities, young people are sometimes transferred "administratively" (without a hearing) to medium- or maximum-security juvenile institutions or mental hospitals. These transfers are often based on the child's behavior or "acting out" in the former institution, rather than on the charge upon which he was originally convicted.

The United States Supreme Court, in *Meachum v. Fano*,[135] determined that a transfer of an adult inmate to a higher level of security within the prison system is not an infringement of the inmate's Fourteenth-Amendment liberty interest requiring a hearing or other due process protections. The Court's holding was based on the absence of either a constitutional right or state-induced expectation to remain at a single level of security once the inmate's liberty has been deprived for violations of the criminal law. However, there may be sufficient differences in expectations between juvenile and adult convicts, including rehabilitative purposes and the use of lesser restrictive alternatives, to conclude that juveniles have greater rights than adults in this area.[136]

While the majority of states permit institutional transfers of juveniles at the discretion of the appropriate youth authority, some procedural rights have recently been extended to inmates of juvenile institutions, although these decisions predate *Meachum*.

In Arizona, for example, the transfer of a child from a drug rehabilitation program to a training school was invalidated.[137] In Texas, a federal court held that arbitrary administrative transfers to maximum-security units without hearings violate the Fourteenth Amendment.[138]

In New York, a child may be transferred only after an administrative hearing at which it is shown that either (1) the transfer is necessary because the child is a serious and evident danger to him/herself and to others to such a degree that a more secure setting is the only alternative; or (2) the treatment and rehabilitative resources are inadequate to handle the behavior of the child and a more secure setting is the only alternative.[139]

Are records of young people in institutions and training schools confidential?

Rarely, even though a child probably has a right to have them kept from disclosure.

Almost every state considers its juvenile court records confidential (see chapter II), but only a few states extend the rule of confidentiality to cover postdispositional records kept by other governmental agencies and institutions.[140]

A significant number of reports and entries in institutional records are filed by doctors, psychiatrists, psychologists, clergymen, and social workers. In a great number of states, communication between a patient or client and many or all of these other professionals are deemed privileged and confidential.[141] Such reports, therefore, should not be disclosed to anyone other than the child himself.

In practice, however, institutional records, including entries made by professionals, are often freely disclosed to juvenile and adult courts, probation officers, other child-caring institutions, welfare offices, the United States armed forces, and public and private employers.

Absconding After Dispositional Decisions

What happens if a young person, who is committed to a juvenile institution or on parole or probation from juvenile court, runs away and is apprehended in another state?

He will most probably be returned to the state from which he ran away and be dealt with there. His return will be facilitated by the Interstate Compact on Juveniles, enacted in every state.[142]

The Interstate Compact also permits states to make agreements that allow for the continuation of a juvenile's parole, probation, and placement or commitment in other states.[143]

If a child who has escaped or absconded is apprehended in another state, is he entitled to a hearing in that state to determine if his return is in his best interest?

No. The question of best interest does not arise in such cases.[144] In fact, if the child is apprehended pursuant to a written requisition for the return of a delinquent juvenile issued by a court in the demanding state, the only issue a judge in the asylum state must determine is whether or not the requisition is in order, which may be determined without a hearing. If the requisition is found to be proper, the asylum state judge may deliver the child to the proper authorities from the demanding state.[145]

If, however, the child is picked up upon reasonable information that he is a delinquent who has escaped or absconded from another state but without a preexisting requisition for his return from the demanding state, a hearing *must* be held to determine whether sufficient cause exists to hold the juvenile for a period up to ninety days to permit a formal requisition to be filed.[146]

What if the child is apprehended in a state where his age makes him no longer subject to the jurisdiction of the juvenile court?

It is likely that he will still be returned to the demanding state if he is currently subject to the continuing jurisdiction of a juvenile court or institution in the demanding state.[147]

If a child has absconded from an institution, can he be prosecuted for the adult crime of escape if he is over the age for juvenile court jurisdiction?

In many states no. Escape from a juvenile facility does not normally constitute criminal escape because the latter is defined as escape from detention imposed for committing a crime and juvenile delinquency is not a crime.[148]

Fines and Restitution

Can a young person be compelled to pay a fine if he is found guilty of a delinquent act?

In an increasing number of states, yes. For many years, children were not usually ordered to pay penalties, including monetary fines.[149] However, in recent years—in accord with the more punitive thrust of juvenile proceedings, in recognition of victims' rights, and out of concern for commitments to help juveniles—fines and restitution have become more common in juvenile court.

Today, in an overwhelming majority of states (including California, Colorado, Illinois, Kentucky, Maine, New York, Virginia, Washington, and Wisconsin) children may be ordered to pay restitution for damages or may be required to work to restore damaged property.[150] In 1978, the United States Supreme Court approved a sentence under the Federal Youth Corrections Act whereby a fine or restitution was as a condition of probation.[151]

In Washington, an appeals court rejected a thirteen-year-old's claim that a sentence of restitution and fifty hours of community service constituted involuntary servitude in violation of the Thirteenth Amendment.[152] In New York, juveniles may be required by the family court to pay for the repair or replacement of damaged or stolen property out of their own earnings or to perform "services for the public good."[153]

In California, a court recently ruled that, while restitution may be required, fines may not be imposed on juveniles,[154] and in Pennsylvania a court ruled that, although it was valid for a court to have ordered probation for a juvenile and ordered his mother to make restitution, it was not permissible to commit the juvenile simply because the mother failed to make restitution.[155]

NOTES

1. 383 U.S. 541 (1966).
2. *See, e.g.*, Cal. Welf. & Inst. Code §701, 702 (Supp. 1982); D.C. Code §16–2317(c)(1981); Ill. Ann. Stat. ch. 37, §705–1(1) (Supp. 1982); N.Y. Fam. Ct. Act §350.1 (1983); *In re Dennis*,1 20 A.D.2d 86, 244 N.Y.S.2d 798 (4th Dept. 1963); *In re Mikkelson*, 226 Cal. App. 467, 38 Cal. Rptr. 106 (1964); *In re J.L.P.*, 25 Cal. App. 3d 86, 100 Cal. Rptr. 601 (1972). *Contra*, *A.S. v. Murphy*, 487 S.W.2d 589 (Mo. Ct. App. 1972).
3. *See, e.g.*, Cal. Welf. & Inst. Code §702 (Supp. 1982); *State in Interest of Simon*, 295 So.2d 473 (La. App. 1974).
4. *People v. Cato*, 4 Ill. App. 3d 1093, 283 N.E.2d 259 (1972).
5. N.Y. Fam. Ct. Act §§350.a(1)-(3) (1983).
6. *See, e.g., A.S. v. Murphy, supra* note 2; *Johnson v. People*, 170 Colo. 137, 459 P.2d 579 (1969).
7. See, e.g., Ohio Rev. Code Ann. §2151.352 (1976); 42 Pa. Cons. Stat. Ann. §6337 (1982); Tex. Fam. Code Ann. §51.10(a)–(b) (1975); Va. Code Ann. §§16.1–266, 16.1–268 (1982); *A.A. v. State*, 538 P.2d 1004 (Alaska 1975). *See also In re Juvenile Appeal*, 39 Conn. Supp. 400, 465 A.2d 1107 (Sup. Ct. 1983).
8. *See, e.g.*, N.Y. Fam. Ct. Act §350.3 (1983). Fla. Stat. Ann. §39.03(3) (Supp. 1981); Cal. Welf. & Inst. Code §706 (Supp. 1982).
9. *See, e.g., Tyler v. State*, 512 S.W.2d 46 (Tex. Civ. App. 1974); *In re J.*, 38 A.D.2d 711, 329 N.Y.S.2d 349 (2d Dept. 1972) (neglect proceeding).
10. *See, e.g., In re Michael C.*, 50 A.D.2d 757, 376 N.Y.S.2d 167 (2d Dept. 1976); *In re Rosmis*, 26 Ill. App. 2d 226, 167 N.E.2d 826 (1960); *State v. Lance*, 23 Utah 2d 407, 464 P.2d 395 (1970). *See also Kent v. U.S.*, 383 U.S. 541 (1966) (waiver hearing); *Mazur v. Lazarus*, 196 A.2d 477 (D.C. App. 1964) (custody proceeding); *U.S. v. Dockery*, 447 F.2d 1178, 1199 (D.C. Cir.) (dissent), *cert. denied*, 404 U.S. 950 (1971).
11. *In re G.S.J.*, 281 N.W.2d 511 (Minn. 1979).
12. Minn. Stat. Ann. §260.155(6).
13. *See, e.g.*, Cal. Welf. & Inst. Code §607 (1971); *People v. Sanchez*, 21 Cal. 2d 466, 132 P.2d 810 (1942); *In re Blakes*, 4 Ill. App. 3d 567, 281 N.E.2d 454 (1972).
14. *In re Maricopa County, Juvenile No. J–86843*, 125 Ariz. 227, 608 P.2d 804 (Ct. App. 1980).
15. N.Y. Fam. Ct. Act §355.3(6) (1983).
16. *Id.* at §353.5(4)(d) (1983).
17. *U.S. v. Hall*, 306 F. Supp. 735 (E.D. Tenn. 1969).

18. *State v. Cassanova*, 494 S.W.2d 812 (Tex. 1973).
19. *See, e.g.*, MASS. GEN. LAWS ANN. ch. 119, §58 (Supp. 1982); VA. CODE ANN. §16.1–285 (1982) (up to 19 years old).
20. *See, e.g, State v. Rice*, 98 Wash. 2d 384, 655 P.2d 1145 (1982) (banc); *U.S. v. Donelson*, 695 F.2d 583 (D.C. Cir 1982); *People ex rel Carey v. Chrastka*, 83 Ill. 2d 67, 413 N.E.2d 1269 (1980); *In re T.D.*, 89 Ill. App. 3d 369, 401 N.E.2d 275 (1980); *In re Appeal, Maricopa County Juvenile No. J–86509*, 124 Ariz. 377, 604 P.2d 641 (1979), *cert. denied*, 445 U.S. 967 (1980); *State v. Gleason*, 404 A.2d 573 (Me. 1979); *In re Eric J.*, 25 Cal.3d 522, 601 P.2d 549, 159 Cal. Rptr. 317 (1979); *U.S. ex rel. Wilson v. Coughlin*, 472 F.2d 100 (7th Cir. 1973); *State v. Sargent*, 305 A.2d 273 (Me. 1973); *In re Blakes*, 4 Ill. App. 3d 567, 281 N.E.2d 454 (1972); *Abernathy v. U.S.*, 418 F.2d 288 (5th Cir. 1969); *Smith v. State*, 444 S.W.2d 941 (Tex. Civ. App. 1969). *But see U.S. ex rel. Sero v. Preiser*, 377 F. Supp. 463 (S.D.N.Y. 1974), *cert denied*, 421 U.S. 921 (1975); *In re Wilson*, 438 Pa. 425, 264 A.2d 614 (1970).
21. *See, e.g.*, CAL. WELF. & INST. CODE §§726, 731 (Supp. 1982); N.C. GEN. STAT. §7A–652(c) (1981); N.Y. FAM. CT. ACT §§353.(5)(6) (1983) (Initial placement for a misdemeanor may be no longer than an adult's maximum sentence; however, placement may be extended by the court, if necessary.)
22. CAL. WELF. & INST. CODE §726 (Supp. 1982).
23. In re Eric J., 25 Cal. 3d 522, 601 P.2d 549, 159 Cal. Rptr. 317 (1979).
24. *People v. Olivas*, 17 Cal. 3d 236, 551 P.2d 375, 131 Cal. Rptr. 55 (1976). *See also M.O.W. v. State*, 645 P.2d 1229 (Alas. 1982).
25. *Eddings v. Oklahoma*, 455 U.S. 104 (1982).
26. *Id.* 455 U.S. at 114.
27. *People v. Spears*, 33 Cal. 3d 279, 188 Cal. Rptr. 454, 655 P.2d 1289 (1983).
28. For an exception, see N.Y. FAM. CT. ACT §§353.2(2),(3) (1983); Uniform Fam. Ct. Rules §2507.10 (1982).
29. *People v. J.R.O.*, 36 A.D.2d 828, 321 N.Y.S.2d 518 (2d Dept. 1971).
30. *Jones v. Commonwealth*, 185 Va. 335, 38 S.E.2d 444 (Va. 1946). *See also In re Mannino*, 14 Cal. App. 3d 953, 92 Cal. Rptr. 880 (1971) (unconstitutional restrictions on adult probationers).
31. *Mempa v. Rhay*, 389 U.S. 128 (1967); *Gagnon v. Scarpelli*, 411 U.S. 778 (1973).
32. *See, e.g.*, ILL. ANN. STAT. ch. 37, §705–3(3) (Supp. 1982); N.C. GEN. STAT. §7A–656 (1981); N.Y. FAM. CT. ACT §360.3(1) (1983); *In re Sneed*, 72 Ill. 2d 326, 381 N.E.2d 272 (1978); *Adams v. Rose*, 551 P.2d 948 (Alas. 1976); *Smith v. Cook*, 105 Ariz. 390, 465 P.2d 370 (1970); *Velasquez v. Pratt*, 21 Utah 2d 229, 433 P.2d 1020 (1968); *People v. Roberson*, 22 Mich. App. 664, 177 N.W.2d 712 (1970).
33. *See, e.g., State ex rel. R.R. v. Schmidt*, 63 Wis. 2d 82, 216 N.W.2d 18 (1974).
34. *See, e.g.*, ILL. ANN. STAT. ch. 37, §705–3(3)(c) (Supp. 1982); NEB. REV. STAT. §43–286(4) (Supp. 1982); N.C. GEN. STATE. 7A–656 (1981);

N.Y. FAM. CT. ACT §360.3(4)(1983); *In re Ames*, 16 Wash. App. 239, 554 P.2d 1084 (1976); *K.E.S. v. State*, 134 Ga. App. 843, 216 S.E.2d 670 (1975); *Naves v. State*, 91 Nev. 106, 531 P.2d 1360 (1975) (entitled to counsel only on a case-by-case basis); *State ex rel. Gillard v. State*, 528 S.W.2d 545 (Tenn. 1975)(same); *State ex rel. D.E. v. Keller*, 251 So.2d 703 (Fla. App. 1971); *Franks v. State*, 498 S.W.2d 516 (Tex. Civ. App. 1973).

35. *Gagnon v. Scarpelli*, *supra* note 31, at 780.
36. *Id*. at 791.
37. *Id* at 789, n.12; *In re Gault*, 387 U.S. 1, 36 (1967).
38. *People v. Roberson*, *supra* note 32. For similar reasoning with an opposite result, *see Naves v. State*, *supra* note 34.
39. *See, e.g.*, N.Y. FAM. CT. ACT §779 (1975).
40. *In re D.E.P.*, 512 S.W.2d 789 (Tex. Civ. App. 1974).
41. *In re Denise C.*, 45 Cal. App. 3d 761, 119 Cal. Rptr. 735 (1975).
42. *Morgan v. MacLaren School, Children's Services Division*, 23 Or. App. 546, 543 P.2d 304 (1975).
43. *G.G.D. v. State*, 97 Wis. 2d 1, 292 N.W.2d 853 (1980).
44. *In re Winship*, 397 U.S. 301 (1970); *K.W.H. v. State*, 596 S.W.2d 248 (Tex. Civ. App. 1980); *People ex rel. C.B.*, 196 Colo. 362, 585 P.2d 281 (1978); *T.S.I. v. State*, 139 Ga. App. 775, 229 S.E.2d 553 (1976); *In re Arthur N.*, 16 Cal. 3d 226, 545 P.2d 1345, 127 Cal. Rptr. 641 (1976); *In re D.E.P.*, *supra* note 40; *In re Taylor*, 268 A.2d 522 (D.C. App. 1970).
45. *See, e.g.*, *In re C.B.*, 196 Colo. 362, 585 P.2d 281 (1978); *In re Maricopa County Juvenile Action No. J–72918-S*, 111 Ariz. 135, 524 P.2d 1310 (1974).
46. *In re John R.*, 92 Cal. 3d 566, 155 Cal. Rptr. 78 (1979).
47. *In re Wayne Anthony J.*, 97 Cal. 3d 776, 159 Cal. Rptr. 106 (1979).
48. *Morrissey v. Brewer*, 408 U.S. 471 (1972); *State ex rel. J.R. v. MacQueen*, 259 S.E.2d 420 (W. Va. 1979); *Walls v. Director of Institutional Services*, 84 Mich. App. 355, 269 N.W.2d 599 (1978); *State ex rel. Bernal v. Hershman*, 54 Wis. 2d 626, 196 N.W.2d 721 (1972); *People ex rel. Silbert v. Cohen*, 29 N.Y.2d 12, 271 N.E.2d 908, 323 N.Y.S.2d 422 (1971); *Morgan v. McLaren School, C.S.D.*, 23 Or. App. 546, 543 P.2d 304 (1975).
49. *See, e.g.*, *State ex rel. Cresci v. Schmidt*, 62 Wis. 2d 400, 215 N.W.2d 361 (1974); *Bernier v. State*, 265 A.2d 604 (Me. 1970); *Loyd v. Youth Conservation Commission*, 287 Minn. 12, 177 N.W.2d 555 (1970).
50. *See, e.g.*, *U.S. v. Ingrams*, 539 F.2d 602 (4th Cir. 1976).
51. *See* Juvenile Court Act, ch. 685, §1, 1959 Minn. Laws 1275 (*repealed* 1980).
52. MINN. STAT. ANN. §260.011(2)(1982). *See also* N.Y. FAM. CT. ACT §301.1(1983) (purpose includes "protection of the community").
53. *See, e.g.*, Wash. Juv. Just. Act of 1977, §§65(1)(a) & (b).
54. *See, e.g.*, IND. CODE ANN. §31–6–4–16 (1980).

55. *See*, N.Y. Fam. Ct. Act §§353.5(3)(5)(1983); *Matter of Quinton A.*, 49 N.Y.2d 328, 402 N.E.2d 126, 425 N.Y.S.2d 788 (1980).
56. *State v. J.K.*, 383 A.2d 283 (1977) *cert. denied*, 435 U.S. 1009 (1978), (*upholding* DEL. CODE ANN. tit. 10, §937 1974).
57. *See* COLO. REV. STAT. §19–1–103 (19.5) (1982 Cum. Supp.). *See also* ILL. ANN. STAT. ch. 37 §§705–12 (Supp. 1982).
58. *See, e.g., In re G.F.*, 455 A.2d 805 (Vt. 1982); *In re Gakin*, 22 Wash. App. 822, 592 P.2d 670 (1979); *Burns v. Siebermann*, 266 N.W.2d 11 (Iowa 1978); *In re Meek*, 236 N.W.2d 284 (Iowa 1978); *In re J.N.*, 279 So.2d 50 (Fla. App. 1973); *A. A. v. State*, 538 P.2d 1004 (Alas. 1975). *See* contra *City and County of Denver v. Juvenile Court*, 182 Colo. 157, 511 P.2d 898 (1973).
59. TEX. FAM. CODE §54.05(b) (1975).
60. CONN. GEN. STAT. ANN. §426–141 (Supp. 1982); ILL. STAT. ch. 37 §§701–2(1), 705–10(1), 705–11 (1972 & Supp. 1982); MASS. GEN. LAWS ANN. ch. 119 §58 (Supp. 1982).
61. N.Y. FAM. CT. ACT §355.3(5)(1983).
62. *Id.* at §§353.5(4)(a)(i)(d)(1983).
63. *See, e.g., Wilson v. Coughlin*, 472 F. 2d 100 (7th Cit. 1973); *J.K. v. state*, 68 Wis. 426, 288 N.W. 2d 713 (1975).
64. *In re Debra A.*, 48 Cal. App. 3d 327, 121 Cal. Rptr. 757 (1975); *B.A.M. v. State*, 528 P.2d 437 (Alaska 1974); *Terrence C. v. New York State Division for Youth*, 45 A.D.2d 825, 357 N.Y.S. 2d 96 (1st Dept. 1974).
65. N.Y. FAM. CT. ACT §353.5(5) (1983).
66. *See, e.g., In re L.L.*, 39 Cal. App. 3d 205, 114 Cal. Rptr. 11 (1974); *In re Michael E.*, 15 Cal. 3d 183, 123 Cal. Rptr. 103, 538 P.2d 231 (1975).
67. *In re Hanan*, 7 Juv. Ct. Digest 20 (1975) (Dist. Ct. Md., Juv. Div., Montgomery Co., Nos. 672–75, 905–75).
68. 42 U.S.C.A. §5633(a)(13) (Supp. 1982).
69. *See, e.g., State v. Grady*, 3 Ohio App. 3d 174, 444 N.E.2d 51 (1981); *Ex parte Leeke*, 184 S.E.2d 80 (S.C. 1971). *But see Osorio v. Rios*, 429 F. Supp. 570 (D.P.R. 1976).
70. *See, e.g.*, ILL. ANN. STAT. ch. 37, §705–10 (Supp. 1982). *See also* KY. REV. STAT. ANN. §208E.140 (1980); MISS. CODE ANN. §43–21–159(3) (1981). *See also* 18 U.S.C.A. §5010(d) (Supp. 1982).
71. *See, e.g., In re Maria A.*, 52 Cal. App. 3d 901, 125 Cal. Rptr. 382 (1975); *In re Haas*, 234 Pa. Super. Ct. 422, 339 A.2d 98 (1975); *In re Rich*, 125 Vt. 373, 216 A.2d 266 (1966); *State ex rel. Londerholm v. Owens*, 197 Kan. 212, 416 P.2d 259 (1966); *Baker v. Hamilton*, 345 F. Supp. 345 (W.D. Ky. 1972); *B.A.M. v. State, supra* note 59.
72. *Wilson v. Coughlin*, 259 Iowa 1163, 147 N.W.2d 175 (1966); *United States ex rel. Murray v. Owens*, 465 F.2d 289 (2d Cir.), *cert. denied*, 409 U.S. 1117 (1973); *Janet R. v. Cory*, 44 A.D.2d 599, 353 N.Y.S.2d 783 (2d Dept. 1974).
73. *See, e.g.*, N.M. STAT. ANN. §32–1–34 (G) (1981).

74. *White v. Reid*, 125 F. Supp. 647 (D.D.C. 1954); *U.S. ex rel. Stinnett v. Hegstrom*, 178 F. Supp. 17 (D. Conn. 1959).
75. *In re Rich*, *supra* note 71, at 269, citing Judge Armon W. Ketcham in Coleman, "The Constitutional Rights of a Juvenile Delinquent," 50 *Women Lawyers J.* 84 (1964).
76. *U.S. v. Riley*, 481 F.2d 1127 (D.C. Cir. 1973).
77. *O.H. v. French*, 504 S.W.2d 269 (Mo. App. 1973); *Wilson v. Coughlin*, *supra* note 72; *Long v. Langlois*, 93 R.I. 23, 170 A.2d 618 (1961). *See also A.B.W. v. State*, 231 Ga. 699, 203 S.E.2d 512 (1974); *Long v. Powell*, 388 F. Supp. 422 (N.D. Ga.), *vacated on other grounds*, 423 U.S. 808 (1975).
78. *See Inmates of Boy's Training School v. Affleck*, 346 F. Supp. 1354 (D.R.I. 1972); *Shone v. Maine*, 406 F.2d 844 (1st Cir.) *vac. as moot*, 396 U.S. 6 (1969); *Boone v. Danforth*, 463 S.W.2d 825 (Mo. 1971). *See also* WASH. REV. STAT. ANN. §13.04.220 (1962).
79. *See, e.g., In re Michael W.*, 102 Cal. App. 3d 946, 162 Cal. Rptr. 744 (1980); *In re John Edward B.*,70 A.D. 2d 1004, 418 N.Y.S. 2d 186 (3d Dept. 1979).
80. *People v. Sandoval*, 70 Cal. App. 3d 73, 138 Cal. Rptr. 609 (1977).
81. *See In Eric J. 25 Cal.* 3d 522, 159 Cal. Rptr. 317, 601 P. 3d 549 (1979).
82. *Wisconsin Industrial School for Girls v. Clark Co.*, 103 Wis. 651, 79 N.W. 422 (1899).
83. *Creek v. Stone*, 379 F.2d 106, 109 (D.C. Cir. 1967). *See also* parallels in civil commitment of mental patients. *Rouse v. Cameron*, 373 F.2d 451 (D.C. Cir. 1966); *Wyatt v. Stickney*, 325 F. Supp. 781 (M.D. Ala. 1971).
84. *Wyatt v. Stickney*, 344 F. Supp. 373 (M.D. Ala. 1972), *modified*, 503 F. 2d 1305 (5th Cir. 1974). *Martarella v. Kelley*, 349 F. Supp. 575 (S.D.N.Y. 1972), 359 F. Supp. 478 (S.D.N.Y. 1973); *Nelson v. Heyne*, 355 F. Supp. 451 (N.D. Ind. 1973), *aff'd*, 491 F.2d 352 (7th Cir.); *cert. den.*, 417 U.S. 976 (1974); *Inmates v. Affleck*, *supra* note 78. *See also O'Connor v. Donaldson*, *supra* note 32.
85. *Wyatt v. Stickney*, 325 F. Supp. 781, 784, 785 (N.D. Ala. 1971).
86. *Martarella v. Kelley*, *supra* note 84; *Inmates v. Affleck*, *supra* note 78; *Nelson v. Heyne*, *supra* note 84; *Morales v. Turman*, 364 F. Supp. 166 (E.D. Tex. 1973); 383 F. Supp. 53 (E.D. Tex. 1974).
87. *Morales v. Turman*, 383 F. Supp. 53 (E.D. Tex. 1974), *rev'd on other grounds*, 535 F.2d 864 (5th Cir. 1976), *rev'd and remanded*, 430 U.S. 322, *remanded on rehearing*, 562 F. 2d 993 (5th Cir. 1977); *Martarella v. Kelley*, *supra* note 84; *Inmates v. Affleck*, *supra* note 59.
88. *Nelson v. Heyne*, 491 F.2d 352, 360 (7th Cir.), *cert. denied*, 417 U.S. 976 (1974); *Morales v. Turman*, *supra* note 86; *Usen v. Sipprell*, 41 A.D.2d 251, 342 N.Y.S.2d 599 (4th Dept. 1973); *In re Lavette M.*, 35 N.Y.2d 136, 316 N.E. 2d 314, 359 N.Y.S.2d 20 (1974).
89. *See, e.g., Usen v. Sipprell*, *supra* note 88.
90. *In re Richard C.*, 43 A.D.2d 862, 352 N.Y.S.2d 15 (2nd Dept. 1974).

91. *Matter of Ilone I.*, 64 Misc. 2d 878, 316 N.Y.S. 2d 356 (Fam. Ct. 1970).
92. *In re Welfare of J.E.C.*, Hennepin County Dist. Ct., Juv. Div. Case No. 75–604 (Feb. 1975).
93. *In re John H.*, 48 A.D.2d 879, 369 N.Y.S.2d 196 (2nd Dept. 1975).
94. *In re Aline D.*, 14 Cal. 3d 557, 536 P.2d 64, 121 Cal. Rptr. 817 (1975); CAL. WELF & INST. CODE §734 (1972).
95. *In re Appeal No. 179*, 23 Md. App. 496, 327 A.2d 793 (1974).
96. *In re Jeannette P.*, 34 A.D.2d 661, 310 N.Y.S. 2d 125 (2nd Dept. 1970). *See also In re Neil M. v. Gregory M.*, 71 Misc. 2d 396, 336 N.Y.S.2d 304 (1972).
97. *Matter of Ort*, 407 N.E.2d 1162 (Ind. Ct. App. 1980). *See also State ex rel. S.J.C. v. Fox*, 268 S.E.2d 56 (W. Va. 1980).
98. *In re Brownlee*, 272 S.E.2d 861 (N.C. 1981).
99. G.S. §7P–646.
100. *Matter of Quinton A.*, *supra* note 55, 49 N.Y.2d at 335. *See also J.K. v. State*, 68 Wis. 426, 228 N.W. 2d 713 (1975).
101. Civil rights actions may be filed pursuant to 42 U.S.C.A. §1983 (Supp. 1981).
102. *See., e.g., Wheeler v. Glass*, 473 F.2d 983 (7th Cir. 1973) (damages awarded a child for cruel and unusual punishment in a mental hospital); *Lollis v. New York State Department of Social Services*, 322 F. Supp. 473 (S.D.N.Y. 1970), 328 F. Supp. 115 (S.D.N.Y. 1971) ($10,000 sought by a training school resident kept in solitary confinement for 14 days). *See also O'Connor v. Donaldson*, 422 U.S. 563 (1975).
103. *Johnson v. Avery*, 393 U.S. 483 (1969); *Procunier v. Martinez*, 416 U.S. 396 (1974).
104. *Morales v. Turman*, 326 F. Supp. 677 (E.D. Tex. 1971).
105. *Jackson v. Bishop*, 404 F.2d 571, 579 (8th Cir. 1968).
106. *Weems v. U.S.*, 217 U.S. 349 (1910).
107. *Wheeler v. Glass*, *supra* note 102.
108. *Ingraham v. Wright*, 430 U.S. 651 (1977); *Baker v. Owen*, 423 U.S. 907 (1975).
109. *See Rennie v. Klein*, 462 F. Supp. 1131 (D.N.J. 1978); *Nelson v. Heyne*, 491 F.2d 352 (7th Cir.), *cert. denied*, 417 U.S. 976 (1974); *Lollis v. New York State Dept. of Social Services*, *supra* note 102.
110. *Nelson v. Heyne*, 355 F. Supp. 451, 454 (N.D. Ind. 1972), *aff'd* 491 F.2d 352 (7th Cir.), *cert. denied*, 417 U.S. 976 (1976) (citing *Jackson v. Bishop*, 404 F.2d 571, 579 (8th Cir. 1968)).
111. *Morales v. Turman*, *supra* note 87.
112. *Morgan v. Sproat*, 432 F. Supp. 1130 (S.D. Miss. 1977); *Pena v. New York Division for Youth*, 419 F. Supp. 203 (S.D.N.Y. 1976); *Morales v. Turman*, *supra* note 87; *Nelson v. Heyne*, *supra* note 110; *Inmates v. Affleck*, *supra* note 78; *Lollis v. Social Services*, *supra* note 102.
113. 9(A) N.Y.C.R.R. §§168.2–168.4.

114. *Nelson v. Heyne, supra* note 109. *See also Morales v. Turman, supra* note 87 (hearings required for solitary confinement extending beyond 5 days).
115. *Inmates v. Affleck, supra* note 78.
116. *Morales v. Turman, supra* note 87.
117. *Morgan v. Sprout, supra* note 112.
118. *Wilson v. Coughlin, supra* note 72; *Nelson v. Heyne, supra* note 110; *Pena v. New York Division for Youth, supra* note 112. *See also Morales v. Turman, supra* note 87 (tear gas and Mace prohibited as forms of punishment); *Naughton v. Bevilacqua*, 458 F. Supp. 610 (D.R.I. 1978) (prolixin could not be used absent a habilitative purpose), *aff'd*, 605 F. 2d 586 (1st Cir. 1979).
119. 9(A) N.Y.C.R.R. §168.3(b).
120. *Wolff v. MacDonnell*, 418 U.S. 539 (1974); *Procunier v. Martinez, supra* note 103.
121. 9(A) N.Y.C.R.R. §171.5.
122. *Morales v. Turman, supra* note 87.
123. *Nelson v. Heyne, supra* note 110. *See also Inmates v. Affleck, supra* note 78.
124. *See, e.g., Wolf v. McDonnell*, 418 U.S. 539 (1974); *Morales v. Turman, supra* note 87.
125. *Tinker v. Des Moines Independent Community School Dist.* 393 U.S. 503 (1969).
126. 9(A) N.Y.C.R.R. §§171.2, 171.3.
127. *Morales v. Turman, supra* note 87, at 101.
128. *Id.* at 100–101.
129. See generally *Connally v. General Const. Ct.*, 269 U.S. 385, 391 (1926); for application to juvenile institutions, *see In re Owens*, 9 Crim. L. Rptr. 2415 (Cir. Ct. Cook Co. Ill. 1971).
130. *Martarella v. Kelley, supra* note 84; *Morales v. Turman, supra* note 87, at 175, 179. In *Wyatt v. Stickney, supra* note 62, the court appointed "human rights committees' to protect the rights of patients to two mental health facilities.
131. A review of newly instituted grievance programs is found in Keating et. al., "Seen But Not Heard: A Survey of Grievance Mechanisms in Juvenile Correctional Institutions," Center for Correctional Justice (Washington, D.C., n.d.).
132. ALASKA STAT. §47.10.080(f) (1979); MINN. STAT. ANN. §260.185 (1982).
133. CAL. WELF. & INST. CODE §§775, 778 (1972 & Supp. 1982); R.I. GEN. LAWS ANN. §14–1–42 (1981).
134. *See, e.g., Allen v. Ricketts*, 236 Ga. 294, 223 S.E.2d 633 (1976); *People ex rel. Arthur F. v. Hill*, 29 N.Y.2d 17, 271 N.E.2d 911, 323 N.Y.S.2d 426 (1971).
135. *Meachum v. Fano*, 427 U.S. 215 (1976).
136. *See, e.g., Montanye v. Haynes*, 427 U.S. 236 (1976).
137. *Gault v. Board of Directors*, 103 Ariz. 401, 442 P.2d 848 (1968).

138. *Morales v. Turman, supra* note 87. *See also Shone v. Maine, supra* note 78.
139. 9(a) N.Y.C.R.R. §§175.1–175.4; *Finner v. Luger,* 73 (W. 552, S.D.N.Y. 1975) (unpublished consent order).
140. *See, e.g.,* N.Y. Soc. Servs. Law §372 (1976 & Supp. 1982).
141. *See, e.g.,* N.Y.C.P.L.R. §§4504, 4505, 4508 (Supp. 1982); CAL. EV. CODE §§912, 992 *et. seq.* (1966 & Supp. 1982); ILL. ANN. STAT. ch. 51 §§5.2 (Supp. 1971), ch. 91 and ½, §406 (1963).
142. *See, e.g.,* N.Y. Unconsol. Laws, tit. 5, §§1801–1806 (1979 & Supp. 1982); CAL. WELF. & INST. CODE §1300 (1972).
143. Interstate Compact on Juveniles, Articles VII, X.
144. *See, e.g., State ex rel. Juv. Dept. of Multnoma Co. v. Edwards,* 15 Ore. App. 677, 516 P.2d 1303 (1973).
145. Interstate Compact on Juveniles, Article V.
146. *Id.*
147. *See, e.g., In Interest of Storm,* 223 N.W.2d 170 (Iowa 1974).
148. *See, e.g., People v. Smith,* 109 Misc. 2d 705, 440 N.Y.S.2d 837 (Crim. Ct. 1981). Contra FLA. STAT. ANN. §39.112 (Supp. 1983).
149. *See, e.g., In re Gonzalez,* 255 Pa. Super. 217, 386 A.2d 586 (1978); *J.E.R. v. State,* 317 So.2d 89 (Fla. Dist. Ct. App. 1975); *In re Malloy,* 114 N.H. 771, 329 A.2d 150 (1974); *In re M.L.*, 64 N.J. 438, 317 A.2d 65 (1974).
150. *See, e.g.,* CAL. WELF. & INST. CODE §§726, 731 (Supp. 1982); COLO. REV. STAT. ANN. §19–3–113(4) (Supp. 1982); *In re J.R.*, 89 Ill. App. 3d 714, 403 N.E. 2d 114 (1980); ME. REV. STAT. ANN. tit. 15 §§3314(1)(B), (1)(E) (1980); N.Y. FAM. CT. ACT. §353.6(1) (1983); WASH. REV. CODE §13.40. 190 (1982); WISC. STAT. ANN. §48.34(5) (Supp. 1982).
151. *Durst v. U.S.*, 434 U.S. 542 (1978).
152. *In re Erikson,* 24 Wash. App. 808, 604 P.2d 513 (1979). *Accord M.J.W. v. State,* 133 Ga. 350, 210 S.E.2d 842 (1974).
153. N.Y. FAM. CT. ACT. §§353.6(1)(1), (b) (1983).
154. *In re Timothy E.*, 99 Cal. App. 3d 949, 160 Cal. Rptr. 256 (1979).
155. *In re Carroll,* 260 Pa. Super. 23, 393 A.2d 993 (1978).

IV

Child Abuse, Neglect, and Termination of the Parent-Child Relationship

Each state has laws that protect children from harm. Through ordinary criminal assault laws, all persons of any age are protected against physical assaults. Child abuse and neglect laws are special in that they protect only children. Broadly speaking, one of the rights of young people is the right to be raised by one's parents free from substantial harm. This right, however, is complicated by the bundle of rights accorded parents to raise their children relatively free from any outside interference.[1] In this chapter this tension between the rights of children and parents will be examined and explained. In addition, this chapter will discuss the circumstances in which the state may exercise one of its most awesome powers—the power to destroy permanently the parent-child relationship.

Do children have the right to be raised by their parents?

The answer to this question is complex. Children do not have the right to live with their parents over their *parents'* objections. Parents may voluntarily surrender their right to their children and give up their custody to third parties, whether or not the children agree with that decision.

However, children and their parents have the *reciprocal* right to live together and remain a family unit.[2] The U.S. Constitution makes no mention whatsoever of either parents or families, but the legal rights of parents to bear children, raise their offspring and guide their family according to their own beliefs are firmly rooted in the first ten amendments to the Constitution (otherwise known as the Bill of Rights). The right of parents to raise their children and the reciprocal right of children to be raised by their parents are therefore regarded as part of the highest law of the land.

The reason why parental and familial rights are accorded such high legal priority, even though they are not articulated in the Constitution, is that our culture has always afforded a great deal of respect to the parent-child relationship, and almost all Western legal codes have accepted the proposition that until children come of age, major decisions regarding their custody and control are left to the discretion of parents.

What is "child abuse"?

No two states have identical legal definitions of child abuse, but there are common aspects among all of them. Virtually every state law considers the infliction of *serious* physical injury upon a child by a parent or custodian to be child abuse. Most laws also include a parent's sexual *intercourse* with, or sexual *molestation* of, a child. Some laws are defined broadly and included conditions when a parent creates a *risk* of serious physical injury or inflicts *psychological* abuse. Still others consider the infliction of *any* injury to be abusive, whether it is "serious" or not.

A typical definition of child abuse is found in the California law. It makes it illegal for

> Any person who, under circumstances or conditions likely to produce great bodily harm or death, willfully causes or permits any child to suffer, or inflicts thereon unjustifiable physical pain or mental suffering, or having the care or custody of any child, willfully causes or permits the person or health of such child to be injured . . . [or for] [a]ny person who, under circumstances or conditions other than those likely to produce great bodily harm or death, willfully causes or permits any child to suffer, or inflicts thereon unjustifiable physical pain or mental suffering. . . .[3]

What is "child neglect"?

In most states, *child neglect* is more loosely defined than child abuse. Generally, it covers situations in which parents do *not* do something that should be done, thereby jeopardizing the health and safety of their children.

Most states consider the failure of parents to supply their children with adequate food, shelter, clothing, and medical care to be child neglect. Abandonment or leaving a child without adequate supervision for a certain length of time are also considered acts of neglect in most states. Thus, if a child suffers from malnutrition because his parents do not feed him, or if he does not get proper medical attention for a wound or injury (regardless of how it was caused) because his parents fail to take him to a doctor, the parents may be charged with child neglect. Similarly, if parents leave their small children unattended overnight or for a longer period of time and make no provisions for someone else to care for them, they may be accused of child neglect.

Many states include still other categories of parental behavior as child neglect. In a number of states the failure to send a child to school is considered neglect, as is a parent's "moral unfitness," use of drugs, or excessive use of alcohol. A parent's conviction of a serious crime may also be deemed neglect in some states.

As stated at the beginning of this answer, *child neglect* is never defined as precisely as abuse; for example, some states define *neglect* as the failure to provide a child with "proper" parental care or the commission of an act that endangers a child's "morals."

Up to what age are children protected by child abuse and neglect laws?

In 44 states the age to which children may be found neglected or abused is 18. In the other states the cutoff age ranges from 16 to 21.

Are children protected by these laws only against the acts of their parents?

No. Most laws hold parents *and persons acting in the role of a parent* responsible for the abuse or neglect of children under their care. New York's law, for example, extends responsibility to a parent "or other person legally responsible for [a child's] care,"[4] and in Maryland, the law encompasses any parent "or other person who has the permanent or temporary care or custody or responsibility for the supervision of a minor child."[5]

Even in states where statutes refer only to parents,

courts have construed this as a reference to any person entrusted with the care and control of a child.[6]

This means that stepfathers or stepmothers, uncles and aunts who regularly care for their nieces and nephews, a parent's live-in boyfriend or girlfriend, or even a baby-sitter may be liable for child abuse.

What constitutes abandonment?

Most state laws include *abandonment* as a condition of child neglect, but it is rarely defined. Most statutes simply state that children are deemed neglected if they are abandoned by their parents, guardians, or custodians. A few statutes are more specific. In Arizona, for example, *abandonment* is defined as the "failure of the parent to provide reasonable support and to maintain regular contact with the child, including the providing of normal supervision. Failure to maintain a normal parental relationship with the child without just cause for a period of six months shall constitute prima facie evidence of abandonment."[7]

In all states, courts will decide whether the specific facts of each case constitutes abandonment or not.

Can children be taken from their parents' custody when the parents fail to provide adequate medical care for them?

Yes. This can come about in a number of ways.

First, parents can be found neglectful for not providing or seeking proper medical care when their children need treatment for illness, injury, or serious physical disorder. Second, they can be charged with neglect for taking a child from a doctor's care or from a hospital before necessary treatment is completed. Third, if parents have been told by doctors or other health professionals that an operation or particular medical treatment is necessary, they might be found neglectful for refusing such treatment. Child-neglect proceedings are frequently invoked to assure that children receive medical treatment to which parents are opposed but which have been deemed necessary by a doctor.[8]

A case arose recently in Massachusetts in which the parents of a child suffering from lymphocytic leukemia were unwilling to submit the child to chemotherapy. The supreme court of that state considered the "primary right" of parents to raise children according to their own consciences, but ruled that parental rights do not give them life-and-death authority over their children. The court ordered treatment over the parents' objections because evidence showed (1) that the disease would be fatal if untreated; (2) that chemotherapy was the only medical treatment offering a hope of cure; and (3) that the risks of the treatment were minimal compared to the consequences of allowing the disease to go untreated. The court pointed to the power of the state to protect children and distinguished its decision in this case, where treatment was necessary to *save* a child's life, from other cases in which medical treatment has been sought merely to briefly *prolong* life.[9]

Do children have the right to receive adequate medical care even if it is contrary to the parents' religious beliefs?

Yes. Although one's religious beliefs are protected by the First Amendment, courts will not permit a parent's religious beliefs to harm his child.

It is important, however, to bear in mind that the state must demonstrate a "compelling" interest to justify interference with parental discretion; this limits the type and degree of intervention that is legally permissible.

Thus, if a parent refuses consent, on religious grounds, to a medically necessary blood transfusion for his child, a court may declare the child to be neglected and authorize that the transfusion be administered. But in the absence of a finding that the parent neglected the child in any other way, no additional court order, such as removing the child from the parent's custody, would be constitutional.[10]

Do children have the right to receive an education?

Yes. Not only do children have the right to receive an education, but in every state parents have a legal *duty* to educate their children. If parents do not ensure that their children receive adequate educational instruction, they may be charged with neglecting the needs of their children.[11] However, a parent's duty does not go beyond enrolling his child in school and making reasonable efforts to assure regular attendance. If the *child* is a truant through no fault of the parent, the child may be punished by the juvenile court (see chapter X for a more in-depth discussion of this subject).

What type of parental misconduct or "immorality" could constitute neglect, such that a court may remove a child from his home?

There is no clear or consistent interpretation of parental immorality or misconduct in the nineteen states that consider it a ground for finding child neglect. Sometimes the laws are read in such a way that when a parent commits adultery, has an illegitimate child, lives with a paramour, or has a drinking problem, it constitutes neglect since the misconduct creates an unstable or improper moral environment for the child. With increasing frequency, however, these interpretations are no longer being made by courts.[12] The question is not whether a parent uses alcohol or commits adultery, but whether the conduct creates deficiencies in adequate child care that require the separation of a child from his parents.[13]

May a child be taken from his home if his parents are found mentally deficient and incapable of raising a child?

Yes, in a number of states.[15] Of course, the court must find that the child is in some way endangered as a result of the parents' deficiencies.

Do young people have the right to be free from child abuse and neglect?

Yes. All children have the right to be protected from physical harm and severe psychological impairment. In addition, every child has the right to be adequately fed, clothed, sheltered, and provided with medical care and educational services.

Generally, it is the responsibility of a child's parents or custodians to provide him with the necessary attributes of life. When they fail to fulfill these responsibilities or prevent a child from receiving them, they may be charged with child abuse or neglect.

What can one do if he suspects that a child is being abused or neglected?

He can report his suspicion to the police or the state or county department of social welfare. A number of states have special toll-free telephone numbers for just this purpose. Generally, the name of the person who makes the report will not be divulged to the family.

Is anyone required to report his suspicion of abuse or neglect?

In every state doctors and hospitals are required to report potentially suspicious child abuse cases and in many states schoolteachers, social workers, and all medical professionals (for instance, dentists and nurses) are required to make reports as well. For these individuals, failure to report reasonable suspicions of child abuse is punishable in most states as a misdemeanor.[15] On the other hand, those who make reports in good faith are rendered free from civil liability.[16]

It is important to note that a report of suspected abuse or neglect does not automatically result in the commencement of legal action. A juvenile or family court will hold a hearing only if a *petition* is filed by an individual or a duly authorized agency. A report is not a petition; it merely alerts the proper authorities that there exists a reasonable suspicion of child abuse or neglect.

Can a child make his own report that he is being abused or neglected?

Yes. Anyone can make such a report.

What happens when a child or a family is reported?

The agency charged with investigating such matters—usually the Department of Social Welfare or the police—will conduct an investigation. The inquiry may include a visit to the child's home and an interview with the parents and perhaps neighbors and a physician in order to determine whether or not a child is or has been abused, neglected or otherwise improperly cared for.

If the investigation reveals evidence of maltreatment, there are a number of options open to the investigating agency: (1) It may file a petition in the appropriate court seeking to have the child declared abused or neglected; (2) it may try to encourage the parents to participate in an educational, training, or rehabilitative program (with the threat of a court petition if they do not cooperate); (3) it may merely encourage the family to accept voluntary help; or (4) it may refer the family or child to another community agency.

If no evidence of improper treatment is found, the agency may do nothing at all. In such cases, of course, the matter will not be referred to court.

Can a child be taken from his home and placed in the custody of any person, family, or agency without a court hearing?

No. No person or agency has the power to remove a child from his home without the approval of the court.

There is an exception to this rule in the case of an emergency. An emergency can be said to exist when conditions (in the home or elsewhere) constitute an extreme danger to the life or safety of the child, such that there is no time to launch an investigation or demand a court hearing. Even in these cases, however, a hearing must be held as soon as possible to determine whether continued separation from the family is necessary.[17]

If a child is alleged to be neglected or abused, what standard of proof must be met before a judicial determination may be made?

Generally, the evidentiary standard is either proof that is "clear and convincing" or proof established by a "preponderance of the evidence."[18] These standards are less exacting than proof "beyond a reasonable doubt," which is required in delinquency cases.[19]

Is a child who is the subject of a neglect, abuse, or dependency hearing entitled to be represented by an attorney?

Yes, in most states.[20] Even though the *Gault* decision requring counsel did not deal with cases of abuse and neglect, its practical effect has been the extension of the right to an attorney for all children—regardless of their age and irrespective of the charge—who are the subject of these proceedings in juvenile and family courts.[21]

Are parents of children alleged to be neglected, abused, or dependent entitled to representation by an attorney as well?

Again, the answer is yes in most states.[22] Counsel for the parent is often provided free of charge if the parent is unable to pay.[23]

What about foster parents or relatives who have temporary custody over a child—are they entitled to take part in dependency hearings involving the child, either personally or through an attorney?

There is no clear answer. The traditional view is that persons having custody of the child who are not themselves charged with child maltreatment have no right to take part in the legal proceedings. Recently, however, a number of courts have granted foster parents "standing" to participate in child protective hearings and dispositional proceedings.[24]

Does a young person have the right to personally appear at a child abuse or neglect hearing and have his own wishes considered?

Normally, courts do not permit children to appear or testify at hearings involving their parents.

Under certain circumstances a judge may permit a child to make his own wishes known with regard to his future placement. Usually a child's "testimony" would not be given in open court but in a judge's chambers. The amount of consideration given to a child's opinion usually increases with his age and maturity (see chapter V).

What happens to children who are found by a court of law to be neglected or abused?

Parents or children who are found to be neglected or abused may be required to participate in rehabilitative programs sponsored by the state or a private child-caring agency. In such cases, the child would remain with his or her parents in the home. If the conditions of neglect or abuse are severe or if the court believes that the interests of the child could best be served by removing him or her from the home, the child may be made a ward of the court (as in California), or placed in the custody of the commissioner of social services (as in New York) and/or placed in the temporary care and custody of some other person such as a friend or relative, a foster home, or an institution that provides care and shelter for neglected and abused children.[25]

If a neglected, abused, or dependent child is placed in an institution, may he be housed with young people who have committed crimes?

Generally, no. In most states dependent children may not be placed in the same facility that houses delinquent children or persons in need of supervision.[26]

What is the "termination of parental rights"?

The termination of parental rights is the permanent severance of the parent-child relationship. When parental rights are terminated the parent and child are no longer legally related; the parent no longer has rights to, or responsibilities for, the child and the child is legally free to be adopted.[27] Not all children whose parents' rights have been terminated are adopted, but they may be adopted without their parent's permission. Children whose parents' rights have been terminated but who are not adopted become wards of the state; they are legally related to no one.

How is the parent-child relationship terminated?

Parental rights may be terminated voluntarily or involuntarily.

The vast majority of terminations are voluntary. This is accomplished when parents surrender the child to a licensed child-care agency or place the child with a relative or friend for private adoption. (For a more detailed discussion of adoption procedures, see chapter V.)

Involuntary termination—the severance of the parent-child relationship without parental consent—is the primary focus of the remainder of this chapter. All terminations made over the objections of parents occur by orders of courts, after hearings conducted pursuant to state laws. These laws vary somewhat from state to state, but there are common threads among them.

For what reasons may a state seek to terminate parental rights?

Before parental rights are terminated, most state laws require proof of gross or long-standing neglect of parental obligations.

Every state law lists abandonment of a child as a condition justifying termination, though this term is defined differently by various state laws and courts. Most states also include repeated or unusually severe acts of neglect or abuse, and parental incapacity or inability to care for children. Many states include mental illness,[28] conviction of a crime affecting the fitness of a parent,[29] and financial nonsupport[30] as conditions justifying termination. A few states even include parental "debauchery," "depravity," adultery, and fornication.[31]

May a state involuntarily terminate the parent-child relationship without prior proof of wrongdoing?

Yes. But in most states, termination may be ordered only if certain conditions have been in existence for a period of time (six months, a year, or more.)

In New York, for example, parental rights can be terminated only if a court finds that express statutory conditions have been in existence for *one continuous year* and (1) the child has been in the care of a licensed child-care agency; (2) the agency has made diligent efforts to encourage the parent-child relationship; (3) the parents have failed to maintain contact with or plan for the future of the child; and (4) the best interests of the child require termination of parental rights.[32] There is no requirement that the original placement of a child in a child-care agency was involuntary or due to a court ruling of abuse or neglect. In other words the *voluntary* placement of a child in foster care may still result in involuntary termination.

Other states have similar requirements. In California, certain conditions must be proven to exist after parents have been involuntarily deprived of their child's custody for *one year* due to most kinds of neglect, or after their child has been voluntarily placed in foster care for *two years*.[33] In Connecticut, the conditions permitting a finding of termination must prevail for *one year* or more. These conditions include (1) abandonment; (2) lack of parental rehabilittation; (3) continuing physical or mental disability of the parent; or (4) absence of an ongoing parent-child relationship.[34]

The wording of these statutes suggests that proceedings to terminate parental rights are usually instituted only after the child has already been under state care or supervision for some time, or only after the parents have had some chance to correct their disabilities. But not all termination proceedings are started after a period of time of "warning" to the parents; some states permit their commencement upon the occurrence of a particularly grave or compelling event such that parental behavior does not fall squarely into any of the enumerated statutory categories. Thus, in California, termination may result (1) if parents are unable to care for their children because of the habitual use of alcohol or drugs; (2) if they have been convicted of a felony or a crime that proves their unfitness; or (3) if they suffer from a severe disability or mental illness such that they are deemed unable to raise children.[35] In Connecticut, immediate termination may be based on the statutory grounds just mentioned, or it may occur if the "totality of circumstances" so requires.[36]

Moreover, in a few states, parental rights may be terminated following an initial court ruling of neglect or abuse, and without a special termination hearing.[37]

Does the state have the duty to provide supportive services to families before the parent-child relationship may be terminated?

Usually. As just mentioned, in most states parental rights may be terminated only after a child has been involuntarily removed from the home or has been a ward of the state for a specified length of time. If the child was removed because of parental abuse, neglect, or some other wrongdoing, the state department of child welfare or another appropriate agency is usually charged with providing the parents supportive or rehabilitative services, such as—

1. counseling;
2. homemaker assistance;
3. parent training;
4. employment training;
5. individual or group therapy;
6. visits with the child.[38]

This duty to provide services is considered so essential in some states that parental rights may not be terminated if services were not first provided, or, conversely, parental rights may be terminated only if services were provided but were either refused or ineffective.[39] Indiana law, for example, requires that before the state involuntarily terminates parental rights it must show that "[r]easonable services have been offered or provided to the parent to assist him in fulfilling his parental obligations, and either that he has failed to accept them or they have been ineffective."[40] Missouri law requires the Division of Family Services or another agency to use "reasonable, diligent and continuing efforts to aid the parent to rectify the conditions."[42]

There are two exceptions to this rule. First, as noted earlier, in a few states parental rights may be terminated upon the immediate conclusion of a neglect or abuse hearing; under such circumstances, obviously, there would be no duty to provide services since there is no time to do so. Second, even in states that require providing rehabilitative services before parental rights may be terminated, the requirement is suspended if there is no possibility that the child's welfare will be improved as a result of such services. Thus, in New York, the law requires the agency to demonstrate that it put forth "diligent efforts to encourage and strengthen the parental relationship," but it adds, "when such efforts will not be detrimental to the best interest of the child."[42] Following this exception, some courts have ruled that, when there is clearly no possibility of rehabilitation, parental rights may be terminated notwithstanding the lack of supportive services, because the welfare of the child could not be served.[43]

May the parent-child relationship be terminated merely because termination is found in a court to be in the child's best interests?

Until recently, courts have refused to terminate parental rights without a clear showing of neglect, unfitness, harm, or abandonment.[44]

In the past decade, however, a few courts have utilized the child's "best interests" as the legal standard for authorizing termination of the rights of parents, even though there has been no showing of parental unfitness,[45] and some states have enacted laws to this effect.[46] A few state laws go so far as to allow an adoption without parental consent if it is in the child's best interest.[47] This means that the state does not have to prove any wrongdoing on the part of the parent or harm or injury to the child—it need only show that it would be in the child's best interests to be involuntarily taken from the custody of his parents. This new trend runs counter to the general rule that a parent's right to custody may not be defeated simply because a child might be better served by having different parents.[48] Language in recent Supreme Court decisions indicates that these state laws and decisions may be unconstitutional if they allow termination without proof that the parents were unfit or that their child suffered some type of harm while under their care.

In 1977, after most of the state-court decisions just alluded to had been decided, the Supreme Court unanimously ruled that the right of natural parents to the care and custody of their children is a "constitutionally recognized liberty interest that derives from blood relationship, state law sanction, and basic human rights."[49] With this opinion, the Supreme Court reaffirmed many cases decided in the past half century that gave constitutional protection to parental rights and that recognized the importance of family integrity. Then, in 1978, the Supreme Court unanimously declared that

> if a State were to attempt to force the breakup of a natural family, over the objections of the parents and their children, without some showing of unfitness and *for the sole reason that to do so was thought to be in the children's best interest*, we should have little doubt that the State would have intruded impermissibly on the "private realm of family life which the State cannot enter" [emphasis added].[50]

Subsequent to this United States Supreme Court decision, the Supreme Court of Montana interpreted its law (which provides for termination based on the best interests standard)[51] in such a manner that termination may be ordered only if a child is found to be abused, neglected or dependent *first;* then, and only then, may his or her future custody be based upon the best interest test. The Court stated that

> the "best interests of the child" test is correctly used to determine custody rights between natural parents in divorce proceedings. However, where third parties seek custody, it has long been the law in Montana that the right of the natural parent prevails until a showing of a forfeiture of this right. . . . This forfeiture can result only where the parent's conduct does not meet the minimum standards of the child abuse, neglect and dependency status.[52]

Similarly, the Massachusetts Supreme Judicial Court expressly overruled an earlier opinion authorizing the "best interests" standard for termination, declaring that the state may not break up a family without proof of parental unfitness.[53]

And in 1979, the highest court in New York cleared up a possible misunderstanding resulting from an earlier case that had been interpreted to stand for the proposition that termination could be based on the best interests standard.[54] The court stated unequivocally:

> A court may not terminate all parental rights by offering a child for adoption when there has been no

> parental consent, abandonment, neglect or proven unfitness, *even though some might find adoption to be in the child's best interests.*[55]

Does there have to be a showing that the child will benefit from a termination order before a court will terminate?

Generally, no. If the grounds for termination are found by a court to exist, termination may be ordered without any inquiry into the effect of such an order on the child. Recently however, a number of courts have ruled that before termination is ordered, the court should determine that the child is adoptable. Only after this showing has been made, these courts have ruled, should an order terminating parental rights be entered.[56]

Are there other constitutional limits to the conditions for which the parent-child relationship may be terminated?

Yes. Because parents have a fundamental right to raise their children, states may only deprive them of that right under *compelling* circumstances. The grounds upon which a state may involuntarily terminate parental rights may not be minor ones, nor may they be defined in overly broad terms such that the scope of potential termination could be interpreted in a way that sanctions termination for less than compelling reasons.

The first major test of overly vague and broad termination statutes was in 1975, when parents challenged an Iowa law that authorized termination for "refusal to give a child necessary parental care and protection" or for parental conduct "likely to be detrimental to the physical or mental health or morals of a child."[57] Pursuant to this statute, the parents' parental rights in four of their five children were terminated, basically because their home was unkempt and the children were often dirty and unruly, even though there was no evidence or judicial finding that the children were harmed in any way. The court terminated their rights because, in the language of the statute, they failed to provide "necessary parental care" and their conduct was "likely to be detrimental" to the children. On appeal a federal court reversed, ruling that the law was constitutionally vague because it (1) did not give "fair warning of what parental conduct is proscribed; (2) permitted . . . arbitrary and discriminatory termination; and

(3) inhibited . . . the exercise of the fundamental right to family integrity."[58]

In another case, the Arkansas Supreme Court held that a state law permitting termination if parents were found deficient in providing a child with "a proper home"[59] was unconstitutionally vague. The court stated that:

> [U]sing any of [the possible] meanings does little to make the words, "a proper home," clearly understandable so that it doesn't mean one thing to one judge, something else to another, and something yet different to still another. What is a proper home? A correct home? A suitable home? A fit home? Is propriety to be determined ethically, socially or economically? Or on the basis of morality? Or prosperity? Is the standard a maximum, a minimum, a mean or an average?[60]

Thus, state laws setting forth grounds for termination that use language as vague or broad as the Iowa and Arkansas statutes are vulnerable to constitutional attack.

On the other hand, a number of state laws have survived legal challenge in state courts, even though their grounds for termination appear almost as vague as those just discussed. A Pennsylvania law that permits termination if a child was "without essential parental care, control or subsistence necessary for his physical or mental well-being,"[61] and a New York statute that permits termination for parental "failure to plan for the future of the child" have been held not to be unconstitutionally vague or broad.[62] Similarly, the Massachusetts standard of "best interest of the child"[63] and the Oklahoma standard that termination may result if a parent "fails to give the child the parental care or protection necessary for his physical or mental health" have survived constitutional attack on vagueness grounds.[64]

Perhaps the reason why many courts are unwilling to find rather imprecise language unconstitutional, when they might rule otherwise in reviewing similarly worded laws not concerned with children, is because, in the words of the Oregon Supreme Court, "what might be unconstitutional if only the parents' rights were involved, is constitutional if the statute adopts legitimate and necessary means to protect the child's interests."[65]

May parental rights be terminated because of low intelligence or mental illness?

Perhaps, if the low intelligence or mental illness is so extreme that it makes parents incapable of caring for their children.

Several courts have held that parents may not be involuntarily deprived of their children without a sufficient showing of harm to the child.[66] A difficult problem arises when a court must decide if parental rights should be terminated when evidence shows that certain parents are incapable of caring for their children due to their mental incapacity, *even though* there is no evidence of any past harm to the children or that the children have suffered under the care of their parents.

Some courts have found low or impaired intelligence alone—without any showing of harm to children—sufficient to justify termination.[67] Other courts have taken the position that a previous judgment of mental incompetence *alone* is sufficient to terminate parental rights.[68]

A number of states, however, do not permit termination merely because parents are thought to be incapable of caring for a child, without some proof that they are *in fact* incapable. The Missouri statute, for example, authorizes termination when a parent has a permanent or irreversible mental condition rendering him unable to form an intent or act knowingly *and* "such parent has substantially and repeatedly neglected the child or failed to give the child necessary care and protection."[69] An an Oregon court ruled that evidence that a mother had an "antisocial personality," and that she was more likely than the average person to abuse her child "someday," was insufficient reason to terminate parental rights. The court required a showing of a present failure to perform her parental role or *substantial certainty* that she would not be able to perform with minimal adequacy.[70]

A middle ground is taken in Nebraska, where the law authorizes termination if "parents are unable to discharge parental responsibilities because of mental illness or mental deficiency, *and* if there are reasonable grounds to believe that such condition will continue for a prolonged indeterminate period."[71]

How strongly must the state prove its case?

At termination proceedings, the state has the burden of proving that parental rights should be terminated. If the state does not prove its case, parental rights will not be terminated.

The question then becomes, how *strongly* does the state have to prove its case: that is, what standard of proof is followed by the court in making its decision? In a criminal trial the state must prove the guilt of the defendant "beyond a reasonable doubt," which is the highest standard of evidence. In a civil trial, one party will win a case if it establishes proof by a "preponderance" of the evidence, which is a less demanding standard. Under this standard, the party seeking to prove its point in court will succeed merely by showing slightly more persuasive evidence on its side than on the other.

In 1982, the United States Supreme Court held that the Constitution requires a state to prove allegations supporting termination of parental rights by *at least* clear and convincing evidence.[72] This standard is less demanding than proof beyond a reasonable doubt but more demanding than proof by a preponderance of evidence. The Supreme Court left it up to the states to adopt the strict "beyond a reasonable doubt" standard, if they so desire. Two states (New Hampshire and Louisiana) already require proof beyond a reasonable doubt to terminate parental rights;[73] and the federal government requires proof beyond a reasonable doubt to terminate the parent-child relationship in child custody proceedings involving Indian families.[74]

In termination proceedings, is a lawyer provided to represent the child?

Many states require courts to appoint a lawyer to represent the child in proceedings to terminate parental rights, even if the child is an infant.[75] Even if state law does not require that a lawyer be appointed, many courts will do so on their own accord.[76] When a lawyer is appointed, it means that he or she is paid by the court; neither the child nor the parents are required to pay the attorney's fees. Children are frequently represented by lawyers in termination proceedings because of the possibility that the child may be permanently separated from his parents and made a ward of the state, and because neither the state (which has charged the parents with abandonment or wrongdoing) nor the parents necessarily represent the interests of the children.

It should be noted that the United States Supreme Court has never considered the question whether children have a constitutional right to counsel in termination proceedings. In 1981, however, the Court ruled that states do not have to provide *parents* with free counsel in these proceedings.[77] In light of this ruling, it is highly questionable that the Court would require states to provide counsel for children. Irrespective of the Supreme Court decision, most states do require counsel for *parents* and *children*, either by statute or by court decision.

However, there are still states that do *not* require separate counsel for the child. In one case in Pennsylvania, the supreme court of that state affirmed an order terminating parental rights over the objection of the parents who thought that the refusal of the lower court to appoint a lawyer for the child made the decision constitutionally defective.[78]

If a lawyer is appointed to represent the child in termination proceedings, must he or she reflect the wishes of the child's parents?

No. The point of having a lawyer represent the child is to have someone available to represent the child's wishes and interests alone. The theory is that the court needs the input and assistance of someone who represents the child and not the state (which seeks termination) or the parents (who may resist it).

However, children who are the subjects of termination proceedings are usually too young to speak for themselves, or if they are old enough to speak they may be unable to articulate or even identify their own interests. Their interests *may* be identical to their parents', or to the state's view, or they may be different from either. Therefore, a lawyer for the child often is required to take an independent role and advocate what the *lawyer* perceives to be the interests of his or her client.

Do families have the constitutional right to receive public assistance benefits at a minimum level to assure that a family can be kept together?

No. It is not unconstitutional for the federal government and states to provide a maximum grant to a family irrespective of the number of members of the family.[79] Poor families may not claim a right to live together if the reason for a separation is that the parents have an inadequate amount of money and public assistance is not sufficient to keep the family together. For this reason, courts have rejected claims by parents, with little or no money of their own, that public assistance benefits, including housing, must be provided in a manner that assures that a parent with a large family will be able to live together.[80]

Do children who are in the state's care have the constitutional right to be returned to their parents or be legally freed for adoption?

No. Children who are in the state's care, either because their parents are unfit or because they have been voluntarily placed by their parents, do not have a constitutional right to be placed for adoption.[81] While children may be kept in the state's care only for compelling reasons, such as an inability of their parents to care for them, once they are properly in the state's care they have no right to insist on being placed with a family permanently.

May children who are in state-supervised foster homes challenge their placement by means of a federal writ of habeas corpus?

No. The United States Supreme Court ruled in 1982, that custody in a foster home is not the type of "custody" (for instance, deprivation of liberty) necessary to authorize use of *federal* habeas corpus.[82] It is probable however that egregious conditions of a child's custody may be challenged in this way.[83] In any event, custody may be challenged through a *state's* habeas corpus remedy.

If children are physically harmed while in state-supervised foster care can the state be sued for monetary damages?

Yes, if the state was negligent in selecting the foster parents or in supervising the placement. Children who are placed in foster care have a right to be kept free from harm. When they are harmed, either by child abuse or sexual abuse, they or their parents may sue those responsible for the harm. This means that the local governmental or private child-care agency responsible for supervising the placement may be sued if the foster parents were inadequately supervised.[84]

NOTES

1. *See, e.g., Meyer v. Nebraska*, 262 U.S. 390 (1923); *Pierce v. Society of Sisters*, 268 U.S. 510 (1925); *Ginsberg v. New York*, 390 U.S. 629 (1968); *Wisconsin v. Yoder*, 406 U.S. 205 (1972); *Moore v. City of East Cleveland*, 431 U.S. 494 (1977); *Santosky v. Kramer* 455 U.S. 745 (1982).
2. *Duchesne v. Sugarman*, 566 F.2d 817, 825 n. 19 (2d Cir. 1977).
3. Cal. Penal Code §273a (Supp. 1982).
4. N.Y. Fam. Ct. Act. §§1012(a) (f)(i) (g) (1981 & Supp. 1982).
5. Md. Ann. Code art. 27, §35A (1982).
6. *See, e.g., Bowers v. State*, 283 Md. 115, 341 (1978); *State v. Smith*, 485 S.W.2d 461 (Mo. App. 1972).
7. Ariz. Rev. Stat. §§8–201(1); 8–546(A)(1) (Supp. 1981–82).
8. *See, e.g., In re Seiferth*, 309 N.Y. 80, 127 N.E.2d 820 (1955).
9. *In re Custody of Minor*, 375 Mass. 733, 379 N.E.2d 1053 (1978). *But see In re Hofbauer*, 47 N.Y.2d 648, 393 N.E.2d 1009 (1979).
10. The constitutional infirmity in excessive or overbroad state action of this sort is that it violates substantive due process of law. *See, e.g.*, N.Y. Soc. Serv. Law §383–b (1976); *People ex rel. Wallace v. Labrenz*, 411 Ill. 618, 104 N.E.2d 769, *cert. denied*, 344 U.S. 824 (1952).
11. *See, e.g.*, N.Y. Fam. Ct. Act. §1012(f)(i)(A) (1981).
12. *See, e.g., In re Cager*, 251 Md. 473, 248 A.2d 384 (1968); *In re Raya*, 255 Cal. App. 2d 260, 63 Cal. Rptr. 252 (1967); cf. *Brim v. Brim*, 532 P.2d 1403 (Okl. Ct. App. 1975).
13. *See, e.g., In re Rinker*, 180 Pa. Super. 143, 117 A.2d 780 (1955).
14. *See, e.g., Todd v. Superior Court, King Co., Juvenile Court*, 68 Wash.2d 587, 414 P.2d 605 (1966); *State ex rel. Paul v. Dept. of Public Welfare*, 170 So.2d 549 (La. Ct. App. 1965).
15. *See, e.g.*, N.Y. Soc. Serv. Law §420 (1976).
16. *See, e.g.*, Mass. Gen. Laws Ann. ch. 119, §51A (Supp. 1982–83); N.Y. Soc. Serv. Law §419 (1976); Ill. Ann. Stat. ch. 23 §2059 (Supp. 1982–83).
17. *See, e.g.*, N.Y. Soc. Serv. Law §417(2) (1976); *York v. Halley*, 534 P.2d 363 (Okla. 1975).
18. *Woods v. Dept. of Social Services*, 11 Md. App. 10, *cert. denied*, 404 U.S. 965 (1971); 272 A.2d 92 *In re Leflure*, 48 Mich. App. 377, 210 N.W.2d 482 (1973); D.C. Code §16–2317(b)(2)(1970).
19. *In re Winship*, 397 U.S. 358 (1970).
20. *See, e.g.*, Cal. Welf. & Inst. Code §679 (Supp. 1982); Minn. Stat. Ann. §260.155(2)(1982); N.Y. Fam. Ct. Act. §249 (1981); Ohio Rev. Code Ann. §2151.352 (1976); Ga. Code Ann. §24A–2001(a) (1981).
21. *See, e.g., In re Orlando F.*, 40 N.Y.2d 103, 386 N.Y.S.2d 64, 351 N.E.2d 711 (1976).
22. *See, e.g., In re Aronson*, 263 Wis. 604, 58 N.W.2d 553 (1953); Conn. Gen. Stat. Ann. §466–135 (Supp. 1982).

23. *See, e.g.*, CAL. CIV. CODE §237.5(b)(1982).
24. *See, e.g.*, *In re Aronson, supra* note 23; *In re B.G.*, 11 Cal.3d 679, 523 P.2d 244, 114 Cal. Rptr. 444 (1974); *Stapleton v. Dauphin Co. Child Care Services*, 228 Pa. Super, 371 324 A.2d 562 (1974). *See also Smith v. Organization of Foster Families*, 431 U.S. 816 (1977).
25. *See, e.g.*, CAL. WELF. & INST. CODE §726, 727 (Supp. 1982); N.Y. FAM. CT. ACT. §§1052–1057 (1981 & Supp. 1982).
26. *See, e.g.*, *Martarella v. Kelly*, 349 F. Supp. 575 (S.D.N.Y. 1972).
27. *See, e.g.*, ILL. ANN. STAT. ch. 40, §1521 (1980); *In re Workman*, 38 Ill. App. 3d 261, 344 N.E.2d 796 (1975).
28. ILL. ANN. STAT. ch. 40, §1510 (Supp. 1982); MO. ANN. STAT. §211.447(2)(2)(g) (Supp. 1982).
29. CAL. CIV. CODE §232(a)(4) (1982); *In re D.S.C.*, 155 Cal. Rptr. 406 (Ct. App. 1979).
30. MO. ANN. STAT. §211.447(2)(f) (Supp. 1982).
31. *See, e.g.*, ILL. ANN. STAT. ch. 40, §1501 (Supp. 1982); MO. ANN. STAT. §211.447(2)(2)(g) (Supp. 1982); MINN. STAT. §260.221(b)(4) (1982).
32. N.Y. FAM. CT. ACT. §614 (Supp. 1982); N.Y. SOC. SERV. LAW §384–b(7) (Supp. 1982).
33. CAL. CIV. CODE §232.1 (1982).
34. CONN. GEN. STAT. §17–43a (Supp. 1982).
35. CAL. CIV. CODE §§232.1(3) (4) (5) (6) (1982).
36. CONN. GEN. STAT. §17–43a (Supp. 1982).
37. *See, e.g.*, KAN. STAT. ANN. §38–824(c) (1981).
38. *See generally* 42 U.S.C.A. §§670–673 (Supp. 1982).
39. *In re Walter B.*, 577 P.2d 119 (Utah 1978); *In re La Freniere*, 420 A.2d 82 (R.I. 1982).
40. IND. CODE 31–6–5–4(3) (1981).
41. MO. ANN. STAT. §211.47(2)(2)(b) (Supp. 1982).
42. N.Y. SOC. SERV. LAW §384–6(7)(a) (Supp. 1982).
43. *See, e.g.*, *M.A. v. P.A.*, 529 P.2d 333 (Colo. Ct. App. 1974).
44. *See, e.g.*, *People ex rel. Portney v. Strasser*, 303 N.Y. 539, 104 N.E.2d 894 (1952); *In re Rinker*, 180 Pa. Super. 143 (1955); *In re Clark's Adoption*, 38 Ariz. 481, 1 P.2d 112 (1931).
45. *See, e.g.*, *In re J.S.R.*, 374 A.2d 860 (D.C. App. 1977); *In re New England Home for Little Wanderers*, 367 Mass. 631, 328 N.E. 2d 854 (Mass. 1975); *In re William L.*, 447 Pa. 322, 383 A.2d 1228 (1978), *cert. denied sub nom.*, *Lehman v. Lycoming County Children's Services Agency*, 439 U.S. 880 (1978).
46. *See, e.g.*, COLO. REV. STAT. ANN. §19–3–111 (1978 & Supp. 1982); MONT. REV. CODE ANN. 841–3–602 (1981); WASH. REV. CODE ANN. §§13–34.190, 26–32.032 *et seq.* (Supp. 1982).
47. *See, e.g.*, D.C. CODE §16-304(e); MASS. GEN. LAWS ANN. ch. 210, §3(a)(ii) (Supp. 1982).
48. *See, e.g.*, *Berrien v. Greene County Dept. of Publ. Welfare*, 216 Va. 241, 217 S.E.2d 854 (1975); *Bennett v. Jeffreys*, 40 N.Y.2d 543, 356 N.E. 2d 277, (387 N.Y.S.2d 821) (1976).

49. *Smith v. Organization of Foster Families*, 431 U.S. 816 (1977).
50. *Quilloin v. Walcott*, 434 U.S. 246, 255 (1978).
51. *See supra* note 50.
52. *In re Fish*, 174 Mont. 201, 569 P.2d 924, 926-28 (1977) (quoting *Henderson v. Henderson*, 568 P.2d 177, 181 (1977)). *See also In re J.P.*, 648 P.2d 1364 (Utah 1982).
53. *In re Custody of a Minor*, 389 N.E.2d 68 (Mass. 1979), expressly overruling *In re New England Home for Little Wanderers, supra* note 45.
54. *Bennett v. Jeffries, supra* note 48.
55. *In re Sanjivini K.*, 47 N.Y.2d 374. 391 N.E.2d 1316, 418 N.Y.S.2d 339 (1979). *See also Corey L. v. Martin L.*, 45 N.Y.2d 383, 380 N.E.2d 266, 408 N.Y.S.2d 439 (1978).
56. *See e.g., In re Juvenile Appeal*, 189 Conn. 66, 454 A.2d 1262 (1983); *In re Elise K.*, 33 Cal. 3d 138, 187 Cal. Rptr. 483, 654 P.2d 253 (1982).
57. IOWA CODE §§232–41(2)(b)(d).
58. *Alsager v. Dist. Court*, 406 F. Supp. 10, 21 (S.D. Iowa 1975), *aff'd*. 545 F.2d 1137 (8th Cir. 1976).
59. ARK. STAT. ANN. 56–182(2)(h).
60. *Davis v. Smith*, 266 Ark. 112, 583 S.W.2d 37 (1979).
61. Adoption Act of 1970 §311(2).
62. *In re William L., supra* note 45; *In re Carl & Annette N.*, 91 Misc.2d 738, 398 N.Y.S.2d 613 (Fam. Ct. 1977), *construing* N.Y. SOC. SERV. LAW §384–b.
63. MASS. GEN. LAWS. ANN. ch. 210 §3.
64. *New England Home for Little Wanderers, supra* note 49; *Matter of Keyes*, 574 P.2d 1026 (Okla. 1977), *appeal dismissed*, 439 U.S. 804 (1978).
65. *State v. McMaster*, 259 Or. 291, 486 P.2d 567 (1971).
66. *See, e.g., Alsager v. Dist. Court, supra* note 61; *Roe v. Conn*, 417 F. Supp. 769 (M.D. Ala. 1976); *In re J.N.M.*, 655 P.2d 1032 (Okla. 1982); *In re David B.*, 91 Cal. App.3d 184, 154 Cal. Rptr. 63 (1979).
67. *See, e.g., In re McDonald*, 201 N.W.2d 447 (Iowa 1972); *States ex rel. Paul v. Dept. of Public Welfare*, 170 So.2d 549 (La. Ct. App. 1965); *In re William L., supra* note 45; *In re Telles*, 87 Cal. App.3d 864, 151 Cal. Rptr. 263 (1978).
68. *See, e.g., People ex rel. Nabsted v. Barger* 3 Ill. 2d 511, 121 N.E.2d 781 (1954); *Strohsahl v. Strohsahl*, 221 App. Div. 86, 222 N.Y.S. 319 (1st Dept. 1927).
69. MO. ANN. STAT. §211.447(2)(2)(g) (Supp. 1982).
70. *In re Wyatt*, 34 Or. App. 793, 579 P.2d 889 (1978).
71. NEB. REV. STATS. SUPP. §43-292(5) (Supp. 1982) (emphasis added); *State v. Metteer*, Neb. Sup. Ct. *in* 5 Fam. L. Rptr. 2670 (June 26, 1979).
72. *Stantosky v. Kramer, supra*, note 1.
73. *State v. Robert H.*, 118 N.H. 713, 393 A.2d 1387 (1978); LA. REV. STAT. ANN. §13:1603(A) (Supp. 1982).

74. 25 U.S.C.A. §1912(f) (Supp. 1982).
75. *See, e.g.*, N.D. CODE §27–20–26 (1974); N.Y. FAM. CT. ACT §241 (1975).
76. *See, e.g.*, *State ex rel. Juvenile Dept. of Multnomah County v. Wade*, 19 Or. App. 314, 527 P.2d 753 (1974); *app. dism.* 423 U.S. 806; *overruled* 547 P.2d 175 (1977); *In re Orlando F.*, 40 N.Y.2d 103, 351 N.E.2d 711, 386 N.Y.S.2d 64 (1964); *In re Fish*, *supra* note 56; *New Jersey Division of Youth & Family Services v. Wandell*, 155 N.J. Super. 302, 382 A.2d 711 (Juv. & Dom. Rel. Ct. 1978); *In re Richard E.*, 21 Cal. 3d 349, 579 P.2d 495; 146 Cal. Rptr. 604 (1978); app. dism. 439 U.S. 1060 (1979).
77. *Lassiter v. Dept. of Social Services* 452 U.S. 18 (1981).
78. *In re D.E.T.*, 484 Pa. 532, 399 A.2d 1063 (1979).
79. *Dandridge v. Williams*, 397 U.S. 471 (1970).
80. *See, e.g.*, *Black v. Beame*, 550 F.2d 815 (2d Cir. 1977).
81. *See, e.g.*, *Child v. Beame*, 412 F. Supp. 593 (S.D.N.Y. 1976); *Smith v. Alameda Co. Social Services Agency*, 90 Cal. App. 3d 929, 153 Cal. Rptr. 712 (1979).
82. *Lehman v. Lycoming County Children's Services Agency*, 458 U.S. 502 (1982). *But see Rhoades v. Penfold*, 694 F.2d 1043 (5th Cir. 1983).
83. 73 L. Ed.2d at 937 n. 12.
84. *See, e.g.*, *Doe v. New York City Dept. of Social Services*, 649 F.2d 134 (2d Cir. 1981); *Brooks v. Richardson*, 478 F. Supp. 793 (S.D.N.Y. 1979).

V

Child Custody, Foster Care, Adoption, and Illegitimacy*

The adult or adults who exercise primary control over the upbringing of a child are said to have "custody" of the child. Custodians may be parents, foster parents, guardians, relatives, institutional personnel, or adoptive parents.

Normally, a child's custody is with his parents. If one parent dies, the surviving parent usually exercises full care and custody of the child. When parents separate or divorce there may be a dispute as to which parent will have custody of the child. If both parents die, or for some reason are unable to exercise proper care, their child may be raised in the custody of relatives, foster, or even adoptive parents.

The methods by which custody is determined, and the rights of children subject to custody disputes, in foster care or after adoption, are the subjects of this chapter.

Custody

Do children have the right to be raised in the custody of their parents?

Yes. Children have the right to be raised in the custody of their parents and, likewise, parents have the right to the custody of their children.[1]

---

*The authors find the word *illegitimate* distasteful, since it would seem to imply that a child bearing that label is someone less than real. But since it is the word that presently denominates the legal status of children of unmarried parents, it is reluctantly used in this chapter.

Do minors have the right to the custody and control over their own children?

Yes. A parent has the right to the custody of his or her child, whether or not the parent is an adult. In the first reported case to address this issue, the Oklahoma Supreme Court ruled in 1920, that simply because a parent was a minor did not mean that she could be denied the right to custody of her child.[2]

The law has not changed since then, and has in fact simplified matters for *married* minors parents, because marriage automatically emancipates minors in every state.[3] Thus, by virtue of being married, minors are considered legal adults. (Of course, to be married in most states, minors need the permission of their parents.)

Parents who are *not* married are also entitled to the custody of their children even if they are minors.

As with adult parents, there may be a contest for the custody of a child between the mother and father, and there may be state action to remove a child if it has been mistreated; but the right of parenthood itself—that is, the right to raise and bring up one own's child—is unaffected by the fact that a parent is not an adult.

What rights do parents have over their children?

Parents have the right to name their children; to determine where they live; what religious faith they should be brought up under; what form of schooling they receive; and in the case of younger children, what food they eat and clothing they wear.[4] Parents also have the right to control and discipline their children.

Naturally, as children grow older, parental control and discipline weaken. This has nothing to do with limits imposed by law, but with the diminishing practical power of parental control as children reach maturity. A parent's right, for example, to determine the religious instruction of his child remains intact, but if a fifteen-year-old refuses to go to church or to say prayers, there is no *legal* recourse for the parent. Parents may impose family-created sanctions, such as withdrawal of an allowance, vacation, or other privileges, but they would get no help from the police or a court in imposing their religious demands on a child who simply refuses to obey. On the other hand, if the child refuses parental demands that are also required by state law, such as the duty to refrain from criminal conduct or the duty to obtain an education, parents may seek legal recourse pursuant to the disobedient child laws discussed in chapter X.

Coupled with the parental rights of custody and control are parental duties to support and nurture their children. If parents are negligent in these duties, or if they abuse or mistreat their children, their custody rights may be temporarily suspended or permanently severed and their children may be placed in the custody of others.

If a child's parents are in the process of getting a separation or divorce, who decides the issue of child custody?

Parents may decide the child custody issue themselves. A common solution is for the mother to have custody, with weekend or biweekly visits by the father. In a growing number of cases, however, parents agree that the father should be granted sole custody or joint custody.

If the matter cannot be solved by agreement, the decision will probably be left to a judge who has the power to grant custody to either parent or order joint custody.

It is important to note that when a custody decision is made, the "losing" parent is not stripped of all rights and duties of parenthood. He or she may still have to support the child, and the parent not granted custody will almost always be granted "visitation" rights; that is, the right to spend some time with the child on a periodic basis.

On what bases are custody decisions made by courts?

In virtually every state judges are bound to make custody decisions based on "the best interests of the child."[5] What this phrase is supposed to mean is that the interest of the child is paramount. In practice however, it is often the case that the child is neither consulted nor represented when a court determines his or her "best interests."

There is no exact formula for deciding the "best interests" of children in custody disputes. Generally, courts will consider—

1. the wishes of the parents;
2. the wishes of the child (if old enough to form an intelligent opinion);
3. the nature of the past relationship between the child and his parents and other siblings;

4. the child's adjustment to the school and community;
5. the mental health of all parties;
6. whether either parent is negligent, abusive, or otherwise unfit or unable to adequately care for children;
7. which parent might best provide a stable environment for the child's development.[6]

Do children have the right to have their wishes considered when a judge determines custody?

It depends. While a child's wishes are not controlling, the current direction of the law is for courts to attach some weight to their preferences. In Georgia, a child's wishes will be followed by the court if the child is 14 years or older.[7] In a handful of other states (including California, Colorado, New Mexico, and Ohio) the law provides that the court *must* consider and give due weight to the preference of a child old enough to form an intelligent opinion.[8] In some states, the court or a state agency may order a social investigation of the child whose custody is in dispute. The resulting report is communicated to the judge and may contain references to the child's wishes, if he is old enough to form an opinion and if the investigator happens to ask.

Most American courts, however, follow the rule that in custody matters a child's preference is not conclusive, but it *may* be considered.[9] If they are of sufficient age and intelligence (there is no exact year—normally 12 or 13 and above), courts often give considerable weight to their wishes. The opinions of children, when ascertained, are not usually taken in the form of sworn testimony in open court. The normal practice is for a judge to examine a child in his or her chambers.[10] While the judge usually strives to create as relaxed an atmosphere as possible, a court stenographer should be present to record the conversation for the record, and in some states attorneys for the parents must be present as well.[11]

Do children have the right to be represented by an attorney in custody cases?

Every court that determines child custody matters has the inherent power to appoint an attorney to represent a child's interests.[12] In practice, however, a child is rarely represented by counsel in divorce and custody proceedings, either because the court merely rubber stamps agreements between the parents, or because they routinely grant custody assuming that the child's interests are fully represented by the parents' attorneys.

In general, a court will decline to appoint counsel for children unless it believes that the child's interests will be different from those of the parents.[13] (This approach was recently reversed by an Illinois appellate court that held that the court must appoint counsel for children *unless* it believes that their best interests are being adequately asserted by counsel for the parents.[14]

While the United States Supreme Court has held that a child accused of a *crime* has a right to counsel, it has yet to guarantee a child's right to legal representation when he or she faces the possibility of being delivered into the custody of a parent or relative contrary to his or her wishes or interests. This disparity was noted by a federal court that stated, "A change of parental bondage during the tender years is hardly less upsetting of one's pattern of life than is the denomination and possible commitment of a child as a juvenile delinquent."[15]

Recently, however, a number of states have begun to provide limited assistance of counsel to children in custody cases, by permitting the judge, district attorney, family court commissioner, or some other person to intervene on behalf of the child in certain circumstances.

In Ohio, for example, a guardian *ad litem* may be appointed when the child needs protection other than that which can be given by either or both parents. In such cases, the guardian *ad litem* focuses on the child's legal rights, his or her welfare while the case is pending, and his or her best interest in custody and support matters, medical care, and education.[16] Similar procedures are available in Rhode Island.[17]

In some states, when a divorce action is commenced, notice of the proceeding must be given to the district or county attorney if there are children of the marriage. The district attorney then has the option to present evidence opposing the divorce if the interests of the children or the "public good" so requires.[18]

In only two or three states is an attorney *required* to be appointed to represent the child in every case involving a custody dispute. The clearest statement of this position was made by the Supreme Court of Wisconsin, which declared that legal representation

> ... is due [to] children who are not to be buffeted around as mere chattels in a divorce controversy, but rather are to be treated as interested and affected parties whose welfare should be the prime concern of the court in its custody determination.[19]

Perhaps the most considerate statute is Colorado's, which permits a court to interview the child in the judge's chambers, to order the probation or welfare department to investigate and report on the child's interests, and to appoint an attorney to represent the child with regard to custody, support, and visitation. Investigators may consult with professionals who have served or treated the child in the past, but such consultations may not take place without the child's permission if he or she is over the age of 16.[20]

After a divorce has been granted, does a child have the right to associate with both parents?

Yes. When one parent is granted custody, the other is usually granted "visitation" rights. From the child's point of view, he or she has the right to periodic visits with the parent who was not awarded custody.[21] In the words of the Wisconsin Supreme Court:

> The paramount reason for visitation is the benefit to be derived by the child from association with its parents. . . . Minor children are entitled to the love and companionship of both parents insofar as this is possible and consistent with their welfare.[22]

The only factor that might prohibit visitation is if the noncustodial parent is negligent or abusive such that visits will be clearly and demonstrably (not just "possibly") detrimental to the child's welfare.

In custody proceedings, does a child have the right to remain with his brothers and sisters?

A child has no clear right to remain with his siblings, but most courts will consider the effect of custody decisions on all the children of a family.

An Idaho court held that, in determining the custody of children, one consideration is the desirability of permitting the children of the family to grow up together and to enjoy each other's love, affection, and mutual companionship.[23] A Texas court paid special attention to the "attributes of brotherly love and affection," and a court in Kentucky held that children of the same parents should live together as members of one family and not lose the benefits of constant association.[24]

After a divorce or separation, must a child always be in the custody of one parent and must the other parent always be a visitor?

No. It is possible that a child may be in the "joint custody" of *both* parents, an arrangement that is gaining favor. Joint custody does not necessarily mean that the child will reside with each parent fifty percent of the time, but it is unlike normal custody arrangements in which the custodial parent enjoys greater rights than the noncustodial parent. Under joint custody, neither parent has greater rights than the other in determining matters such as place of residence, education, religion, or medical care. Naturally, joint custody requires a great deal of cooperation between the parents and is probably unworkable if they have major differences.

Joint custody is more often achieved by agreement than by court order. This is due to the fact that parents who resort to the courts to solve their custody arrangements are not often well disposed to working out the many problems that joint custody could involve over time. This led New York's highest court to observe:

> Joint custody is encouraged primarily as a voluntary alternative for relatively stable, amicable parents behaving in a mature civilized fashion. As a court-ordered arrangement imposed upon already embattled and embittered parents, accusing one another of serious vices and wrongs, it can only enhance familial chaos.[25]

Other courts, however, are becoming more tolerant of court-ordered joint custody under favorable circumstances.[26] As one New Hampshire Supreme Court judge recently stated in a dissenting opinion:

> The sole parent not only has to fulfill all family functions, but has little release from his or her burden. Thus one parent becomes overburdened

> and the other, in a sense, under burdened. [T]he children who are free to develop full relationships with both parents fare best after divorce. Joint custody avoids subjecting the child completely to one parent's will, and instead affords the child in-depth exposure to both parents.[27]

In Michigan, a statute was recently enacted authorizing courts to award joint custody, and in California and Nevada, laws have been passed that provide that when parents have agreed to be joint custodians, courts will presume that joint custody is in the best interest of the children if there is a subsequent court contest.[28] About ten other states also permit courts to award joint custody under certain circumstances.[29]

Many observers have also become increasingly supportive of the joint custody concept.[30]

After a divorce, does a child still have the right to be supported by his parents?

Yes. Parents are always obligated to support their children—commensurate with their ability and with the needs of their children—whether or not they have custody.[31] The form and amount of support may be based upon an agreement between the parents or, if they are unable to come to terms, it can be ordered by a court.

In a custody dispute between a parent and a nonparent, does a child have the right to remain with his natural parent?

A child has no absolute right to remain in anyone's custody, but in most states, when the legal dispute is between a parent and nonparent, the parent, if fit, has the primary right to custody.[32] Thus, if custody is to be awarded a nonparent, it must be proven in court that it would not only be in the child's best interests, but that custody with the parent would be detrimental to the health or safety of the child due to parental unfitness.[33] The sole fact that a child's interest might be "better" served in the custody of a nonparent should not constitute grounds for transferring custody from the natural parent.[34]

Once a child is in the legal custody of one parent, is there anything to prevent the other parent from "snatching" the child back?

Until recently, the problem of "child-snatching" by noncustodial parents was not treated seriously by law enforcement officials. In the past few years, however, a number of states as well as the federal government have taken steps to strengthen laws designed to discourage these acts.

About half of all states have laws making child-snatching a criminal offense—usually a misdemeanor—and in some states it becomes a felony if the child is removed from the state, injured or kept for a certain length of time.[35] Most importantly, all states have adopted the Uniform Child Custody and Jurisdiction Act (UCCJA), or laws almost identical to it, which is intended to provide uniformity among states so that noncustodial parents will not unlawfully abduct their children, take them to a different state and initiate a new custody proceeding there. The UCCJA requires courts to defer to custody orders rendered in other states.

In addition, in December 1980, the Federal Parental Kidnapping Prevention Act was enacted, which requires state courts to abide by child custody decrees issued in other states.[36] The act also directs the Federal Bureau of Investigation to help apprehend parental child-snatchers, and permits the use of the Federal Parent Locater Service—which was previously used only to locate parents who had not paid child support obligations—to assist in locating parental abductors.

Do children have the right to disregard a visitation order and not visit with a parent after a divorce?

Ordinarily, no. Unless there are truly extraordinary circumstances, courts will protect the noncustodial parent's right to visit his or her children, even when the children object. Thus, courts will require the custodial parent to exert reasonable authority over the child to compel him or her to visit with the noncustodial parent.[37]

Foster Care and Adoption

What is "foster care"?

Generally, foster care means a noninstitutional, family type, substitute parent-child relationship for a limited period during which the chid's parents are unable to provide care.[38] A foster child can be any child temporarily living with an adult who is not the child's natural parent. A foster parent may be a relative, a friend, or a stranger. A child in extremely short-term custody, such as a child in the temporary care of a baby-sitter or a relative while the parents are on vacation, could not be said to be in foster care. On the other hand, there is no clear point at which a short-term relationship turns into foster care.

Foster care may be established by mutual consent between the natural parents and foster parents, or between the natural parents and a child-care agency. This could happen for any number of reasons, including a parent's poor health, emotional illness, dire economic circumstances, drug or alcohol problems, or imprisonment. Not all foster care is voluntary; it may come about against the wishes of the natural parents if a court orders them to place their child in foster care. This may occur when parents are suspected, or have been found by a court, to have neglected or abused their children, or because the children have been found to be delinquent or in need of supervision.

What is a "foster home"?

There are several types of foster homes and each serves a different function.

"Emergency" homes, for example, receive children for short-term care, perhaps for only a few days, pending a court hearing. Children removed from parents by the police or social welfare workers due to emergency or life-threatening conditions are usually placed in this type of foster home.

Family or "group homes," as another type, may house from two to eight children with one set of foster parents, and are frequently used for older or adolescent children who need longer foster care.

Is foster care meant to be temporary?

In most cases, yes. The foster parent-child relationship is viewed as a temporary relationship to provide the child with the benefits of a family setting (instead of institutionalized care) when residence out of the natural home is necessary. The ultimate goal is to reunite the child with his or her parents or, when necessary, to place the child in a permanent, adoptive relationship.

But this design does not always square with actual practice. Very often children are kept in foster care for many years longer than necessary.[39] As a result of remaining with the same foster family over a period of years, children and foster parents often develop deep emotional bonds.

If a child is in foster care under supervision of a child care agency, can the agency remove the child from foster parents on the grounds that the foster parents and the child have become too attached?

Yes. Since foster care ultimately is designed to reunite the child with the natural parents, agencies may move a child from one foster home to another if foster parents "become too emotionally involved with the child."[40]

If parents voluntarily place their children in foster care, can they have them returned on demand?

It depends. Some states provide that parents have the right to have their child returned on demand;[41] but when the department or agency does not want a child returned, it may file a petition in court alleging that the natural parents are unfit. When this is done the natural parents often are unsuccessful in obtaining the speedy return of their child, and, at times, they are unsuccessful in securing the return at all.[42]

What happens to children whose parents want them back but whose foster parents also want to keep them?

In some states, foster parents may prevail if they have maintained custody over a child for some time, and they can prove that it is in the "best interests" of the child to remain with them.[43] This theory has been bolstered in recent years by the proposition that foster parents may, in time, become a child's "psychological parents," more deserving of the child's affections than their natural parents.[44] But in other states, courts require proof that the child will be harmed if they are returned to the natural parents before they will allow foster parents to retain custody.[45]

If children have been in foster care for a period of time, do foster parents have the right to adopt them?

They have the right to *attempt* to adopt their foster children by legal means, but of course they have no guarantee of success. If the natural parents are still legal parents, no adoption can take place without their permission or until their parental rights are involuntarily terminated. Generally, the legal standard for terminating parental rights is severe due to the fundamental right of family integrity (see chapter IV).

As discussed in chapter IV, the trend is toward allowing termination of parental rights and adoption when it is found that doing so is in the child's "best interests." This trend allows for what might be called no-fault termination of parental rights. The most common situation in which courts enter no-fault terminations is when children have lived with foster parents for a significant period of time and consider the foster parents to be their "real" or only parents. In these circumstances, some courts have permitted adoption even where the natural parents are not unfit and have not abandoned the children. Thus, when the no-fault theory applies, the longer foster parents retain custody, the greater likelihood they will be permitted to adopt the children.

Surprisingly, it is often the child-care agency that opposes adoption by the foster parents. When a public child-welfare agency has legal custody of children in foster care, it is responsible for making decisions about the child's future. For many years, courts have routinely supported agency decisions. Only recently have courts been willing to overrule them. Nonetheless, an agency's view on the propriety of foster parents adopting still carries great weight in court proceedings.[46] One court, for example, held that an agency had the power to remove a child from one set of foster parents and to place the child for adoption by a second set of parents. The foster parents from whose home the child was removed objected to the proposed adoption and sought to adopt the child themselves. The court had little difficulty siding with the agency on the strength of a state law that stated, "[W]here a parent or parents place a child with an agency, only the prospective parents selected by the agency may adopt the child."[47]

Are foster parents given a preference to adopt once the children are adoptable?

Not necessarily. Because the agency usually has legal custody of the children and places them only temporarily with foster parents, the agency is allowed to choose the adoptive parents. Frequently, agencies give children to one set of parents for temporary foster care and then choose a different couple to adopt. Because foster care is temporary, agencies use different criteria for selecting foster parents than for choosing adoptive parents. Criteria for temporary foster parents include such things as the ability to provide a safe and healthy environment. For adoptive parents, however, other factors are included—the psychological characteristics of the parents, their financial ability, their race, age and religion, and the size of the family.

A few states, however (including New York), give a statutory "preference" to foster parents to adopt the foster children who have remained in their home for at least eighteen months.[48] California grants a preference for custody (and ultimately adoption) to the "person or persons in whose home the child has been living in a wholesome and stable environment," if a court finds that return of custody to the natural parents would be detrimental to the child.[49]

Is an agreement between foster parents and a child-care agency that the foster parents will not adopt the foster child enforceable in court?

Usually, but courts may allow the adoption notwithstanding the existence of such an agreement. Since courts attempt to do what is in the child's "best interests," foster parents who agreed not to adopt when they took the child into their home have sometimes been allowed to adopt a child who has stayed with them for a significant period of time.[50]

Do courts generally monitor the placement of children in foster care?

No. Because the social services agency is legally charged with (and presumed to be) acting in the best interests of the child, courts and legislatures rarely deem it necessary to protect children from needless shifting from one foster home to another. Similarly, they have not required a review of the length of time a child stays in foster care before being returned to their natural parents or adopted.

Recent recognition that children have been harmed by the needless prolongation of foster care has led a number of states to require a periodic judicial review of the status of children in foster care.[51] In addition, Congress has passed laws that required states to supervise the care of foster children and to periodically review the necessity of retaining each child in foster care.[52]

Is periodic review of foster care arrangements constitutionally required?

The answer is uncertain. The United States Supreme Court recently upheld New York's practice of reviewing the foster care arrangement of each child every eighteen months, and it is clear that there is no constitutional requirement to review foster care arrangements more frequently than that.[53] But it is unclear if New York's schedule is required as a minimum. (If it is, most state foster care systems would be unconstitutional, since few states require any review.)

A federal court in Massachusetts recently ruled that a periodic review of each child in foster care is required by federal law.[53a]

Do local or state governments make any effort to monitor the placement of children in foster care other than by periodic court review?

Only a few jurisdictions have established mechanisms for investigating problems raised by parents. In New York City, for example, the Department of Social Services has created a Parents' Rights Unit to monitor placements and to help parents maintain relationships with children in foster care. Illinois and Texas also have special units to investigate complaints by parents or others concerning children in placement.

What is "AFDCFC"?

The Aid to Families with Dependent Children Foster Care program (AFDCFC) authorizes federal subsidies for the care and support of children who have been removed from their homes and made wards of the state, after a court has determined that their homes do not provide for their welfare.[54]

Are children who live in relatives' homes that serve as foster homes entitled to AFDCFC payments?

Yes. The United States Supreme Court held that children living with relatives may not be excluded from the AFDCFC, because that would conflict with Congress's preference that children who need foster care be cared for by relatives when feasible.[55]

May children be placed in foster care out of state?

Yes, if the out-of-state placement is necessary to meet the individual child's needs. In addition, some states require the out-of-state facility to meet the placing state's internal standards of suitability, or the requirements of the Inter-State Compact on the Placement of Children.[56] But the practice of out-of-state placements is coming under increasing attack, and some states are curtailing the practice.[57]

If children are treated poorly in foster care, may they sue the agency that exercises control over them?

Courts are becoming more agreeable to the notion that a government agency may be liable for negligence in the placement of children.

A New York court, for example, ruled that a county may be held responsible for its negligence in placing a three-year-old child in the care of persons who abused the child.[58] And a federal court in Pennsylvania ruled that a child could sue county welfare officials for their failure to provide him with adequate care and treatment that would have enabled him to return home.[59]

In some states, however, courts may consider their departments of child welfare and commissioners of social services immune from such liability,[60] or simply not responsible for foster parent wrongdoing.[61]

Adoption

What is "adoption"?

Adoption is a legal procedure whereby the relationship between a child and his natural parents is permanently terminated and a new parent-child relationship arises with all the rights, duties, and other attributes of a natural one. Adoption differs from foster care, in which the custody of the child is *temporarily* transferred to another and where many rights and duties of the natural parent-child relationship remain.

In order to effectuate an adoption, the law goes so far as to "falsify" the child's original birth certificate by creating a new one that lists the adoptive mother and father as the natural parents of the child.

How does a child become adopted?

Any child who is to be adopted, whether born in or out of wedlock, must be "freed" for adoption by both natural parents. Generally there are two methods for freeing a minor child for adoption during the lives of his natural parents: by voluntary termination (parental consent), or by involuntary termination of parental rights.

What is "voluntary termination of parental rights"?

This is more commonly known as voluntarily surrendering a child for adoption. Once surrendered by his or her parents, a child may be adopted.

What is "involuntary termination of parental rights"?

Involuntary termination of parental rights is discussed in detail in chapter IV. In brief, parental rights may be terminated by a court for reasons of abandonment, persistent child neglect, or parental unfitness. Termination of parental rights results in the permanent severance of all aspects of the parent-child relationship. Once their rights have been terminated, parents are no longer responsible for child support and lose all rights to child custody and visitation. They also lose the right to consent to their child's adoption; thus, their child may be adopted without their consent.

What happens to a child whose parents' parental rights have been terminated?

Until they are adopted, such children become wards of the state or a licensed child-care agency. This means the child has no parents but does have a guardian. The legal status of the child is similar to that of an orphan except that an orphan is likely to have living relatives. As a rule, once parental rights are terminated, whether by voluntary or involuntary means, no legal relationship exists between the parents and the child or between the relatives of the parents and the child. There are two possible exceptions to this principle, visitation with, and inheritance from, grandparents.

Do natural parents have the right to choose who will adopt their child?

Not necessarily. If parental rights have been terminated involuntarily or if the parent has surrendered the child to the state or a licensed child-care agency, the parent's choice as to who should adopt the child will not be determinative. The agency or the court, in its role as surrogate parent, will decide which adoptive family will serve the child's best interests. The power of the state is so great that even when a *private* placement occurs—that is, when the parents personally place the child with a new set of parents—the adoption must still be approved by a court with the standard for approval being the child's best interests.

If a child is surrendered for adoption, may the natural parents later revoke their surrender and seek the child's return?

Only under limited circumstances. In many states, there is a short "waiting period" (from six to nine months depending on the state) during which the natural parents may change their minds and ask for their child's return, if the final adoption decree has not been rendered.[62]

After that point, however, parents have no right to regain custody of their child unless it can be demonstrated that the surrender occurred because of duress or a complete lack of understanding. Even then, if a certain period of time has passed with the child in the custody of his or her adoptive parents, he will probably not be returned to the natural parents.

What circumstances might constitute duress or lack of understanding?

The definitions vary among the states. All states allow for revocation of a surrender if it was given under *physical* duress.[62a] Accordingly, one court revoked a surrender because a minor parent was told by her own parents that she could not continue to live in her parents' home unless she surrendered her child for adoption.[63] Duress might also be present if a parent was paid a large amount of money as an inducement to surrender the child. However, if the duress was less direct or the parent claims, for example, that unemployment problems or sickness led to the surrender, courts may rule differently.[64] In one case, a mother's complaint that unsettling influences in her personal life, including an unhappy marriage, divorce, quarrels with parents and relatives with whom she and her child were living, and financial and health problems, all added up to duress, was not sustained by a court.[65]

Generally, a court will revoke a surrender if it can be proven that the parent did not fully understand the nature and consequences of the surrender. Age may be a factor in finding that the surrender was not voluntary. (When a mother is a minor, courts will be particularly sensitive to the possibility that the surrender was not a voluntary act.)[66]

What if the natural parent is a minor? Can she surrender her own child for adoption without first obtaining her parent's consent?

It depends on the state. In a number of states and in the District of Columbia a young person may consent to the adoption of her own child—which is to say that the young mother's parents cannot prevent the adoption[67]—while in other states the consent of a minor's parents is required.[68] In some states parental consent is necessary only if the minor is unmarried.[69] In most states, if the parents are minors and married, the consent of *both* husband and wife are required, but if the minor mother is unmarried, her consent alone may be sufficient.[70] In all states, however, if the unmarried father is available, he must at least be notified and given a chance to appear at a hearing before the adoption of his child may take place.[71] And in some states, if the unmarried father has maintained a sufficient relationship with the child, his consent will be required.[72]

If children become eligible for adoption, do foster parents who have cared for them for a long period of time have a right to adopt them?

Not necessarily. It is common practice in many states for foster parents, upon first receiving a child from an agency, to sign an agreement that they will not try to adopt their foster child. Even when they have not signed such a form, and when the child later becomes eligible for adoption, the agency or a court retains the power to determine whether permanent adoption by the foster couple should be allowed. Practically, if a child has been in foster care for a long period of time and if the child considers his or her foster parents "psychological parents," adoption by the foster parents may be permitted. But the adoption still may be disallowed, and the child may be removed from the home of the foster parents, if factors such as race, health, age, or other condition, such as problems in the family, lead a court to conclude that the adoption is not in the child's best interests.[73]

Can a child be adopted by parents of a different religion?

Yes, but some states require that the child be adopted by parents of the same religion as the natural parents "so far as consistent with the best interests of the child and where practicable."[74] Religious matching is required, where feasible, on the premise that natural parents have the right to determine the religious upbringing of their child, even if they are no longer the primary custodians. However, religious matching is never rigidly applied, even in states that recognize the principle.

May minor children adopt other children?

No. A person cannot adopt another unless he or she is at least 18 years of age.[75]

May a child be adopted over his or her own objection?

Most states require that a child over a certain age (usually 12 or 14) consent to his or her own adoption before it will be approved.[76]

Do children have the right to appeal from an adverse decision in an adoption proceeding?

It depends on the state. In states where the child is considered a party to the proceedings, yes. But in most states, children may not appeal since they are only the *subjects* of the proceeding, not parties to it.[77]

Do siblings who are adopted have the right to remain together after a divorce?

They do not have a "right" per se. But the same presumption in favor of siblings being raised together after a divorce applies to adopted children as well as to natural children.[78]

Does a child who is about to be adopted have the right to an attorney?

In some states, courts are without the power to conduct adoption proceedings until a guardian *ad litem* or an attorney has been appointed to represent the child.[79] The attorney or guardian ad litem has a duty to protect the child's interests by obtaining and bringing forth evidence that may have a bearing on the child's welfare.

Does an adopted child have the right to inherit from his adoptive parents?

Yes. Moreover, most state statutes confer upon an adopted

child the right to inherit from his adopting parents' next of kin as well.[80]

In one case, an adopted child's parents died only six months after the temporary decree of adoption was entered. Even though the final order had not become effective, the court upheld the adopted child's right to inherit.[81]

Does an adopted child have the right to inherit from his natural grandparents?

The answer depends on the wording of the state's adoption laws.[82] In states where a statute merely confers on an adopted child all the rights of a natural child, courts have held that it does not prohibit an adopted child from inheriting from his natural grandparents, when the natural parents have predeceased them.[83]

However, when a statute states that the rights and duties between adoptive children and natural parents are *terminated* upon adoption, the right to inherit from natural grandparents is less secure;[84] and when a statute expressly terminates inheritance from an adopted child's natural parents, the right to inherit from natural grandparents no longer exists.[85]

The modern view is that just as adoption creates an entirely new parent-child relationship, it extinguishes all ties between the adopted child and his or her natural relatives. Under this view, the child has no rights with regard to natural parents, including the right to inherit from them or from *their* parents.[86]

Does the child of an adopted child have the right to inherit from his parents' adoptive parents (his "adoptive" grandparents)?

Yes. Since an adopted child inherits from his adoptive parent, the adopted child's child succeeds to the inheritance rights of his parents, the originally adopted child.[87]

This occurs pursuant to interpretations of most adoption contracts and statutes that grant adopted children the right to inherit from adopting parents.[89]

Once children are adopted, do they have the right to visit with their natural grandparents?

It depends on the state. Generally, the rule is that once an adoption is final, all rights between the child and parents become severed. By extension, all rights between the child and grandparents would also disappear. Thus, if the adoptive parents desired to restrict or curtail visitation between the child and his or her natural grandparents, they could do so.[89] Of course, if the adoptive parents have no objection, visitation may take place.

Recently, some states have made exceptions to this general rule. In California, when a parent has died and a step-parent adopts the child, grandparents (on the side of the deceased parent) have a statutory right to seek visitation.[90] And in New Jersey, New York, and Ohio, courts have ruled that adoption does not extinguish the visitation rights of grandparents if they can demonstrate that it would be in the child's interest to visit with them.[91]

Do adopted children have the right to learn the identity of their natural parents?

In the vast majority of states, adoption records are sealed and may be opened, if at all, only by a court order upon a showing of "good cause."[92]

But in several states (including Alabama, Kansas, Montana, Pennsylvania, and South Dakota) original birth records or records in the adoption proceeding are available to an adoptee when he or she becomes an adult without the necessity for court review or approval.[93] And in at least nine states—California, Connecticut, Iowa, New Hampshire, North Carolina, Ohio, Rhode Island, South Carolina, and Virginia—an adoptee has the right to discover information (but not the identity) about the natural parents relating to physical and mental history for medical reasons.[94]

Why are limits placed on adoptees' rights to learn the identity of their natural parents?

There are a number of reasons offered for sealing adoption records. First, sealed records protect adopted children from the stigma of their adopted status, and they protect adopted children who were born to unmarried parents from the stigma of illegitimacy. Second, sealed records protect the adoptive family from possible intrusion into their lives by the natural parents. They also help insulate adoptive parents from fears that the child they have raised as their own might transfer his or her affections and loyalty to the natural parents at a later date. Third, sealed records protect the natural parents from future intrusion into their lives by the adopted child. Many adopted children are born of unwed teenage mothers who later married without telling their husbands of their past; since these women relied on the promise of sealed records, their lives might be severely disrupted if they were suddenly confronted with the appearance of an adopted child. Fourth, it is often argued that a promise of secrecy is necessary to encourage parents to surrender their children to authorized agencies. For a variety of reasons, parents who have given up a child for adoption may never want anyone they know to find out. If the information could be brought out years later, this might discourage parents from surrendering unwanted children for adoption.

Proponents of making birth records available to adoptees dispute all of these reasons. First, they claim that many natural parents would not object to meeting their adult child if the child wished. Moreover, if the adoptee is denied access to records because of the feelings of the natural parents, then natural parents should be contacted to determine their wishes before any request is denied. Also, they argue, respecting the wishes of natural parents has nothing to do with revealing certain nonidentifiable information to the adoptee such as relevant medical information. But even this is frequently withheld. Finally, many adoptees claim that preventing access to birth records is emotionally harmful to them. If providing adoptees access to records will be distressful to the natural parents, then it is they who should suffer rather than the adoptees.

In states that permit a court order to open sealed adoption records, what conditions might fulfill the "good cause" requirement?

Even in states that permit the unsealing of adoption records upon a showing of "good cause," courts are reluctant to disclose the identity of natural parents to adult adoptees. Mere curiosity about one's parentage will not suffice.[95]

More compelling needs, however, may qualify, depending on their severity and the subjective judgments of judges. The South Carolina Supreme Court, for example, recently ruled that an adoptee's deep emotional need to know the truth, which caused him to become emotionally unstable, was not sufficient reason to disclose the identity of his natural parents.[96] And in New York, the state's highest court recently ruled that while a "desire to learn about one's ancestry should not be belittled," unless there are "concrete psychological problems" found to be connected to the lack of knowledge about ancestry, the adoptee has not shown "good cause" to justify opening the records.[97]

On the other hand, a lower New York Court ruled that adoption records may be released if the adoptee can demonstrate medical or psychological necessity beyond mere curiosity. In that case, the adopted person feared that she might be subject to a disease caused by a dangerous drug her mother took during pregnancy.[98] A Louisiana court recently ruled that an adoptee's right of inheritance from natural parents might be a compelling reason for opening the records (although the court stated that the actual identity of the parents was to remain anonymous).[99] And in the District of Columbia, where the test is whether disclosure would promote or protect the adoptee's welfare rather than "good cause," a court ruled than an adult adoptee's "genealogical bewilderment" was sufficient.[100]

Do courts ever permit adoptees to obtain certain information about their natural parents without disclosing their identity?

Yes. In fact, this seems to be a growing trend, especially when the "good cause" shown for information is medical in nature. In these cases the court may appoint an attorney or an officer of the court to find out the essential information and to reveal all necessary facts to the adult adoptee *except* the names or identity of the natural parents.[101]

Are laws that restrict adoptees' access to their birth records constitutional?

Yes. Courts have consistently ruled that confidentiality statutes are constitutional because legislatures may rationally conclude that sealed adoption records serve valid state interests in promoting adoptions.[102]

What is an "open adoption"?

An open adoption is a modern alternative to traditional adoptions, because after a child is adopted, he or she still retains a relationship with the natural parents. This permits the child and the adoptive parents to benefit from the security of an adoption order while permitting the natural parents to retain visitation rights and to remain involved in the child's life to a limited extent. The "all or nothing" alternative of ordinary adoptions forces many natural parents to oppose the adoption of their child even in circumstances where they do not want actual custody. The classic case of this sort arises after a divorce and after a proposed adoption by a stepparent. Open adoptions are rare, and they will be granted only on the consent of all parties. It is possible that these adoptions will become more popular in the next few years.

Illegitimacy

Historically, children born to unmarried parents had no claim to support from their parents and no rights of inheritance. According to English common law, from which much of American law stems, an illegitimate child was considered *filius nullius*, or "child of no one." As such, he or she enjoyed far fewer rights than legitimate children.

Legal discrimination against illegitimate children existed in America until the recent past. In the last few years, however, a number of laws that treated illegitimate children differently from legitimate children have been declared unconstitutional by the United States Supreme Court.

Even with recent changes in the law, illegitimate children are still treated differently than legitimate children in certain circumstances. Similarly, the rights and obligations of the *parents* of illegitimate and legitimate children differ in some respects as well, especially in the realms of child custody and in the disposition of property and money when a parent dies.

What makes a child illegitimate?

A child is considered illegitimate when he or she is born to a woman who is not married to the child's biological father at the time of birth. Conversely, a legitimate child is one born to a woman who is married to the child's biological father.

Is the term "illegitimate" still in use today?

Yes. Statutes and courts today still use the terms *legitimate* and *illegitimate* to describe the legal status of children. In some state codes, children born of unmarried parents are still referred to as bastards.

If the parents marry after the child is conceived but before it born, is the child considered illegitimate?

No. A child is considered illegitimate only when *born* to unwed parents. Therefore, parents who marry during the mother's pregnancy will not be considered the parents of an illegitimate child.

Is it possible for an illegitimate child to become legitimate?

Yes. In every state there is at least one way this can happen. Not all the state laws are the same, however.

The most common way that illegitimate children may be later *legitimized* is for the biological parents of the child to marry each other after the child's birth. This is the manner permitted in California, New York, Florida, Connecticut, and Michigan, among other states.[103]

In some states (such as Massachusetts) not only must the parents marry each other but the father must acknowledge his paternity as well, either in writing or before a notary.[104] And in other states acknowledgment alone, with or without marriage, is sufficient (as in Michigan, Alabama, and Wisconsin).[105]

Does an illegitimate child have the right to be supported by his parents?

Yes. The parental duty to support children extends to all children, legitimate or not.

In 1973, the United States Supreme Court overturned a Texas law that stated that there was no parental duty to support illegitimate children even though there was a duty to support legitimate children.[106] In that case a mother sued on behalf of her illegitimate children for support from their father. The Supreme Court stated that there is no justification for denying a substantial right to a child (the right to support) simply because his or her father and mother have not married. The Court also held that a state may not deny illegitimate children benefits accorded to legitimate children.

Does an illegitimate child have the right to be supported by public assistance?

Yes, assuming other family financial qualifications are met. In 1973, the United States Supreme Court struck down a New Jersey law that made families eligible for public assistance only if the household contained two *married* adults and at least one minor child.[107] According to the state, the purpose of the law was to preserve and strengthen "traditional family life." The Supreme Court disagreed and found it denied illegitimate children equal protection of the law since the benefits of public assistance are indispensable to the health and well-being of illegitimate as well as legitimate children.[108]

What is the "Aid to Families with Dependent Children (AFDC) program"?

The AFDC is part of the federally sponsored Social Security program. Families are eligible for AFDC money if there are children under age 18 in the home, or under age 21 and attending school, and the children are deprived of support because of the death, absence, or incapacity of one or both parents. Today such payments are made on behalf of 1 of every 8 children under age 18 in the United States.[109] As stated earlier, AFDC funds are available to families whether children are legitimate or illegitimate.

Are all children born out of wedlock eligible for AFDC money?

No. They must meet certain qualifications. If a child (whether born out of wedlock or not) lives with both parents and both are able to support the child, the child does not come within the guidelines of the federal law. So long as one or both of the child's parents are available and able to support the child, they are obligated to support the child, and the family is ineligible for AFDC money.[110]

Do illegitimate children have the right to sue for damages for the wrongful death of their parents?

Yes. In the first case of its kind, in 1968, the United States Supreme Court overturned a Louisiana law that prohibited illegitimate children from suing for the wrongful death of their mother.[111] On the same day the Supreme Court also held that a mother has the right to sue for the wrongful death of her illegitimate child.[112] In both cases the Court concluded that it is unfair to punish a child for the activity of his parents, and that illegitimate children are entitled to the equal protection of the laws as guaranteed by the Fourteenth Amendment.

Subsequently, a number of states changed their laws that

discriminated against illegitimate children in the distribution of proceeds from a wrongful death action.[113]

If a child wishes to sue for the wrongful death of his father, how does he establish proof of paternity?

Paternity can be established in several ways. In some states, if the father of an illegitimate child obtained an order of filiation or a statement of paternity within a certain period of time after his child's birth, this will suffice to establish the fact that he was the natural parent.

In some cases, the father's payment of support in the past operates as an acknowledgment of paternity so that more formal statements, such as declarations of paternity or orders of filiation are not prerequisites for a child to sue for the wrongful death of a father.[114] In one case, a Nevada court allowed illegitimate children to sue for the wrongful death of their father when his only admission of paternity was his public acknowledgment of the fact and his plan to marry the children's mother.[115] In Arizona, the issue of paternity can be established in a pretrial hearing within the wrongful death action.[116]

Do illegitimate children have the right to recover workman's compensation and similar benefits from their parents?

Yes. The United States Supreme Court recently struck down a state law that allowed only legitimate children residual benefits of their father's workman's compensation.[117] The purpose of workman's compensation, the Court stated, is to provide for the support of a man's dependents, but the states' classification, which discriminated against (unacknowledged) illegitimate children, bore no rational relation to that purpose.

Do illegitimate children have the right to recover Social Security benefits from their parents?

Yes, but certain requirements must be met. Any child may inherit Social Security support through insured parents if the child is under eighteen (or under twenty-two for a full-time student). The child must also be dependent at the time of the parent's death. A child is considered *dependent*, as defined in the Social Security Act, if the insured parent was living with the child or contributing to the child's support at the time of the parents' death.

Legitimate children do not have to prove their "dependency" in order to receive Social Security benefits, but illegitimate children must do so, *unless*—

1. they are adopted by the deceased;
2. their parents married each other after the child was born;
3. the father acknowledged in writing that the child was his;
4. the father was declared the father by a court or was ordered by a court to pay support for the child;
5. the child was entitled to inherit from the father under the state law governing interstate inheritance.[118]

Even though the Social Security Act does not require legitimate children to prove their "dependency," the Supreme court ruled that this difference does not discriminate against illegitimate children since the distinction is a "reasonable" one related to the administration of the Social Security Act.[119]

Does an illegitimate child have the right to receive disability insurance from his parents under the Social Security Act?

Yes. Until recently, the Social Security Act contained a provision whereby illegitimate children who were not later legitimated, or who could not inherit under state intestacy laws, could under no circumstances receive benefits from disabled wage-earning parents. This was found unconstitutional by the Supreme Court as a violation of the equal protection of the laws, since other illegitimate children were not so barred from recovery.[120]

Unlike the previously discussed section of the Social Security Act that requires certain illegitimate children to prove their dependency on the insured, this section was found objectionable because it provided no mechanism for proof of dependency at all.

How does the government classify illegitimate children of noncitizens for immigration purposes?

Under the Immigration and Nationality Act of 1957, a

child or a parent of a United States citizen or a lawful permanent resident is granted a "special preference" for immigration and labor purposes.[121] However, the Act grants special preference only to parents of legitimate children and to mothers—not fathers—of illegitimate children. Therefore, the father of an illegitimate child who is a United States citizen or a permanent resident alien is not entitled to special preference as a parent. This distinction was recently reviewed by the United States Supreme Court and found to be constitutional.[122]

Can an illegitimate child inherit money and property from his mother if the mother dies without a will (intestate)?

Yes. In virtually every state, illegitimate and legitimate children have the same rights to inherit from their mothers. If a single mother dies without a will, her estate will automatically be inherited by her children, legitimate or illegitimate.

Can an illegitimate child inherit money and property from his father if the father dies without a will?

It depends on the law in each state. A number of states make it more difficult for illegitimate children than for legitimate children to inherit from their fathers who die without a will. This unequal treatment is usually supported by the argument that paternity is difficult to prove. The United States Supreme Court has applied rather uneven standards in a number of cases, ruling that some state laws that limit the right of inheritance of illegitimate children are constitutional while other state laws are not.

The Court, for example, declared unconstitutional an Illinois law that prohibited a child born to unmarried parents from inheriting from the intestate father if the father had not "acknowledged" the child and had not married the child's mother.[123] But recently the Court upheld a New York law, which restricts the rights of illegitimate children to inherit from their fathers who die intestate unless the father obtains a court order declaring his paternity before his child reaches the age of two; if he fails to do this, the child cannot inherit from the father if he dies without a will.[124] The Supreme Court ruled that this law is rational, and therefore not unconstitutional, because the state has an interest in requiring proof, during a father's lifetime, that he is the father of the illegitimate child. The Supreme Court distinguished New

York's law from the Illinois inheritance statute because the latter, which required a father's acknowledgment *and* marriage, unduly burdened the rights of illegitimate children and bore little relation to the state's interest in having estates pass correctly.

The state of the law seems to be that states may make rules that restrict the intestate succession of estates from fathers to their illegitimate children even when no such rules apply to the succession of estates from fathers to their legitimate children. But these rules must bear some rational relation to the state interest in identifying actual fathers and in avoiding unnecessary disputes over the inheritance of property and money. Once an illegitimate child has been acknowledged by the father, the child must be permitted to share in the estate if the father died without a will.[125]

Therefore, the rights of inheritance of illegitimate children—and the equal right of fathers of illegitimate children to have their estates inherited by them—depend on the laws of each state.

Generally, what are the requirements in most states for fathers to have their estate inherited by their illegitimate children if they die intestate?

There is no consistency among various state laws.

Twenty states had laws similar to the Illinois law just discussed that was struck down by the Supreme Court. Most of those states—including Connecticut, Massachusetts, Ohio, Pennsylvania, Texas, and the District of Columbia, which required acknowledgment *and* marriage as a prerequisite for inheritance, are now in the process of rewriting their laws to conform with constitutionally acceptable guidelines.

Fifteen states (including Michigan, Minnesota, New York, and Wisconsin) permit inheritance if the father acknowledges the child in writing. Interestingly, even though the Supreme Court ruled that New York's inheritance law was constitutionally permitted, as just discussed, the legislature changed the law shortly afterward so that now fathers can pass their estate to their illegitimate children if they obtain an order of filiation during their lifetime (not within two years of the child's birth as the old law required), if they sign an instrument acknowledging paternity, provided it is witnessed and filed according to law, or if paternity has been established.[126]

Eleven sates (including Colorado, Delaware, Florida,

and Indiana) permit inheritance if the father later marries the mother, is declared the father by a court, or if paternity is established after his death by convincing proof. To meet this latter test, the father must not have refused to support the child and he must have openly treated the child as his own.

In five states (including California) "open and notorious" recognition of an illegitimate child by the father during his lifetime is sufficient.

What if the father of an illegitimate child dies having written a will and specifies that the child is to inherit all or part of his estate?

This presents no problem. So long as the child is mentioned by name in the will, the child will inherit accordingly. An adult has the right to will his property to anyone—be it his child, friend, or chambermaid—or to any organization or charity he desires. Thus a father can designate an illegitimate child as the beneficiary of his estate just as he can designate anyone else. (This does not always mean that a designated beneficiary will inherit the entire estate because in some states the law requires that a certain percentage of a person's estate must be given to his surviving spouse or children even if the will directs otherwise.)

Can a state limit the time within which a paternity action may be brought?

Probably, but the length of time may not be too short. A number of states do have such limitations, including Texas which has a four year statute of limitations in paternity cases.[127] Recently, the United States Supreme Court declared unconstitutional a two-year statute of limitations in such cases, reasoning that this time is too short to protect illegitimate children who wish to bring paternity cases.[128] In 1980, the Florida Supreme Court declared unconstitutional that state's four-year statute of limitations,[129] and in 1981, the Montana Supreme Court struck down a three-year statute of limitations.[130]

NOTES

1. *See, e.g., Meyer v. Nebraska,* 262 U.S. 390 (1923); *Pierce v. Society of Sisters,* 268 U.S. 510 (1925); *Spence-Chapin Adoption Service v.*

Polk, 37 A.D.2d 718, 324 N.Y.S.2d 238 (2nd Dept. 1971); *Stanley v. Illinois*, 405 U.S. 645 (1972).

2. *Coats v. Benton*, 80 Okla. 93, 194 P. 198 (1920).
3. *See, e.g., Ditmar v. Graham*, 157 Mass. 73, 31 N.E. 706 (1892); *Gillikin v. Burbage*, 263 N.C. 317, 139 S.E.2d 753 (1965).
4. *Wisconsin v. Yoder*, 406 U.S. 205 (1972); *Pierce v. Society of Sisters*, *supra* note 1; *State v. Garber*, 197 Kan. 567, 419 P.2d 896 (1966), *cert. denied*, 389 U.S. 51 (1967); *Knowlton v. Baumhover*, 182 Iowa 691, 166 N.W. 202 (1918); *People ex rel. Portnoy v. Strasser*, 303 N.Y. 539, 104 N.E.2d 895, 105 N.Y.S.2d 905 (1952); *Daily v. Minnick*, 117 Iowa 563, 91 N.W. 913 (1902); *Eaton v. Libbey*, 165 Mass. 218, 42 N.E. 1127 (1896); *Jech v. Burch*, 466 F. Supp. 714 (D. Hawaii 1979).
5. *Ford v. Ford*, 371 U.S. 187 (1962); *Garvey v. Garvey*, 233 S.W.2d 48, 50–51 (Mo. Ct. App. 1950).
6. *See, e.g., In re Marriage of Little*, 26 Wash. App. 814, 614 P.2d 240 (1980); OHIO REV. CODE §§3109.04 (Supp. 1981).
7. GA. CODE ANN. §19–9–1 (1981).
8. CAL. CIV. CODE §4600 (Supp. 1982); COLO. REV. STAT. §14–10–124 (1) (1974); OHIO REV. CODE §3109.04(1) (Supp. 1981); N.M. STAT. ANN. §40–4–9 (1978).
9. *See, e.g., Gillespie v. Gillespie*, 40 Hawaii 315 (1953); *Obey v. Degling*, 37 N.Y.2d 768, 337 N.E.2d 601, 375 N.Y.S.2d 91 (1975); *Butler v. Perry*, 210 Md. 332, 123 A.2d 453 (1956); *Callen v. Gill*, 7 N.J. 312, 81 A.2d 495 (1951); *Goldstein v. Goldstein*, 115 RI. 152, 341 A.2d 51 (1975); *Hursh v. Klugman*, 256 Minn. 113, 97 N.W.2d 425 (1959).
10. *See, e.g., Flanagan v. Flanagan*, 123 Ill. App. 2d 17, 259 N.E.2d 610 (1970); *Gantner v. Gantner*, 39 Cal. 2d 272, 246 P.2d 923 (1952).
11. *Williams v. Cole*, 590 S.W.2d 908 (Mo. 1979); *Forbes v. Wettman*, 598 S.W.2d 231 (Tex. 1980).
12. *See, e.g.*, Hansen, "Guardians Ad Litem in Divorce and Custody Cases: Protection of the Child's Interests," 4 *J. Fam. L.* 181 (1964).
13. *Lewis v. Lewis*, 271 Pa. Super. 519, 414 A.2d 375 (1979), *cert. denied*, 449 U.S. 877 (1980); *Mackey v. Mackey* (Cal. Ct. App.), 7 F.L.R. 2332 (March 24, 1981)).
14. *Pierson v. Bloodworth*, 81 Ill. App. 3d 645, 401 N.E.2d (1980).
15. *See Brown v. Chastain*, 416 F.2d 1012, 1027 (5th Cir. 1969) (Rives, C.J., dissenting), *cert. denied*, 397 U.S. 951 (1970).
16. *Barth v. Barth*, 12 Ohio Misc: 141, 225 N.E.2d 866 (1967); Ohio Civ. Rule 17(B) (1982).
17. *Zinni v. Zinni*, 103 R.I. 417, 238 A.2d 373 (R.I. 1968).
18. *See, e.g.*, 18 MICH. STAT. ANN. §25.121 (1974).
19. *Wendland v. Wendland*, 29 Wis. 2d 145, 138 N.W.2d 185, at 191 (1965).
20. COLO. REV. STAT. §§14–10–116, 14–10–126, 14–10–127 (1974 & Supp. 1982).
21. *Lewis v. Lewis*, 301 S.W.2d 861 (Mo. App. 1957).
22. *Block v. Block*, 15 Wis. 2d 291, 112 N.W.2d 923 (1961).

23. *Brashear v. Brashear,* 71 Idaho 158, 228 P.2d 243 (1951).
24. *Penn v. Abell,* 173 S.W.2d 483 (Tex. Civ. App. 1943); *Howard v. Howard,* 307 Ky. 452, 211 S.W.2d 412 (1948); See also *Pact v. Pact,* 70 Misc. 2d 100, 332 N.Y.S.2d 940 (Fam. Ct. 1972).
25. *Braiman v. Braiman,* 44 N.Y.2d 584, 378 N.E. 2d 1019, 407 N.Y.S.2d 449 (1978). See also *In re Marriage of Neal,* 92 Cal. App. 3d 834, 155 Cal. Rptr. 157 (1979).
26. *See, e.g., Beck v. Beck,* 86 N.J. 480, 432 A.2d 63 (1981); *Zinni v. Zinni, supra* note 17; *Winn v. Winn,* 143 Cal. App. 2d 184, 299 P.2d 721 (1956); *Perotti v. Perotti,* 78 Misc. 2d 131, 355 N.Y.S.2d 68 (1974).
27. *Starkeson v. Starkeson,* 119 N.H. 78, 397 A.2d 1043 (N.H. 1979).
28. MICH. COMP. STAT. ANN. §722.26a (Supp. 1982); CAL. CIV. CODE §4600.5 (Supp. 1982); REV. STAT. §§125.134, 125.125 (1981).
29. Connecticut, Iowa, Hawaii, Kansas, Kentucky, New Jersey, Nevada, North Carolina, Oregon, Texas, and Wisconsin.
30. *See, e.g.,* Baum, "The Best of Both Parents," *N.Y. Times Magazine,* p. 45 (Oct. 21, 1976); M. Galber, *Co-Parenting* (1978); M. Roman and W. Haddad, *The Disposable Parent* (1978).
31. *Anderson v. Anderson,* 437 S.W.2d 704 (Kansas Ct. App. 1969); *Commonwealth ex rel. Kaplan v. Kaplan,* 236 Pa. Super. 526, 344 A.2d 578 (1975); *Commonwealth ex rel. Gitman v. Gitman,* 428 Pa. 387, 237 A.2d 181 (1967); *Hecht v. Hecht,* 189 Pa. Super. 276, 150 A.2d 139 (1959).
32. *Guardianship of Smith,* 42 Cal. 2d 91, 265 P.2d 888 (1954); *In re Klugman,* 256 Minn. 113, 97 N.W.2d 425 (1959); *People v. Free Synagogue Child Adoption Committee,* 194 Misc. 332, 85 N.Y.S.2d 541 (1949), *appeal dismissed,* 275 A.D. 823 91 N.Y.S.2d 926 (1st Dept. 1949); *Hall v. Hall,* 367 So.2d 162 (La. App. 1979).
33. *See, e.g.,* CAL. CIV. CODE §4600 (Supp. 1982); *In re B.G.,* 11 Cal. 3d 679, 114 Cal. Rptr. 444, 523 P.2d 244 (1974).
34. *See* contra the much denounced holding of *Painter v. Bannister,* 258 Iowa 1390, 140 N.W.2d 152, *cert. denied,* 385 U.S. 949 (1966), where custody of a child was awarded to his grandparents in Iowa because Iowa farm life would better serve the interests of the child than the "bohemian" mode of life of his widowed father in California. *See also In re Hernandez,* 249 Pa. Super. 274, 376 A.2d 648 (1977).
35. *See, e.g.,* ALASKA STAT. §11.41.300 (Supp. 1982); CAL. PENAL CODE §278.5 (Supp. 1982); ME. REV. STAT. ANN. tit. 17–A, §303 (Supp. 1982); N.M. STAT. ANN. §30–4–4 (1978); 18 PA. CONS. STAT. ANN. §2904 (1973); WASH. REV. CODE ANN. §9A.40–050 (1977).
36. 28 U.S.C.A. §1738a (Supp. 1982).
37. *See, e.g., Commonwealth v. Lotz,* 188 Pa. Super. 241, 146 A.2d 362 (1958).
38. *See, e.g., Smith v. Organization of Foster Families for Equality & Reform,* 431 U.S. 816 (1977).
39. Fanshel, "The Exit of Children from Foster Care: An Interim

Research Report," 50 *Child Welfare* 65 (1971); *Smith v. O.F.F.E.R.*, *supra* note 38.

40. *In re Jewish Child Care Assn. of New York*, 5 N.Y.2d 222, 156 N.E.2d 700, 183 N.Y.S.2d 65 (1959).
41. *See, e.g.*, CAL. WELF. & INST. CODE §16552 (1980).
42. *See, e.g., In re Juvenile Appeal (Anonymous) v. Commissioner of Children & Youth Services*, 177 Conn. 648, 420 A.2d 875 (1979), *In re New England Home for Little Wanderers*, 367 Mass. 788, 328 N.E.2d 854 (1975).
43. *See, e.g., In re Juvenile Appeal (Anonymous) v. Commissioner, supra* note 42; *Ross v. Hoffman*, 33 Md. App. 333, 364 A.2d 596 (1976); *In re New England Home for Little Wanderers, supra* note 42; *In re J.S.R.*, 374 A.2d 860 (D.C. App. 1977); *In re J. & J.W.*, 134 Vt. 480, 365 A.2d 521 (1976); *Painter v. Bannister, supra* note 34.
44. *See* Goldstein, Freud, and Solnit, *Beyond the Best Interests of the Child* (1973).
45. *See, e.g., In re B.G.*, 11 Cal. 3d 679, 523 P.2d 244, 114 Cal. Rptr. 444 (1974): *Bennett v. Jeffries*, 40 N.Y.2d 543, 356 N.E.2d 277, 387 N.Y.S.2d 821 (1976); *In re LaRue*, 244 Pa. Super. 218, 366 A.2d 1271 (1976).
46. *See, e.g., Drummond v. Fulton County Dept. of Family & Children's Services*, 563 F.2d 1200 (5th Cir. 1977), *cert. denied*, 437 U.S. 910 (1978); *Keyes v. County Dept. of Public Welfare*, 600 F.2d 693 (7th Cir. 1979).
47. *In re Adoption of Runyon*, 268 Cal. App. 2d 918, 74 Cal. Rptr. 514 (1969).
48. N.Y. SOC. SERV. LAW §§ 374 (1)(a), 383 (3) (Supp. 1982).
49. CAL. CIV. CODE §4600 (Supp. 1982).
50. *See, e.g., Knight v. Deavers*, 259 Ark. 45, 531 S.W.2d 252 (1976); *In re Adoption by Alexander*, 206 So.2d 452 (Fla. Dist. Ct. App. (1968).
51. *See, e.g.*, N.Y. SOC. SERV. LAW §392(2) (Supp. 1982).
52. 42 U.S.C.A. §§608 (1974 & Supp. 1982); 45 CFR §223.110 (1981).
53. *Smith v. O.F.F.E.R., supra* note 38.

53a. *Lynch v. King*, 550 F. Supp. 325 (D. Mass. 1982).

54. 42 U.S.C.A. § 608.
55. *Miller v. Youakim*, 440 U.S. 125 (1979).
56. *Sinhogar v. Parry*, 74 A.D.2d 204, 427 N.Y.S.2d 216, (1st Dept. 1980), *mod.*, 53 N.Y.2d 424, 425 N.E.2d 826, 442 N.Y.S.2d 438 (1981).
57. *See, e.g., In Interest of V.M.C.*, 369 So.2d 660 (Fla. Dist. Ct. App. 1979).
58. *Bartels v. County of Westchester*, 76 A.D.2d 517, 429 N.Y.S.2d 906 (2nd Dept. 1980).
59. *Cameron v. Montgomery Co. Child Welfare Services*, 471 F. Supp. 761 (E.D. Pa. 1979). *See also Koepf v. County of York*, 198 Neb. 67, 251 N.W.2d 866 (1977); *Elton v. Co. of Orange*, 3 Cal. App. 3d 1053,

84 Cal. Rptr. 27 (1970); *Vonner v. State Dept. of Public Welfare*, 273 So.2d 252 (La. 1973).

60. *See, e.g., Pickett v. Washington County*, 31 Or. App. 1263, 572 P.2d 1070 (1977).
61. *See e.g., Parker v. St. Christopher's Home*, 77 A.D.2d 921, 431 N.Y.S.2d 110 (2nd Dept. 1980).
62. *See, e.g., Martin v. Ford*, 224 Ark. 993, 277 S.W.2d 842 (1955); *In re Adoption of Lauless*, 216 Or. 188, 338 P.2d 660 (1959); *Wright v. Fitzgibbons*, 198 Miss. 471, 21 So.2d 709 (1945); *Scarpetta v. Spence-Chapin Adoption Service*, 28 N.Y.2d 185, 269 N.E.2d 787, 321 N.Y.S.2d 65, *cert. denied*, 404 U.S. 805 (1971). *In re Anderson*, 99 589 Idaho 2d 805, 957 (1978). Contra *Bailey v. Mars*, 138 Conn. 593, 87 A.2d 388 (1952); *Duncan v. Harden*, 234 Ga. 204, 214 S.E.2d 890 (1975); *Barwin v. Reidy*, 62 N.Y. 183, 307 P.2d 175 (1957).

62a. *See, e.g., People ex rel. Drury v. Catholic Home Bureau*, 34 Ill. 2d 84, 213 N.E.2d 507 (1966).

63. *See In re Sims*, 30 Ill. App. 3d 406, 332 N.E.2d 36 (1975). Contra *In re Adoption of Griambrone*, 262 So.2d 566 (La. App. 1972).
64. For cases that allowed the revocation, *see, e.g., In re D.*, 408 S.W.2d 361 (Mo. App. 1966); *In re G.*, 389 S.W.2d 63 (Mo. App. 1965). For cases that disallowed the revocation, *see Barwin v. Reidy*, *supra* note 62; *In re Surrender of Minor Children*, 344 Mass. 230, 181 N.E. 2d 836 (1962).
65. *Regenold v. Baby Fold, Inc.*, 68 Ill. 2d 419, 369 N.E. 2d 858 (1977), *appeal dismissed*, 435 U.S. 963 (1978).
66. *Janet G. v. New York Foundling Hospital*, 94 Misc. 2d 133, 403 N.Y.S.2d 646 (Fam. Ct. 1978).
67. ARIZ. REV. STAT. ANN. §8–106 (Supp. 1982); D.C. CODE ANN. §16–304 (Supp. 1978); KAN. STAT. ANN. §59–2102 (1976); MD. ANN. CODE, art. 16, §74 (1973); N.Y. DOM. REL. LAW §111 (1977) *People ex rel C. v. Spence-Chapin Services*, 6 FLR 2411 (1980).
68. MICH. COMP. LAWS ANN. §710.43 (Supp. 1982). *See also* IND. CODE ANN. §31–3–1–6 (1980).
69. MINN. STAT. ANN. § 259.24 (1982).
70. *See, e.g.*, N.Y. DOM. REL. LAW §111 (1977).
71. *Stanley v. Illinois*, 405 U.S. 645 (1972).
72. N.Y. DOM. REL. LAW §111a(d) (Supp. 1982).
73. *See, e.g., Drummond v. Fulton County*, *supra* note 46.
74. *See Dickens v. Ernesto*, 30 N.Y.2d 61, 281 N.E.2d 153, 330 N.Y.S.2d 346, *appeal dismissed*, 407 U.S. 917 (1972). *See also* MASS. GEN LAWS ANN. ch. 210, §5B (Supp. 1982); ILL. ANN. STAT. ch. 40, §1519.
75. *See* Wadlington, "Minimum Age Differences as Requisite for Adoption," 1966 *Duke L. J.* 392.
76. *See, e.g.*, ARIZ. REV. STAT. ANN. §8–106; OKLA. STAT. ANN. tit. 10, §60.11 (1966); N.Y. DOM. REL. LAW §11 (1977 & Supp. 1982); ILL. ANN. STAT. ch. 40, §1514 (1980).

77. *See e.g., Durham v. Barrow*, 600 S.W.2d 756 (Tex. 1980).
78. *See e.g., Albright v. Commonwealth ex rel. Fetters*, 421 A.2d 157 (Pa. 1980); *In re Iverson*, 83 Ill. App.3d 493, 404 N.E.2d 411 (1980).
79. *See, e.g.*, Mo. Rev. Stat. §453.020 (Supp. 1983).
80. *See* 2 Am. Jur. 2d 941 §100 et. seq. (1962).
81. *Williams v. Nash*, 247 Ark. 135, 445 S.W.2d 69 (1969).
82. *See generally* 60 A.L.R.3d 631, 636–642 §§3–6 (1974).
83. *In re Darling's Estate*, 173 Cal. 221, 159 P. 606 (1916); *In re Wilson's Estate*, 95 Colo. 159, 33 P.2d 969 (1934); *In re Gourlay's Estate*, 173 Misc. 930, 19 N.Y.S.2d 122 (Surr. Ct. 1940). *See* contra *Young v. Bridges*, 86 N.H. 135, 165 A. 272 (1933).
84. Inheritance allowed: *In re Benner's Estate*, 109 Utah. 172, 166 P.2d 257 (1946). Inheritance disallowed: *Wailes v. Curators of Central College*, 366 Mo. 932, 254 S.W.2d 645 (1953).
85. *Kerlin v. Kenny*, 239 Ind. 142, 155 N.E.2d 389 (1959); *Thornberry v. Timmons*, 406 S.W.2d 151 (Ky. 1966); *Franz v. Florence*, 131 N.E.2d 630 (Ohio 1954); *In re Estates of Donnelly*, 81 Wash. 2d 430, 502 P.2d 1163 (1972).
86. *In re Estates of Donnelly, supra* note 85.
87. 94 A.L.R.2d 1202, §2; 1203, §3 (1964).
88. *See, e.g., In re Grace's Estate*, 88 Cal. App. 2d 956, 200 P.2d 189 (1948); *Pointer v. Lucas*, 131 Ind. App. 10, 169 N.E.2d 196 (1960); *Gillian v. Guarantee Trust Co.*, 186 N.Y. 127, 78 N.E. 697 (1906). Apparently, only one case indicates the contrary, *Harle v. Harle*, 109 Tex. 214, 204 S.W. 317 (1918).
89. *See In re Fox*, 567 P.2d 985 (Okla. 1977).
90. Cal. Civ. Code. §197.5 (1982).
91. *Mimkon v. Ford*, 66 N.J. 426, 332 A.2d 199 (1975); *People ex rel. Simmons v. Sherman*, 98 Misc. 2d 328, 414 N.Y.S.2d 83 (1979); *Graziano v. Davis*, 50 Ohio App. 2d 83, 361 N.E.2d 525 (1976).
92. *See e.g.*, N.Y. Dom. Rel. Law §114 (1977); Mich. Comp. Laws Ann. §710.67 (Supp. 1982).
93. *See, e.g.*, Ala. Code 26–10–4 (1977); Kan. Stat. Ann. §59–2279 (1976); S.D. Codified Laws Ann. §25–6–15 (1976).
94. *See, e.g.*, Conn. Gen. Stat. Ann. §§45–58a *et. seq.* (1981 & Supp. 1982); Va. Code §63.1–236 (1980).
95. *Matter of Linda F.M.*, 95 Misc. 2d 581, 409 N.Y.S.2d 638 (1978); *aff'd*, 72 A.D.2d 734, (1st Dept. 1980); *aff'd*, 52 N.Y.2d 236, 418 N.E.2d 1302, 437 N.Y. 2d 283 (1981). For a slight loosening of this standard, *see Mills v. Atlantic City Dept. of Vital Statistics*, 148 N.J. Super. 302, 372 A.2d 646 (1977).
96. *Bradey v. Children's Bureau of South Carolina*, 275 S.C. 622, 274 S.E.2d 418 (1981).
97. *Linda F.M. v. Dept. of Health*, 52 N.Y. 2d 236, 418 N.E.2d 1302, 437 N.Y.S. 2d 283, *appeal dismissed*, 454 U.S. 806 (1981).
98. *In re Application of Hayden*, 106 Misc. 2d 849, 436 N.Y.S.2d 541 (1981).

99. *Massey v. Parker,* 369 So.2d 1310 (La. 1979).
100. *In re Female Infant,* 5 F.L.R. 2311 (1979).
101. *See, e.g., Chattman v. Bennett,* 57 A.D.2d 618, 393 N.Y.S.2d 768 (1977); *Application of Maples,* 563 S.W.2d 760 (Mo. 1978).
102. *See, e.g., Alma Society v. Mellon,* 459 F. Supp. 912 (S.D.N.Y. 1978), *aff'd.,* 601 F.2d 1225 (2nd Cir. 1979), *cert. denied,* 444 U.S. 995 (1979); *In re Linda F.M., supra* note 97; *Schecter v. Boren,* 535 F. Supp. 1, (W. Okla. 1980); *Mills v. Atlantic City Dept. of Vital Statistics, supra* note 95.
103. CAL. CIV. CODE §7004 (Supp. 1982); CAL. PROB. CODE §255 (Supp. 1982); N.Y. DOM. REL. LAW §24 (1977); FLA. STAT. ANN. §742.091 (Supp. 1981); CONN. GEN. STAT. ANN. §45–274 (1981); MICH. COMP. LAWS ANN. §702.83 (1968).
104. MASS. GEN. LAWS ANN., ch. 190, §7 (Supp. 1982).
105. ALA. CODE §26–11–2 (Supp. 1982); WIS. STAT. ANN. §767.60 (Supp. 1982); MICH. COMP. LAWS ANN §702.83 (1968).
106. *Gomez v. Perez,* 409 U.S. 535 (1973).
107. *New Jersey Welfare Rights Organization v. Cahill,* 414 U.S. 619 (1973).
108. *Id.*
109. L. Platky, *Aid to Families with Dependent Children: An Overview* 17 (Social Security Bulletin, Oct. 1977).
110. *See King v. Smith,* 392 U.S. 309 (1968).
111. *Levy v. Louisiana,* 391 U.S. 68 (1968). *See also In re Estate of Perez,* 69 Misc. 2d 538, 330 N.Y.S.2d 881 (Surr. Ct. 1972).
112. *Glona v. American Guarantee & Liability Insurance,* 391 U.S. 73 (1968).
113. *See, e.g.,* N.Y. Est. Powers & Trusts Law §5–4.4, 5–4.5 (1981).
114. *In re Estate of Perez, supra* note 111.
115. *Weaks v. Mounter,* 88 Nev. 118, 493 P.2d 1307 (1972).
116. *Hurt v. Superior Court,* 124 Ariz. 45, 601 P.2d 1329 (1979).
117. *Weber v. Aetna Casualty & Surety Co.,* 406 U.S. 164 (1972). *See also Foy v. Vann,* 386 So.2d 1141 (Ala. Civ. App. 1979).
118. 42 U.S.C.A. §§402(d)(1) (d)(3); 416(h)(2) (h)(3) (1974 & Supp. 1982).
119. *Matthews v. Lucas,* 427 U.S. 495 (1976). *But see Davis v. Richardson,* 342 F. Supp. 588 (D. Conn.), *aff'd.* 409 U.S. 1069, (1972); *Griffin v. Richardson,* 346 F. Supp. 1226 (D. Md.), *aff'd.* 409 U.S. 1069 (1972).
120. *Jiminez v. Weinberger,* 417 U.S. 628 (1974).
121. 8 U.S.C.A. §§1101(b)(1)(D) (b)(2) (1970 & Supp. 1982).
122. *Fiallo v. Bell,* 430 U.S. 787 (1977).
123. *Trimble v. Gordon,* 430 U.S. 762 (1977). *See also Adkins v. McEldowney,* 280 S.E.2d 231 (W.Va. 1981).
124. *Lalli v. Lalli,* 439 U.S. 259 (1978).
125. *In re Brown,* 388 So.2d 1151 (La. 1980), *cert. denied,* 450 U.S. 998 (1981).
126. N.Y. Est. Powers & Trusts Law §4–1.2 (1981).
127. TEX. FAM. CODE ANN. §13.01 (Supp. 1982).

128. *Pickett v. Brown*, 76 L.Ed. 2d 372 (1983). *See also Mills v. Habluetzel*, 456 U.S. 91 (1982).
129. *Florida ex rel. Gillespie v. West*, 378 So.2d 1220 (Fla. 1979).
130. *Montana v. Wilson*, 634 P.2d 172 (Mont. 1981).

VI

Access to Courts: Suing and Being Sued

Every person has the right to sue another. Generally, age is not a bar to the recovery of damages (usually money) if one can prove that another person, corporation, or governmental body intentionally or negligently caused him harm, injury or some other loss. However, there are a few exceptions to this rule.

How does a child go about bringing a lawsuit against another person?

Just like anyone else. Usually this entails a visit with a lawyer who will advise him about the law and the probability of success. If the child is under the age of majority in his state (see Appendix A), he lacks what is called the legal capacity to sue. This does not mean that a child is barred from access to the courts; it means that a person over the age of majority must bring the suit for him, in the child's name. Depending on the state and the circumstances, the person who brings the suit may be a lawyer, parent, guardian, or "next friend."[1] The parent, guardian, or next friend is entitled to hire a lawyer to litigate the case. Generally, the person who brings the suit for the young person does not have to be appointed by the court.

Do children have the right to sue their parents for negligent or injurious conduct?

It depends on the state and on the reason for the lawsuit. Tradition and a ninety-year-old legal concept—the "intrafamily tort immunity rule"—have prevented children in bringing lawsuits for injuries caused by parental negligence (careless) or willful conduct. This limitation is based on the assumption that lawsuits brought by one family member against another destroy family unity, pose a threat to parental authority, and foster collusive lawsuits in which family members scheme to defraud insurance companies or others.[2]

At least twenty-nine states have abolished or limited parental immunity where the child wants to sue a parent for injuries sustained due to the parent's negligence. Situations that most commonly result in lawsuits by children against their parents are automobile accidents where the driver's negligence injures his child who is a passenger in the same car. Other cases typically involve instances where a parent injures his child when backing a car out of a driveway or when carelessly operating a power lawn mower.

What are the twenty-nine states in which children have the right to sue their parents for injuries sustained due to the parents' negligence?

The *extent* of the limitation of parental tort immunity varies from state to state, and in many states the role of parental immunity is not clearly defined. The immunity rules have been abolished or limited in Alaska, Arizona, California, Connecticut, Delaware, Florida, Iowa, Illinois, Kansas, Kentucky, Maine, Massachusetts, Michigan, Minnesota, Montana, New Hampshire, New Jersey, New York, North Carolina, North Dakota, Pennsylvania, Rhode Island, South Carolina, Virginia, West Virginia, Washington, and Wisconsin.[3] Three states never adopted the immunity in the first place—Hawaii, Nevada, and Vermont.

In abolishing parental immunity, the California Supreme Court took note of the fact that parents, though they have the right to discipline their children, have no right to act negligently toward them. Most importantly, the court affirmed the doctrine that an injured person, regardless of age or family position, has a fundamental right to be compensated for injuries caused by another.[4] In abolishing parental immunity, New York's highest court rejected the argument that families would be undermined by allowing children to sue their parents.[5] The court stated that, because automobile liability insurance is widespread and compulsory, the true parties to family litigation often are not the child and his parent but the injured child and an insurance company. In rebutting the argument that abolition of the immunity doctrine will foster collusion to defraud insurance companies or others, courts of many states have noted that the possibility of fraud exists in every liability case, not just those between members of a family.

The role of parental immunity in the remaining states is unclear: it has been abrogated at least in automobile negligence cases. The most common exceptions to total abrogation that have been adopted were listed by the Supreme Court of Wisconsin.[6] That court abrogated the doctrine except "(1) where the alleged negligent act involves an exercise of parental authority over the child; and (2) where the alleged negligent act involves an exercise of ordinary parental discretion with respect to the provision of food, clothing, housing, medical and dental services, and other care."[7] Arizona, Kentucky, and Michigan have expressly adopted these exceptions, while Alaska and New Jersey have referred favorably to them.

Other states (including Delaware, Iowa, Kansas, Maine, Massachusetts, and Washington) feel that there may be areas of parental authority and discretion where the immunity still applies but have been unwilling to define those areas.

Generally, courts are concerned that families will be split apart if children are allowed to sue their parents for negligent supervision alone, or for simply being incompetent parents. Courts have noted that parents should not be sued for wrong decisions concerning their child's welfare. This may be seen more clearly if this type of negligence is contrasted with negligence in automobile negligence cases. In automobile cases, it may be said that the duty breached by the parent was owed to the world at large and not solely to the child. Thus, while a court would allow a suit by a child who was a passenger in a car driven negligently by a parent, it might prohibit a suit against the parent by a child who was hit by a car driven by a stranger when the child was on a bike in the street because his parent negligently left the front gate open.[8]

At least three states—Delaware, Florida, and Massachusetts—limit the abrogation to the extent of insurance coverage.

For those states that allow children to sue their parents, can children sue for injuries sustained due to the parents' negligent supervision in their duties as parents?

Not in every state. In New York, for example, a child may sue a parent for negligence where the duty is ordinarily owed apart from the family relation, in such examples as negligently driving a car.[9] Since *all* drivers owe a duty to drive carefully, drivers who happen to be parents may be sued by their children. But New York does not allow suits by children who seek damages from their parents based on a breach of a special duty owed by a parent to care and raise the child.[10] Most states do not make this distinction.[11]

Even in states where parent-child immunity exists, are there still situations in which parents may be held liable for acts causing harm or injury to their children?

Yes. Even where parental immunity is in force, lawsuits are usually permitted on behalf of children against other members of their own family—

1. for damage to one's property (as distinguished from a personal injury);[12]
2. for personal injury resulting from a parent's *willful or malicious action* (as distinguished from negligent action);[13]
3. for matters involving cases against the estate of deceased parent;[14]
4. for claims against the employer of a parent for torts committed during the scope of a parent's employment;[15]
5. for cases against parents in their business capacity.[16]

In discussing a child's right to recover for the malicious act of his parent, the California Supreme Court states, "While it may seem repugnant to allow a minor to sue his parent, we think it more repugnant to leave a minor child without redress for the damages he has suffered by reason of his parent's willful or malicious misconduct."[17]

Moreover, in states that honor the intrafamily immunity rule a child may still be permitted to recover compensation from his parents for negligence if the child becomes "emancipated" before bringing the suit.[18]

How does a child achieve emancipated status in order to sue his parents?

The issue of emancipation must be determined by a court. Even in states that bar intrafamily suits for negligence, courts have been quite willing to grant emancipation for the limited purpose of permitting lawsuits if the facts warrant.[19] The facts warranting emancipation include those indicating that a child is financially independent, that he or she lives alone or pays his or her own room and board, and/or that he or she is totally or partially free from parental control and discipline (see chapter VII).

In a New Hampshire case a sixteen-year-old child was found to be sufficiently emancipated so that he could sue, even though he was living at home and attending high school, since he was working during his summer vacation for his father, receiving the same wage as other workers and paying for his own board.[20] In another case, a Connecticut court held that the fact that a twenty-year-old girl lived at home and did not pay for room and board would not automatically prohibit a finding of emancipation since she had her own source of income, paid for her clothing, medical care, and music lessons and was relatively free of parental control.[21]

What about other members of the family? Does a child have the right to sue them for negligence or injury?

Yes. Curiously, children may sue their minor brothers and sisters for their tortious conduct, even though they may be prohibited from suing their parents.[22] (In New York, however, no lawsuit may be brought by a younger sibling against an older one based on the negligent supervision of the younger child.)[23]

In every state, uncles, aunts, and more distant relatives may be sued. Moreover, children are permitted to sue people who stand in the place of parents, or those who have custody of them. Courts, for example, have upheld the right of children to sue their stepfathers, adoptive parents, and grandparents, even in states where the law does not permit children to sue their natural parents.[24]

Can children sue their parents for emotional and psychological injuries caused by inadequate parenting?

Probably not. The few courts that have considered such claims have rejected them, ruling that questionable parenting that does not result in *physical injury* is not tortious conduct for which children may sue.[25]

Can a child sue for damages resulting from a tort committed against the mother before the child was born?

In many states, yes. Over the past ten years a number of states have recognized that a child has a cause of action for damages for injuries resulting from a tort committed against the mother before the child was born.[26] New York does not permit such a cause of action;[27] but it does allow lawsuits for damages inflicted on a developing fetus.[28] A number of states (including Michigan and New Jersey) permit similar suits.[29] In the words of the New Jersey Supreme Court:

> [J]ustice requires that the principle be recognized that a child has a legal right to begin life with a sound mind and body. If the wrongful conduct of another interferes with that right, and it can be established by competent proof that there is a causal connection between the wrongful interference and the harm suffered by the child when born, damages for such harm should be recoverable by the child.[30]

Do children have the right to recover monetary damages if their parent is injured by the negligence of another person?

Generally, no. In order to recover damages, a person needs to show that he or she was *personally* harmed. This does not mean that only persons who are *directly* injured may sue. Indirect harms are recognized. A spouse, for example, of an injured person may sue third parties for causing the injury on the theory that the spouse has been indirectly harmed by the loss of companionship of their husband or wife. This theory of loss of companionship (or "consortium") is rarely applied to children who sue third parties for injuring their parents.[31] This is because children do not have a legal right to a parent's companionship or custody. At least three courts, however, have recognized this cause of action by children.[32]

Similarly, courts do not allow actions by children against a lover of one of their parents on a theory of alienation of affection—taking the love of the parent away from the child.[33]

In some states, children who actually witness the negligent injury of a parent may recover damages for fright or emotional shock—but only if they were near the scene of the accident and if the shock resulted from a direct emotional impact of observing the injury. On occasion, courts have allowed similar suits for seeing brothers or sisters injured.[34]

Does a child have the right to sue another person for defamation of character (libel and slander)?

Yes. Defamation is an injury of one's reputation. Usually,

one's reputation is injured when someone tells untruthful or malicious things about him to others and his earning capacity or standing in the community is lowered ("de-famed"). In most states a child has a right to recover damages (usually money) for the defamation of his character by others.[34a] A young person's reputation is just as deserving of protection as that of an adult.[35]

Generally, the defamation is called libel if it appears as words or pictures printed in a newspaper, book, or magazine, and it is called slander if it is spoken. Naturally, slander is more difficult to prove than libel.

Young people have sued others who have defamed them by written or spoken words that charged (1) that a boy had venereal disease (contained in a letter to the boy's father);[36] (2) that a girl committed theft (told by a shopkeeper to the girl's father);[37] (3) that an unmarried girl was pregnant;[38] and (4) that a minor "hangs around in a disreputable part" of town (printed in a local newspaper).[39]

Can a child be sued for negligence or intentional injury?

Yes. Children as well as adults may be found liable for injuries carelessly or intentionally caused.[40] It may be difficult, however, to obtain monetary damages from children because they are not likely to have their own financial resources. For this reason, persons harmed by children often attempt to sue the parents, who are more likely to be able to pay any damages. (Parents are not obliged to pay money owed by their children that are assessed against them as damages in lawsuits.)

If a child is sued, how is he notified of the action?

Notice of a lawsuit is usually personally handed to the person being sued in the form of a "summons."

If a child is being sued, the summons must bear his name. If he is below a certain age (generally fourteen years old), service upon his parents or guardian will suffice. If the child is above that age, however, most states require that he be personally served as well.[41] In these states if *only* the child *or* the parent is served, the summons may be defective.[42]

If a child is sued, how does he defend himself?

If a child is sued for negligence or in some other civil

action, the judge must appoint someone to represent him.[43] Usually this person is called a guardian *ad litem* and, if he is not a lawyer himself, he may hire a lawyer to defend the child. A guardian *ad litem* is not a guardian in the usual sense of the word; that is, one who takes custody of a child or watches over his property; a guardian *ad litem* acts on behalf of the child for the sole purpose of serving as his representative in the legal action. If a guardian *ad litem* is not appointed by the court, a child against whom a decision has been rendered has the right to a new trial.[44] Normally, all proceedings will be suspended until a guardian *ad litem* has been appointed.[45] In many states, if a child is fourteen years of age or older, he may personally ask the court to have a guardian *ad litem* appointed.[46]

In most states, if a guardian *ad litem* or some other person has been appointed to represent a child, the case may not be settled between the parties without approval of the court.

If a child is sued for negligence, is he held to the same standard of care as adults?

No. Even though children are liable for injuries they cause, they are not expected to conduct themselves with the same degree of care as adults. Courts usually hold a child responsible for the amount of care exercised by children of a like age, experience, and development, or the measure of care that a child of the same age would ordinarily exercise under similar circumstances.[47]

In some jurisdictions, an old rule is used: children under the age of 7 are incapable of negligence; children between the ages of 7 and 14 are presumed incapable of negligence but the presumption is rebuttable and grows weaker as the child nears the age of 14; and children over the age of 14 are presumed capable of negligence but are allowed to rebut the presumption.[48]

If a child injures another person or destroys another person's property, is the child's parent liable for the amount of damages?

Only under some circumstances. Generally, the mere fact of parenthood does not render a parent liable for the acts of his child. Thus, if a child is involved in an accident caused by his carelessness or lack of judgment, his parents are probably not responsible for paying the damages resulting from that accident.[49]

But there are situations in which parents will be held liable for part or all of the damages caused by their children. Parents, for example, may be held liable for the acts of their children if it is shown that the child *worked* for the parent and was negligent while acting as an agent or employee of his employer-parent.[50] Thus, a Massachusetts court found a father liable for personal injuries caused to another by his child while riding a bicycle because at the time of the accident the child was a "servant" of his father, acting within the scope of his employment with his father's grocery business as a delivery boy.[51]

Also, parents may be held liable if they actually directed the child in causing damage to others, or if parents consented to, or sponsored, the child's actions.[52]

In a few states, parents may be liable for the negligent acts of their children if they are negligent in failing to exercise proper control or supervision over their child, with knowledge that injury to another is a possible consequence of their child's conduct. As an example of this legal principle, a Florida court ruled that a parent may be liable to others for entrusting to a child a bicycle which, because of the child's young age, inexperience, and lack of judgment may be a source of danger to others. In this case, a woman was struck from behind by a five-year-old child riding a two-wheeled bicycle on a sidewalk. The child was riding without supervision only five days after the father had removed training wheels from the bike.[53]

What if damages or injuries caused by a child are not the result of an accident but are intentionally inflicted?

Parents may be liable for damages caused by the intentional or willful acts of their children in two situations.

First, parents may be found liable if they had knowledge of the destructive tendencies of their child and did not exercise proper care or control to prevent such outbreaks.[54] If parents are found to have violated this "duty of care," they may be held responsible for the full amount of damages caused. Proving liability, however, is not easy. In an Arizona case, for example, a fourteen-year-old boy assaulted a woman and her two daughters with a hammer. The woman sued the boy's parents but failed to establish sufficient evidence to show that the parents knew that their son would commit the assault or that they should have known of their child's propensity for violence.[55] In a California case, a person was shot by a child who stationed himself on a hill and fired at passing motorists. The injured person sued the boy's parents and at the trial produced a psychiatrist who testified that the child was a paranoid schizophrenic, and that the symptoms should have been observed by his parents and precautions should have been taken. The court disagreed, ruling that testimony by the psychiatrist alone was not sufficient to warrant holding the parents liable.[56]

Second, many states have recently passed laws making parents financially liable for intentional or willful acts of their children that cause damage or injury to others.[57] These laws require parents to pay *regardless* of whether they knew or should have known of their children's propensity to cause damage. They have been enacted as a result of the much-publicized "wave" of juvenile crime, with the belief that parents will exercise greater control over their children's behavior if they know they are liable for damages caused by their children's intentional or illegal acts.

The most common form of parental liability is reimbursement for property damage, although some states also require payment of medical expenses for personal injuries.

Unlimited liability, however, is probably unconstitutional.[58] Many states set limits on the amount of parental liability. In New York, for example, parental liability is limited to $1,500 for most property damage inflicted by children, and $5,000 for willful damage to houses of religious worship done by children over 10 and less than 18 years old.[59] In Texas, which imposes liability on parents for damages not to exceed $5,000, a court held that parents were responsible for $15,000 worth of damage when their child did damage in excess of $5,000 to three different homes.[60]

Moreover, in some states, parents are liable only if they fail to exercise due diligence in supervising and controlling their child.[61]

A challenge to Connecticut's parental liability law, which imposes a maximum liability of $1,500, was rejected by that state's supreme court.[62] The parents contended that, among other things, the law was unfair. The court ruled that "[i]t seems fair and equitable to put the responsibility on the parent who may be at least partly to blame for the child's conduct, rather than the innocent injured party."[63]

If a parent leaves a gun or other dangerous instrument where a child finds it and uses it to injure someone else, may the parent be held liable for the injury caused by the child?

Yes. In one case, parents were found guilty of negligence when their 7-year-old child shot his 4-year-old brother with a pistol that was left in an unlocked automobile glove compartment.[64] In another case, a father had purchased a gun for his 10-year-old son and taught him never to point it at anyone and to use it only in the basement. The father was, nevertheless, found negligent because he left it in an open cabinet where his son found it and accidentally shot his playmate while playing with the gun in the basement.[65]

On the other hand, if parents entrust a gun to a child who, for example, has a hunting license, they might not be found liable for injuries caused by the child since they could have assumed that the child was schooled in the use of firearms.[66]

Does a parent have the right to refuse to testify against his child? Must a child testify against a parent?

Some states have some form of legislation that protects husbands and wives from being forced to testify against each other in certain circumstances. But no laws exist that protect parents and children from testifying against each other. Thus, the only answer that can be given to these questions is that unless a court in an individual case grants protection, the testimony may be compelled.

In New York, for example, a well-known civil rights lawyer was summoned before a federal grand jury to disclose the address of his daughter. He refused, claiming a "parent-child privilege." He was threatened with contempt of court for refusing to provide the information and the matter went to court. The judge denied the lawyer's claim, stating:

> [The father] invokes the "parent-child privilege." But there is no such thing. All of us, whether as parents or children, may empathize over the imaginable prospect of being asked to incriminate those close to us. However, that is not necessarily the

> situation here and it would not in any event justify enforcement of the novel privilege now asserted.[67]

On the other hand, two other cases from New York suggest that concepts of family privacy and common decency may protect the parent-child relationship from forced testimonial disclosure. In the first case, the mother of a sixteen-year-old was called before a grand jury because the prosecutor wanted to find out whether or not her son, who was suspected of committing an act of arson, had made any admissions to her. An appellate court ruled that the legislature had not created a "parent-child privilege," but that

> communications made by a minor child to his parents within the context of the family relationship may, under some circumstances, be within the "private realm of family life which the state cannot enter." ... It would be difficult to think of a situation which more strikingly embodies the intimate and confidential relationship which exists among family members than that in which a troubled young person, perhaps beset with remorse and guilt, turns for counsel and guidance to his mother and father. There is nothing more natural, more consistent with our concept of the parental role, than that a child may rely on his parents for help and advice.[68]

The court did not rule that the mother in this case was free from her obligation to answer questions from the grand jury, but it did suggest that some of her communication with her son may be "privileged" and therefore nondisclosable in the interest of family privacy.

And, following this case, a New York County Court judge ruled that the father of a son who was charged with criminally neligent homicide, because he was in an automobile accident in which another person died, need not divulge the conversation he had with his son shortly after the accident.[69] In deciding to protect the family relationship, the judge stated, "The confidences extended between parent and child are just as sacrosanct as between a doctor and a patient or a priest and penitent."

Even more recently, a federal court in Nevada ruled that

the parent-child privilege is applicable even to adult children. In a broad ruling the court held that a person may not be compelled to testify about conversations had, or information obtained through, the parent-child relationship. The broad sweep of language in the opinion is likely to influence courts that consider this issue in the future. The court reasoned:

> There can be little doubt that the confidence and privacy inherent in the parent-child relationship must be protected and sedulously fostered by the courts. While the government has an important goal in presenting all relevant evidence before the court in each proceeding, this goal does not outweigh an individual's right of privacy in his communications within the family unit, nor does it outweigh the family's interests in its integrity and inviolability, which springs from the rights of privacy inherent in the family relationship itself. There is no reasonable basis for extending a testimonial privilege for confidential communications to spouses . . . yet denying a parent or child the right to claim such a privilege.[70]

NOTES

1. *See, e.g.*, Mo. Rules Civ. Prac. 52.02(a) (1976).
2. Discussed in *Gibson v. Gibson*, 3 Cal. 3d 914, 479 P.2d 648, 92 Cal. Rptr. 288 (1971).
3. *Hebel v. Hebel*, 435 P.2d 8 (Alaska 1967); *Streenz v. Streenz*, 106 Ariz. 86, 471 P.2d 282 (1970); *Sandoval v. Sandoval*, 128 Ariz. 11, 623 P.2d 800 (1981); *Gibson v. Gibson, supra* note 2; CONN. GEN. STAT. ANN. §52–572c (Supp. 1982); *Williams v. Williams*, 369 A.2d 669 (Del. 1976); *Ard v. Ard*, 414 So.2d 1066 (Fla. 1982); *Tamashiro v. De Gama*, 51 Hawaii 74, 450 P.2d 998 (1969); *Peterson v. City & County of Honolulu*, 51 Hawaii 484, 462 P.2d 1007 (1970); *Illinois National Bank & Trust Co. v. Turner*, 83 Ill. App.3d 234, 403 N.E.2d 1256 (1980); *Cummings v. Jackson*, 57 Ill. App.3d 68, 372 N.E.2d 1127 (1978). *But see Thomas v. Chicago Board of Education*, 77 Ill. 2d 165, 395 N.E.2d 538 (1979); *Turner v. Turner*, 304 N.W.2d 786 (Iowa 1981); *Nocktonick v. Nocktonick*, 227 Kan. 758, 611 P.2d 135 (1980); *Rigdon v. Rigdon*, 465 S.W.2d 921 (Ky. 1971); *Black v. Solmitz*, 409 A.2d 634 (Me. 1979); *Sorensen v. Sorensen*, 369 Mass. 350, 339 N.E.2d 907 (1975); *Plumley v. Klein*, 388 Mich. 1, 199 N.W.2d 169 (1972);. *Sileski v. Kelman*, 281 Minn. 431, 161 N.W.2d 631 (1968); *Anderson v. Steam*, 295 N.W.2d 595 (Minn. 1980);

Transamerica Insurance Co. v. Royle, 51 L.W. 243 (Mont. 1983); *Rupert v. Stienne*, 90 Nev. 397, 528 P.2d 1013 (1974); *France v. APA Transport Co.*, 56 N.J. 500, 267 A.2d 490 (1970); *Briere v. Briere*, 107 N.H. 432, 224 A.2d 588 (1966); *Gelbman v. Gelbman*, 23 N.Y.2d 434, 245 N.E.2d 192, 297 N.Y.S.2d 529 (1969); N.C. GEN. STAT. §1–539.21 (Supp. 1981); *Nuvelle v. Wells*, 154 N.W.2d 364 (N.D. 1967); *Falco v. Pados*, 444 Pa. 372, 282 A.2d 351 (1971); *Silva v. Silva*, 446 A.2d 1013 (R.I. 1982) *Elam v. Elam*, 275 S.C. 132, 268 S.E.2d 109 (1980); *Smith v. Kauffman*, 212 Va. 181, 183 S.E.2d 190 (1971); *Wood v. Wood*, 135 Vt. 119, 370 A.2d 191 (1977); *Merrick v. Sutterlin*, 93 Wash. 2d 610 P.2d 891 (1980); *Lee v. Comer*, 224 S.E.2d 721 (W. Va. 1976); *Goller v. White*, 20 Wis. 2d 402, 122 N.W.2d 193 (1963).

4. *Gibson v. Gibson*, *supra* note 2.
5. *Gelbman v. Gelbman*, *supra* note 3.
6. *Goller v. White*, *supra* note 3.
7. 20 Wis. 2d at 413, 122 N.W.2d at 198.
8. *See e.g.*, *Sandoval v. Sandoval*, *supra* note 3.
9. *Gelbman v. Gelbman*, *supra* note 3.
10. *Holodook v. Spencer*, 36 N.Y.2d 35, 364 N.Y.S.2d 859, 324 N.E.2d 338 (1974).
11. *See e.g.*, *Peterson v. City of Honolulu*, *supra* note 3; *Gabel v. Koba*, 1 Wash. App. 684, 463 P.2d 237 (1969); *Howes v. Hansen*, 56 Wis. 2d 247, 201 N.W.2d 825 (1972).
12. *See, e.g.*, *Signs v. Signs*, 156 Ohio St. 566, 103 N.E.2d 743 (1952).
13. *See e.g.*, *Mahnke v. Moore*, 197 Md. 61, 77 A.2d 923 (1951).
14. *See, e.g.*, *Davis v. Smith*, 253 F.2d 286 (3rd Cir. 1958); *Brown v. Cole*, 198 Ark. 417, 129 S.W.2d 245 (1939); *Brennecke v. Kilpatrick*, 336 S.W.2d 68 (Mo. 1968) (*en banc*).
15. *See, e.g.*, *Stapleton v. Stapleton*, 85 Ga. App. 728, 70 S.E. 2d 156 (1952).
16. *See, e.g.*, *Signs v. Signs*, *supra* note 12.
17. *Emery v. Emery*, 45 Cal. 2d 421, 427, 289 P.2d 218, 224 (1955).
18. *See, e.g.*, *Lancaster v. Lancaster*, 213 Miss. 536, 57 So.2d 302 (1952); *Logan v. Reaves*, 209 Tenn. 631, 354 S.W.2d 789 (1962).
19. *Carricato v. Carricato*, 384 S.W.2d 85 (Ky. Ct. App. 1964).
20. *Dunlop v. Dunlop*, 84 N.H. 352, 150 A. 905 (1930).
21. *Wood v. Wood*, 135 Conn. 280, 63 A.2d 586 (1948). See also *Wurth v. Wurth*, 322 S.W.2d 745 (Mo. 1959).
22. W. Prosser, *The Law of Torts* (4th ed.) §122 (cases cited p. 866, note 81).
23. *Smith v. Sapienza*, 52 N.Y.2d 82, 417 N.E. 2d 530, 436 N.Y.S2d 236 (1981).
24. *Bricault v. Dereau*, 21 Conn. Sup. 486, 157 A.2d 604 (1960); *Brown v. Cole*, 198 Ark. 417, 129 S.W.2d 245 (1939); *Willkins v. Kane*, 74 N.J. Super. 414, 181 A.2d 417 (1962); *See* contra *Wooden v. Hale*, 426 P.2d 679 (Okl. 1967).
25. *Burnette v. Wahl*, 284 Or. 705, 588 P.2d 1105 (1978).

26. *See e.g., Douglas v. Hartford*, 542 F. Supp. 1267 (D. Conn. 1982); *Renslow v. Mennonite Hospital*, 67 Ill. 2d 348, 367 N.E.2d 1250 (1977); *Lazermich v. General Hospital*, 6 FLR 2865 (M.D.Pa. 1980); *Anonymous v. Physician*, 6 FLR 2565 (Conn. 1980); *Bergstreser v. Mitchell*, 577 F.2d 22 (8th Cir. 1978); *Jorgensen v. Meade Johnson Laboratory*, 483 F.2d 237 (10th Cir. 1973); *Sylvia v. Gobeille*, 101 R.I. 76, 220 A.2d 222 (1966).
27. *Albala v. City of New York*, 54 N.Y.2d 269, 429 N.E.2d 786, 445 N.Y.S.2d 108 (1981).
28. *Woods v. Lancet*, 303 N.Y. 349, 102 N.E.2d 691 (1951).
29. *See, e.g., Grodin v. Grodin*, 102 Mich. App. 396, 301 N.W.2d 869 (1981); *Smith v. Brennan*, 31 N.J. 353, 157 A.2d 497 (1960).
30. *Smith v. Brennan, supra* note 29, 31 N.J. at 364–65, 157 A.2d at 503.
31. *See e.g., Salin v. Kloempkin*, 332 N.W.2d 736, (Minn. 1982); *Borer v. American Airlines, Inc.*, 19 Cal. 3rd 441, 563 P.2d 858, 138 Cal. Rptr. 302 (1977); *Morgel v. Winger*, 290 N.W.2d 266 (N.D. 1980); *Roth v. Bell*, 24 Wash. App. 92, 600 P.2d 602 (1979): *De Angelis v. Lutheran Medical Center*, 84 A.D.2d 17, 445 N.Y.S.2d 188 (2d Dept. 1981); *Norwest v. Presbyterian Intercommunity Hospital*, 7 FLR 2025 (Ore. 1982); *Russell v. Salem Transport Co.*, 61 N.J. 502, 295 A.2d 862 (1972); *Hoffman v. Dautel*, 189 Kan. 165, 368 P.2d 57 (1962).
32. *See Berger v. Weber*, 82 Mich. App. 199, 267 N.W.2d 124 (1978) *modified* 411 Mich. 1, 303 N.W.2d 424 (1981); *Weitl v. Moes*, 311 N.W.2d 259 (Iowa 1981); *Ferriter v. Daniel O'Connell's Sons*, 413 N.E.2d 690 (Mass. 1980).
33. *See, e.g., Bock v. Linquist*, 278 N.W.2d 326 (Minn. 1979).
34. *See, e.g., Steward v. Hall*, 17 Ill. 71 (1855); *Hurst v. Goodwin*, 114 Ga. 585, 40 S.E. 764 (1902); *Munden v. Harris*, 153 Mo. App. 652, 134 S.W. 1076 (1911).

34a. *See, e.g., Rickey v. Chicago Transit Authority*, 100 Ill. App.3d 439, 428 N.E.2d 596 (1981); *Dillon v. Legg*, 441 P.2d 912 (Cal. 1968).

35. *Van Wiginton v. Pulitzer Publishing Co.*, 218 F. 795 (8th Cir. 1914).
36. *King v. Pillsbury*, 115 Me. 528, 99 A. 513 (1917).
37. *Roper v. Great Atlantic & Pacific Tea Co.*, 164 A.2d 478 (D.C. Mun. App. 1960).
38. *Vigil v. Rice*, 74 N.M. 693, 397 P.2d 719 (1964).
39. *Land v. Tampa Times Publishing Co.*, 68 Fla. 546, 67 So. 130 (1914).
40. *See, e.g., Stevens v. Stevens*, 172 Ky. 780, 189 S.W. 1143 (1916); *Swoboda v. Nowak*, 213 Mo. App. 452, 255 S.W. 1079 (1923).
41. *See, e.g., White v. White*, 294 Ky. 563, 172 S.W.2d 72 (1943).
42. *Frost v. Blackwood*, 408 P.2d 300 (Okla. 1965); *Leahy v. Hardy*, 225 A.D. 323, 232 N.Y.S. 543 (3rd Dept. 1929); *Smith v. Canada*, 290 S.W.2d 463 (Ky. 1956); *Akley v. Bassett*, 189 Cal. 625, 209 P. 576 (1922).
43. *See, e.g.*, Mo. Rules Civ. Proc. 52.02(e) (1976).
44. *Cox v. Wrinkle*, 267 S.W.2d 648 (Mo. 1954).

45. *See, e.g., Maloney v. Schandelmier,* 65 Mont. 531, 212 P. 493 (1923); *In re Thomas' Trust,* 33 A.D.2d 990, 307 N.Y.S.2d 312 (4th Dept. 1970).
46. *See, e.g.,* N.Y. Civ. Prac. Law §1202(a) (1976); *Maloney v. Schandelmier, supra* note 45.
47. *Richards v. Relles,* 144 Cal. App. 2d 416, 301 P.2d 7 (1956); *Kuhns v. Bragger,* 390 Pa. 331, 135 A.2d 395 (1957).
48. *Kuhns v. Bragger, supra* note 47; *Stephens v. Stephens,* 170 Ky. 780, 189 S.W. 1143 (1916).
49. *Lastowski v. Norge Coin-O-Matic,* 44 A.D.2d 127, 355 N.Y.S.2d 432 (1974); *Parsons v. Smithy,* 109 Ariz. 49, 504 P.2d 1272 (1973); *Aetna Insurance Co. v. Richardell,* 528 S.W.2d 280 (Tex. Civ. App. 1975). *See* contra *Turner v. Bucher,* 308 So.2d 270 (La. 1975).
50. *Broadstreet v. Hall,* 168 Ind. 192, 80 N.E. 145 (1907); *Mirick v. Suchy,* 74 Kan. 715, 87 P. 1141 (1906); *Davis v. Littlefield,* 97 S.C. 171, 81 S.E. 487 (1914).
51. *Altoonian v. Muldonian,* 277 Mass. 53, 177 N.E. 830 (1931).
52. *See, e.g., Hopkins v. Droppers,* 184 Wis. 400, 198 N.W. 738 (1924); *Langford v. Shu,* 258 N.C. 135, 128 S.E.2d 210 (1962); *Guilbeau v. Guilbeau,* 326 So.2d 654 (La. 1976).
53. *Southern American Fire Insurance Co. v. Maxwell,* 274 So.2d 579 (Fla. Dist. Ct. App.), *cert. denied,* 279 So.2d 32 (1973).
54. *See, e.g., Spector v. Neer,* 262 So.2d 689 (Fla. 1972); *Caldwell v. Zaher,* 344 Mass. 590, 183 N.E.2d 706 (1962); *Steinberg v. Cauhois,* 249 A.D. 518, 293 N.Y.S. 147 (1937).
55. *Parsons v. Smithey, supra* note 49.
56. *Reida v. Lund,* 18 Cal. App. 3d 698, 96 Cal. Rptr. 102 (1971).
57. *See, e.g.,* 11 PA. CONS. STAT. ANN. §§2001–05 (Supp. 1982); N.Y. Gen. Obl. Law, §3-112 (Supp. 1982); *General Insurance Co. of America v. Faulkner,* 259 N.C. 317, 130 S.E.2d 645 (1963); *Kelly v. Williams,* 346 S.W.2d 434 (Tex. Civ. App. 1961); *Mahaney v. Hunter Enterprizes, Inc.,* 425 P.2d 442 (Wyo. 1967). *See* contra *In re Weiner,* 176 Pa. Super. 255, 106 A.2d 915 (1954).
58. *Corley v. Lewless,* 227 Ga. 745, 182 S.E.2d 766 (1971).
59. N.Y. Gen. Obl. Law §3–112 (Supp. 1982); N.Y. Rel. Corp. Law §28 (Supp. 1982).
60. *Buie v. Longspaugh,* 598 S.W.2d 673 (Tex. Civ. App. 1980). *See also In re Sorrell,* 20 Md. App. 179, 315 A.2d 110 (1974); *In re Appeal No. 769, Sept. 1974,* 25 Md. App. 565, 335 A.2d 204 (1975); Md. H.B. 639 (1980); *Hyman v. Davis,* 453 N.E.2d 336 (Ind. Ct. App. 1983).
61. N.Y. Gen. Obl. Law §3–112 (Supp. 1982).
62. *Watson v. Gradzik,* 34 Conn. Sup. 7, 373 A.2d 191 (1977). *See also Hayward v. Ramick,* 285 S.E.2d 697 (Ga. 1982); *Bryan v. Kitamura,* 529 F. Supp. 394 (D. Hawaii 1982).
63. 373 A.2d at 192 (quoting *General Insurance Co. v. Falkner,* 259 N.C. 317, 322, 120 S.E.2d 645, 49–50 (1963). See also *Board of Education of Piscataway v. Caffiero,* 431 A.2d 799 (N.Y. 1981).

64. *Valence v. State*, 280 So.2d 651 (La. Ct. App.); *cert. denied*, 282 So.2d 517 (1973).
65. *Gerlat v. Christianson*, 13 Wis. 2d 31, 108 N.W.2d 194 (1961).
66. *See, e.g., Conley v. Long*, 21 Misc. 2d 759, 192 N.Y.S.2d 203 (1959).
67. *In re Kinoy*, 326 F. Supp. 400–406 (S.D.N.Y. 1970). *See also In re Terry W.*, 59 Cal. App.3d 745, 130 Cal. Rptr. 913 (1976).
68. *In re A. & M.*, 61 A.D.2d 426, 403 N.Y.S.2d 375 (4th Dept. 1978). But see, *In re Grand Jury Proceedings: Starr*, 647 F.2d 511 (5th Cir. 1981).
69. *People v. Fitzgerald*, 101 Misc. 2d 712, 422 N.Y.S.2d 309 (West. Count Ct. 1979).
70. *In re Agosto*, 553 F. Supp. 1298, 1325 (D. Nev. 1983).

VII

Age of Majority and Emancipation

What does the "age of majority" mean?

The term *age of majority* describes the age at which one becomes an adult in the eyes of the law. For most legal purposes, the terms child, infant, minor, or juvenile are used interchangeably to denote those who have not yet attained the age of majority.

How old does one have to be to attain the age of majority?

Each state determines its own age of majority. In most states the age is 18.

Until 1971, the age of majority in almost every state was 21. Since the enactment in that year of the Twenty-Sixth Amendment—which gave 18-year-olds the right to vote in federal elections—all but a few states have lowered the age of majority from 21 to 18. (See Appendix A for a list of the age of majority in every state.)

When a child reaches the age of majority, is he given all the rights of an adult?

Not necessarily. The effect of the age of majority, even within the same state, varies with respect to the activity involved. Even though one may attain the age of majority he does not necessarily gain *all* the rights afforded adults.

In the state of Washington, for example, the age of majority is 18, and upon a child's eighteenth birthday he is granted *most* of the rights of an adult. But in order to buy, possess or drink alcoholic beverages in Washington State, one must be 21; on the other hand, children qualify for drivers' licenses at age 16, two years below the age of majority.

In New York, the age of majority is also 18 for many purposes, but one assumes the right to buy, possess and consume alcoholic beverages only at 19. Juvenile court jurisdiction in New York, however, terminates when a child reaches the age of 16. When 16- and 17-year-olds in New York are arrested and sent to trial, they are treated as adults (or adult "youthful offenders") even though they have not attained the general age of majority.

Moreover, a young person under the age of majority is subject to a dual set of disabilities: he is denied by the *state* certain rights enjoyed by adults, and he may be denied various attributes of personal freedom by his *parents* as well.

The state has the power to set ages of qualification for the following activities:

- voting
- serving on a jury
- marrying without parental consent
- buying, possessing and drinking alcoholic beverages
- making a contract and drawing a will
- working for wages
- obtaining a license to drive a motor vehicle
- attending school
- receiving juvenile court treatment for illegal or criminal conduct
- using the courts to sue another person
- receiving medical care without parental consent

Parents generally have the right to—

1. custody (which includes determining the place the child shall live);
2. receive earnings of their children;
3. discipline (so long as they do not use excessive force);
4. consent or withhold consent to their child's desire to marry or to obtain a driver's license;
5. determine religious training and education;
6. determine overall style of life, which may include exercising a reasonable degree of control over friends kept, food eaten, entertainment, and the style of clothes and hair.[1]

The power of the state and parents over the life of young people has diminished in recent years as adolescents have obtained a degree of liberty and self-determination.[1a] Of course, by virtue of their special status, children are also *granted* certain rights that are not given to persons over the age of majority, such as the right to be supported by their parents and to receive an education, and the right to be free from neglect and abuse.

Can a state set different ages of majority for males and females?

No. The age of majority must be the same for both sexes.

In *Stanton v. Stanton*, the United States Supreme Court held that different ages of majority based on *gender* violates the equal-protection clause of the Fourteenth Amendment.[2] *Stanton* involved a Utah statute that set the age of majority at 21 for boys and 18 for girls. In declaring this distinction void, the Supreme Court stated,

> [N]o longer is the female destined solely for the home and the rearing of the family, and only the male for the marketplace and the world of ideas. . . . If a specified age of majority is required for the boy in order to assure him parental support while he attains his education and training, so, too, it is for the girl.[3]

It is important to note that the Court did not say that the age must be 18 or that it must be 21, but that whatever the state legislature decides the age to be, it must be the same for both males and females.

May states prescribe different ages of qualification for other rights and activities based on sex?

This was not made clear by the Supreme Court, since *Stanton* only dealt with the general age of majority and its effect on the child's right to receive support. In other areas, including the right to marry and to engage in sex, states often maintain different age qualifications for males and females. Each distinction on the basis of sex must be justified by a state as necessary or important; it may not be based on stereotypical concepts about men and women; for example, in recent years, the Supreme Court has ruled that states may not prohibit only males (allowing females) between 18 and 20 from purchasing alcoholic beverages.[4] States may, however, criminally punish only teenage males for engaging in premarital sex with females of the same age.[5]

What does "emancipation" mean?

Emancipation is a legal term used to describe the condition whereby children, before reaching majority, are released from some or all of the disabilities of childhood and receive the rights and duties of adulthood. Emancipation also may release parents from their rights and duties, including the right to the custody and control of their child; the right to receive their child's services and earnings; and the duty to support, maintain, protect, and educate their child.[6]

Are there degrees of emancipation?

Yes. Emancipation may be complete or partial. Complete emancipation results from an agreement between the parents and child or a court declaration that extinguishes the right and duties of the parent and child.

Partial emancipation, on the other hand, results when (1) a child is freed from *some* of his parents' control and rights during the child's minority; (2) a child is freed from all of his parents' rights during *part* of the period of his minority; or (3) a child is freed from *some* of his parents' rights for *part* of his minority.[7]

Under partial emancipation, a child may be allowed to keep his earnings and still receive some degree of parental support.[8]

In order to insure that a child is fully cared for, courts are prone to find partial rather than complete emancipation.[9] As an example of the reluctance of courts to find complete emancipation, a Pennsylvania court held that an eighteen-year-old was only partially emancipated, even though he had a job and an independent source of income, and paid board and otherwise disposed of his money as he pleased.[10]

How does a child become emancipated?

The most common form of emancipation takes place automatically when a young person reaches the age of majority. Emancipation *before* that age may be obtained in one of two ways: first, it may be granted by a court; second, a child may, under other conditions, become emancipated in whole or in part by implication, consent, agreement, or fact, even without permission or approval of a court.[11]

How, and under what conditions, will a court declare a child emancipated?

Historically, emancipation was a privilege granted to parents, not children. Parents could—and still can—petition a court for a declaration of emancipation so that they could be released from their legal obligation to support, maintain and educate their children.

Today, in most states, parents still must consent to a judicial decree of emancipation, even though in some cases courts will find that outrageous behavior of parents toward children (such as abandonment of parental duties) constitutes *implied* consent, thereby emancipating children even though formal or express consent was never granted.[12] In Missouri, for example, a child must receive either the express or implied consent of both parents or the parent having custody to be declared emancipated.[13]

In determining whether a child should be emancipated, a court (or a jury)[14] will consider factors such as the age of the child, whether he lives at home,[15] and whether the child is free from the authority and control of his or her parents.[16] Most important, however, are the following financial considerations:

1. the child's employment and source of income;[17]
2. his ability to spend money without parental permission;[18]
3. whether the child pays room and board if living at home;[19]
4. whether the child pays his own debts;[20]
5. whether the parents have listed the child as a dependent for tax purposes.[21]

It is important to remember that in most cases the right to obtain a judicial declaration of emancipation is a right that belongs to the parent rather than the child.[22] In some cases a child's guardian or next friend will petition the court for an order of emancipation, but usually for a specific purpose only, such as the right to sue a parent in jurisdictions where this is otherwise prohibited.

What conditions constitute automatic emancipation?

Marriage and membership in the armed forces usually emancipate a child automatically, even when he or she is below the age of majority and even if no court has granted a decree. This is because marriage and membership in the armed forces drastically change the nature of the family relationship and bestow a degree of independence on the child.[23]

Some states have laws that provide automatic emancipation at a certain age *for a specific purpose only*. California, for example, emancipates some children at age fifteen for the purpose of obtaining medical care and treatment without parental consent.[24] In New York and other states, children are considered emancipated at all ages for the purpose of suing their parents or other members of their family.[25] In such cases, however, the child is granted no other right of emancipation beyond the stated purpose of the law.

What conditions might constitute emancipation by implication, agreement, or some other means?

Complete or partial emancipation may be established without the benefit (or bother) of obtaining judicial approval if the child and parent agree to the establishment of certain conditions, such as leaving home and establishing an independent household:[26] (1) if the parents consent to these conditions or acquiesce by not demanding that the circumstances change; (2) if parents require their child to pay room and board; or (3) if parents actually force their child out of the home and require that the child support himself.[27]

Can a young person file his own petition for emancipation?

Only in Arkansas, California, Connecticut, Kansas, Louisiana, and Oklahoma; and even in these states, the right to file a petition does not guarantee a decree of emancipation. Courts still have the discretion to deny petitions if they think that the qualifications are not met or if emancipation would not be in the child's best interest.

In Arkansas, circuit and chancery courts may "emancipate" any person 16 or older for the purpose of transacting business. This type of emancipation is not total; it only permits 16- and 17-year-olds to sign binding contracts, write wills and inherit property.[28]

In Kansas, a minor of any age may file a petition for

emancipation. Upon proof that the child is of sound mind, is able to conduct his or her own affairs, and that emancipation will promote the child's interests, a court may grant a decree of emancipation for *any* or *all* of the following purposes: (1) to sign binding contracts; (2) to own and sell real estate and personal property; (3) to inherit property; and (4) to sue and be sued in his own name.[29]

In Louisiana, a minor may file a petition for emancipation but the parents must consent, unless the ground for emancipation is parental mistreatment or nonsupport. If the court finds that the minor is capable of managing his own affairs, it will declare the child emancipated, with full power to perform all activities as though the child were an adult.[30]

In Oklahoma, district courts have the authority to grant minors the rights of majority, but only to the extent of entering into binding contracts and transacting other business.[31] The court must be satisfied that the child is of sound mind, is able to transact his own affairs, and that the child's interests would be promoted by this partial emancipation.

There is little evidence, however, that many young people are emancipated under the laws of these states. Moreover, none of them permit *total* emancipation without parental consent or unfitness. Two modern statutes—California's and Connecticut's, both in existence for only a few years—permit emancipation for all purposes without parental consent.

In California, young people may petition the court for emancipation if they are married, on active duty with the armed forces, or living separate from their parents and managing their own financial affiars. Emancipation is virtually automatic when it is based on marriage or service in the armed forces. But if emancipation is based on a child's living apart from his parents, a court must find that: (1) the child is sixteen or older; (2) emancipation would be in the child's best interest; (3) the source of the minor's income is not derived from illegal activity; and (4) the child is living apart from the parents either with their consent or acquiescence. (*Acquiescence* means that even if the parents have not given their consent they have done nothing to encourage their child's return.) If emancipation is granted, a child will be considered an adult for the purposes of—

1. consenting to medical, dental, and psychiatric care;
2. entering into binding contracts;

3. suing and being sued in his own name;
4. establishing residency;
5. buying or selling real property;
6. enrolling in a school or college;
7. applying for a work permit.[32]

In Connecticut, any minor sixteen or older may petition for emancipation if he is married, is on active duty with the armed forces, or is living apart from his parents with or without their consent and is managing his or her own financial affairs. A court may also declare a child emancipated if the facts indicate that the parent-child relationship has irretrievably broken down. Once emancipated, the child may do all the acts just listed in the California law, as though he or she were an adult.[33]

The major differences between the California and Connecticut statutes are that, in Connecticut, children may be living apart from their parents without their consent (while California requires parental acquiescence, a subtle difference), and in Connecticut a court may emancipate children if the relationship with their parents has totally broken down, regardless of the existence of other factors, such as a place of residence other than the parents, or their source of income. Moreover, in Connecticut, *parents* may petition the court for their children's emancipation, a provision not found in the California law.

In both states, emancipation not only frees the child of most of the legal disabilities of being a minor; it also frees parents of their obligation to support their children. Thus, when children become emancipated, they give up their right to parental support.

Are emancipated minors permitted to go to public school?

Yes. In most states, young persons above the compulsory education age who have not finished high school have a right to go to school until they reach eighteen or nineteen whether or not they live at home. Some local school boards have attempted to bar emancipated minors who do not live at home, but this discrimination has been held to be unconstitutional. A school district policy in Georgia, for example, permitted married minors but not emancipated single minors to attend high school. The school board argued that the policy was needed to restrict attendance to students who live with their parents so that the school could contact an adult in the event of academic or disciplinary problems, and that an emancipated minor's unconventional living arrangements might be a bad influence on impressionable students. A federal court rejected these arguments.[34]

NOTES

1. Courts customarily abstain from determining disputes between parents as to the proper upbringing of their child. *Kilgrow v. Kilgrow,* 268 Ala. 475, 107 So.2d 885 (1958); *People ex rel. Sisson v. Sisson,* 271 N.Y. 285, 2 N.E.2d 660 (1936). They often refuse to entertain cases involving "style of life" disputes between parents and their children as well. See Arthur and Kalitowski, "Child v. Parent: Residence, Education, and Dates," 24 *Juv. Justice* 34 (1974). *But see* contra *Roe v. Doe,* 29 N.Y.2d 188, 272 N.E.2d 567, 324 N.Y.S.2d 71 (1971).

1a. *See, e.g., Belloitti v. Baird,* 443 U.S. 622 (1979).

2. 428 U.S. 7 (1975).
3. *Id.* at 14, 15.
4. *Craig v. Boren,* 429 U.S. 190 (1976).
5. *Michael M. v. Superior Court,* 450 U.S. 464 (1981).
6. 59 Am. Jur. 2d, Parent and Child, §§93–101; *Gimlett v. Gimlett,* 629 P.2d 450 (Wash. 1981); *Accent Service Co. v. Ebsen,* 306 N.W. 2d 575 (Neb. 1981).
7. *See* S. Katz, W. Schroeder, and L. Sidman, "Emancipating Our Children—Coming of Legal Age in America," 7 *Fam. L. Q.*211 (1973); *Vaupel v. Bellach,* 261 Iowa 376, 379–80, 154 N.W.2d 149, 150–151 (1967).
8. *Turner v. Turner,* 441 S.W.2d 105 (Ky. Ct. App. 1969).
9. *Vaupel v. Bellach, supra* note 7.
10. *Detwiler v. Detwiler,* 162 Pa. Super 383, 57 A.2d 426 (1948).
11. *See, e.g.,* CAL. CIV. CODE §204 (1982). *But see* ARGONAUT INSURANCE EXCHANGE V. KATES, 137 Cal. 2d 158, 289 P.2d 801 (1955).
12. *Mahnke v. Moore,* 197 Md. 61, 77 A.2d 923 (1951); *Cogwill v. Boock,* 189 Ore. 282, 218 P.2d 445 (1950); *Spurgeon v. Mission State Bank,* 151 F.2d 702, 704 (8th Cir. 1945).
13. *Royall v. Legislation & Policy Division,* 610 S.W.2d 377 (Mo. Ct. App. 1980).
14. *Wood v. Wood,* 135 Conn. 280, 63 A.2d 586 (1948); *Wurth v. Wurth,* 322 S.W.2d 745 (Mo. 1959).
15. Fitzgerald v. Valdez, 77 N.M. 769, 427 P.2d 655 (1967).
16. *Gillikin v. Burbage,* 263 N.C. 317, 139 S.E.2d 753 (1965).
17. *Schoenung v. Callet,* 206 Wis. 52, 238 N.W. 852 (1931).
18. *Lafkin v. Harvey,* 131 Minn. 238, 154 N.W. 1097 (1915).
19. *Wurth v. Wurth, supra* note 14.

20. *Carricato v. Carricato*, 384 S.W.2d 85 (Ky. Ct. App. 1964).
21. *Wadoz v. United National Indemnity Co.*, 274 Wis. 383, 80 N.W.2d 262 (1957).
22. 39 Am. Jur. 2d, Parent and Child, §93; *Matter of Bates v. Bates, supra* note 6.
23. *Allen v. Arthur*, 139 Ind. App. 460, 220 N.E.2d 658 (1966); *Iroquois Iron Co. v. Industrial Commission*, 249 Ill. 106, 128 N.E. 289 (1920); CAL. CIV. CODE §204 (1982).
24. CAL CIV. CODE §34.6 (1982) (*see* discussion in chap. 8).
25. *Gelbman v. Gelbman*, 23 N.Y.2d 434, 245 N.E.2d 192, 297 N.Y.S.2d 529 (1969).
26. *Rounds Brothers v. McDaniel*, 133 Ky. 669, 676, 118 S.W. 956, 958 (1909); *Carricato v. Carricato, supra* note 20.
27. *Smith v. Gilbert*, 80 Ark. 525, 98 S.W. 115 (1906).
28. ARK. STAT. ANN. §34–2001 (Supp. 1979).
29. KAN. STAT. ANN. §§38–108, 109 (1981).
30. LA. CODE CIV. PROC., art. 3991 *et. seq*. (1961 & Supp. 1982).
31. OKLA. STAT. ANN. tit. 10, §§91–93 (Supp. 1982).
32. CAL. CIV. CODE §§60–70 (1982).
33. CONN. GEN. STAT. ANN. 46b–150 *et. seq*. (Supp. 1982).
34. *Street v. Cobb County School Dist*. 520 F. Supp. 1170 (N.D.Ga. 1981).

VIII

Medical Care, Contraception, Abortion, and Pregnancy

In general, no doctor, surgeon, nurse, or other medical professional may treat a patient of any age without his or her consent. Technically, if a physician operates on or even touches a patient without consent, the physician may be liable for assault or battery.

Traditionally, children have been deemed legally incapable of consenting to their own medical care or treatment.[1] Accordingly, only a child's parents (or guardians) may provide the necessary consent for medical treatment; without it, a doctor or medical professional who provides treatment will risk liability. This often prevents children from seeking essential medical care and inhibits doctors and other medical professionals from providing necessary treatment. These rules have begun to change, and most states now recognize special circumstances that permit children to obtain, and physicians to render, medical services without the permission of a parent or guardian. Moreover, a number of states have lowered the age at which minors are deemed capable of providing independent consent to medical treatment.

This chapter describes the legal rights of, and limitations on, young people obtaining medical care. It must be emphasized that the focus is on what the law says, and not necessarily on what will happen in "real life." While the legal rights of young people to obtain medical care without parental consent or knowledge have grown in the past decade, many practical obstacles still remain. For social, moral, and financial reasons, many hospitals and doctors will not treat young people without parental consent even when the law permits them to do so. It is hoped that as more medical personnel and more young people become familiar with the rights described in this chapter, it will become easier to realize the theoretical gains that have been made in recent years that have given adolescents greater autonomy.

Medical Care

At what age may a young person see a doctor and receive medical care without parental permission?

Generally, it is assumed that the age is the same as "the age of majority" in each state (see Appendix B). This, however, is not always so.

A number of state laws permit a young person to consent for medical treatment at an age *lower* than the age of majority. In Alabama, for example, it is set at 14, in Oregon it is 15, and in Rhode Island and South Carolina the age of consent is 16.[2] A few states set no minimum age at all and allow consent based on factors other than age.

What are the exceptions to the rule that medical care may be given children only with parental consent?

In all states, a child may be treated without parental consent in the case of an *emergency*.

Children who are *emancipated* may be treated on their own consent alone.

In some states, children who are deemed *mature minors* also may be treated upon their own request.

Finally, special types of medical care, such as treatment for drug or alcohol, venereal disease, prenatal care, or an abortion, may be obtained by a child without parental consent under certain circumstances.

What is a medical "emergency"?

An emergency is a situation in which medical care is required immediately and the parents or guardians of the child cannot be reached in time to provide consent. To qualify as an emergency however, the child's life need not be threatened. It is enough that a delay in treatment may increase the risk to the patient's health or that treatment is necessary to alleviate physical pain or discomfort.[3]

What is an "emancipated minor"?

As explained more fully in chapter VII, the determination of when a minor becomes emancipated varies from state to state, but ordinarily occurs when a minor marries, joins the armed forces, is declared emancipated by a court of law or, in some states, has a residence and manages his or her own financial affairs.

In a number of states, the law expressly permits emancipated minors to consent to their own medical care and treatment without permission from parents. These states include Alabama, Alaska, California, Colorado, Delaware, Florida, Idaho, Illinois, Indiana, Maryland, Minnesota, Mississippi, Montana, Nebraska, Nevada, New Jersey, New Mexico, North Carolina, Oklahoma, Pennsylvania, and Virginia.[4]

In California and Colorado, the law provides that any person who is married, regardless of age, or any person who is at least fifteen years old who is living separate from his parents or guardians for *any* length of time, and is managing his own financial affairs, regardless of the *source* of his income, may consent to hospital, medical, surgical, and dental care for himself.[5]

In Nevada, the young person need not be financially independent of his or her parents but must have lived separately from the parents for at least four months.[6]

In a number of other states, any young person who is, or has been, married or who has had a child may consent to medical care without the permission of anyone else.[7]

What is a "mature minor"?

A *mature minor* generally means a child intelligent enough to understand and appreciate the nature and consequences of a specific medical treatment. Factors to be considered in determining whether a child might qualify as a mature minor are age, intellectual maturity, and the expected benefits of the proposed treatment. If a physician or medical professional believes that a child is a mature minor, he or she may provide medical treatment without first obtaining the consent of the child's parents. (Of course, as stated at the outset of this chapter, simply because a child is a mature minor does not mean that he will be able to locate a physician willing to treat him without parental consent.)

A number of states (including Arkansas, Idaho, Mississippi,

and Nevada) provide by statute that young people, regardless of age, who have "sufficient intelligence to understand and appreciate the consequences of the proposed surgical or medical treatment or procedures" may consent themselves.[8] This doctrine has been granted judicial recognition in a number of other states (including Washington, Kansas, Michigan, and the District of Columbia).[9] The United States Supreme Court has endorsed the mature minor exception in the context of sexually related medical care.[10]

If a young person consents to his own medical treatment, will the doctor be liable to lawsuits if it turns out that the child misrepresented his right to consent?

Probably not. A number of states now provide *statutory immunity* to physicians who treat children without obtaining the consent of their parents, who relied on the good-faith representation of the child that he was of age, emancipated, or for some other reason did not need parental permission.[11]

Contraception

Are contraceptives legal?

Yes. In 1965, the United States Supreme Court said that states could not prohibit doctors from prescribing contraceptive devices to married couples since it would interfere with the right of privacy of those desiring them.[12] In 1972, the Court expanded this ruling by holding that a statute that prohibited the prescription of contraceptives to unmarried persons was unconstitutional.[13]

Do minors have the right to seek and obtain over-the-counter birth control devices without prior parental consent?

Yes. Generally, over-the-counter birth control devices (condoms and vaginal foams) are available to anyone who wishes to buy them, regardless of age. Laws that made it illegal to sell nonprescription birth control devices to minors were struck down a few years ago by the United States Supreme Court because they violated a minor's right to privacy. The Court held that

> in a field that by definition concerns the most intimate of human activities and relationships, deci-

sions whether to accomplish or to prevent conception are among the most private and sensitive. . . . Restrictions on the distribution of contraceptives clearly burden the freedom to make such decision.[14]

If a drugstore (or any store) is permitted to sell nonprescription birth control devices to minors, there is no legal duty on the part of store owners or employees to inform the parents of a minor who purchases them.

Do minors have the right to obtain prescription birth control devices without parental consent?

Most states have laws permitting minors access to prescription contraceptives in some circumstances, though these laws are difficult to categorize. In Alaska, California, Colorado, the District of Columbia, Kentucky, Maryland, Minnesota, North Carolina, Oregon, Tennessee, and Virginia, minors of any age may obtain birth control devices from doctors willing to prescribe them. In Georgia, Louisiana, and Mississippi, any female regardless of age may obtain these devices. And in Arkansas, Idaho, Massachusetts, Mississippi, and Nevada, the minor, regardless of age, need only be of sufficient intelligence to understand the consequences to obtain birth control prescriptions. Other states use age as the criterion for consent; in Delaware, for example, a person need be 12 years old; in Alabama and Hawaii, 14 years; and in Kansas, Rhode Island, South Carolina, and Texas, the young person must be 16 years old.

Several states (including Illinois, Maine, and Pennsylvania) permit doctors to give prescriptions whenever in their opinion there would be a serious health hazard if the minor were not treated. In these states minors do not have a clear *right* to obtain medical assistance, but if doctors are willing to cooperate, the minors will be able to be treated.

In the states that have no laws governing this issue, the question remains whether treatment for contraception falls under the general rule that prior parental consent is required for all medical care for children, or whether sex-related medical treatment (including prescription birth control devices) qualifies as an exception based on a child's right to privacy.

May public clinics require parental consent before prescribing birth control devices to minors?

The answer is uncertain. In a number of states, local welfare departments are required or permitted to distribute birth control information and devices to minors of childbearing age without the consent of their parents.[15] In addition, federal law mandates that states offer family-planning services and supplies to *all persons* of childbearing age, without regard to marital status or age, who are eligible for Medicaid or Social Security payments.[16] It is unclear whether states may require the written consent of a minor's parents before such services and supplies may be furnished.[17]

A federal court has declared unconstitutional Utah's regulation that permitted state officials, funded by Social Security money, to provide contraceptive services and supplies to minors only with the permission of a parent or guardian.[18] Because these state regulations conflicted with federal laws mandating supplies without regard to age or marital status, the Utah regulations were declared illegal. The federal court went even further, however, and held that minors have a constitutional right to access to contraceptives that cannot be abridged by parental consent requirements.[19] The Supreme Court affirmed the holding of the district court, declaring Utah's regulations to be unconstitutional, but *only* on the grounds that they were in conflict with federal law.[20] The Supreme Court has yet to rule on the constitutional right of minors to obtain prescription contraceptive devices.

Do minors have the right to obtain birth control devices without their parents being notified?

The issue is currently being litigated in many courts throughout the country.

In the majority of states (including Colorado, Florida, Illinois, Maine, Mississippi, and Tennessee) the law permits *doctors* to provide birth control information and to prescribe contraceptives to patients of any age without parental consent or notification.[21] In other states, physicians may prescribe contraceptives, but the statutes expressly *permit* notification to the parents.[22] In those states that permit young people to consent to *general* medical care, they may obtain prescription contraceptives as a specific type of general care.

Many states have established voluntary birth control clinics that distribute contraceptives to minors without notifying parents. In Michigan, a group of parents went to court challenging such a clinic, not on the grounds that it dispensed birth control devices, but because the clinic failed to *inform* the parents that their children were being treated.

The court ruled against the parents, holding that a state may provide birth control information and devices to persons of any age without giving notice to anyone.[23] In deciding the case, the court observed:

> Though the state has somewhat broader authority to regulate the conduct of children than that of adults, minors do possess a constitutionally protected right of privacy. . . . As with adults, the minors' right of privacy includes the right to obtain contraceptives. . . . The desire of the parents to know of such activities by their children is understandable. However, the only issue . . . is whether there is a constitutional obligation on the Center to notify them.

While this decision, if followed by other courts, would indicate that states may establish a voluntary birth control clinic that distributes contraceptives to minors without notifying parents, this does not mean that when states *require* parental notification, such a requirement violates the minor's constitutional rights. To understand this statement, however, two historical developments must be discussed. First, in 1981, Congress passed a law that provides money to create demonstration projects, to be funded by the federal government, which would provide counseling and medical service to adolescents.[24] As a condition of receiving money under this law, the demonstration project must agree to provide parental *notification* and, in most circumstances, *consent*, before administering family planning services to adolescents. This law reflects Congress's concern that parents play a direct role in the lives of their adolescent children. To date, however, this law has had a modest effect on state practices since it affects *only* those programs funded under the act. The much greater amount of federal money that goes to recipients of Social Security dollars in the form of Aid to Families with Dependent Children (AFDC) or Medicaid, still is covered by the mandate that medical supplies be given to adolescents without parental involvement.[25]

Early in 1983, federal regulations were issued requiring that facilities receiving federal money notify the parents of unemancipated minors within 10 working days that prescriptions for birth control have been dispensed to their children. These regulations would have applied to nearly 5,000 family planning clinics serving a total of 615,000 people age 17 and under.[26] However, the regulations never went into effect. After being declared unconstitutional by two federal courts of appeals,[27] they were withdrawn by the secretary of health and human services.[28]

Are doctors susceptible to lawsuits if they provide contraceptive devices to minors?

No case has been discovered where a doctor was found liable for damages resulting from the prescription of contraceptives to a minor of any age without parental consent.

Abortion

May a minor obtain an abortion without the consent of her parents?

Yes. A more complete understanding of this answer requires a brief historical account of legislation and litigation concerning this issue.

When the United States Supreme Court ruled in 1973, that states could not prohibit abortions if performed through the second trimester (twenty-four weeks) of a woman's pregnancy,[29] the question of whether the decision applied to *unmarried minor* females remained unanswered. Many states began to pass laws covering this situation, some of which made it impossible for unmarried minor females to obtain an abortion without obtaining prior parental consent.

In 1976, the Supreme Court struck down a Missouri statute that made it a crime for a physician to perform an abortion on an unmarried minor without parental permission.[30] The Missouri law was so strict that it gave parents an absolute veto over their daughter's decision to abort. It was this fact—that a minor female had no recourse whatsoever if her parents withheld permission—that made the law constitutionally unacceptable. The Court stated, "Any independent interest a parent may have in the termination of their daughter's pregnancy is no more weighty than the right of privacy of the competent minor mature enough to have become pregnant."

In 1979, the Supreme Court reviewed a Massachusetts

law that required parental consent but also provided that, if consent was denied, the minor female could petition a court, which had the power, after a hearing, to overrule her parents' decision if it believed that termination of the child's pregnancy was in her best interest. Under the Massachusetts law, the minor's parents had a right to be present at the hearing and offer their reasons for denying consent.

The Supreme Court ruled that this law also was unconstitutional for two main reasons: first, because it permitted a court to deny the child's right to an abortion even if she was mature and fully competent to make an independent decision; second, because it required parental consultation in all cases and left no room for a child to seek court permission without first notifying her parents.[31]

The Supreme Court differentiated a child's decision to terminate a pregnancy from other types of decisions for which parental consent is required. The Court noted that the pregnant minor's options are much more limited than, say, a minor unable to obtain parental consent to marry. The Court stated:

> A minor not permitted to marry before the age of majority is required simply to postpone her decision. . . . A pregnant adolescent, however, cannot preserve for long the possibility of aborting, which effectively expires in a matter of weeks from the onset of pregnancy. . . . Moreover, the potentially severe detriment facing a pregnant woman is not mitigated by her minority. Indeed, considering her probable education, employment skills, financial resources, and emotional maturity, unwanted motherhood may be exceptionally burdensome for a minor. . . . In sum, there are few situations in which denying a minor the right to make an important decision will have consequences so grave and indelible.

In 1983, the Supreme Court upheld a Missouri law that requires all nonemancipated minors to obtain parental or judicial consent for an abortion unless the minor is found by the Court to be mature enough to make her own decision.[32] As a result of this decision, it is constitutional to require unemancipated minors to obtain parental consent provided the minor has the right to go to court and seek a judical declaration that an abortion should be performed without the necessity of parental consent. Where this is done, the court *must* grant permission if it finds that the minor is mature enough to make her own decision. If the court finds that the minor is not mature enough to do this, it nonetheless must give permission if, in the court's own view, the abortion would be in the child's best interests.

Does this mean that every unmarried woman under the age of eighteen has an absolute right to consent to an abortion without any parental involvement whatever?

No. In 1981, the Supreme Court ruled that a Utah law requiring physicians to notify parents "if possible" before performing an abortion on an immature, unemancipated minor is constitutional.[33] In Utah, a physician is required to notify parents "if under the circumstances, in the exercise of reasonable diligence, he can ascertain their identity and location and it is feasible or practicable to give them notification."[34] The Supreme Court was careful, however, to emphasize that it ruled only that this law is constitutional when the minor is *immature and unemancipated*. Moreover, the Utah law only requires *notice*, which can be given even *after* the abortion is performed. Under this law, parents do not have a right to veto and need not be consulted by the physician to determine their views on the propriety of the abortion. The Supreme Court recognized that a notice requirement "may inhibit some minors from seeking abortions," but ruled that the law was nonetheless constitutional as applied to immature children.

In 1983, the Court stated that a notice requirement as applied to a mature or emancipated child would be unconstitutional.[35] Thus, a minor who could demonstrate her capacity for mature judgment has a constitutional right to obtain an abortion without her parents' knowledge if she believes that notification would not be in her best interests.

A number of states (including Maine, Maryland, Minnesota, Montana, Nebraska, Nevada, and Rhode Island) have laws that require parental notification of the abortion decision in at least some circumstances.[36]

Do parents have the right to force their minor daughter to terminate her pregnancy if she opposes?

No. The same right of a minor child that permits her to

obtain an abortion without parental consent also guarantees the right of a child *not* to abort if she so desires.[37]

Pregnancy

If an unmarried young woman decides against an abortion, and elects to bear her child, can she receive medical care and treatment related to pregnancy without the consent of her parents?

Yes. In almost every state pregnant females may consent to most pregnancy-related health services.[38]

In a very few states, however, the pregnant minor must first reach a certain age, such as 14 in Hawaii and 12 in Delaware[39] (see Appendix D).

Once the child is born, of course, the minor mother may consent for the medical treatment of herself and her child, whether or not she is married.[40]

Venereal Disease, Alcohol, and Drug Addiction

May a minor seek and receive treatment for venereal diseases (syphilis, gonorrhea, herpes simplex, and so forth) without his parents' permission?

Yes. In virtually every state there are special provisions that permit minors of any age to obtain free medical care for venereal diseases or suspected venereal diseases without parental consent.[41]

A few states still have age requirements, but most of these are either 12 or 14[42] (see Appendix D).

May young people receive treatment for drug or alcohol addictions without parental consent?

Yes, in many states.[43] Such treatment is usually rendered free of charge as well.

In a few states, the young person must be at least a certain age, such as 12 in Vermont.[44]

Disclosure to Parents

If a young person receives treatment of any kind from a doctor without prior parental consent, will his parents have to know about it after the treatment is rendered?

Not necessarily. In every state, communication between a doctor and patient is considered "privileged";[45] that is, information communicated to or discovered by a physician (or nurse, dentist, surgeon, and so forth) cannot be disclosed by the physician to anyone other than the patient or to persons authorized by the patient. The medical profession considers confidentiality a high, ethical standard.[46] Recent judicial interpretations of the doctor-patient privilege indicate that it extends to minors.[47]

Despite the existence of the doctor-patient privilege, there are some instances in which physicians may—or must—relay information about a patient to others. The degree of confidentiality of a minor's medical care depends on the age of the patient and the type of treatment.

With regard to general medical treatment, a number of states permit physicians to use their own judgment in advising parents that their child is seeking treatment.[48] A Minnesota law permits doctors to inform parents when failure to inform them may jeopardize the health of the child, and in Kentucky, disclosure to parents is permitted when it would be beneficial to the minor's health.[49] In California, the law protects the rights of the child by stating that a physician may contact the parents only if the child indicates where they live.[50] In Nevada a doctor does not have to notify a parent when the doctor believes such efforts would jeopardize treatment.[51]

As discussed earlier, notice to parents of an immature and unemancipated minor's intent to abort may lawfully be required by state law.

In many states, doctors must inform public health agencies about cases of venereal disease,[52] but these reports are usually kept confidential and are not disclosed to parents. In some states, the law permits a doctor to treat a child for venereal disease without informing the child's parents,[53] and in many other states, including New York, the law *prohibits* notification of any treatment for venereal disease.[54]

Finally, federal drug and alcohol regulations, which prohibit disclosure of treatment regardless of the age of the patient, may make it unlawful to states to permit disclosure.

Court-Ordered Treatment

If a parent refuses to provide necessary medical treatment for a child can a court require the treatment?

Yes. When a child urgently needs medical attention and the parents refuse to provide it, even if their objection is based on religious grounds, a court may order necessary care, treatment, or surgery. A common example occurs when a court orders a blood transfusion to save the life of a child over the objections of parents who base their refusal on their religious beliefs.[55] (Parents who fail to secure necessary medical services for their children may be liable to a finding of *neglect*, pursuant to most statutory definitions of that term[56] (see chapter IV)).

As the Supreme Court said in another context, parents are free to become martyrs themselves, but they are not free to make martyrs of their children.[57]

Under what conditions will a court order treatment of a child over parental objections?

Almost every court will require treatment if the life of the child is endangered.

For conditions that are less than life-threatening there is no clear rule, but courts often consider the risk of the operation involved, the psychological impact of the untreated disease or condition on the child, and the wishes of the child.

A few illustrations will demonstrate the different approaches courts have taken on this issue. In 1942, a Washington court refused to order the amputation of a child's deformed arm when medical testimony indicated that the operation was dangerous, even though it would enable the child to lead a normal life.[58] In 1955, a New York court refused to order corrective surgery of a boy's harelip and cleft palate even though the operation involved little risk and could become more difficult with time.[59] In the latter case, the parents objected to the operation for religious reasons, but the court based its decision on the right of the child, then fourteen years of age, to make up his own mind.

But opposite decisions have been reached also. In a 1970

New York case, the mother of a boy whose face was disfigured objected to cosmetic surgery since it would involve blood transfusions to which she objected on religious grounds. Despite the fact that an operation was not necessary to preserve the life or health of the child, the court ordered surgery, since without it the boy would be unable to lead a normal, useful life.[60] And in 1972, an Iowa court ordered the surgical removal of a child's tonsils and adenoids over the religious objections of the father, who preferred medication as the treatment. The court reasoned that it had the duty to preserve the health of a child even though there was no evidence of an immediate threat to his life or limb.[61]

How does a court order medical treatment over parental objection?

Usually the matter is brought to the attention of the court by a hospital where the child is located. If the court decides to order treatment, it may temporarily suspend the rights of the parent to control and care for the child and appoint a guardian—often the superintendent of the hospital—who then gives consent for the treatment or surgery.[62]

Do parents have the authority to have their children sterilized?

Not without court approval. Although parents have the right and duty to care for their child's health, their authority is not absolute. If sterilization is to be performed at all, it may be done only in accordance with state law and with court approval; parents alone do not possess this extraordinary power.[63]

Courts generally do not grant parents permission to have their children sterilized unless there is a compelling reason, such as severe mental or physical retardation. Connecticut law, for example, permits parents to seek medical authorization for sterilization of inmates in state institutions for the mentally incompetent.[64] A number of courts have ruled that unless a statute specifically empowers a court to authorize sterilizations, there is no authority to do so.[65] Recently, however, several courts have concluded that the general *parens patriae* grant of power to juvenile or probate courts is sufficient to authorize a judge to order sterilization of incompetents when parents request it and there is a compelling reason to require such a drastic operation.[66]

Civil Commitments

Can young people be placed in mental institutions by their parents without a prior court hearing?

Yes, if the mental hospital's medical staff concludes that the child is in need of care and treatment. The United States Supreme Court recently held that extensive precommitment procedures, such as a court hearing at which the child would be represented by an attorney or other representative who would be in a position to oppose the planned placement, are not constitutionally required.[67]

While the decision has been considered by many to be a blow against the due process rights of children, it conforms to the general theory stated at the outset of this chapter that parents have the right to determine their child's medical needs. According to Chief Justice Burger, who wrote the opinion of the Supreme Court:

> Our jurisprudence historically has reflected Western civilization concepts of the family as a unit with broad parental authority over minor children. Our cases have consistently followed that course; our constitutional system long ago rejected any notion that a child is "the mere creature of the State" and, on the contrary, asserted that parents generally "have the right, coupled with the high duty, to recognize and prepare [their children] for additional obligations." Surely, this includes a "high duty" to recognize symptoms of illness and to seek and follow medical advice. The law's concept of the family rests on a presumption that parents possess what a child lacks in maturity, experience and capacity for judgment required for making life's difficult decisions. More important, historically it has recognized that natural bonds of affection lead parents to act in the best interests of their children. Most children, even in adolescence, simply are not able to make sound judgments concerning many decisions including their need for medical care and treatment. Parents can and must make those judgments.[68]

The Supreme Court did require, however, that a hospital staff physician, in addition to the child's parents, decide that a child is in need of medical care, and that the physician's decision be "independent"; that is, free from parental influence and based on sources of information traditionally relied upon by physicians, including consultation with behavioral specialists. The Court also held that a "neutral fact finder" must make a preadmission inquiry into the child's background, using all available sources, including parents, schools, and social agencies, as well as an interview with the child. Finally, the Court ruled that once a child is committed, his continuing need for commitment must be reviewed periodically by a "similarly independent procedure."

Even though the Court ruled that court hearings are not constitutionally required, this does not mean that states are prohibited from establishing procedures stricter than those set forth by the Court. Some states, for example, stipulate that parents may commit children only if they are under a certain age, such as 12 or 13, and that if children over this age are to be committed by their parents, they must give their own consent.[69] Other state laws provide that children may be committed by their parents but, if they are over a certain age, they may obtain their own release.[70] Michigan law states that if a child objects he or she must receive a hearing within 7 days after filing an objection.[71]

May a child obtain psychiatric or psychological treatment without parental consent?

In some states, yes. In Virginia, for example, a minor is considered an adult for the purpose of consenting to mental health related treatment.[72] In states that emancipate minors for these purposes, however, it remains to be determined whether parents may obtain access to such records and who is to pay for the services.

Payment

Who is financially responsible for a young person's medical bills?

Ordinarily parents are obliged to pay for the medical care and treatment of their children.[73] In a New Jersey case that illustrates this rule, a young person went to get medical care for a sprained ankle that his parents refused to treat. The court held that the parents had to pay the doctor for all expenses incurred.[74]

A minor who consents to medical treatment because he claims to be "emancipated" or a "mature minor" (see chapter VII) will be liable for any medical bills. Almost every statute that permits an emancipated minor to consent to medical care without parental permission also states that the contract made with the doctor or hospital is *not* subject to the usual right of a minor to disaffirm.[75]

If a young person is part of a family health insurance plan, may he charge medical bills to the insurance company, even if treatment was received without parental consent?

Probably. Under most insurance plans, every member of the family is considered "an insured," and state insurance laws ordinarily provide that "an insured" party may file a claim for payment to him or herself or to the party who extended the medical services.[76]

Most insurance policies require claims filed with doctors or hospitals to be signed by the *patient* (rather than the policy holder, which in the case of most family insurance policies would be the parent). The only other necessary elements for payment are that the child be listed as a dependent beneficiary and that the policy identification number be written on the form. (Of course, if a child files a claim under a policy held by a parent, it is likely that information regarding the nature of the medical treatment will be disclosed to the parent.)

NOTES

1. *See, e.g., Bonner v. Moran,* 126 F.2d 121 (D.C. Cir. 1941); *Lacey v. Laird,* 166 Ohio St. 12, 139 N.E.2d 25 (1956).
2. Ala. Code §22–8–4 (1977); Oreg. Rev. Stat. §109.640 (1981; R.I. Gen. Laws §23–4.6–1 (1979); S.C. Code Ann. §20–7–280 (Supp. 1982).
3. Prosser, *Torts,* 103 (4th ed. 1971).
4. Ala. Code §22–8–4 (1977); Alaska Stat. §09.65.100(a)(5) (Supp. 1982); Cal. Civ. Code §34.6 (1982); Colo. Rev. Stat. §13–13–22–103 (Supp. 1982); Del. Code Ann. tit. 13, §707 (Supp. 1981); Fla. Stat. Ann. §743.01 (Supp. 1981); Idaho Code §32–101 (Supp. 1980); Ill. Ann. Stat. ch. 111, §4501 (1978); Ind. Code Ann. §16–8–4–1 (1973); Md. Health-Gen. Code Ann. §20–102 (1982); Minn. Stat. Ann.

§144.341 (Supp. 1982); MONT. CODE ANN. §41–1–402)(1)(b)(1981); NEB. REV. STAT. §38–101 (1974); NEV. REV. STAT. §129.030(1)(a)(1981); N.J. STAT. ANN. §9:17A–1 (1976); N.M. STAT. ANN. §24–10–1 (1981); N.C. GEN STAT. §90.21.5 (1981); OKLA. STAT. ANN. tit. 63, §2602(a)(2) (Supp. 1982); PA. STAT. ANN. tit. 35 §10101 (1977); VA. CODE §54–352.2 (1982).

5. CAL. CIV. CODE §34.6 (1982); COLO. REV. STAT. §13–22–103(2) (Supp. 1982).
6. NEV. REV. STAT. §129.030(1)(a)(1981).
7. *See, e.g.*, ALA. CODE §22–8–4 (1977); COLO. REV. STAT. §13–22–103 (Supp. 1982); IND. CODE ANN. §16–8–4–1 (1973); MINN. STAT. ANN. §144.342 (Supp. 1982); N.J. STAT. ANN. §9:17A–1 (1976); N.Y. PUB. HEALTH LAW §§2504 (1977).
8. ARK. STAT. ANN. §82–363(g) (1976). *See also* IDAHO CODE §39–4302 (1977); MISS. CODE ANN. §41–41–3(h) (1981); NEV. REV. STAT. §129.030 (1981).
9. *Smith v. Seibly*, 72 Wash. 2d 16, 431 P.2d 719 (1967); *Younts v. St. Francis Hospital*, 205 Kan. 292, 469 P.2d 330 (1970); *Bakker v. Welsh*, 144 Mich. 632, 108 N.".94 (1906); *Bishop v. Shurly*, 237 Mich. 76, 211 N.W. 75 (1926); *In re P.J.*, 12 Crim. L. Rptr. 2549 (D.C. Sup. Ct. Feb. 1, 1983); but see *Bonner v. Moran, supra* note 1, where the court refused to apply the doctrine when used to supply the consent of a person *other* than the child receiving treatment.
10. *See, e.g., Bellotti v. Baird*, 443 U.S. 622 (1979).
11. *See, e.g.*, ALA. CODE §22–8–7 (1977); GA. CODE ANN. 31–9–6 (1982); IDAHO CODE §39–4302 (1977); PA. STAT. ANN. tit. 35, §10105 (1977).
12. *Griswold v. Connecticut*, 381 U.S. 479 (1965).
13. *Eisenstadt v. Baird*, 405 U.S. 438 (1972).
14. *Carey v. Population Services Intl.*, 431 U.S. 678 (1977).
15. *See, e.g.*, N.Y. SOC. SERV. LAW §350 (1)(e)(1976).
16. 42 U.S.C.A. §§602(a)(15) (Supp. 1982), 1396d(a)(4)(c) (1976); 45 C.F.R. §1392.21 (a)(1981).
17. *See, e.g., T. H. v. Jones*, 425 F. Supp. 873 (D. Utah 1975), *aff'd men.*, 425 U.S. 986 (1976). A number of Supreme Court justices have indicated that minors have a constitutional right to obtain prescription contraceptive devices. *See Carey v. Population Services International*, 435 U.S. 678, 691–99 (1977)(Justice Brennan, Marshall, Stewart, and Blackmun). But one justice stated that he would describe as "frivolous" the "argument that a minor has the constitutional right to put contraceptives to their intended use." *Id.* at 713 (Justice Stevens).
18. *T.H. v. Jones, supra*, note 17.
19. Id. 425 F. Supp. at 880–880.
20. *Jones v. T.H.*, 425 U.S. 986 (1976).
21. *See, e.g.*, COLO. REV. STAT. §13–22–105 (1974); FLA. STAT. ANN. §381.382(5)(1973); ILL. ANN. STAT. ch. 111 1/2, §§4651(1) (Supp.

1982); ME. REV. STAT. ANN. tit. 22 §1908 (1980); MISS. CODE ANN. §41–42–7 (1981); TENN. CODE ANN. §53–4607 (1977).
22. *See, e.g.*, OKLA. STAT. ANN. tit. 63 §2602(B)(Supp. 1982); OREG. REV. STAT. §109.640 (1981).
23. *Doe v. Irwin*, 615 F2d 1162 (6th Cir. 1980), *cert. denied*, 449 U.S. 829 (1980).
24. 42 U.S.C. §§300A *et. seq*. (1982).
25. *See* 42 U.S.C.A. §§602(a)(15)(Supp. 1982), 1396d(a)(4)(C) (1974); 45 C.F.R. §1392.21(a)(1981).
26. *N.Y. Times*, Jan. 25, 1983, P. A3, col 1–2.
27. *Planned Parenthood v. Heckler*, 712 F.2d 650 (D.C. Cir. 1983); *State of New York v. Heckler*, 719 F.2d 1191 (2d. Cir. 1983).
28. *N.Y. Times*, Dec. 1, 1983, p. B13, Col. 3–4.
29. *Roe v. Wade*, 410 U.S. 113 (1973).
30. *Planned Parenthood v. Danforth*, 428 U.S. 52 (1976).
31. *Bellotti v. Baird*, *supra* note 10.
32. *Planned Parenthood Assn. of Kansas City v. Ashcroft*, 76 L. Ed. 2d 733 (1983).
33. *H.L. v. Matheson*, 450 U.S. 398 (1981).
34. Id. at 405.
35. *City of Akron v. Akron Center for Reproductive Health, Inc.*, 76 L. Ed. 2d 687, 710, m. 31 (1983).
36. *See, e.g.*, ME. REV. STAT. ANN. tit. 22 §1597 (1980); MD. HEALTH-GEN. CODE ANN. §20–103 (1982); MINN. STAT. ANN. §144.343 (Supp. 1982); MONT. CODE ANN. §50–20–107(a)(b)(1981); NEB. REV. STAT. §28–333 (Supp. 1979); NEV. REV. STAT. §442.255 (1981); R.I. Gen. Laws §23–4.7–6 (Supp. 1982).
37. *See, e.g., In re Smith*, 16 Md. App. 209, 295 A.2d 238 (1972).
38. *See, e.g.*, ALA. CODE §22–8–6(1977); ALASKA STAT. §09.65.100(a) (4) (Supp. 1982); ARK. STAT. ANN. §82–363(d) (1976); CAL. CIVIL CODE §34.5 (1982); DEL. CODE ANN. tit. 13 §708(a)(1981); FLA. STAT. ANN. §743.065(1) (Supp. 1981); GA. CODE ANN. §31–9–2(5)(1982): KAN. STAT. ANN. §38–123 (1981); KY. REV. STAT. ANN. §214.185(1)(1982); MD. HEALTH GEN. ANN. CODE §20–102 (1982); MINN. STAT. ANN. §144.343(1) (Supp. 1982); MISS. CODE ANN. §41–41–3(i)(1981); MO. ANN. STAT. §431.061(1)(4) (a) (Supp. 1983); MONT. CODE ANN. §41–1–402(c) (1981); N.J. STAT. ANN. §9:17A–1 (1976); N.M. STAT. ANN. §24–1–13 (1981); N.C. GEN. STAT. §90–21.5(a)(ii) (1981); OKLA. STAT. ANN. tit. 35 §10103 (1977); UTAH CODE ANN. §78–14–5(4)(f) (1977); VA. CODE §54–325.2(D)(2) (1982).
39. *See, e.g.*, DEL. CODE ANN. tit. 13, §708(a)(1981); HAWAII REV. STAT. §577A–2 (Supp. 1981).
40. See Statutes listed *supra* note 7.
41. *See, e.g.*, ALASKA STAT. §09.65.100(a)(4) (Supp. 1982); CONN. GEN. STAT. ANN §19–89a (1977); N.J. STAT ANN. §9:17 A–4 (1976); N.Y. PUB. HEALTH LAW §2305 (Supp. 1982).
42. *See, e.g.*, ALA. CODE §22–16–9 (1977); CAL. CIV. CODE §34.7 (1982); DEL. CODE tit. 13, §708 (1981); IDAHO CODE §39–3801 (1977).

43. *See, e.g.*, COLO. REV. STAT. §13–22–102 (1973); ALA. CODE ANN. §22–8–6 (1977); CAL. CIV. CODE §34.7 (1982); MINN. STAT. ANN. §144.343 (Supp. 1982); MASS. GEN. LAWS ANN. ch. 112, §12E (Supp. 1982); MICH. COMP. LAWS §722.51 (Supp. 1981); 21 U.S.C.A. §1175 (1981).
44. *See, e.g.*, VT. STAT. ANN. tit. 18 §4226 (Supp. 1971); TEX. FAM. CODE ANN. §35.03 (1975).
45. *See, e.g.*, N.Y. CIV. PRAC. LAW §4504 (Supp. 1982); CAL. EVID. CODE §§990–1007 (1966 & Supp. 1982); ILL. STAT. ANN. ch. 51, §5.1 (Supp. 1982).
46. The American Medical Association *Principles of Medical Ethics* §9 (1971) reads: "A physician may not reveal the confidences entrusted to him in the course of medical attendance . . . unless he is required to do so by law or unless it becomes necessary in order to protect the welfare of the individual or of the community."
47. *See, e.g., Roberts v. Superior Court*, 9 Cal. 3d 330, 508 P.2d 309, 107 Cal. Rptr. 309 (1973).
48. *See, e.g.*, N.J. STAT. ANN. §9:17A–5 (1976).
49. MINN. STAT. ANN. §144.346 (Supp. 1982); KY. REV. STAT. §214.185 (1982).
50. CAL. CIV. CODE §34.6 (1982).
51. NEV. REV. STAT §129.030 (1981).
52. *See, e.g.*, N.Y. PUB. HEALTH. L. §2300 (1977).
53. *See, e.g.*, ARK. STAT. ANN. §82–631 (1976); FLA. STAT. ANN. §384.061 (1973); GA. CODE ANN. §31–17–7 (1982); HAWAII REV. STAT. tit. 31 §577A–3 (Supp. 1981); ILL. ANN. STAT. ch. 111, §4505 (Supp. 1982); KAN. STAT. ANN §65–2892 (1980); LA. REV. STAT. §40–1065.1 (1977); MAINE REV. STAT. ANN. tit. 32 §3292 (1978); MICH. COMP. LAWS ANN. §333.5257 (1980); MO. REV. STAT. §431.062 (Supp. 1983); DEL. CODE ANN. tit. 13, §708 (1981).
54. N.Y. PUB. HEALTH L. §2306 (1977).
55. *Jehovah's Witnesses in the State of Washington v. King Co. Hospital*, 278 F. Supp. 488 (W.D. Wash. 1967) *aff'd per curiam*, 390 U.S. 598 (1968).
56. *See, e.g., State v. Pericone*, 37 N.J. 463, 181 A.2d 751, *cert. denied*, 371 U.S. 890 (1962).
57. *Prince v. Massachusetts*, 321 U.S. 158, 170 (1943).
58. *In re Hudson*, 13 Wash. 2d 673, 126 P.2d 765 (1942).
59. *Matter of Seiferth*, 309 N.Y. 80, 127 N.E.2d 820, 137 N.Y.S. 2d 35 (1955). *See also In re Green*, 448 Pa. 338, 292 A.2d 387 (1972); 452 Pa. 373, 307 A.2d 279 (1973).
60. *In re Sampson*, 65 Misc. 2d 658, 317 N.Y.S.2d 641 (Fam. Ct. Ulster Co. 1970); *aff'd*. 37 A.D.2d 668, 323 N.Y.S.2d 253 (3rd Dept. 1971); *aff'd per curiam* 29 N.Y.2d 900, 328 N.Y.S.2d 686 (1972).
61. *In re Karwath*, 199 N.W.2d 147 (Iowa 1972).
62. *See, e.g., State v. Pericone, supra*, note 60.
63. *See, e.g., A.L. v. G.R.H.* 163 Ind. App. 636, 325 N.E.2d 501 (1975), *cert. denied*, 425 U.S 936 (1976).

64. Conn. Gen. Stat. §19–569g.
65. *See, e.g., Hudson v. Hudson,* 373 So. 2d 310 (Ala. 1979); *Guardianship of Kemp,* 43 Cal. App. 3d 758, 118 Cal. Rptr. 64 (1974); In re S.C.E., 378 A.2d 144 (Del. Ch. 1977); *A.L. v. G.R.H.*, supra note 67; *In re M.K.R.*, 515 S.W.2d 467 (Mo. 1974).
66. *See, e.g., Wentzel v. Montgomery General Hospital Inc.*, 447 A.2d 1244 (Md. 1982); *In re Moe,* 385 Mass. App. 555, 432 N.E.2d 712 (1982); *In re A.W.*, 637 P.2d 366 (Colo. 1981); *C.D.M. v. State,* 627 P.2d 607 (Alaska 1981); *In re Grady,* 85, N.J. 235, 426 A.2d 467 (1981); *Guardianship of Eberhardy,* 102 Wis. 2d 539, 307 N.W. 2d 881 (1981).
67. *Parham v. J.R.*, 442 U.S. 584 (1979).
68. Id. at 602–03.
69. *See, e.g.*, W. Va. Code §27–4–1(b) (1980).
70. *See, e.g.*, Idaho Code §§66–318, 320; N.Y. Mental Hyg. Law §89.13(b) (1978).
71. Mich. Stat. Ann. §14.800(417) (1980).
72. Va. Code §54–325.2(d)(4) (1982).
73. Medical care constitutes one of the "necessaries" of a child's life. *See* 59 Am. Jur. 2d, Parent & Child §87; Clark, *Domestic Relations* §6.3 (1968).
74. *Greenspan v. Slate,* 12 N.J. 426, 97 A.2d 390 (1953).
75. *See, e.g.*, Cal. Civ. Code §34.6 (1982); Colo. Rev. Stat. §13–22–103 (Supp. 1982); Minn. Stat. Ann. §144.347 (Supp. 1982).
76. *See, e.g.*, N.Y. Ins. Law §164 (1966 & Supp. 1982); Ill. Ann. Stat. tit. 73, §767.60(b) (1965 & Supp. 1982).

IX

Work, Contracts, and Money

Does a child have the right to work?

Yes. But in every state there are a number of laws that restrict the type of jobs that children may hold, the age at which they may hold them, and the hours of employment, along with other qualifications and restrictions.

These laws, usually called child labor laws, came into existence about sixty years ago when children were often exploited as cheap sources of labor and put to work for long hours at dangerous and unhealthy jobs. Some recently enacted child labor laws are designed to protect the educational interest of children as well as their health and safety.

Specifically, what do typical child labor laws permit and require?

Every state has its own law, and no two are exactly alike. Each person should consult the state employment office or department of labor to find out the exact provisions in a particular state. State employment or labor offices may be found in all state capitals, with branch offices in most large cities. It may be possible to obtain a booklet from school guidance counselors that describes that state's child labor law.

Two state laws—Illinois and New York—are typical of child labor laws in larger industrial states.

Illinois. Generally, children between the ages of 14 and 16 may be employed outside school hours and during school vacations so long as the work is not dangerous, hazardous, or otherwise prohibited by law or regulation. Hazardous and dangerous jobs include work in

1. bowling alleys;
2. pool or billiard rooms;
3. skating rinks;
4. amusement parks;
5. garages and filling stations;
6. mines;
7. quarries;
8. plants that manufacture explosives;
9. sawmills;
10. steel mills;
11. foundries;
12. hot-rolling mills;
13. the operation of power-driven machinery for punching, shearing, or bending metal;
14. as a bellboy in a hotel;
15. any place or establishment where liquors are served, sold for consumption on the premises, manufactured, or bottled.

Illinois recognizes certain exceptions to the 14-year-old age requirement. Children over 12 may be employed in agricultural pursuits. There are no age restrictions for those engaged in the sale or distribution of magazines and newspapers during hours when school is not in session, or for work in and around a minor's own home or the home of another. In addition, minors over the age of 12 may work as golf caddies, and minors under 10 may work as theatrical performers when accompanied on the job by their parents.

Illinois restricts the hours of employment so that no person under 16 may work more than 8 hours per day or more than 48 hours per week. Hours of employment are also forbidden between 7:00 P.M. and 7:00 A.M., or after 9:00 P.M. in the summer.

Children under 16 need an Illinois employment certificate in order to work in all occupations except agriculture, the sale and distribution of magazines and newspapers, work in and around the home, and as a golf caddy. Persons and businesses employing minors must keep employment certificates on record. They are obtainable from the city or county superintendent of schools, and are revocable by the principal of the minor's school if the principal believes the employment is interfering with the optimum physical, intellectual, and moral development of the minor. In order to get a certificate, the child must provide—

1. parental permission;
2. a statement of intention from the prospective employer setting forth the nature of the occupation;
3. a birth certificate;
4. a baptismal record or some other proof of age;
5. a statement of physical fitness signed by a public health or school physician.[1]

New York. Children between the ages of 14 and 16 may work after school hours and during vacations. Children 16 and older who do not attend school may work full time. Children 12 years or older may harvest berries, fruits and vegetables, sell and deliver newspapers and magazines outside school hours (with parental permission and a certificate requiring a doctor's and school principal's approval), but one must be 14 to sell newspapers on the street. Children 12 or older also may work for their parents or guardians in the home or outdoors in work not connected with a business. There are no age restrictions for child performers or models so long as parental consent and a special permit are obtained, and a special exception exists for the employment of children who are 15 and who can no longer profit from further schooling.

New York prohibits minors from working in a number of occupations, depending on the age of the child. Persons under 18 may not work

1. in tunnels and mines;
2. in the operation of hoists and locomotives;
3. in construction work as operators of certain types of cranes;
4. in dry-cleaning establishments as supervisors of dry dyeing and deterging rooms;
5. in the use or storing of explosives;
6. in any construction work;
7. in any occupation involved in the operation of most power-driven machinery (including circular and band saws);
8. in slaughterhouses or meat-packing plants;
9. in the manufacture of brick products;
10. in logging, mining, or quarring occupations;

11. in packing paints or leads;
12. in the use of any poisonous or radioactive substance.

Window cleaning or selling or handling alcoholic beverages are also prohibited. In addition to all of these restrictions, children under 16 may not be employed in a factory (except in delivery and clerical jobs in an enclosed office), in painting or exterior cleaning jobs, or as a peddler.

New York also restricts the *hours* that children may work. For 14- and 15-year-olds attending school, the maximum number of hours one may work is 3 hours on a school day and 8 hours on other days, with no work permitted between 7:00 P.M. and 7:00 A.M. For 16-year-olds attending school, the limit is 4 hours on school days, 8 hours on other days, with no work permitted from midnight to 6:00 A.M. For children 16 and 17 who are not in school the limit is an 8-hour day, a 48-hour week, and a maximum of 6 days per week with no work permitted from midnight to 6:00 A.M. Newspaper carriers aged 12 to 18 may work only 4 hours on school days and 5 hours on other days with no work allowed between 7:00 P.M. and 5:00 A.M.

New York, like Illinois, requires an employment certificate for all children under 18 before they may begin work, even if the child has graduated from high school or is working for his parents. There are different types of certificates in New York depending on the age of the child and the type of employment. To obtain a certificate a minor must submit written permission from a parent, proof of age, and a certificate of physical fitness from a doctor. Employment certificates are *not* required for caddies and baby-sitters over 13, farm workers over 16, children working for their parents in the home or doing work not connected with a business, or college students 16 or 17 years of age who work for the college. Lawn and garden workers may have to get an employment certificate depending on the age of the applicant and whether or not power tools are used.[2]

Are there any exceptions to these restrictions?

Yes. Most states make exceptions to many of the rules just mentioned for farm and agricultural work, for domestic work (for instance, housecleaning, baby-sitting), and for work in and around a home (yard work and chores in one's own house) performed by children.

In addition, many states permit children to work in specific jobs even below the specified age limit. There are often special provisions making it possible for a child to be a newsboy or newsgirl or a golf caddy at age 12 or 13, or an actor or actress at any age with parental supervision.

Moreover, restrictions on evening employment are sometimes lifted during nonschool nights and summer months.

Do children need special permits to work?

Yes. Most states require children to obtain employment certificates. These are usually obtained from state employment or labor offices or school superintendents, depending on the state.

In most states, it is not only illegal for children to work without an employment certificate, but illegal as well for an employer to hire a child who does not possess one.

What must one do to obtain an employment certificate?

The certificate must be obtained by the child himself. The child is usually required to furnish written permission from his parents or guardian, proof of age in the form of a birth certificate or baptismal record, and information about the prospective job or a note from the prospective employer. Several states require permission from the child's school principal and others demand a note from a doctor stating that the child is physically fit to work.

Are children entitled to receive a fair or minimum wage?

Federal law currently provides for a $3.35 per hour minimum wage for employees whose work or work product is related to interstate commerce.[3] There are, however, a number of exceptions to the federal minimum wage law that affect young people. Generally, the law does not apply to agriculture workers, many state and local government employees, employees of certain retail or service establishments, and domestic service employees (these are just some of the important exceptions to the law).[4] In addition, employers may petition for certificates that enable them to pay certain employees subminimum wages.[5] These employees include apprentices, handicapped individuals, messengers, patient workers in hospitals, and student-employees of educational institutions.[6]

In addition, there are state minimum wage laws, which apply where federal law is inapplicable. But just as there are exceptions to federal employment laws, there are also exceptions to these state minimum wage laws (excepted jobs typically include caddying, baby-sitting, and domestic work); and some states permit employers to establish wage scales slightly lower than the minimum hourly rate for minors, students, learners, and apprentices. In New York, for example, the minimum wage is $3.35 per hour but employers may apply for a special permit that allows them to pay less per hour to certain employees under the age of 18.[7] In Illinois, the minimum wage for adults is $2.30 per hour, but the minimum wage for employees under 18 years of age is $1.95 per hour.[8]

It should be remembered that no law prevents an employer from paying children wages *greater* than the minimum rate, nor are children prohibited from asking for a higher wage or from quitting if they think they are not paid enough. The minimum wage merely requires an employer to pay his employees *at least* that amount.

Are employers allowed to pay higher wages to boys than to girls?

No. Federal law prohibits employers from differentiating rates of pay on the basis of sex when males and females are employed in the same establishment at jobs requiring equal effort, skill, and responsibility, performed under similar working conditions.[9]

Domestic and agricultural workers are usually not covered by equal-pay laws.

Are children protected by laws prohibiting discrimination generally?

Yes. In many states, discrimination in employment is prohibited because of race, creed, national origin, disability, sex, or marital status.

What should young people do if they are not receiving a fair or minimum wage or are discriminated against on the basis of race or sex?

They should report the violation to the local offices of the state and federal departments of employment or labor. If a young person is receiving an illegally low wage, they will help him get a proper wage and collect back payments.

Unpaid wages for regular and overtime work should also be reported.

Reports of wage or job discrimination on account of race or sex should also be made to the Equal Employment Opportunity Commission (EEOC). Most reports to the EEOC must be made within 180 days of the date of discrimination. (See the American Civil Liberties Union handbook *The Rights of Women*, by Susan D. Ross and Ann Barcher.)

If a child is found to have been discriminated against, he may be able to recover back wages, and the employer may have to pay the young person's legal fees as well.[10]

Does the federal government regulate child labor?

Yes. In 1938, Congress enacted the Fair Labor Standards Act[11] that prohibits an employer from using "oppressive child labor" in the production of goods to be used in interstate commerce. Courts have interpreted what constitutes interstate commerce very broadly, so that most employers in the United States are covered by the law. Different types of jobs have different age restrictions. Generally, persons under 14 may not work other than as actors or performers. Persons 14 to 16 may work in a number of nonmanufacturing occupations if employment does not interfere with school.

Persons under 18 may not be hired for positions—

1. in or about plants manufacturing or storing explosives or articles containing explosive components:
2. in coal or other mining operations;
3. in logging operations or sawmills, lath mills, shingle mills, or cooperage-stock mills;
4. in occupations involving exposure to radioactive substances or ionizing radiations;
5. in the operation of elevators or other power-driven hoisting apparatus;
6. in the operation of power-driven woodworking, bakery, paper products, metal-forming, punching, or shearing machines;
7. in or about slaughtering and meat-packing establishments and rendering plants;
8. as motor vehicle drivers and helpers;
9. in the manufacture of bricks, tile, and kiln-dried products;
10. as operators of circular saws, band saws, and guillotine shears;

11. in wrecking, demolition, and ship-breaking operations;
12. in roofing or excavation operations.

Are young people penalized for violating child labor laws?

No. The penalty for violation is imposed against the employer. Because of the possibility of penalites, employers are frequently reluctant to hire a young person without proof of age.

Are children entitled to fringe benefits?

Yes. Employers who have agreed to pay employee wage supplements to adults, such as vacation pay or holiday pay, health benefits, and reimbursement for expenses, must pay them to child employees as well. Part-time work, however, may not qualify for such benefits. In any case, an agreement on fringe benefits should be reached between a young person and his employer before he or she actually begins work.

Are children entitled to workman's compensation if injured while working?

Yes. If a minor is injured in an *on-the-job* accident in the course of his employment, the injury is covered by workman's compensation. Occupational diseases are also included.

If injured, the young person should report the accident immediately to the employer who in turn must report it to the Workman's Compensation Board.

Benefits may include weekly cash payments for the time lost on the job as well as necessary medical care to which an employee is entitled even if there is no job time lost. Compensation may be less than the full weekly wage, usually at a fraction of about two thirds the normal rate.

If a child is injured at a job in which he is employed illegally (for example, a job prohibited by law for minors since it is dangerous or hazardous), he may be entitled to compensation over and above the normal amount.

In most states, jobs of baby-sitting and casual yard or housework are not covered by workman's compensation.

Do minors qualify for unemployment insurance if they get laid off?

Yes, but only if they meet the requirements set for all workers, which usually consist of working a minimum number of weeks before being laid off, not having voluntarily quit the job, nor having been fired for misconduct. Moreover, the employer must be one who qualifies under the law. The exact qualifications are available from State Unemployment offices, usually a division of the State Department of Labor or Employment.

Generally, part-time workers and *those who work after school or during vacations* are excluded from receiving unemployment insurance, as are baby-sitters, golf caddies, and, in many states, *all* children under the age of fourteen.

Must children apply for and obtain Social Security cards?

Yes. Anyone who works, regardless of age, has to have a Social Security number and a card. Payroll deductions will also be made for Social Security purposes and this money is not refundable until age sixty-five, even if income tax withholdings are returned.

Are there any special programs designed to find work for young people?

Yes. Many state Employment offices provide free placement for young applicants seeking work. The federally funded Manpower Services program, Job Corps, Federal Comprehensive Employment and Training Act (CETA), and work-study programs conducted through schools may provide some help in this area.

Do young people have the right to be supported by their parents?

Absolutely. This is one of the most secure rights a child has. Parents, whether or not they are married to each other, have a legal duty to support their children.

There is no specific amount of support to which children are entitled, so long as their basic needs of adequate food, shelter, clothing, education, and medical care are being satisfied. If parents are living apart, however, due to separation or divorce, they may disagree on the amount each is willing to pay for child support, in which case an exact weekly or monthly dollar amount may be determined by agreement or by a court.

In most states, stepparents have no legal duty to support their stepchildren, unless they adopt them.

The age at which the right to support terminates is usually eighteen or twenty-one, depending on the state, or sometimes sooner if the child becomes emancipated.[12]

Do young people have the right to be supported by their parents to enable them to obtain a college education?

Probably not. The most common rule is that when children reach the age of majority, they have no further right to parental support, and in no case does the duty to support a child include the duty to pay for a child's college education.[13]

Curiously, some children of divorced or separated parents may establish the right to a parent-sponsored college education if "special circumstances" require it,[14] or if the terms of a separation agreement provide that one or both parents will provide support payments for a college education.[15]

Do children have the unqualified right to keep their own earnings?

No. As explained earlier, children have the legal right to be supported by their parents. This entails the right to receive food, clothing, shelter, medical care, and an education. The other side of this rule is that parents are entitled to the services and income of their children in exchange for their duty of support.

This rule was much more meaningful in preindustrial times when a child was viewed as the "property" of the parent and as an "extra pair of hands" around the farm or home. But the parental right still exists, and a young person's earnings are not always exclusively his own since his parents have the right to claim the earnings as their own.

In response to this situation a few states have enacted laws that permit children to keep their earnings unless the parent takes some affirmative action. In California, for example, the wages of a minor may be paid to him unless his parents or guardians give the employer notice that the wages are claimed by them.[16] In New York, what an employer pays to a child cannot be claimed by a parent unless the parent gives written notice of a claim to his child's earnings within thirty days after the employment starts.[17]

There are a number of other ways by which the parental right to his child's earnings may be mitigated. First, and most practical, a young person can make an agreement with his parents that the money he earns is to be his very own, to save, spend, or dispose of as he wishes. This results in a "partial emancipation" of the child but does not affect any other aspects of the parent-child relationship.[18]

Second, it may be "understood" that the earnings a minor receives are exclusively his even without an express agreement between him and his parents. This understanding usually becomes effective when the child has earned money in the past and his parents have permitted him to keep it without demanding all or part of it for themselves,[19] or when parents are able to support their child but do not, and the child supports himself with his own source of income[20] (see chapter VII).

Third, marriage or living away from home even before attaining the age of majority may extinguish the right of a young person's parents to claim his earnings (see Chapter VII).

Fourth, some states permit child "prodigies"; that is, young entertainers, models, or athletes, to keep their own earnings or at least to have them kept in a special fund until they reach their age of majority and are free from parental control.[21] These employment contracts, however, may only be entered into with the consent of the child's parents or guardians.

Of course, money earned by minors that is subject to claims made by parents is not to be confused with money *given* to children or placed *in trust* for them or *inherited* by them. This money cannot be claimed by anyone other than the child who has the right to ownership upon reaching the age of majority.

Do children have to pay income taxes?

Yes. If an individual receives income, regardless of age, he must pay income taxes, and taxes may be withheld from a young person's paycheck. Of course, if the total yearly income is less than a certain amount (depending on whether or not certain deductions are claimed) the money withheld from a minor's paycheck may be refunded in part or in whole the following year.

Does a young person have the right to open a bank account in his own name?

Yes. A young person may deposit and withdraw his own

money from a bank account without the consent or prior approval of an adult. However, bank accounts established by an adult "in trust" for a child cannot be drawn from by the child nor claimed until he reaches the age of majority. Such an account will be managed by an adult "trustee" who has specific duties to preserve or utilize the funds for a special purpose, such as the education of the child.

Do young people have the right to apply for and be granted welfare benefits?

If they are living with one or both parents, or another adult who is caring for them, young people may receive welfare benefits indirectly through payments made to the adult, usually in the form of aid to dependent children, funded in large part by the federal government.

If a young person lives alone, however, the answer is not as clear. In the first place, since the age up to which a child may be taken to court for simply leaving home without parental approval in most states is 18 (see chapter X), it would be difficult for any child below the age of 18 to establish a home of his own without running afoul of the law. In the second place, welfare officials are very reluctant to provide assistance to young people who, in their opinion, are still legally entitled to support from their parents. Thus in some state or county welfare departments, there may be a blanket policy to turn away *all* young applicants, even if such blanket restrictions may be illegal. It is therefore important for any young person who believes that he or she is entitled to welfare to obtain the refusal in writing, and then to consult a lawyer to determine if a hearing should be requested to contest the denial.

In New York (which is actually an atypical state because there a young person can leave home at age 16 and yet has the right to parental support until age 21) courts have ruled that if a child voluntarily leaves home without parental permission, the parents may be excused from their duty to support and the young person may receive welfare benefits in his own name, if the economic and work-related qualifications are met.[22]

In most states, however, the receipt of public assistance by a child will not extinguish the duty of his or her parents to provide support if the child remains in the home of either or both parents.[23]

Do minors have the right to make contracts?

Generally, no, but it often depends on the type of contract.

A contract is an agreement between two or more people. An agreement does not have to be written to be a contract; under certain circumstances oral or spoken agreements may be as valid and binding as one that is written and signed.

Most states do not consider a contract binding against a young person if one of the parties to the agreement is a minor. The fact that it is not binding does not mean that it cannot be fully performed by all parties; it means that if the child later wishes to "disaffirm" the contract (back out of it), he may do so. Therefore, minors can enforce contracts against adults but they can choose to break contracts themselves.[24]

Since a minor has the right to disaffirm or repudiate a contract, many adults are reluctant to enter into agreements with children. A party to a contract may therefore insist upon the signature of a child's parent on a contract in order to bind the parent since an adult may not disaffirm or repudiate contractual obligations.

What happens if a child disaffirms a contract?

If the contract was for an item of sale—a bicycle, for example—the child must return the bicycle upon disaffirmance, whereupon he is entitled to receive his money back, less the amount of "depreciation" (wear and tear) which occurred while the child used the bicycle. The law does not permit a child to disaffirm the contract and enjoy the benefits of it at the same time.[25]

The privilege to disaffirm a contract, however, must be exercised within a reasonable period of time,[26] and it is unlikely that a contract could be disaffirmed if it was entered into with a minor's own misrepresentation that he was of the age of majority.[27]

Are there exceptions to a child's right to disaffirm contracts?

Yes. Contracts that may be disaffirmed by minors are called voidable. Voidable contracts operate with all the binding force of normal contracts, until the minor chooses to disaffirm. Only upon disaffirmation is the contract void. Other contracts made by minors are *void* from the moment they are made. Void contracts have no validity and cannot be enforced by anyone. Still others are not subject to disaffirmation; they are fully operable and binding on everyone even though one of the parties is a minor.

What types of contracts are void when made by minors?

Leases are void contracts when made or signed by a minor. In some states marriage contracts are also void if one or both of the parties are below the age at which marriage is permitted in a state (see appendix D). Not all such marriages are void. Some are *voidable;* that is, valid unless and until someone contests their validity.

What types of contracts are fully binding when made by minors?

Examples of binding contracts not subject to a minor's disaffirmance are those made when a minor enlists in the armed forces, when a minor enters a marriage contract (assuming he is of the age permitted to marry), and when a minor signs a driver's license.

In some states contracts made by minors in the course of their own business are binding if the contracts are fair and reasonable.[28] In most states, contracts entered into by minors for educational loans and automobile or motorcycle insurance are binding and not subject to future disaffirmance.[29] There are also special rules for the creation of binding contracts by children engaged in theatrical, modeling, or athletic pursuits.[30]

Contracts made by minors for "necessaries" are also binding on them and their parents.[31]

What are "necessaries"?

Necessaries are goods or services that provide for the health and welfare of the child, such as food, clothing, shelter, and medical care. When a child agrees to purchase necessaries and they are not being provided to the child by his parents, the contract is binding on the child and his parents and it may not be disaffirmed by either.[32] Similarly, if a parent does not support his child, he is liable for the reasonable value of necessaries supplied to a person who is caring for the child.

Can a young person make a will?

No. A person must reach the age of majority before he can execute a valid will.

What happens to the money and property of a child if he dies?

In most states, if a child dies without a will, the money and property will go to his parents. If both parents are dead, the money or property will go to his or her sisters and brothers. If the child is married and dies without a will, the estate will go to his spouse and children.

Does a young person have the right to inherit money or property from someone who has died?

Absolutely. There are two ways in which a person may inherit from another. First, he may be mentioned in the will of a person who has died. Second, one may inherit if he or she is related to a person who has died without leaving a will.

While the money or property will belong to the child, he will not be able to take it or spend it as he chooses until he reaches the age of majority. The will of the person from whom the child inherits the money will probably designate someone to be the guardian or trustee of the child's inheritance; in most cases the guardian is the surviving parent. If the will does not name someone, a probate or surrogate court judge will appoint someone to act in this capacity.[33] The guardian or trustee has the responsibility of safeguarding the money until the child comes of age or utilizing it for the care and education of the child.

How does a young person inherit money or property from someone who has died without leaving a will?

It depends on the laws of inheritance in each state as well as the number of relatives who are living at the time of the death of the person who left no will.

Normally, the child of a parent who dies without a will inherits a fraction of the "estate" (the total amount of the money and property) of the dead parent. The fraction is usually dependent on whether or not the child has a surviving parent and sisters and brothers. Of course, amounts and fractions may differ in different states.

Can a child be disinherited by his parents?

Yes. A child can be "disinherited" (receive *no* money or property from his or her parents when they die) if he is mentioned in the will by name or by class ("children") as being disinherited. If the child is not mentioned by name or by class, he may be able to contest the disinheritance, depending on the law in each state.

Of course, as just discussed, if the parent dies leaving no will at all, then the child may inherit a certain portion of the estate automatically.

Does a young person have the right to own real estate?

Yes, but ownership does not confer the right of management or control. A child may not rent, sell, or otherwise manage real property until he reaches the age of majority. Until that time the control of his property is usually the duty of a guardian or trustee who must manage it for the benefit of the child.

NOTES

1. ILL. ANN. STAT. ch. 48, §31.1 et seq. (Supp. 1982).
2. N.Y. ED. LAW §§3215–3230 (1981); N.Y. LABOR LAW §130 *et. seq*. (Supp. 1981).
3. Fair Labor Standards Act, 29 U.S.C.A. §206(a)(1)(1978).
4. *See* 29 U.S.C.A. §§206(a)(5)(1978), 213 (1965 & Supp. 1982); *National League of Cities v. Usery*, 426 U.S. 833 (1976).
5. 29 U.S.C.A. §213(a)(7)(Supp. 1982).
6. 29 C.F.R. §§519–529 (1982).
7. N.Y. LABOR LAW §§6521(1) 655(5)(c) (Supp. 1978).
8. ILL. ANN. STAT. ch. 48, §1004(a) (Supp. 1982).
9. 29 U.S.C.A. §206 (d) 1(1978). *See also* Title VII of the 1964 Civil Rights Act, 42 U.S.C. §§2000(e) *et. seq*. (1981); for examples of similar state laws, *see* ILL. REV. STAT. ch. 48 §1004(b) (Supp. 1982); N.Y. LABOR LAW §194 (Supp. 1981).
10. *Asaro v. Lillenfeld*, 36 N.Y.S.2d 802 (N.Y.C.Ct. 1942).
11. 29 U.S.C. §§201 et seq. (1976 & Supp. 1980).
12. *See, e.g.*, N.Y. FAM. CT. ACT. §413 (Supp. 1981); *Lyle v. Lyle*, 72 A.D. 2d 549, 421 N.Y.S.2d 98 (2nd Dept. 1979); *Davenport v. Davenport*, 356 So. 2d 205 (Ala. Civ. App. 1978); *In re Stephen K.*, 289 Md. 294, 424 A.2d 153 (1981); *Behr v. Behr*, 46 N.C. App. 694, 266 S.E.2d 393 (1980); *Spears v. Spears*, 382 So.2d 572 (Ala. Civ. App. 1980).
13. *See, e.g.*, *Philips v. Philips*, 339 So. 2d 1299 (La. App. 1976).
14. *See, e.g.*, *Kaplan v. Wallshein*, 57 A.D. 2d 828, 394 N.Y.S. 2d 439 (2nd Dept. 1977).
15. *See, e.g.*, *Bethune v. Bethune*, 46 N.Y.2d 913, 387 N.E.2d 1220, 414 N.Y.S. 2d 905 (1979); *Carpenter v. Carpenter*, 25 N.C. App. 235, 212 S.E.2d 911 (1975).
16. CAL. CIV. CODE §212 (1982).

17. N.Y. GEN. OBL. LAW §3–109 (1978).
18. 59 Am. Jur.2d, Parent and Child §46 (1971).
19. *Rounds Brothers v. McDaniel*, 133 Ky. 669, 118 S.W. 959 (1909).
20. 165 A.L.R. 723.
21. *See, e.g.*, N.Y. GEN. OBL. LAW §3–105 (1978); CAL. CIV. CODE §36 (1982).
22. *Parker v. Stage*, 43 N.Y. 2d 128, 371 N.E. 2d 513, 400 N.Y.S. 2d 794 (1977), relying on *Roe v. Doe*, 29 N.Y. 2d 188, 272 N.E. 2d 567, 342 N.Y.S. 2d 71 (1971).
23. *See, e.g., French v. French*, 599 S.W.2d 40 (Mo. Ct. App. 1980).
24. 2 Williston, *Contracts*, ch. 9 (3rd ed., 1959).
25. *See, e.g., Pieri v. Nebbia*, 178 Misc. 388, 34 N.Y.S.2d 317 (Monroe Co. Ct. 1942).
26. *See, e.g.*, REV. CODE WASH. §26.28.030 (1961); *Wuller v. Chuse Grocery Co.*, 241 Ill. 398, 89 N.E.796 (1909); *Washington Street Garage v. Maloy*, 230 A.D. 266, 243 N.Y.S. 467 (4th Dept. 1930).
27. *See, e.g.*, REV. CODE WASH. §26.28.040 (1961).
28. *See, e.g.*, N.Y. GEN. OBL. LAW §3–101(2) (1978).
29. *See, e.g.*, N.Y. ED. LAW §681 (Supp. 1981).
30. CAL. CIV. CODE §36(a)(1) (1982).
31. *See, e.g.*, CAL. CIV. CODE §36(1) (Supp. 1974).
32. 2 Williston, *Contracts*, §241 (3rd ed., 1959); *Girls Latin School of Chicago v. Hart*, 317 Ill. App. 382, 46 N.E.2d 118 (1943); *Auringer v. Cochrane*, 225 Mass. 273 114 N.E. 355 (1916).
33. *See, e.g.*, MO. REV. STAT. §456.225 (1982).

X

Status Offenses: Children "In Need of Supervision"

What is a child "in need of supervision"?

When the first juvenile court was established in Illinois in 1899, delinquency was defined in terms of criminal and penal laws. Shortly thereafter, the definition was expanded to include children who were "incorrigible," those who associated with "undesirable" friends, and even young people who exhibited "bad habits," such as idleness, immorality, and waywardness. Such laws have a long history in American jurisprudence. In 1654, the Massachusetts Bay Colony provided for corporeal punishment by whipping children who behaved disrespectfully and disobediently toward their parents.[1] Today every state empowers its juvenile courts to exercise authority over children who do not commit crimes but who are "incorrigible," "ungovernable," or "beyond control" of their parents or custodians. Children who fall into this category are often called status offenders since they harm no one other than themselves and are punished for merely "being" something. Most status offenses of children are not illegal if committed by adults. Children are therefore subject to possible punishment and loss of liberty for acts that are not prohibited for adults.

Courts and commentators often justify the existence of status offenses by referring to their effect of identifying predelinquent children and preventing them from committing delinquent or criminal acts in the future.[2]

In most states, the noncriminal jurisdiction exists in a category separate from delinquency[3] under which young people may be determined persons in need of supervision (PINS), children in need of supervision (CINS), minors in need of supervision (MINS), or wayward children. In the other states, it is included in the broad definition of *delinquency*.[4]

Are laws prohibiting juvenile status offenses constitutional?

Yes, but they have been under attack for two decades.

Many lawyers feel that laws that make children in need of supervision subject to the authority of juvenile courts are unconstitutional because they—

1. fail to give young people adequate notice of prohibited behavior;
2. are overly broad and vague;
3. deny young people equal protection of the laws since adults are not subject to their restrictions;
4. permit arbitrary and capricious enforcement;
5. serve no legitimate state purpose;
6. punish children for a status rather than for specific acts.

Those who attack the constitutionality of such laws base part of their arguments on a number of recent courts decisions that held adult status offenses unconstitutional,[5] and upon decisions that have found that laws that define criminal conduct in overly broad terms are vague and therefore void.[6]

Statutes that subject children in need of supervision to the power of the court and to a possible loss of liberty are continuously under attack in numerous state and federal courts. Moreover, a growing number of national organizations have recommended that status offenses be removed from the jurisdiction of juvenile courts. These include (1) the President's Task Force on Juvenile Delinquency and Youth Crime; (2) the White House Conference on Children; (3) the National Council of Crime and Delinquency; and (4) the Joint Commission of the American Bar Association-Institute of Judicial Administration Juvenile Justice Standards Project.[7] Confirming this trend, the 1974 federal Juvenile Justice and Delinquency Prevention Act provides funds for states that submit plans for the decarceration of status offenders and for the development of facilities to deal with runaway youths outside the law enforcement and juvenile justice system.[8]

Nevertheless, almost every challenge to the constitutionality of a persons in need of supervision statute has been denied by the courts.[9] In viewing a Texas statute that defined a child in need of supervision as one who "habitually so deports himself as to impair or endanger the morals or health of himself or others," the court found that the term *morals* was not unconstitutionally vague since it conveyed sufficient specificity to the average person.[10]

However, *parts* of definitions of status offenders have been declared invalid. A federal court found California's statutory reference to minors "in danger of leading an idle, dissolute, lewd, or immoral life" unconstitutionally vague.[11] Since then, the statute was redrafted to eliminate references to immoral behavior, and similar wording has been stricken from the Washington, D.C., CINS statute as well.[12] The statutes themselves, however, remain and are in full force.

What are some of the prohibited acts or conditions that may constitute a status offence?

The definition of *persons in need of supervision* varies by state but it usually includes the status of being "incorrigible," "beyond control," "habitually disobedient," or truant from school. In many cases it may mean staying away from home, smoking, drinking, glue-sniffing, or violating curfew regulations. Some states make children subject to the jurisdiction of the juvenile court if they are merely *in danger* of becoming in need of supervision.

The Ohio statute is typical of many. It classifies as "unruly" any child:

> . . . who does not subject himself to the reasonable control of his parents, teachers, guardian or custodian, by reason of being wayward or habitually disobedient; who is an habitual truant from home or school; who so deports himself as to injure or endanger the health or morals of himself or others; . . . who is found in a disreputable place, visits or patronizes a place prohibited by law, or associates with vagrant, vicious, criminal, notorious, or immoral persons. . . .[13]

California defines a status offender as

> any person under the age of 18 years who persistently or habitually refuses to obey the reasonable and proper orders or directions of his parents, guardian,

custodian, or who is beyond the control of such persons. . . .[14]

New York defines a person in need of supervision as a person under 16 who does not attend school as required by law or "who is incorrigible, ungovernable or habitually disobedient and beyond the lawful control of parent or other lawful authority" or who possesses marijuana.[15]

Is a single act of "ungovernable" behavior sufficient to support a finding that a young person is in need of supervision?

Not usually. A number of statutory definitions of *PINS offenses* require a showing of "habitual" disobedience or repeated truancy or unruliness. A single act, therefore, rarely constitutes legal grounds for a judge to find a juvenile in need of supervision.[16]

In California, truancy must reach a habitual level to come under the jurisdiction of the court.[17] Even then, a habitual truant may not be found in need of supervision unless he is also shown to be unresponsive to additional services offered to correct his truancy.[18]

Are there defenses that may justify behavior that is alleged to constitute a status defense?

Yes. In a number of jurisdictions the prohibited conduct must be engaged in "without justification." In others, the disobedience must be in reaction to "reasonable" demands of a parent or guardian. Therefore, if a child can show that the behavior complained of was justified, he may be able to win his case. A young person may also attempt to prove that he was pressured or under considerable duress to act the way he did. In one case of this nature, a student was able to convince the court that his truancy was due to harassment by other boys at school.[19] Moreover, if a young person can show that his parents make unreasonable demands, such as requiring him to be home on weekend evenings at very early hours or refusing to permit him to associate with any friends, his disobedience may not justify a finding that he is in need of supervision.

In fact, a young person may be successful in showing that his parents are so unreasonable or arbitrary that it is they who are in need of supervision, not him.[20] (Such cases are rare and will not be accepted by juvenile courts unless the parental behavior is actually harmful to the child.)[21] If so, the PINS petition may be withdrawn and replaced by a neglect petition[22] (see chapter IV). There is a certain risk to this approach, because if parental neglect is found, the child may still be subject to removal from the home (for the purpose of protection rather than for punishment or treatment).

Who has the authority to charge a young person with a status offense?

Usually the power to file a PINS petition against a young person is granted to police officers, probation officers, school officials, parents, guardians, and custodians of a child.

Do young people charged with status offenses have all the due process rights that are granted juveniles charged with delinquency?

No. In 1967, the United States Supreme Court, in *In re Gault,* held that young people in juvenile court were guaranteed many of the constitutional rights granted adult criminal defendants[23] (see chapter I). However, the *Gault* decision, and some of those to follow, were confined in application to charges that render young people subject to commitment, or charges alleging delinquent conduct only. Therefore, some procedural guarantees extended to young people charged with being delinquent are not given to those charged with status offenses.

In all states, for example, young people accused of being juvenile delinquents must be found guilty by proof "beyond a reasonable doubt,"[24] but those alleged to be in need of supervision may be found guilty only by a "preponderance" of the evidence or by "clear and convincing" evidence.[25] (In a few states [including Colorado, Indiana, Massachusetts, New York, and Texas] young people charged with status offenses do have the right to be found guilty by proof established beyond a reasonable doubt.)[26] In some states, young people taken into custody for status offenses are not protected from self-incrimination, unlike delinquents.[27]

Most other procedural guarantees, however, are extended to PINS and delinquents alike. In most states young people charged with a status offense have the right to receive adequate notice of the specific acts they are alleged to have committed,[28] the right to a hearing, and the right to have hearsay testimony excluded from evidence.[29]

Do young people charged with status offenses have the right to an attorney?

Normally, yes. Strictly speaking the *Gault* decision only required counsel for children in proceedings that render them subject to the loss of liberty.[30] But since children charged with status offenses are usually rendered liable to placement away from home, commitment to an institution, or placement on probation, the right to counsel should be firmly established.[31] Nonetheless, a number of courts have held that counsel is not required in these cases.[32]

If arrested or taken in custody for a status offense, may young people be held in detention centers with delinquents?

No. Because of a federal law that prohibits allocating federal moneys to states for criminal justice programs that incarcerate children in need of supervision in detention facilities,[33] most states today prohibit the placement of nondelinquents in such facilities.[34] The theory of the federal law, and the recent trend restricting the use of detention of children in need of supervision, is that such persons rarely present a danger to society and deserve to be treated humanely. For these reasons, the federal law requires that states that want to obtain federal criminal justice money must place noncriminal offenders in facilities that are the least restrictive alternatives appropriate to the needs of the child and the community. Moreover, these facilities must be in reasonable proximity to the family and the home communities of such children and provide them with a variety of rehabilitative services.

If a judge finds a young person to be in need of supervision, may he commit the child to a training school?

In most states, yes, but not the first time the child is adjudicated. The same federal law just referred to prohibits the placement of noncriminal offenders in secure detention and correction facilities. Training schools are typically, but not always, secure correctional facilities. Thus, states that desire to comply with federal law (the vast majority) place restrictions on committing children in need of supervision to training schools.

A number of states simply prohibit the placement of status offenders in secure training schools.[35] In a few states, children found guilty of noncriminal conduct may not be committed to training schools unless placement in other nonsecure facilities is fully explored first. In West Virginia, a juvenile court cannot send a habitual runaway child to a secure facility used to house delinquents. Other PINS children may be committed to a secure facility only if they are "so ungovernable or antisocial that no other reasonable alternative exists."[36] In New Jersey, no PINS child may be committed, except for the purpose of mental health treatment.[37] And in North Carolina, a status offender may not be committed to a training school unless there is no other suitable placement that he will accept.[38]

In other states (including Illinois) a child in need of supervision may not be sent *directly* to a training school. However, if he later violates an order of the court, such as running away from a court-ordered, nonsecure placement, or violating court-ordered terms of probation, he may then be committed.[39] In still other jurisdictions (including the District of Columbia and Tennessee) a status offender may be placed in a training school only upon a *second* supervisory adjudication.[40]

Generally, young people found "guilty" of status offenses are subject (and have the right) to the same dispositional alternatives as delinquents. These include (1) probation; (2) placement with his own or another family or with a private agency or a foster home; (3) commitment to a state farm, camp; or (4) with the restrictions just mentioned, to a training school.

If a PINS child is sent to an institution and runs away, may the child be found guilty of contempt or escape and be placed in a more secure institution as a result?

It depends on the state. In New York, the answer is that such children cannot be charged with escape because PINS children cannot be sentenced to a secure facility in the first place. In other words, there can be no "escape" from a nonsecure setting.[41] The law appears to be similar in California and New Jersey.[42] In Pennsylvania, a court has held that it is not criminal contempt of court for a PINS to run away chronically.[43] However, in Washington, an appeals court recently held that running away constitutes civil contempt of court that in turn authorizes more severe sanctions.[44]

In Florida, truants and runaways found "guilty" of their first "offense" are classified as dependent children who may not be incarcerated. However, a second adjudication for ungovernability, including running away from a court-ordered placement, results in classification as a *delinquent*.[45]

Some states also provide that status offenders who are found guilty of violating probation may be committed as delinquents. However, a New Mexico court has ruled that a PINS child cannot be committed for a violation of probation for conduct (such as glue sniffing) which is not criminal in itself.[46]

May children who have never committed a criminal act be classified as delinquents?

In a number of states, yes. As just indicated, Florida classifies as delinquent all children who are twice adjudicated in need of supervision. Other states (including California, Georgia, and Montana) define *delinquent behavior* as the violation of probation or any court order by a PINS child.[47] In still other states (including Indiana, Minnesota, and South Carolina) the definition of *delinquency* includes noncriminal as well as criminal misbehavior.[48]

May PINS children be placed together with delinquent children?

In most states, yes. Some states absolutely prohibit the placement of noncriminal offenders with delinquents.[49] Others prohibit only an initial placement of such children together, but permit subsequent commingling if the PINS child continues to get into trouble.[50]

May females be held subject to juvenile court jurisdiction for status offenses at an older age than boys?

No. In every state girls and boys may be declared in need of supervision by juvenile courts, but no state may legally make one sex liable for status offenses for a longer period of time than the other. Until 1971, for example, in New York, girls were subject to juvenile court jurisdiction over status offenders until age 18 while boys were only liable until 16. This was declared unconstitutional as a violation of the Fourteenth Amendment's guarantee of equal protection of the laws.[51] Similar provisions in other states have also been changed or struck down.[52] Therefore, while the age may differ according to the state, boys and girls within each state must be subject to the same jurisdictional age definition for status offenders.

Can young people take advantage of PINS laws and have themselves declared "incorrigible" in order to "divorce" their parents?

As described in chapter VII, a number of states permit young people to become emancipated before reaching 18. This question focuses on those states that do not have such emancipation laws. It asks whether young people who do not get along with their parents can go to court and claim they are "incorrigible" because they refuse to obey their parents' instructions.

PINS statutes were passed to broaden and enforce parental authority. Accordingly, unless parents, or some other adult, claims that the child is incorrigible, it is a misuse of a PINS statute to permit the young person him or herself to invoke the court's jurisdiction. In any event, such cases do occur, but very rarely. The young person runs the risk that a court will agree that he or she is incorrigible and order a placement not to the liking of the youth. Two courts that have considered the question have disagreed, one allowing the youth to be declared incorrigible, the other dismissing the case.[53]

NOTES

1. *See* the brief history described in *Commonwealth v. Brasher,* 359 Mass. 550, 552, 270 N.E.2d 389, 391 (1971).
2. *See, e.g., In re Presley,* 47 Ill.2d 50, 56, 264 N.E.2d 177, 179 (1970); *S.S. v. State,* 299 A.2d 560, 570 (Me. 1973); Polier, "The Future of the Juvenile Court," 26 *Juv. Just.* 3 (1975).
3. At least 35 jurisdictions separately categorize status offenses. *See, e.g.,* CAL. WELF. & INST. CODE §601 (Supp. 1981); N.Y. FAM. CT. ACT §712(b) (1983); ILL. ANN. STAT. ch. 37, §702–3 (1982).
4. *See, e.g.,* MINN. STAT. ANN. §260.015(5) (Sup. 1982); S.C. CODE ANN. §§20–7–390, 20–7–400 A (1) (Supp. 1982); W. VA. CODE ANN. §49–1–4 (1980).
5. *Robinson v. California,* 370 U.S. 660, (1962); *Powell v. Texas,* 392 U.S. 514, (1968); *Alegata v. Commonwealth,* 353 Mass. 287, 295, 231 N.E.2d 201, 206 (1967).
6. *See, e.g., Gesicki v. Oswald,* 336 F. Sup. 371 (S.D.N.Y. 1971), *aff'd.* 406 U.S. 913 (1972). In this case the New York "wayward minor"

statute overturned by the court contained the vague phrase "morally depraved... or in danger of becoming morally depraved." The *Gesicki* decision, however, disavowed any intent to question the validity of similar juvenile court provisions. 336 F. Supp. at 377, n. 7.

7. The President's Commission on Law Enforcement and Administration of Justice, Task Force Report: Juvenile Delinquency at 27 (1967); White House Conference on Children Report to the President, at 382 (1970); Policy Statement, National Council on Crime and Delinquency (1974)(contained in 21 *Crime and Delinquency* 97 1975). Similar recommendations have been made by the Maryland Department of Juvenile Services Master Plan; Hawaii Justice Master Plan; California Assembly Interim Committee on Criminal Procedure; Legal Aid Society of New York, Juvenile Rights Division; American Civil Liberties Union, Juvenile Rights Project; and David L. Bazelon, Chief Judge of the Circuit Court of Appeals in Washington, D.C. One major organization favoring retention of the status jurisdiction is the National Council of Juvenile Court Judges.
8. 42 U.S.C. §§5633(a)(12), 5711 (Supp. 1981).
9. *In re R*. 274 Cal. App. 2d 749, 79 Cal. Rptr. 247 (1969); *Commonwealth v. Brasher, supra* note 1; *E.S.G. v. State*, 447 S.W.2d 225 (Tex. Civ. App. 1969), *cert. denied* 398 U.S. 956 (1970); *Patricia A. v. City of New York*, 31 N.Y.2d 83, 286 N.E.2d 432, 335 N.Y.S.2d 33 (1972); *District of Columbia v. B.J.R.*, 332 A.2d 58 (D.C. Ct. App. 1975), *cert. denied* 421 U.S. 1016 (1975); *In re Napier*, 532 P.2d 423 (Okl. 1975); *Blondheim v. State*, 84 Wash. 2d 874, 529 P.2d 1096 (1975); *Sheehan v. Scott*, 520 F.2d 825 (7th Cir. 1975); *In re Gras*, 337 So.2d 641 (La. App. 1976); *In re E.B.*, 287 N.W.2d 462 (N.D. 1980).
10. *E.S.G. v. State, supra* note 9.
11. *Gonzalez v. Mailliard*, 42 U.S. Law Week 3574, (N.D. Cal. 1971), striking down Cal. Welf. & Inst. Code §601 (1971), *vac. and rem.*, *Mailliard v. Gonzalez*, 416 U.S. 918, (1974), *reinstated*, No. 50424 (N.D. Cal. 1975)(summarized in 9 Clearing House Rev. 496 (Nov. 1975)).
12. Cal. Welf. & Inst. Code §601 (Supp. 1982); D.C. Code §16–2301 (1973), superceding D.C. Code §§11–1551(a)(1)(H) (I) (1976).
13. Ohio Rev. Code Ann. §2151.022 (1978). *See also* Kan. Stat. Ann. §38–802(d)(1) (Supp. 1981).
14. Cal. Welf. & Inst. Code §601 (Supp. 1982).
15. N.Y. Fam. Ct. Act §712(b) (1983).
16. *See, e.g., In re McMillan*, 21 N.C. App. 712, 205 S.E.2d 541 (1974); *In re D.J.B.*, 18 Cal. App. 3d 782, 96 Cal. Rptr. 146 (1971); *In re O.*, 31 N.Y.2d 730, 290 N.E. 2d 145 338 N.Y.S.2d 105 (1972). In some instances if a single act is serious, a court may find a child in need of supervision without evidence of repeated behavior. *See, e.g., In re S.*, 12 Cal. App. 3d 1124, 91 Cal. Rptr. 261 (1971).
17. Cal. Ed. Code §46010 (1978).
18. Cal. Welf. & Inst. Code §601(b) (Supp. 1982).

19. *Board of Education of Detroit v. Marable*, 282 N.W.2d 221 (Mich. App. 1979); *People v. Y.D.M.*, 197 Colo. 403, 593 P.2d 1356 (1979).
20. *In re G.*, 28 Cal. App. 3d 76, 104 Cal. Rptr. 585 (1972).
21. *People v. Allen*, 22 N.Y.2d 465, 239 N.E.2d 879, 293 N.Y.S.2d 280 (1968)
22. *In re Lloyd*, 33 A.D.2d 385, 308 N.Y.S.2d 419 (1st Dept. 1970).
23. *In re Gault*, 387 U.S. 1 (1967).
24. *In re Winship*, 397 U.S. 359 (1970).
25. *See, e.g.*, GA. CODE ANN. ch. 12A §2201(c) (Supp. 1981); *In re Henderson*, 199 N.W.2d 111 (Iowa 1972); D.C. CODE ANN. §16–2317 (C)(2) (Supp. 1979) (preponderance); TENN. CODE ANN. §37–279(c) (Cum. Supp. 1981) (clear and convincing). For reasoning by a court that rejected the beyond a reasonable doubt standard, *see In re Potter*, 237 N.W.2d 401 (Iowa 1970).
26. COLO. REV. STAT. ANN. §19–3–106(1)(1981); IND. CODE §31–6–3–1 (1979); MASS. ANN. LAWS ch. 119, §39G (1981); *Richard S. v. City of New York*, 27 N.Y.2d 802, 264 N.E.2d 353, 315 N.Y.S.2d 861 (1970); TEX. FAM. CODE §54.03(f) (1975).
27. *See, e.g., In re Spaulding*, 273 Md. 690, 332 A.2d 246 (1975); *In re Henderson, supra* note 25. *See* contra N.M. Ct. Rule 60 (providing for the exclusion of illegally seized evidence and involuntary confessions in PINS cases).
28. TEX. FAM. CODE ANN. §54.03(e) (1975); *In re R.*, 73 Misc.2d 390, 341 N.Y.S.2d 998 (Fam. Ct. (1973).
29. *Gilbert v. Commonwealth*, 214 Va. 142, 198 S.E.2d 633 (1973).
30. *In re Gault*, 387 U.S. (1967).
31. *See, e.g.*, N.Y. FAM. CT. ACT §249 (1983); IND. CODE §31–6–3–1 (1980). *See* contra *In re Walker*, 282, N.C. 28, 191 S.E.2d 702 (1972).
32. The Juvenile Justice Delinquency and Prevention Act of 1974, 42 U.S.C. §5633 (12) (Supp. 1982).
33. *See, e.g., In re Walker*, 282 N.C. 28, 191 S.E. 2d 702 (1972). *M.J.M. v. Dept. of Health & Rehab. Serv.*, 397 So. 2d 755 (Fla. Ct. App. 1981); *In re R.R.*, 417 N.E. 2d 237 (Ill. Ct. App. 1981). *But see In re K.S.Y.*, 416 N.E. 2d 736 (Ill. Ct. App. 1981).
34. *See, e.g.*, Cal. Rules of Ct., R. 1326 (1980); N.Y. EXEC. LAW §§501, 510 (1982); N.Y. FAM. CT. ACT §720(3) (1983). *See also D.B. v. Tewksbury*, 545 F. Supp. 896 (D. Or. 1982); *State ex rel. H.K. v. Taylor*, 289 S.E.2d 673 (W. Va. 1982); *Benitez v. Collazo*, 1 Nat'l. Juv. Law Rptr. 75 (D.P.R. 1982).
35. *See, e.g.*, ALAS. REV. STATE. §47.10.010 (1980); MD. CTS. & JUD. PROC. CODE ANN. §3–823(b)(1980); MISS. CODE ANN. §43–21–607 (f) (1981); N.Y. EXEC. LAW §§501, 510, 511, (Supp. 1981); TEX. FAM. CODE §54.04(d) (1982).
36. *State ex rel. C.A.H. v. Strickler*, 251 S.E.2d 222 (Sup. Ct. Apps. W.Va. 1979), relying on *State ex rel. Harris v. Calendine*, 223 S.E. 2d 318 (Supp. Ct. Apps. W.Va. 1977).
37. *State in Interest of K.P.*, 400 A.2d 84 (N.J. App. 1979).

38. *Matter of Hughes*, 273 S.E. .2d 324 (N.C. Ct. App. 1981).
39. ILL. REV. STAT. ch. 37 §§702–2, 3 (Supp. 1972); *People v. Sekeres*, 48 Ill.2d 431, 270 N.E.2d 7 (1971); *Vann v. Scott*, 467 F.2d 1235 (7th Cir. 1972).
40. D.C. CODE ANN. §16–2320(d) (1979); TENN. CODE ANN. §37–232 (Cum. Supp. 1982).
41. *Matter of Freeman*, 103 Misc.2d 649, 426 N.Y.S.2d 948 (Fam. Ct. 1980); *In re Sylvia H.*, 78 A.D.2d 857, 433 N.Y.S.2d 29 (2nd Dept. 1980).
42. *In re Ronald A.S.*, 69 Cal. App. 3d 866, 138 Cal. Rptr. 387 (1977); *Matter of Mary D.*, 95 Cal. App. 3d 34, 156 Cal. Rptr. 829 (1979); *State in Interest of M.S.*, 129 N.J. Super. 61, 322 A.2d 202 (1974), *aff'd* 139 N.J. Super. 503, 354 A.2d 646 (1976).
43. *Pennsylvania v. Theresa S.*, 281 Pa. Super 400, 422 A.2d 53 (1980). *See* contra *L.A.M. v. State*, 547 P.2d 827 (Alas. 1976).
44. *State v. Norlund*, 31 Wash. App. 725, 644 P.2d 724, (1982); *See also In re Darlene C.*, 301 S.E.2d 136 (S.C. 1983).
45. FLA. STAT. ANN. §39.01(10)(Cum. Ann. Supp. 1981); *D.H. v. Polen*, 396 So. 2d 1189 (Fla. Ct. App. 1981); *R.M.P. v. Jones*, 419 So. 2d 618 (Fla. 1982); see also, *In re Dowell*, 17 N.C. App. 34, 173 S.E.2d 301 (1972).
46. *State v. Doe*, 619 P.2d 194 (N.M. Ct. App. 1980).
47. *See* CAL. WELF. & INST. CODE §602 (West. Supp. 1982); GA. CODE ANN. §24A–401(e)(2)(Supp. 1982); MONT. REV. CODES §41–5–201 (Supp. 1981).
48. *See, e.g.*, IND. CODE ANN. §31–6–4–1 (Supp. 1980); MINN. STAT. ANN. §260.015(5)(Supp. 1982); S.C. CODE ANN. §20–7–390 (Supp. 1981).
49. *See, e.g.*, Mass. Ann. Laws ch. 119, §39G (1982).
50. CAL. WELF. & INST. CODE §§602, 730, 777 (Supp. 1982); D.C. CODE ANN. §16–2320(d)(1979).
51. *In re Patricia A.*, *supra* note 9.
52. *See, e.g., Lamb v. Brown*, 456 F.2d 18 (10th Cir. 1972).
53. *See, In re Snyder*, 85 Wash. 2d 182, 532 P.2d 278 (1975) (upholding jurisdiction); *Illinois v. Polovchak*, 104 Ill. App. 3d 03, 432 N.E.2d 873 (1981) (rejecting jurisdiction); *affirmed on other grounds*, 97 Ill. 2d 212, 454 N.E.2d 258 (1983).

XI

Miscellaneous Rights and Disabilities of Adolescents

Young people are denied many of the social and political rights enjoyed by adults. There are laws prohibiting young people from drinking alcoholic beverages, serving on juries, purchasing sexually explicit material and even engaging in sexual intercourse. These are just a few activities in which the right to participate is gained only upon the attainment of a certain age.

Laws regulating the social and political conduct of children are in a state of rapid change, and prohibitions vary from state to state. This chapter addresses many of the laws that affect only, or chiefly, adolescents. Although a number of other topics discussed in other chapters, notably contraception, abortion, and pregnancy, could have been placed in this chapter, the issues discussed here do not neatly fit in any of the other chapter headings. The reader is encouraged to turn to the graphs in the Appendexes that state the exact age at which rights are gained in each state.

The Rights of Adolescents

Do children have constitutional rights?

Yes. Although the answer to this question was less certain before 1967, it is now clear that children enjoy fundamental rights that are protected by the Constitution. This does not mean that *all* of the rights in the Constitution belong to children, or that *all* children have the same constitutional rights. Applications differ depending on a number of factors.

Why are children not always entitled to the full constitutional protection that adults receive under similar circumstances?

There are two related reasons for this. First, a child may lack the maturity, experience, or capacity necessary to exercise a right that adults ordinarily enjoy. Second, the state may exercise power over the lives of children in order to maximize their potential for development into healthy functioning adults in circumstances that the state could not act if it were regulating the conduct of adults. This answer requires a brief explanation.

American constitutional law is founded on the principle of minimum state restriction of the individual's freedom. Developed from the reasoning of philosophers such as John Locke and, later, Thomas Jefferson, the Bill of Rights is written in language that limits the government's authority; that is, "Congress shall make no law . . . abridging the freedom of speech, or of the press; . . . The right of the people to be secure in their persons, houses, papers and affects, against unreasonable searches and seizures, shall not be violated. . . ." There are two sources of power that the government may authorize as encroachment on an individual's freedom: the *police* power and the *parens patriae* power. The police power is the state's power to prevent its citizens from harming one another and to promote all aspects of the public welfare (generally referred to as the "health, safety, and welfare" of society). The parens patriae power is the state's paternalistic power to protect the welfare of individuals who lack the capacity to act in their own best interests. The two groups most affected by the exercise of the parens patriae power are children and mental incompetents.

Acting under either of these powers, or a combination of the two, state laws restrict the freedom of, or impose limitations on, children in ways that would be unconstitutional if done to adults. Obvious examples of their application include compulsory education or child labor laws. But even as the state restricts the freedom of children in these ways, children possess many constitutional rights that limit the way in which the state may enact and enforce laws against them.

Do adolescents have greater rights than very young children?

Yes. It is important to remember that the presumption underlying exercise of the parens patriae power is that the individual lacks the capacity to act in his or her own best interest. People do not magically attain the ability to care for themselves upon reaching the age of 18. If it is clear that three-month-olds don't have this capacity, it is equally clear that a great number of seventeen-year-olds do. Once it can be shown that a state-imposed restriction on an individual's freedom is based on the faulty premise that the individual affected does not have the capacity to make intelligent decisions for him or herself, the justification for the restriction is diminished. For this reason, adolescents have many rights to make decisions for themselves that younger children do not have.

First-Amendment Freedoms

Which constitutional rights do adolescents enjoy that are greater than rights enjoyed by young children?

Young people have the constitutional right to the freedom of speech, expression, and thought—the core qualities of the First Amendment—which may not be abridged by the state except for "compelling" reasons. In 1969, the Supreme Court declared that grammar and high school students "may express their opinions, even on controversial subjects."[1] This right exists because the value of openly expressed speech from *all* sources, including young people, contributes to the freedom and competition of ideas for the entire society.

The area of First-Amendment rights that has resulted in the fewest rights accorded to young people is obscenity. Even in this area, however, young people have definite constitutional rights; they are less broad than adults' rights, however, and states may curtail expression more extensively when it reaches minors. Although adults have a constitutional right of privacy to possess obscene materials in their own home,[2] young people have no comparable right.[3] Nonetheless, speech that is not "obscene as to youths . . . cannot be suppressed solely to protect the young from ideas or images that a legislative body thinks unsuitable for them, even when material contains nudity."[4]

Do young people have the right to purchase or obtain pornographic material?

No. Virtually every state makes the sale and distribution of pornographic or obscene material (books, magazines, films, and so forth) illegal, *regardless* of the age of the purchaser. In addition, most states have laws that contain strict definitions of sexually explicit material considered "harmful to minors,"[5] and stiff penalties for those convicted of selling or distributing pornographic materials to minors.[6] Therefore, some materials, though deemed suitable for adult consumption, may not be disseminated to minors.[7]

A typical statute defines the term *harmful to minors* as the representation of nudity, sexual conduct, sexual excitement, or sadomasochistic abuse when it (a) predominantly appeals to the prurient, shameful, or morbid interests of minors; and (b) is patently offensive to prevailing standards in the *adult* community with respect to what is suitable for minors; and (c) is utterly without redeeming social importance for minors.[8]

The ages under which it is illegal to sell or distribute indecent, obscene, or pornographic materials to young people vary by state; in many states it is one or two years below the age of majority (see appendix J).

It is important to note that most state laws do not make it illegal for *minors* to purchase or possess obscene materials; instead, they prohibit the *dealer* from selling or distributing to the child. But a minor's misrepresentation of his age may be illegal.[9]

Is it constitutional to prohibit the distribution of books or films that visually depict sexual performances by children under sixteen but which are not obscene?

Yes. Virtually every state prohibits the production of child pornography. In addition, at least twenty states prohibit the *sale* or *distribution* of nonobscene materials depicting sexual performances by children under a certain age.[10] Normally, the First Amendment prohibits any restriction on nonobscene materials, but the United States Supreme Court recently upheld such laws against a challenge that they violated the First Amendment.[11] The Court repeated its long held view that states have a compelling interest in protecting minors and, specifically, that the "prevention of sexual exploitation and abuse of children constitutes a government objective of surpassing importance."[12] Since the Court found that using children as subjects of pornography is harmful to the child's psychological, emotional, and mental well-being, it concluded that restricting the *distribution* as well as the *production* of such materials is constitutional.

Does a young person's parent have the right to stop pornographic materials from being sent through the mail to the house?

Yes. Federal law grants the right of a person to require a commercial mailing house to remove his name and the name of minors under nineteen residing in the same household from mailing list(s).[13] The law was enacted to protect the rights of families to protect themselves and their children from receiving unsolicited pornographic materials through the mail.

Curfews

What is a "curfew"?

A curfew is a law, regulation, or ordinance in effect in a specified geographical area that restricts access to the streets and public places during the evening and night hours by certain or all people. Generally, curfew laws apply only to young people.[14]

Few curfew laws are in effect on a state-wide basis. Most state statutes merely enable counties, cities, or smaller localities to impose their own restrictions on the movement of children during the night. Some states and many localities have no curfew laws at all, and there may be different local laws within the same state.

Restricted hours and the ages of young people subject to curfew laws vary widely. In San Francisco, for example, children under the age of 18 may not loiter in a public place between 11:00 P.M. and 6:00 A.M.[15] Dauphin County, Pennsylvania, restricts access to the streets after 10:00 P.M. for children under 12, after 10:30 P.M. for those under 14, and after 11:00 P.M. for young people between the ages of 14 and 18.[16]

Most curfew laws permit young people to be on the streets or in public places after hours *when in the company of an adult*. Some laws permit young people to be out after hours if they have their parents' permission.

What happens if a child violates a curfew law?

He may be stopped or picked up by the police. What happens then depends on how serious the policeman considers the matter. If the young person has a valid excuse for being out late, the officer may do nothing or merely give a warning. In other cases, the offending child may be picked up and either taken home to his or her parents or to the police station. If the child is taken into custody, he or she may later be released to his or her parents or charged with an act of delinquency or the status of being in need of supervision (see chapter X).

In some states and localities, a child must violate a curfew law more than once before he can be formally charged with an offense or taken into court.

May a young person be arrested by the police for a curfew violation?

Usually, but not necessarily. In several states (including New York) the police may only arrest young people when there is probable cause to believe they committed an act that would be a crime if committed by an adult.[17] Since curfews do not apply to adults, violation of a curfew is not a crime. Using this reasoning, a court in New York dismissed a charge of resisting arrest against an accused delinquent since the arrest itself was illegal, and in New York the crime of resisting arrest is not established unless the arrest was lawful.[18]

How can young people find out what the curfew laws are (if any) in his community?

They should ask a policeman, a probation officer, a city or local official, such as the mayor or town supervisor, or an official or guidance counselor at school.

Is it a violation of curfew if a young person is a passenger in an automobile or driving a car during restricted hours?

Usually.[19] Where the curfew flatly restricts being out after a certain hour, even being in a car is considered a violation.

Are curfews constitutional?

Some are and some are not. A number of courts have found curfew laws too broad, too vague, or simply unnecessary intrusions on parental prerogatives. Other courts have found them permissible.

Curfew laws are penal laws. To be valid, a penal law must be clear enough to be understood by those subject to its provisions. Laws that do not meet this test are often found to violate the Fourteenth Amendment's guarantee of due process of law because their terms are so vague that they do not provide adequate notice of the prohibited activity. In the past decade, a number of laws that prohibited *loitering* or *vagrancy* (by adults) have been declared void for reasons of vagueness, since these terms are incapable of precise definitions.[20] Many curfew laws contain similarly vague terms and are therefore subject to the same constitutional scrutiny. Laws in Hawaii and Oklahoma have been declared void for this reason.[21]

In other locations, curfew laws have been overturned for more substantive reasons. As early as 1898, a city ordinance in Graham, Texas, which made it unlawful for persons under twenty-one to be on the streets after nine P.M., was struck down since it unlawfully usurped the functions of *parents*.[22] More recently, curfew laws in California and Florida have been declared void since they violated children's rights of liberty and freedom of travel.[23]

In overturning a Seattle curfew, the Supreme Court of Washington stated, "Prima facie, mere sauntering or loitering on a public way is lawful and the right of any man, woman or child."[24] The court then went on to cite a United States Supreme Court opinion that walking, strolling, wandering, and even loafing and loitering in public places "are historically part of the amenities of life as we have known them."[25]

A Portland, Oregon, curfew was struck down on the ground that it gave the police the power to arrest a person on the suspicion that he had no lawful purpose for merely being somewhere, when the true standard for arrest should be probable cause that a crime has been committed.[26] Similarly, the Seattle curfew mentioned earlier was found to exceed the lawful scope of police power because it made no distinction between conduct calculated to cause harm and conduct that is essentially innocent.[27]

There is no clear trend respecting courts' views on the constitutionality of curfew laws and ultimately it may be necessary for the United States Supreme Court to decide whether such laws are indeed constitutional. Recently a federal appeals court declared juvenile curfew law in Louisiana unconstitutional.[28] The curfew prohibited persons under 17 from being on the streets from 11:00 P.M. to 4:00 A.M. on Sunday through Thursday night, or 1:00 A.M. to 4:00 A.M. Friday or Saturday night unless on an emergency errand or accompanied by a parent or other responsible adult. The court did not rule that *all* curfews are per se unconstitutional, but only that the particular curfew being challenged was too broad and interfered with a young person's constitutional right to association, employment, and travel, and that it violated the parent's constitutional right to raise children free from state interference as well.

Generally, laws that restrict juvenile activities are upheld because courts conclude that such laws aid parents in raising their children. But curfew laws that prohibit outside activities even with parental permission cannot be said to *enforce* parental authority since, in fact, these laws *replace* such authority. Using this reasoning, a second federal court, in a decision reversed by an appeal court on other grounds, recently declared unconstitutional a New Hampshire curfew that restricted access to public streets, except for specific activities, by persons under age 16 from 10:00 P.M. to 5:00 A.M.[29] The court found that the law violated both the child's and parent's constitutional rights.

Nonetheless, not all curfew laws have been declared void when challenged: several have withstood recent constitutional attack.[30] In one of these cases, the United States Supreme Court refused to review the decision of a lower federal court upholding a curfew ordinance on the grounds that it was a reasonable means of furthering the following four legitimate state goals: (1) protection of children from each other and from other persons on the street during the nighttime hours; (2) enforcement of parental control and responsibility for children; (3) protection of the public from nocturnal mischief by minors; and (4) reduction in the incidence of juvenile criminal activity.[31]

Marriage

Do young people have the right to get married?

Yes, but they may need parental permission or approval from a judge, or approval from both, if they are below a certain age.

In California, for example, men and women can get married without anyone's permission if they are over 18. If they are under 18 they must obtain the consent of their parents and of the superior court.[32]

In New York, people over the age of 18 may marry on their own agreement. If the male is between the ages of 16 and 18, and if the female is between the ages of 14 and 18, written parental consent is necessary. Furthermore, if the female is between the ages of 14 and 16, permission from a court must be secured as well. In New York, no male under 16 or female under 14 may be permitted to marry under any circumstances.[33]

The ages at which marriages are permitted in each state are listed in Appendix E.

Are laws that restrict a minor's right to marry constitutional?

Yes. A federal court in *Moe v. Dinkins*,[34] the first case of its kind, recently upheld New York's scheme just described. The plaintiffs in *Dinkins* included a 15-year-old girl and a 17-year-old boy who wished to marry but did not have parental consent. The girl was 8 months pregnant. They claimed that the law violated their constitutional right to marry and that it resulted in their becoming parents of an illegitimate child. The court rejected their claims and ruled that laws that require parental consent are valid. Requiring parental consent, reasoned the court, ensures that at least one mature person will participate in the decision to marry; and the state has a legitimate interest, in light of the importance of the decision to marry, to ensure that the decision is not reached hastily. The court of appeals affirmed the *Dinkins* decision, ruling that minors do not have a fundamental right to marry.[35] So long as there exists a rational basis for a restriction, the court held, laws restricting marriage by age requirements are constitutional.

What happens if a minor marries without the necessary consent of his parents or the judge?

In some states the marriage is considered absolutely void; that is, nonexistent in the eyes of the law. In other states, however, such marriages are valid, but *may* be voided if a court so declares upon someone's protest or challenge; if no one challenges the marriage, it is valid. In many states, if the young person stays married beyond the age where consent is no longer needed, the marriage may become valid automatically and it may not be challenged on the basis that it was entered into illegally.

Alcohol, Tobacco, and Headshops

What is an "alcoholic beverage"?

An alcoholic beverage is any drink that contains a certain amount of alcohol. The amount necessary to qualify a drink as an "alcoholic beverage" varies from state to state, but is usually any amount over half of one percent of the contents.[36] Generally, all wines, beers, "hard" liquors, and liqueurs are alcoholic beverages.

Do minors have the right to purchase alcoholic beverages?

No. Every state prevents young people from *purchasing* alcoholic beverages, either by making it illegal for minors to buy them or by making it illegal for adults to sell them, or both. Not every state, however, makes it a crime merely to *drink* or *possess* alcohol. In some states it is illegal for young people to drink alcohol only if they are outside the home or in public places (these laws imply that it is legal for minors to drink liquor supplied by their parents in the home). In others it is permissible to participate in the drinking of alcohol or spirits in the course of a religious observance (for instance, sipping wine at Communion, Passover, or Sabbath).

The age at which it becomes legal to buy, possess and drink alcoholic beverages is determined by each state. Many states that lowered their age of majority from 21 to 18 kept the age at which it is permitted to buy, possess and drink alcoholic beverages at 21. A number of states that allowed persons under 21 to drink have raised the age in recent years because of a disproportionately high percentage of drunken driving by 18- and 19-year-olds. New York, for example, has recently raised the legal age from 18 to 19, and New Jersey has raised it from 19 to 21. The age requirements in each state are listed in Appendix C.

It is lawful to prohibit only young men from purchasing alcoholic beverages?

No. In 1976, the United States Supreme Court ruled

unconstitutional an Oklahoma law that prohibited the sale of 3.2-percent beer to males under the age of 21 and to females under the age of 18.[37] The Court held that such discrimination solely on the basis of gender violated the guarantee of equal protection of the law. As a result of this decision, states may prohibit the purchase of alcoholic beverages below an age they see fit, but the age must be uniform for men and women.

What if there is liquor or beer in a car controlled by a minor?

In some states, it is illegal for minors merely to transport liquor, even if sealed or unopened, in automobiles unless accompanied by a parent or unless they are being transported for a lawful business purpose.[38] Moreover, if beer cans or bottles are opened, or if the seal on a bottle of liquor is broken, those in the automobile may be found guilty of a crime, even if they are not drinking or intoxicated.[39]

Are minors permitted to work in bars or taverns?

No. Almost every state prohibits the employment of minors in nightclubs, bars, taverns, or any place where drinks are being served or consumed.[40]

Do minors have the right to purchase and possess tobacco products?

As with alcohol, it depends on the state. Moreover, a number of states distinguish between the *sale* of tobacco products and their *possession*. In many states, it is illegal for adults to sell tobacco products to young people under a certain age, but it is legal for young people to possess and smoke them. The ages and scope of prohibited activity in each state are listed in Appendix F.

Generally, tobacco products include cigarettes, cigars, pipe and rolling tobacco, and snuff.

If a minor is married, are laws restricting sales to minors applicable?

Yes. It is no defense to a charge of violation of state law that the minor was married.[41]

Is it lawful for a state to prohibit the sale or display of drug-related print materials in "head shops" to minors?

Generally, no. Young people have First-Amendment rights to *information*. Recognizing these rights, a federal court declared unconstitutional a Georgia law that prohibited, among other things, advertising, describing, or displaying to persons under 18, "any machine, instrument, tool . . . or device . . . to introduce into the human body . . . [or] to enhance the effect on the human body."[42] The state's purpose in enacting the law was to reduce teenage drug use. The court recognized the legitimacy of the state's interest but emphasized that the law improperly restricted *information*.

Hitchhiking

Is it against the law to hitchhike?

It depends on the state. In some states hitchhiking is totally illegal, in others it is not prohibited at all, and in still others it is legal under certain conditions. In New York and California, for example, hitchhiking is not permitted on freeways, thruways, parkways, bridges, tunnels, and other limited-access highways, or on ramps leading to and from freeways and thruways, but it *is permitted* from the side of other roads if the hitchhiker stands off the roadway (usually the paved portion of the road) when soliciting a ride.[43] Moreover, in many states special circumstances may justify hitchhiking; such as during emergencies or illness. At least thirty-three states prohibit hitchhiking in certain places depending on where the hitchhiker stands.

Perhaps no other laws are so randomly enforced as those concerning hitchhiking. In some states and localities hitchhiking is overlooked by law enforcement officials but in others it is strictly or even discriminatorily enforced. Local custom and the appearance of the hitchhiker often play an important role in determining how hitchhiking laws are enforced.

Statutory Rape

What is "statutory" rape?

Rape is defined as sexual intercourse with another person without the other person's consent. But in each state the law defines (by statute) the age below which females are deemed *incapable* of forming consent. Therefore, even though a female may *in fact* consent to sexual intercourse, she may still be found to have been raped *in law*, because she is considered without capacity to consent if she is below a certain age. Sexual intercourse with females below this age may result in prosecution for statutory rape even though both parties may consent.

The ages below which females may not consent to sexual intercourse are listed for each state in Appendix G.

In most states, the age of the female is the sole factor to be considered, but in a few states a male may not be found guilty of statutory rape unless he is also *above* a certain age, specified by statute. As indicated in Appendix F, a growing number of states have an age of consent for females *and* males alike.

In some states, if statutory rape cannot be proved, one may be charged with impairing or corrupting the morals of a minor, depending on the age of the parties.

Is it constitutional to make statutory rape a crime that punishes only males?

Yes. In 1981, the United States Supreme Court, in *Michael M. v. Superior Court*, upheld the constitutionality of a California law that makes it a crime for a man to engage in sexual intercourse with a "female not the wife of the perpetrator, where the female is under the age of 18 years."[44] Even though it is unlawful in California to have sexual intercourse with underage females with no corresponding crime for sexual intercourse by females, and underage males, the Court found that the law does not unlawfully discriminate between males and females.

> We need not be medical doctors to discern that young men and young women are not similarly situated with respect to the problems and the risks of sexual intercourse. Only women may become pregnant, and they suffer disproportionately the profound physical, emotional, and psychological consequences of sexual activity.[45]

Is it constitutional to punish only a male for statutory rape when both the male and female are the same age?

Yes. In *Michael M.*, the male and female were both under 18. The Court upheld the law even as applied to that case, reasoning that the age of the man is irrelevant since the harm sought to be protected by the law is the prevention of illegitimate teenage pregnancy, and 16-year-olds are as capable of causing pregnancy as men over 18.[46]

Is it constitutional for a state law to punish males, but not females, for statutory sex-related crimes other than rape?

There is no clear answer to this. Many states prohibit sexual touching when females are below a certain age. Courts that considered the constitutionality of such laws before *Michael M*. found them to be unconstitutional. An Oklahoma law, for example, permitted boys to be found guilty of a crime (molesting children) at age 16 but under the same law girls were liable for prosecution only if they were 18 or older.[47] This distinction was found unconstitutional because an Oklahoma court could find no rational relationship between the differing age thresholds, and no evidence that the age distinctions furthered the goal of discouraging child molestation.[48]

Similarly, a federal court of appeals declared unconstitutional a New Hampshire statutory rape law that would appear to be constitutional in light of the *Michael M*. decision, reasoning that many of the harms of teenage sex apply equally to both sexes.[49] The *Michael M*. decision emphasized a state's legitimate interest in protecting females from unwanted *pregnancy*. Accordingly, laws that punish only males who engage in sexually related activity other than intercourse must be justified on grounds different from the reasoning of the decision in *Michael M*.

Voting and Juries

Do 18-year-olds have the right to vote?

Yes, in all federal elections.[50] In most states, young people may vote in state and local elections at age 18 as well. In a few states, however, the age qualification for voting in state elections is older than 18, even though 18-year-olds may vote in all national elections (see Appendix G).

Do 18-year-olds have the right to register and vote in their college communities?

In most states the answer is yes, as determined by opinions of state attorneys general[51] or by virtue of federal or state court decisions.[52]

In a few states, however, it has been determined that election boards may examine potential student voters about facts surrounding their claims of residency or the "locus of their primary concerns," even though nonstudents are not so questioned.[53]

Do young people have the right to serve on local juries?

Only those young people over a certain age, which is eighteen in most states (see Appendix H).

School

Is it legal for a young person to quit school?

All states have compulsory education laws that require daily attendance at school or some equivalent form of instruction. A young person may leave school only upon reaching a certain age or upon graduating from high school, whichever occurs first. The age requirement varies by state (see Appendix I).

In some states a young person may quit school at an earlier age if he has a full-time job, and in almost every state school is not compulsory for children who are physically or mentally unable to attend classes or benefit from instruction.

Do young people who are in the United States illegally have the right to a free public education?

Yes. It is unlawful for a state to deny to school-age children, who are not legally admitted aliens, the right to attend public school on the same basis as all other children.[54] However, if children move into a school district for the sole purpose of attending school there and they are not living with their parents, it is not unconstitutional to charge them tuition.[54a]

May local school boards remove books that it deems offensive from the library shelves of high schools?

No. More precisely, the United States Supreme Court recently ruled that local school boards may not remove books from school library shelves *merely* because they dislike the ideas contained in those books.[55] This decision does not mean that students have constitutional rights to ensure that a particular book or series of books is *placed* in their school library or that decisions to remove books based on sound educational policy may not occur. But once books are already in a school library, they may not be removed for reasons that offend the First Amendment.

The Draft

Do young people have to register with the Selective Service?

Only young men. Since 1980, all males between the ages of 18 and 26 are required to register with the Selective Service.[56] Failure to register is punishable by imprisonment for up to 5 years and/or a fine up to $10,000.[57]

Is it constitutional to require men but not women to register?

Yes. In 1981, the United States Supreme Court upheld Congress's decision not to require women to register for military service.[58] Recognizing that Congress had the power to conclude that women should not be drafted for combat military duty, the Court refused to second-guess Congress's decision not to require women to register.

Electronic Games

Are there laws that restrict young people from using electronic games?

Yes. A number of cities and localities in the United States restrict access by young people to places in which electronic games are played. One such law for the city of Mesquite, Texas provides:

> It shall be unlawful for any owner, operator or displayer of coin-operated amusement machines to allow any person under the age of seventeen (17) years to play or operate a coin-operated amusement

machine unless such minor is accompanied by a parent or legal guardian.[59]

The constitutionality of these laws is being challenged in many states. In one recent decision, the United States Supreme Court avoided a ruling on constitutional grounds;[60] but a federal court of appeals declared the law to be unconstitutional because there is no substantial connection between the law and any legitimate state purpose.[60a]

Many of these laws have been passed in response to the tremendous popularity of electronic games with young people. The Supreme Court of Hawaii, finding these games to be of skill and accuracy rather than chance, declared such a law to be void.[61]

Housing

Is it lawful for landlords to refuse to rent apartments to families with children?

It may be. No definitive judicial ruling on this point has been made, but most courts that have considered the question have allowed landlords to discriminate against families with young children.[62] The problem is growing nationally. In Atlanta, Cincinnati, and Dallas, to name just a few cities, a very large percentage—reported to be as large as sixty to seventy percent—of apartment complexes refuse to rent to families with young children. In the absence of a state law or local ordinance banning such discrimination, landlords are permitted to rent to whomever they wish. Discrimination in housing on the basis of race, color, religion, sex, or national origin is prohibited by federal law, but not on the basis of age or status as a family.[63]

At least nine states—Arizona, Connecticut, Delaware, Illinois, Massachusetts, Michigan, Minnesota, New Jersey, and New York—and the District of Columbia have enacted laws prohibiting discrimination in rental housing against families with children.[64] In addition, a greater number of cities have passed similar ordinances.[65]

Recently, in two very important rulings, courts have declared that discrimination based upon age is illegal. In one case, the California Supreme Court ruled that landlords who refuse to rent to families with children violate California's Unruh Civil Rights Act.[66] In deciding the case, the court said:

> A society that sanctions wholesale discrimination against its children in obtaining housing engages in suspect activity. Even the most primitive society fosters the protection of its young; such a society would hardly discriminate against children in need for shelter.[67]

In the second case, a federal appeals court ruled, for the first time, that an adults-only policy of renting in Los Angeles infringed upon the fundamental right of family members to live together, and required a compelling justification for the discrimination.[68] In deciding the case, the court held that such discrimination may violate the federal Fair Housing Act.[69]

NOTES

1. *Tinker v. Des Moines Independent Community School Dist.* 393 U.S. 503, 513 (1969).
2. *Stanley v. Georgia*, 394 U.S. 557 (1969).
3. *Ginsberg v. New York*, 390 U.S. 629 (1968); *F.C.C. v. Pacifica Foundation*, 438 U.S. 726 (1978).
4. *Erznoznick v. City of Jacksonville*, 422 U.S. 205, 213-14 (1975).
5. *Ginsberg v. New York, supra* note 3; *Ballas v. Symm*, 494 F.2d 1167 (5th Cir. 1974).
6. *See, e.g.*, N.C. GEN. STAT. §§14–190.7, 14–190.8 (1981).
7. *Bookcase, Inc. v. Broderick*, 18 N.Y.2d 71, 271 N.Y.S.2d 947 (1966).
8. *See, e.g.*, N.H. REV. STAT. ANN. ch. 571–B:1(VI) (Supp. 1981); N.Y. PENAL L. §235.20(6) (1980) (emphasis added).
9. *See, e.g.*, N.M. STAT. ANN. §§30–37–6, (1978).
10. *See, e.g.*, COLO. REV. STAT. §18–6–403 (Supp. 1981); MASS. GEN. LAWS ANN. ch. 272, §29A (Supp. 1982); N.Y. PENAL L. §263.05 (Supp. 1981).
11. *New York v. Ferber*, 458 U.S. 747 (1982).
12. *Id.* 458 U.S. at 757.
13. Title III of the Postal Revenue and Federal Salary Act of 1967, 81 Stat. 645, 39 U.S.C. §4009, sustained in *Rowan v. U.S. Post Office*, 397 U.S. 729 (1970).
14. *See* "Juvenile Curfews: A Policy Statement. National Council on Crime and Delinquency," in *Crime and Delinquency* 136 (April 1972).

15. S.F. MUNIC. CODE, P.C. 539a.
16. Ch. VI, Ord. No. 662, Borough of Middletown, County of Dauphin, Commonwealth of Pa. (1975).
17. *See, e.g.*, N.Y. FAM. CT. ACT §305.2 (1983).
18. *In re Michael G.*, 99 Misc. 2d 699, 416 N.Y.S.2d 1016 (Fam. Ct. 1979).
19. *In re Francis W.*, 42 Cal. App. 3d 892, 117 Cal. Rptr. 277 (1974).
20. *Papachristou v. City of Jacksonville*, 405 U.S. 156 (1972); *Ricks v. District of Columbia*, 414 F.2d 1097, 1103-4, 1107 (D.C. Cir. 1968).
21. *In re Doe*, 54 Hawaii 647, 513 P.2d 1385 (1973), striking down a Honolulu ordinance that prohibited a child under 18 from loitering in public places between 10:00 P.M. and sunrise unless accompanied by a parent; *Hays v. Municipal Court of Oklahoma City*, 487 P.2d 974 (Okl. Crim. App. 1971), striking down an Oklahoma City ordinance that made it a crime for any person under 16 to loaf or loiter on the streets between 9:00 P.M. and 6:00 A.M.
22. *Ex parte McCarver*, 46 S.W. 936 (Tex. Ct. Crim. App. 1898).
23. *Alves v. Justice Court*, 148 Cal. App. 2d 419, 306 P.2d 601 (1957); *W.J.W. v. State*, 356 So.2d 48 (Fla. Dist. Ct. App. 1978).
24. *City of Seattle v. Pullman*, 82 Wash. 2d 794, 514 P.2d 1059 (1973); *citing Commonwealth v. Carpenter*, 325 Mass. 519, 521, 91 N.E.2d 666, 667 (1950) (emphasis added).
25. *City of Seattle v Pullman, supra* n. 24, at 1064, *citing Papachristou v. City of Jacksonville, supra* note 4, at 164.
26. *City of Portland v. James*, 251 Or. 8, 444 P.2d 554 (1968).
27. *City of Seattle v. Pullman, supra* n. 24.
28. *Johnson v. City of Opelousas*, 658 F.2d 1065 (5th Cir. 1981).
29. *McCollester v. City of Keene, New Hampshire*, 514 F. Supp. 1046 (D.N.H. 1981), *rev'd on other grounds*, 668 F.2d 617 (1st Cir. 1982).
30. *In re Nancy C.*, 28 Cal. App. 3d 747, 105 Cal. Rptr. 113 (1972); *Bykofsky v. Borough of Middletown*, 401 F. Supp. 1242 (H.D. Pa. 1975); *aff'd*, 535 F.2d 1245 (3rd Cir. 1976), *cert. denied*, 429 U.S. 964 (1976); *People v. Chambers*, 66 Ill. 2d 36, 360 N.E.2d 55 (1976).
31. *Bykofsky v. Borough of Middletown, supra* n. 30.
32. CAL. CIV. CODE §4101 (Supp. 1982).
33. N.Y. DOM. REL. LAW §15 (1977).
34. *Moe v. Dinkins*, 533 F. Supp. 623 (S.D.N.Y. 1981).
35. *Moe v. Dinkins*, 669 F.2d 67 (2d Cir. 1982); *cert. denied*, 103 S. Ct. 61 (1982).
36. *See, e.g.*, CAL. BUS. & PROF. CODE §23004 (1964).
37. *Craig v. Boren*, 429 U.S. 190 (1976).
38. *See, e.g.*, CAL. VEH. CODE §23224 (Supp. 1982).
39. *See, e.g.*, *id.* at §§23222, 23223 (Supp. 1982).
40. *See, e.g.*, CAL. BUS. & PROF. CODE §§25663, 25665 (1964).
41. *State v. Garman*, 250 Iowa 166, 93 N.W.2d 105 (1958).
42. *High Ol' Times v. Busbee*, 456 F. Supp. 1035 (N.D. Ga. 1978), *aff'd*, 621 F.2d 141 (5th Cir. 1980) (striking GA. CODE §26–9912).

43. N.Y. VEH. & TRAF. LAW §1157 (1970); CAL. VEH. CODE §21957 (1971).
44. *Michael M. v. Superior Court of Sonoma County,* 450 U.S. 464 (1981) upholding Cal. Penal Code §261.5). *See also People v. Whidden,* 51 N.Y.2d 457, 415 N.E.2d 927, 434 N.Y.S.2d 937 (1980).
45. 450 U.S. at 471.
46. *Id.* at 475.
47. 21 OKLA. STAT. §1123.
48. *Matter of D.H.W.,* 614 P.2d 81 (Okla. Crim. App. 1980).
49. *Meloon v. Helgemoe,* 564 F.2d 602 (1st Cir. 1977), *cert. denied,* 436 U.S. 950 (1978).
50. U.S. Const., amend. XXVI, upheld in *Oregon v. Mitchell,* 400 U.S. 112 (1970).
51. Massachusetts, Louisiana, Florida, Idaho, Georgia, Oklahoma, Pennsylvania, Connecticut, Maryland, Illinois, Missouri, West Virginia, Kansas, Rhode Island, Nevada, and Oregon.
52. *See, e.g., Jolicoeur v. Mihaly,* 5 Cal. 3d 565, 96 Cal. Rptr. 697, 488 P.2d 1 (1971); *Wilkins v. Bentley,* 385 Mich. 670, 189 N.W. 2d 423 (1971); *Anderson v. Brown,* 332 F. Supp. 1195 (S.D. Ohio 1971); *Johnson v. Darrell,* 337 F. Supp. 138 (S.D. Ind. 1971); *Bright v. Baesler,* 336 F. Supp. 527 (E.D. Ky. 1971).
53. *Ramey v. Rockefeller,* 348 F. Supp. 780 (E.D.N.Y. 1972).
54. *Plyler v. Doe,* 457 U.S. 202 (1982).
54a. *Martinez v. Bynum,* 75 L.Ed. 2d 879 (1983).
55. *Board of Education v. Pico,* 457 U.S. 853 (1982).
56. 50 U.S.C. App. §453 (Supp. 1982).
57. *Id.* at 462 (1981).
58. *Rostker v. Goldberg,* 453 U.S. 57 (1981).
59. Section 5 of Ordinance 1353 of the Code of the City of Mesquite, reproduced in *City of Mesquite v. Aladdin's Castle, Inc.,* 455 U.S. 283 (1982).
60. *City of Mesquite v. Aladdin's Castle, Inc., supra* note 59.
60a. *Aladdin's Castle, Inc. v. City of Mesquite,* 701 F.2d 524 (5th Cir. 1983).
61. *State v. Bloss,* 62 Hawaii 147, 613 P.2d 353 (1980).
62. *See, e.g., Riely v. Stoves,* 22 Ariz. App. 223, 526 P.2d 747 (1974); *Flowers v. John Burnham and Co.,* 21 Cal. App.3d 700, 98 Cal. Rptr. 644 (1971); *White Egret Condominium, Inc. v. Franklin,* 379 So.2d 346 (Fla. 1979).
63. 42 U.S.C. § 3604 (1976). *But see* 12 U.S.C. §1713(b)(1980).
64. ARIZ. REV. STAT. ANN. §33–1317 (Supp. 1982); CONN. GEN. STAT. §47a–2a (Supp. 1982); DEL. CODE ANN. tit. 25, §6503 (1975); D.C. CODE ANN. §6–2231 (1980); ILL. ANN. STAT. ch. 68, §3–104 (Supp. 1982); MASS. GEN. LAWS ANN. ch. 151B, §4(11)(Supp. 1982); MICH. COMP. LAWS ANN. §§37.2101–2804 (Supp. 1982); MINN. STAT. ANN. §363.03, subd. 2 (Supp. 1982); N.J. STAT. ANN. §2A:42–101 (Supp. 1982); N.Y. REAL PROP. LAW §§236, 237 (Supp. 1981).
65. *See, e.g.,* Philadelphia, Pa., Ordinance 130 (July 7, 1980); Seattle, Wash., Ordinance 108, 205 (May 18, 1979).

66. *Marina Point Ltd. v. Wolfson*, 30 Cal. 3d 721, 640 P.2d 115, 180 Cal. Rptr. 496 (1982) (interpreting CAL. CIV. CODE §51 (Supp. 1981)).
67. 640 P.2d at 129.
68. *Halet v. Wend Investment Co.*, 672 F.2d 1305 (9th Cir. 1982).
69. 42 U.S.C. §§3601–3631 (1976).

APPENDIX A

Legal Organizations Involved in Defending the Rights of Young People

The following list of legal organizations, which is incomplete, should be explained. There are a number of public and private law offices that represent children either free of charge or for a minimal fee. (Most of the organizations on the following pages provide legal services without charge.) On the other hand, the mere presence of an organization on this list does not guarantee that it is in a position to offer assistance. There are a number of financial, jurisdictional, geographic, and policy reasons that may not permit an organization listed here to grant the particular legal aid a reader may need. If contacted by telephone, by mail, or in person, however, they may be able to transfer a request to an appropriate local agency or to an organization more directly involved with defending the rights of young people.

National

Youth Law Center
693 Mission St.
San Francisco, CA 94105
415-495-6420

National Juvenile Law Center
3701 Lindell Blvd.
P.O. Box 14200
St. Louis, MO 63178
314-652-5555

American Civil Liberties Union
Children's Rights Project
132 W. 43 St.
New York, NY 10036
212-944-9800

Children's Defense Fund
Legal Division
1520 NH. Ave., N.W.
Washington, DC 20036
202-483-1470

NAACP Legal Defense Fund
10 Columbus Circle
New York, NY 10019
212-586-8397

Alabama

Legal Aid Society of Birmingham
3700 Fourth Ave. S., Suite 201
Birmingham, AL 35023
205–595–2501

Alabama Civil Liberties Union
P.O. Box 447
Montgomery, AL 36101
205–262–0303

Alaska

Alaska Civil Liberties Union
1247 8th Ave.
Anchorage, AL 99501
907–276–7133

Arizona

Arizona Civil Liberties Union
1433 North First St.
Phoenix, AZ 85004
602–254–3339

Public Defender of Maricopa County
Juvenile Defender Office
3125 W. Durango St.
Phoenix, AZ 85009
602–269–4230

Community Legal Services
903 North 2nd St.
Phoenix, AZ 85004
602–258–3434

The Navajo Nation
Navajo Children's Legal Services
P.O. Box 1593
Tuba City, AZ 86045

Southern Arizona Legal Aid
Family Law Unit
155 E. Alameda
Tucson, AZ 85701

Association for Youth Development
2125 S. Torrey
Pines Circle
Tuscon, AZ 85710

Arkansas

Northwest Arkansas Legal Services
Bldg. D, 530 North College
Fayetteville, AR 72701

Ozark Legal Services
26 E. Center
Fayetteville, AR 72701

Legal Aid Bureau of Central Arkansas
624 Malvern Ave.
Hot Springs, AR 71901

Arkansas Civil Liberties Union
P.O. Box 2832
Little Rock, AR 72203
501–374–2660

Public Defender
6th Judicial District of Arkansas
318 Wallace Bldg.
Little Rock, AR 72201
501–661–4685

Arkansas Legal Services
P.O. Box 2038
Little Rock, AR 72203

Arkansas Juvenile Justice Institute
Association of Arkansas Counties
118 National Old Line Blvd.
Little Rock, AR 72201

Legal Aid/Central Arkansas
Hall Bldg.
Little Rock, AR 72201

Central Arkansas Legal Services
209 W. Capitol Ave., Suite 36
Little Rock, AR 72201

Legal Services Northeast Arkansas
202 Walnut St.
Newport, AR 72112

California

San Mateo County Bar Association
Private Defender Program
Juvenile Court Branch
21 Tower Rd.
Belmont, CA 94002
415–573–2127

Berkeley Youth Alternatives
2141 Bonar St.
Berkeley, CA 94702

Inyo County Public Defender's Office
148 North Main St., Suite 200
Bishop, CA 93514
714–873–5912

Fresno County Public Defender
Juvenile Division
744 S. 10th St.
Fresno, CA 93721
209–488–3634

Imperial County Public Defender
120 North 8th St.
El Centro, CA 92243
714–339–4510

Solano County Public Defender Office
Hall of Justice
550 Union Ave.
Fairfield, CA
707–429–6254

ACLU of Southern California
633 S. Shatto Pl.
Los Angeles, CA 90005
213–487–1720

Los Angeles County Public Defender
19–513 Criminal Courts Bldg.
210 W. Temple St.
Los Angeles, CA 90012
213–974–2801

Loyola Law Clinics
1441 W. Olympic Blvd.
P.O. Box 15019
Los Angeles, CA 90015
213–736–1103

California Association of Black Lawyers
849 S. Highland Blvd.
Los Angeles, CA 94102

California Rural Legal Services
P.O. Box 2600
Marysville, CA 95901

Public Defender of Stanislaus County
Juvenile Unit
2215 Blue Gum Ave.
Box 3428
Modesto, CA 95353
209–571–6444

Legal Assistance Agency
1005 Jefferson St.
Napa, CA 94558

Legal Aid Society of Alameda
Domestic Relations Unit
1815 Telegraph Ave.
Oakland, CA 94612

Public Defender of Alameda County
Juvenile Unit
400 Broadway, Rm. 202A
Oakland, CA 94607

Legal Aid Society
2357 San Pablo Ave.
Oakland, CA 94612

Public Defender of Orange County
Juvenile Unit
301 City Dr. S., Rm. 2110
Orange, CA 92668
714–634–7366

Family Information Center
P.O. Box 1087
Rohnert Park, CA 94928
707–795–2177

Public Defender of Sacramento
Juvenile Unit

9701 Kiefer Blvd.
Sacramento, CA 95826

Juvenile Prison Law and Legal Counseling Clinic
3200 5th Ave.
Sacramento, CA 95817

California Rural Legal Services
328 Cayuga St.
Salinas, CA 93901

Monterey County Defender
P.O. Box 539
Salinas, CA 93902
408–758–4621

San Bernardino County Public Defender
Juvenile Office
900 E. Gilbert
San Bernardino, CA 92415
714–383–1975

Defenders Program of San Diego, Inc.
Juvenile Division
2851 Meadowlark Dr.
San Diego, CA 92123
714–277–6315

ACLU of Northern California
1663 Mission St., 4th Fl.
San Francisco, CA 94103
415–621–2488

National Center for Youth Law
693 Mission St., 6th Fl.
San Francisco, CA 94105
415–495–6420

Youth Law Center
1663 Mission St., 5th Fl.
San Francisco, CA 94103
415–543–3379

Public Defender, City and County of San Francisco
Juvenile Court Division
375 Woodside Dr.
San Francisco, CA 94127
415–731–7470

Legal Services for Children
149 Ninth St.
San Francisco, CA 94103
415–863–3762

Public Defender of Santa Clara County
70 W. Hedding
San Jose, CA 95110
408–998–5121

Public Defender of Alameda County
Juvenile East Office
2200 Fairmont Dr., Rm. 292
San Leandro, CA 94578
415–577–1097

Office of Public Defender
Santa Barbara County
Juvenile Office
4500 Hollister Ave.
Santa Barbara, CA 93110
805–967–7814

Youth Advocates Inc.
300 Bridgeway
Sausalito, CA 94965

San Joaquin County Public Defenders Office
24 South Hunter, Rm. 201
Stockton, CA 95202
209–944–2361

Colorado

Colorado Civil Liberties Union
815 E. 22 Ave.
Denver, CO 80205
303–861–2258

ACLU Mountain States Regional Office
2160 S. Holly
Denver, Co 80222
303–753–1214

Colorado State Public Defender
1575 Sherman St., Suite 718

Denver, Co 80203
303–866–2661

Guardian Ad Litem Program
Children's Legal Clinic
1764 Gilpin St.
Denver, Co 80220
303–333–1946

Public Defender's Office
331 14th St.
Denver, Co 80202
303–893–8939

Denver Legal Aid
770 Grant, Suite 5
Denver, CO 80203

Eastside Legal Services
2130 Downing St.
Denver, CO 80205

Connecticut

Division of Public Defender Services
4th Judicial District
Juvenile Unit
785 Fairfield Ave.
Bridgeport, CT 06604
203–579–6599

Division of Public Defender Services
3rd Judicial District
Juvenile Matters
67 Main St.
Danbury, CT 06810
203–797–4405

Connecticut Civil Liberties Union
22 Maple Ave.
Hartford, CT 06114
203–247–9823

Legal Aid Society of Hartford County, Inc.
Child Advocacy Unit
525 Main St.
Hartford, CT 06103
203–722–6360

Child Law Unit
New Haven Legal Assistance Association, Inc.
399 Temple St.
New Haven, CT 06511

Delaware

ACLU of Delaware
903 French St.
Wilmington, DE 19801
302–654–3966

Community Legal Aid Society, Inc.
103 W. 7 St.
Wilmington, DE 19801

District of Columbia

ACLU of the National Capitol Area
600 Pennsylvania Ave., S.E., Suite 301
Washington, DC 20003
202–544–1076

Children's Defense Fund
Legal Division
1520 New Hampshire Ave., N.W.
Washington, DC 20036
202–483–1470

FLOC—Child Advocacy Center
1341 G St., N.W., Suite 505
Washington, DC 20005
202–638–4031

Public Defender Service for the District of Columbia
451 Indiana Ave., N.W.
Washington, DC 20001
202–628–1200

Legal Aid Society of D.C.
666 11th St., N.W., Suite 300
Washington, DC 20001

National Network of Runaway Youth
1705 Desales St., N.W.
Washington, DC 20036

Children's Legal Rights
2008 Hillyer Pl., N.W.
Washington, DC 20009

Florida

Public Defender
6th Judicial Circuit Juvenile Office
14500–49th St. North
Clearwater, FL 33520
813–448–3904

Florida Institutional Legal Services, Inc.
2614 S.W. 34 St.
Gainesville, FL 32608
904–377–4212

Southern Legal Counsel
115 N.E. 7 Ave., Suite A
Gainesville, FL 32601

Indian Legal Services
633 Forest St.
Hollywood, FL 33024

Jacksonville Area Legal Aid
Family Law Unit
604 Hogan St.
Jacksonville, FL 32202

Office of the Public Defender
4th Judicial Circuit of Florida
Duval County Courthouse, Rm. 221
330 E. Bay St.
Jacksonville, FL 32202
904–633–6820

Jacksonville Legal Aid, Inc.
205 E. Church St.
Jacksonville, FL 32202
904–356–8371

Three Rivers Legal Services
817 W. Duval St.
Lake City, FL 32055

Office of the Public Defender
Juvenile Division
3300 N.W. 27 Ave.
Miami, FL 33142
305–638–6241

ACLU of Florida
7210 Red Rd., Rm. 208
South Miami, FL 33143
305–666–2950

Legal Aid Society of Orange City
121 S. Court St.
Orlando, FL 32801

Office of the Public Defender
9th Judicial Circuit
250 N. Orange Ave., Suite 900
Orlando, FL 32801
305–420–3109

Public Defender
1st Judicial Circuit
Juvenile Justice Center
2929 N. L St.
Pensacola, FL 32502

Public Defender
2058 Main St.
Sarasota, FL 33577
813–953–6615

Center for Children and Youth
102 S. Calhoun St.
Tallahassee, FL 32301

Legal Aid Bureau of Hillsborough County
311 N. Morgan St.
Tampa, FL 33602
813–272–5870

Georgia

Georgia Legal Services Program
Albany Regional Office
309 Pine Ave.
Albany, GA 31708

Georgia Legal Services Program
Americus Regional Office

P.O. Box 1469
123 W. Church St.
Americus, GA 31709

Laurens County Public Defender Program
P.O. Box 2035
Court Square Station
Dublin, GA 31021
912–275–0142

Public Defender
DeKalb County Juvenile Court
3631 Camp Circle
Decatur, GA 30032
404–294–2794

ACLU of Georgia
88 Walton St., N.W.
Atlanta, GA 30303
404–523–5398

ACLU Southern Regional Office
52 Fairlie St., N.W., Suite 355
Atlanta, GA 30303
404–523–2721

Atlanta Legal Aid Society
151 Spring St., N.W.
Atlanta, GA 30335

Atlanta Legal Aid Society
1131 Capitol Ave., S.W.
Atlanta, GA 30315

Hawaii

ACLU of Hawaii
217 S. King St., Suite 307
Honolulu, HI 96813
808–538–7336

Legal Aid Society of Hawaii
1164 Bishop St., 11th Fl.
Honolulu, HI 96813

Idaho

Idaho Civil Liberties Union
Boise Valley National Chapter
P.O. Box 968
Boise, ID 83701
208–384–2807

Southeast Idaho Chapter of ACLU
2810 Holly Pl.
Idaho Falls, ID 83401

Idaho Legal Aid Service Inc.
503 W. 19 St.
P.O. Box 1136
Idaho Falls, ID 83401

Pocatello Chapter of ACLU
Idaho State University
P.O. Box 8134
Pocatello, ID 83209

Shoshone County Public Defender's Office
524 Bank St.
Wallace, ID 83873
208–556–1507

Illinois

ACLU of Illinois
220 S. State St., Suite 816
Chicago, IL 60604
312–427–7330

Cook County Public Defender
Juvenile Division
1100 S. Hamilton Ave.
Chicago, IL 60612
312–738–8557

Legal Assistance Foundation of Chicago
Legal Assistance for Juveniles
343 S. Dearborn St.
Chicago, IL 60604
312–341–1070

Legal Advocacy Service
4753 N. Broadway, Suite 1118
Chicago, IL 60640

West Town Legal Services
2150 W. North Ave.
Chicago, IL 60647

Legal Assistance Foundation
106 N. Vermillion, Rm. 275
Danville, IL 61832

DeKalb County Public Defender's Office
317 E. Locust St.
DeKalb, IL 60115
815–758–6626

Public Defender of Jo Daviess County
295 Sinsinawa Ave.
E. Dubuque, IL 61028
815–747–3123

Whiteside County Public Defender's Office
114 E. Main St.
Morrison, IL 61270
815–772–7441

Jackson County Public Defender's Office
Jackson County Courthouse
Murphysboro, IL 62966
618–684–2151

Winnebago County Public Defender
Winnebago County Courthouse, Suite 245
Rockford, IL 61101
815–987–2536

Indiana

Legal Services Organization of Indiana
P.O. Box 1539
Bloomington, IN 47401

Project Justice and Equality, Inc.
475 Broadway, Suite 504
Gary, IN 46402
219–883–0384

Indiana Civil Liberties Union
445 N. Pennsylvania St., Suite 604
Indianapolis, IN 46204
317–635–4056

Indiana Civil Liberties Union
Calumet Chapter (NW IN)
P.O. Box 2521
Gary, IN 46403
219–939–0663

Indiana Public Defender Council
802 State Office Bldg.
Indianapolis, IN 46204

Legal Services Organization of Indianapolis
107 N. Penn St., Suite 300
Indianapolis, IN 46205

Public Defender, State of Indiana
309 W. Washington St., Suite 501
Indianapolis, IN 46204
317–232–2475

Iowa

Iowa Civil Liberties Union
American Civil Liberties Union
102 E. Grand, Suite G–100
Des Moines, IA 50309
515–243–3576

Polk County Legal Aid Society
102 E. Grand Ave.
Des Moines, IA 50312

Youth Law Center, Inc.
405 Shops Bldg.
Des Moines, IA 50309
515–244–1172

Lee County Public Defender
707–½ Ave. G
Fort Madison, IA 52627
319–372–3887

Cerro Gordo County Public Defender's Office
608 Brick and Tile Bldg.
Mason City, IA 50401
515–423–4181

Kansas

ACLU of Kansas and Western Missouri
8001 Conser, Suite 221
Overland Park, KS 66204
913-648-4534

Kansas Legal Services
112 W. 6 St.
Topeka, KS 66603

Kentucky

Northeast Kentucky Legal Services
P.O. Box 1573
Ashland, KY 41101

Northern Kentucky Legal Aid
302 Greenup St.
Covington, KY 41011

Office for Public Advocacy
State Office
State Office Bldg. Annex, 3rd Fl.
Frankfort, KY 40601
502-564-5211

Fayette County Legal Aid, Inc.
317 W. Short St.
Lexington, KY 40507
606-253-0593

Kentucky Civil Liberties Union
809 S. Fourth
Louisville, KY 40203
502-581-1181

Louisville-Jefferson County
Public Defender Corporation
200 Civil Plaza
701 W. Jefferson St.
Louisville, KY 40202
502-587-3800

Kentucky Youth Advocates, Inc.
2024 Woodford
Louisville, KY 40205

Legal Aid Society, Inc.
425 N. Muhammed Ali
Louisville, KY 40202

Western Kentucky Legal Aid
23 W. Center
Madisonville, KY 42431

Northeastern Kentucky Legal Services
P.O. Box 679
Morehead, KY 40351

Western Kentucky Legal Services, Inc.
401 W. Third St.
P.O. Box 478
Owensboro, KY 42301

Western Kentucky Legal Aid
501 S. 7th
Paducah, KY 42001

Louisiana

Advocate for the Developmentally Disabled
201 Medical Center
4550 North Blvd.
Baton Rouge, LA 70806
504-927-2320

Juvenile Justice Program
P.O. Box 44102
Capitol Station
Baton Rouge, LA 70804

ACLU of Louisiana
348 Baronne St., Suite 324
New Orleans, LA 70112
504-522-0617

Advocate for the Developmentally Disabled
333 St. Charles Ave., Suite 1221
New Orleans, LA 70130
504-522-2337

Orleans Indigent Defender Program

Juvenile Court
421 Loyola Ave.
New Orleans, LA 70112
504–523–0619

Tulane Law Clinic
Tulane University School of Law
7031 Freret St.
New Orleans, LA 70118
504–865–5153

Advocate for the Developmentally Disabled
103 Lucia Lane
Shreveport, LA 71106
318–688–4414

Maine

Maine Civil Liberties Union
97A Exchange St.
Portland, ME 04101
207–774–5444

Maryland

Legal Aid Bureau Inc.
100 Cathedral St.
Annapolis, MD 21401

Maryland Juvenile Law Clinic
500 W. Baltimore St.
Baltimore, MD 21201
301–528–7354

Legal Aid Bureau, Inc.
Family Law Center
341 N. Calvert St.
Baltimore, MD 21202

South Area Youth Services
P.O. Box 33088
District Heights, MD 20028

Guardian Ad Litem Project
237 Old Clay Rd. 202
Laurel, MD 20810

Legal Aid Bureau
P.O. Box 146
Upper Marlboro, MD 20772

ACLU of Maryland
744 Dulaney Valley Ct., Suite 4
Towson, MD 21204
301–337–9233

Massachusetts

ACLU of Massachusetts
47 Winter St.
Boston, MA 02108
617–482–3170

Greater Boston Legal Services
Juvenile Law Project
85 Devonshire St., 6th Fl.
Boston, MA 02109
617–367–2880

Task Force on Children Out of School, Inc.
d/b/a Massachusetts Advocacy Center
2 Park Square, 7th Fl.
Boston, MA 02116
617–357–8431

Mass Defender Committee
120 Boylston St.
Boston, MA 02116

Children's Advocate
21 James St.
Boston, MA 02118

Legal Services for Cape Cod
35 Winter St.
Hyannis, MA 02601

The Legal Services Institute
470 Centre St.
Jamaica Plain, MA 02130

North Shore Child Law Project
P.O. Box 710
Lynn, MA 01903

Greater Boston Legal Services
46 Gould Ave.
Walden, MA 02148

Western Massachusetts Legal Services
150 North St.
Pittsfield, MA 01201

Michigan

Legal Services of South East Michigan
153 N. Main
Adrian, MI 49221

Legal Services of Northern Michigan
117B State St.
Alpena, MI 49707

Washtenaw County Public Defender
Juvenile Court Sub-Office
2270 Platt Rd.
Ann Arbor, MI 48104
313–994–1716

Clinic Law Project
420 N. 4th Ave.
Ann Arbor, MI 48104

ACLU of Michigan
1701 David Whitney Bldg.
1553 Woodward Ave.
Detroit, MI 48226
313–961–4662

Wayne County Juvenile Defenders Office
51 W. Warren Ave., Suite 314
Detroit, MI 48201

Michigan Legal Services
900 Michigan Bldg.
220 Bagley Ave.
Detroit, MI 48226

Legal Aid and Defender Association of Detroit
Juvenile Defender Office
51 W. Warren, Suite 314
Detroit, MI 48201
313–832–2600

Legal Services of Eastern Michigan
352 S. Saginaw, Suite 403
Flint, MI

Legal Aid of Western Michigan
Family Law Center
430 Federal Square Bldg.
Grand Rapids, MI 49503

Justice for Juveniles
Michigan Council on Crime and Delinquency
300 N. Washington
Lansing, MI 48933

Allen Briggs
U.P. Legal Services
P.O. Box 188
Ontonagon, MI 49953

Michigan Indian Legal Services
733 E. 8 St., Suite B–6
Traverse City, MI 49684

Minnesota

Legal Aid Service
302 Ordean Bldg.
Duluth, MN 58802

Minnesota Civil Liberties Union
628 Central Ave.
Minneapolis, MN 55414
612–378–9392

Hennepin County Office of the Public Defender
C-2200 Government Center
Minneapolis, MN 55487
612–348–7530

Legal Rights Center, Inc.
808 E. Franklin Ave.
Minneapolis, MN 55404
612–871–4886

Guardian Ad Litem Program
350 S. 5 St., No. 507
Minneapolis, MN 55415

Mississippi

ACLU of Mississippi
528 N. State St.
Jackson, MS 39201
601–355–6464

Children's Defense Fund
Mississippi Project
P.O. Box 1684
Jackson, MS 39205

Jackson Public Defender
P.O. Box 2384
200 E. Pascagoula
Jackson, MS 39205
601–969–7156

Mississippi Legal Services Coalition
120 N. Congress St., Rm. 712
Jackson, MS 39201

Northern Mississippi Rural Legal Services
P.O. Box 618
Lexington, MS 39095

East Mississippi Legal Services
P.O. Box 1931
Meridian, MS 39301

Southern Mississippi Legal Services
P.O. Box 1654
Pascagoula, MS 39567

Indian Legal Services
Tribal Office Bldg.
Rt. 7, Box 21
Philadelphia, MS 39350

Missouri

Public Defender
Courthouse, 3rd Fl.
Benton, MO 63736
314–545–3574

Public Defender
34th Judicial Circuit Courthouse
Caruthersville, MO 63830

Office of the Public Defender
21st Judicial Circuit
St. Louis County Courthouse
7900 Carondelet
Clayton, MO 63105
314–889–2778

Mid-Missouri Legal Services Corporation
217 Strollway Centre
111 S. 9th St.
Columbia, MO 65201
314–442–0116

Public Defender
24th Judicial Circuit
3 S. Jefferson
Farmington, MO 63640

Public Defender
10th Judicial Circuit Courthouse
Hannibal, MO 63401

N.E. Missouri Legal Services
Federal Bldg.
801 Broadway
Hannibal, MO 63401

Public Defender
23rd Judicial Circuit
P.O. Box 156
Hillsboro, MO 63050

Public Defender's Office
32nd Judicial Circuit Courthouse
Jackson, MO 63755
314–243–3949

Legal Aid of Western Missouri
Juvenile Office
Juvenile Court Bldg.
625 E. 46
Kansas City, MO 64108
816–556–5426

Legal Aid of Western Missouri
P.O. Box 1086
St. Joseph, MO 64502

ACLU of Eastern Missouri
5756 W. Park Ave.
St. Louis, MO 63110
314-647-4554

National Juvenile Law Center
3701 Lindell Blvd.
P.O. Box 14200
St. Louis, MO 63178
314-652-5555

Montana

ACLU of Montana
P.O. Box 3012
Billings, MT 59103
406-248-1086

Montana Legal Services
2822 3rd Ave., N., Suite B12
Billings, MT 59101

Youth Court Defender Office
208 W. Park
Butte, MT 59701
406-792-9141

Montana Legal Services Association
510 First Ave. N.
Great Falls, MT 59401

Montana Legal Services Association
126 3rd St.
Harve, MT 59501

Juvenile Defender
2225 11th Ave., Suite 21
Helena, MT 59601

Flathead County Public Defender
30 Fifth St. E.
Kalispell, MT 59901
406-755-6500

Montana Legal Services Association
519 Main St.
Miles City, MT 59301

Nebraska

Nebraska Civil Liberties Union
511 Anderson Bldg.
P.O. Box 81455
Lincoln, NB 68501
402-476-8091

Legal Services
800 Anderson Bldg.
Lincoln, NB 68508

Public Defender's Office
555 S. 10 St.
Lincoln, NB 68508
402-471-7631

Nevada

Nevada State Public Defender
Capitol Complex
Carson City, NV 89710
702-885-4880

Clark County Public Defender
Juvenile Office
3401 E. Bonanza Rd.
Las Vegas, NV 89101
702-649-3611

Clark County Legal Services
2031 McDaniel St.
N. Las Vegas, NV 89030

ACLU of Nevada
2437 Westfield Ave.
Reno, NV 89509
702-356-6279

New Hampshire

New Hampshire Civil Liberties Union
11 S. Main
Concord, NH 03301
603-225-3080

New Jersey

ACLU of New Jersey
Camden Office
501 Cooper St.
Camden, NJ 08120
609-365-3796

Camden Regional Legal Services, Inc.
326 Market St.
Camden, NJ 08102

Legal Service Corporation
123 Main St.
Flemington, NJ 08822

ACLU of New Jersey
38 Walnut St.
Newark, NJ 07102
201-642-2084

Office of the Public Defender
1180 Raymond Blvd.
Newark, NJ 07102

Department of the Public Advocate
Child Abuse Section
520 E. State St.
Trenton, NJ 08625
609-292-0220

New Mexico

ACLU of New Mexico
1330 San Pedro Dr., N.E., Rm. 110
Albuquerque, NM 87110
505-266-5915

Legal Services Bureau
600 Second St., N.W.
Albuquerque, NM 87102

Northern New Mexico
P.O. Box 756
520 Camino Del Pueblo
Bernalillo, NM 87004

Cliff Rees
New Mexico Legal Services
The Onate Bldg.
Espanola, NM 87532

DNA Peoples Legal Services
P.O. Box 116, Crownpoint
Navajo Nation, NM 87313

New Mexico Public Defender Department
215 W. San Francisco St.
Santa Fe, NM 87501
505-827-5344

Community Law Center
P.O. Box 2328
Santa Fe, NM 87501

New York

New York State Defenders Association, Inc.
150 State St.
Albany, NY 12207
518-465-3524

Cornell Legal Aid
Myron Talor Hall
Ithaca, NY 14853

New York Civil Liberties Union
84 Fifth Ave., Suite 300
New York, NY 10011
212-924-7800

The Legal Aid Society
Juvenile Rights Division
15 Park Row, 21st Fl.
New York, NY 10038
212-619-3890

The Legal Aid Society
Juvenile Rights
175 Remsen St.
Brooklyn, NY 11201
212-237-7900

The Legal Aid Society
Juvenile Rights

900 Sheridan Ave.
Bronx, NY 10451
212–681–1701

The Legal Aid Society
Juvenile Rights
60 Lafayette St.
New York, NY 10013
212–577–3586

The Legal Aid Society
Juvenile Rights
90–04 161st St.
Jamaica, NY 11432
212–291–1500

The Legal Aid Society
Juvenile Rights
42 Richmond Terrace
St. George, SI, NY 10301
212–981–0219

National Conference of Black Lawyers
Juvenile Defense
126 W. 119 St.
New York, NY 10026
212–864–4000

Advocates for Children of New York, Inc.
29–28 41st Ave.
Long Island City, NY 11101
212–729–8866

Covenant House
460 41st St.
New York, NY 10036
212–613–0349

Community Action for Legal Services, Inc.
335 Broadway
New York, NY 10013
212–431–7200

Legal Aid Society of Nassau County
33 Willis Ave.
Mineola, NY 11501
516–294–2600

Franklin County Public Defender's Office
8 Harrison Place
P.O. Box 46
Malone, NY 12953
518-483-2631

Public Defender Office of Dutchess
28 Market St.
Poughkeepsie, NY 12601
914-485-9730

Legal Aid Society of Rochester, Inc.
65 Broad St.
Rochester, NY 14614
716–232–4090

Statewide Youth Avd. Inc.
429 Powers Bldg.
Rochester, NY 14614
716–454–5419

Onondaga County
Legal Services
2121 S. State Ct.
Syracuse, NY 13205

Essex County Assigned Counsel Program
P.O. Box 305
Ticonderoga, NY 12883
518–585–6756

North Carolina

North Carolina
Civil Liberties Union
P.O. Box 3094
Greensboro, NC 27402
919–273–1641

North State Legal Services
P.O. Box 246
Pittsboro, NC 27312

North Dakota

Missouri Valley Chapter of ACLU
P.O. Box 2463
Bismarck, ND 58501

Red River Valley Chapter of ACLU
717 Cherry St.
Grand Forks, ND 58201

Ward County Chapter of ACLU
Political Science Division
Minot State College
Minot, ND 58701

Ohio

Stark County Legal Aid Society
306 N. Market Ave.
Canton, OH 44702

Greater Cleveland Chapter ACLU
1223 W. 6th St., 2nd Fl.
Cleveland, OH 44113
216–781–6276

Juvenile Division
Public Defender Office
Marion Bldg.
1276 W. Third St.
Cleveland, OH 44113

Street Law Program
Cleveland Marshall College of Law
18th and Euclid Ave.
Cleveland, OH 44115

University Legal Center
Case Western Reserve University
1901 Ford Dr.
Cleveland, OH 44106
216–386–2766

Institute for Child Advocacy
2800 Euclid Ave.
Cleveland, OH 44115

Legal Aid Society of Cleveland
1223 W. 6 St.
Cleveland, OH 44113

Cleveland Legal Aid
3408 Loraine Ave.
Cleveland, OH 44113

Free Legal Clinic
Safe Space Station
Runaway Youth Services
12321 Euclid Ave.
Cleveland, OH
216–421–2000

Legal Aid Society of Cincinnati
901 Elm St.
Cincinnati, OH 45202

ACLU of Ohio
360 S. Third St., Suite 150
Columbus, OH 43215
614-228-8951

Franklin County Public Defender
400 S. Front St.
Columbus, OH 43215
614–462–3690

Ohio Legal Rights Service
8 E. Long St., 6th Fl.
Columbus, OH 43215
614–466–7264

Legal Aid Society of Dayton
117 S. Main St., Rm. 525
Dayton, OH 45402

Office of the Public Defender
10 E. Pine St.
Mount Vernon, OH 43050

Huron County Public Defender
30 E. Seminary St.
Norwalk, OH 44857
419–668–3702

Lake County Public Defender Office
270 E. Main St., #50
Painesville, OH 44077
216–357–5777

College of Law Legal Clinic
College of Law
2801 W. Bancroft St.
Toledo, OH 43606

Youngstown Chapter
112 W. Commerce St.
Youngstown, OH 44503

Southeastern Ohio Legal Services
333 Market St.
Zanesville, OH 43701

Oklahoma

ACLU of Oklahoma
P.O. Box 799
Oklahoma City, OK 73101
405-524-8511

Legal Aid of W. Oklahoma
980 Leonhardt Pl.
(228 Robert S. Kerr)
Oklahoma City, OK 73102

Grain County Legal Aid
Society, Inc.
P.O. Box 924
Stillwell, OK 74960

Tulsa County Public Defender
Juvenile Court Division
315 S. 25 W. Ave.
Tulsa, OK 74127
918-584-2561

Oregon

Public Defender Services of Lane
County, Inc.
1025 Willamette St., #200
Eugene, OR 97401
503-484-2611

ACLU of Oregon
601 Willamette Bldg.
534 S.W. 3 Ave.
Portland, OR 97204
503-227-3186

Office of the Public Defender
2285 Court St.
Baker, OR 97814
503-523-6414

Oregon Legal Services Corporation
Juvenile Rights Project
408 S.W. 2nd, Suite 412
Portland, OR 97204
503-242-1411

Community Law Project
1628 S.E. Ankeny
Portland, OR 97241
503-233-4747

Pennsylvania

Delaware County
Legal Assistance, Inc.
410 Welsh St.
Chester, PA 19013

Bucks County Public Defender
Court House, 6th Fl.
Doylestown, PA 18901
215-348-2911

Laurel Legal Services
320 Market St.
Kittanning, PA 16201

Dauphin County Public Defender's
Office
112 Market St.
Blackstone Bldg., 8th Fl.
Harrisburg, PA 17101
717-255-2746

Pennsylvania Legal Services
Blackstone Bldg.
112 Market St., 6th Fl.
Harrisburg, PA 17109

Public Defender's Office
Blair County Courthouse, Annex #1
Holidaysburg, PA 16648
814-695-5541, Ext. 380

Central Pennsylvania
Legal Services
Stevens House
10 South Prince St.
Lancaster, PA 17603

Keystone Legal Services, Inc.
10 South Grand St.
Lewistown, PA 17044

Public Defender of Delaware County
Juvenile Division Courthouse
Fronefield Bldg.
Media, PA 19063

ACLU of Pennsylvania
Juniper Bldg.
1324 Walnut St.
Philadelphia, PA 19107
215–735–7103

Juvenile Law Center of Philadelphia
112 South 16 St., Suite 703
Philadelphia, PA 19102
215–563–1933

Defender Association of Philadelphia
121 North Broad St.
Philadelphia, PA 19107
215–568–3190

Legal Services Corporation
101 N. 33 St., Rm. 404
Philadelphia, PA 19119

Child Advocacy Unit
1801 Vine St., Rm. 234
Philadelphia, PA 19103

Public Defender of Children County
204 E. Water St.
Lock Haven, PA 17745
717–748–4154

Montgomery County Public Defender
Montgomery Court House
Sweden and Main Streets
Norristown, PA 19401
215–278–3295

ACLU of Pennsylvania
Greater Pittsburgh Chapter
237 Oakland Ave.
Pittsburgh, PA 15213
412–681–7736

Neighborhood Legal Services
Child Advocacy Unit
300 South Craig St.
Pittsburgh, PA 15213
412–687–5800

Public Defender's Office of Allegheny County
Penn-Liberty Plaza
1520 Penn Ave.
Pittsburgh, PA 15222
412–355–5801

Pennsylvania Child Advocate
700 Fifth Ave.
Pittsburgh, PA 15219

Public Defender Office
Schuylkill County Courthouse
Pottsville, PA 17901
717–622–5570

Tioga County Public Defender's Office
118 Main St.
Wellsboro, PA 16901
717–724–1906

Luzerne County Public Defender
Luzerne County Courthouse
Wilkes-Barre, PA 18711
717–825–1754

Public Defender's Office
Lycoming County Court House
Williamsport, PA 17701
717–327–2367

Rhode Island

Rhode Island Civil Liberties Union
212 Union St., Rm. 408
Providence, RI 02903
401–831–7171

South Carolina

ACLU of South Carolina
533–B Harden St.

Columbia, SC 29205
803–799–5151

Alston Wilkes Advocacy for Youth
2215 Devine St.
P.O. Box 363
Columbia, SC 29202
803–799–4807

Public Defender Corporation of Darlington County
P.O. Box 201
109 E. College Ave.
Hartsville, SC 29550
803–332–3331

South Dakota

Public Defender's Office
Pennington County Courthouse
Rapid City, SD 57701
605–394–2181

South Dakota National Chapter—ACLU
P.O. Box 95
Sioux Falls, SD 57101
605–331–2154

Minnehaha County Public Defender
413 North Main
Sioux Falls, SD 57102
605–335–4243

Tennessee

Legal Services of Upper East Tennessee, Inc.
325 W. Walnut St.
Johnson City, TN 37601
615–928–8311

Memphis Area Office of ACLU
81 Madison Bldg., Suite 1501
Memphis, TN 38103
713–869–0265

Memphis Area Legal Services
Juvenile Services
Dermon Bldg., Suite 316
46 N. 3rd St.
Memphis, TN 38103

ACLU of Tennessee
P.O. Box 120160
Nashville, TN 37212
615–383–9525

Legal Services of
Nashville and Middle TN, Inc.
1512 Parkway Towers
404 James Robertson Pkwy.
Nashville, TN 37219

Public Defender of Metropolitan Nashville and Davidson County
Juvenile Office
210 Metro Howard Office Bldg.
Nashville, TN 37210
615–259–5546

Vanderbilt Legal Aid Society
Vanderbilt University Law School
Nashville, TN 37240
615–322–6630

Texas

Texas Civil Liberties Union
600 W. 7 St.
Austin, TX 78701
512–477–5849

University of Texas School of Law Clinical Program
727 E. 26 St.
Austin, TX 78705
512–471–5151

Travis County Juvenile Defender
P.O. Box 1748
Austin, TX 78767
512–473–9590

Child and Youth Project
2710 Stemmons Freeway
Dallas, TX 75207

Dallas Child and Youth Project
University of Texas
5323 Harry Hines Blvd.
Dallas, TX 75235

Family Law Unit
100 Main St.
Fort Worth, TX 76102

Houston Chapter of ACLU
1256 W. Gray
Houston, TX 77019
713-524-5925

Gulf Coast Legal Foundation
Suite 400 2601 Main
Houston, TX 77002

Legal Services
1601 Metro Tower
Lubbock, TX 79401

Utah

DNA Legal Services
Box 488
Mexican Hat, UT 84531

Utah Legal Services
453 24th St.
Ogden, UT 84401

ACLU of Utah
632 Judge Bldg.
8 E. Broadway
Salt Lake City, UT 84111
801-521-9289

Utah Legal Services, Inc.
Office at Juvenile Court
3522 S. 700 W.
Salt Lake City, UT 84111

Utah Legal Services
637 E. 4 S.
Salt Lake City, UT 84102
801-328-8891

Vermont

Office of the Public Defender
S. Winooski Ave.
Burlington, VT 05041

Vermont Legal Aid, Inc.
180 Church St.
P.O. Box 562
Burlington, VT 05401

Vermont Civil Liberties Union
43 State St.
Montpelier, VT 05602
802-223-6304

Office of the Juvenile Defender
State Office Bldg.
141 Main St.
Montpelier, VT 05602
802-828-3168

Virginia

Fairfax Legal Aid Society
4029 Chain Bridge Rd.
Fairfax, VA 22030

Virginia Legal Aid Society
P.O. Box 427
Lynchburg, VA 24505

ACLU of Virginia
112A North 7 St.
Richmond, VA 23219
804-644-8022

Youth Advocacy Clinic
University of Richmond
School of Law
Richmond, VA 23173
804-285-6370

Washington

Island County Defenders
Association
P.O. Box 520

Coupeville, WA 98239
206–678–5303

Youth Services of Kittitas County
P.O. Box 523
Ellensburg, WA 98926

Northwest Intertribal Court System
P.O. Box 676
LaConner, WA 98257
206–466–3163

Evergreen Legal Services
Cowlitz-Wahkiakum Office
1417 15th St., #8
Longview, WA 98632

Evergreen Legal Services
Institutional Legal Services Project
P.O. Box A
Medical Lake, WA 99022

Clallam-Jefferson Public Defender
206 South Lincoln
Port Angeles, WA 98362
206–452–3307

ACLU of Washington
2101 Smith Tower
Seattle, WA 98104
206–624–2180

Juvenile Law Office
1500 E. Adler
Seattle, WA 98122

Seattle-King Defender Association
Juvenile Division
1350 E. Fir St.
Seattle, WA 98122
206–323–6810

Spokane County Public Defender's Office
Spokane County Courthouse
Spokane, WA 99260
509–456–4246

Pierce County Department of Assigned Council
945 Market St., Rm. 334
Tacoma, WA 98402
206–593–4787

West Virginia

West Virginia Civil Liberties Union
P.O. Box 1509
Charleston, WV 25301

West Virginia Public Legal Services
1900 Washington St. E., Rm. A–217
Charleston, WV 25305
304–348–3905

West Virginia Legal Services
119–½ Third St.
Elkins, WV 26241

West Virginia Legal Services
P.O. Box 689
Lewisburg, WV 24901

Juvenile Advocates, Inc.
138–½ Chestnut St.
Morgantown, WV 26505
304–291–5156

West Virginia Legal Services
207 Main St.
Webster Springs, WV 26288

Appalachian Research and Defense Fund
P.O. Box 1519
Williamson, WV 25661

Wisconsin

Youth Policy and Law Center, Inc.
30 W. Mifflin St., Rm. 904
Madison, WS 53703
608–263–5533

Wisconsin Civil Liberties Union
983 N. Water St., Suite 800
Milwaukee, WS 53202
414–272–4032

State Public Defender
Juvenile Division
1417 North Wauwatosa Ave.
(North 76 St.)
Milwaukee, WS 53213
414–257–7728

Youth Policy and Law Center, Inc.
436 W. Wisconsin Ave., Rm. 306
Milwaukee, WS 53203
414–224–9508

Legal Aid Society Public Defender
Juvenile Division
1417 N. 76 St.
Wauwatosa, WS 53213

Legal Aid Society of Milwaukee
Guardian Ad Litem Office
Children's Court Center
10201 Watertown Plank Rd.
Wauwatosa, WS 53226
414–257–7159

Wyoming

Laramie Chapter of ACLU
418 S. 12
Laramie, WY 82070
307–745–3729

APPENDIX B

Age of Majority

	Age of Minority	Age Below Which Young People May Be Subject to Juvenile Court Jurisdiction for Criminal Conduct
Ala.	19	18
Alaska	18	18
Ariz.	18	18
Ark.	18	18
Calif.	18	18
Colo.	18	18
Conn.	18	16
Del.	18	16
D.C.	18	18
Fl.	18	18
Ga.	18	17
Hawaii	18	18
Idaho	18	18
Ill.	18	17
Ind.	18	18
Iowa	18	18
Kans.	18	18
Ky.	18	18
La.	18	17
Maine	18	18
Md.	18	18
Mass.	18	17
Mich.	18	17
Minn.	18	18
Miss.	21[a]	18
Mo.	18	17
Mont.	18	18

Nebr.	19	18
Nev.	18	18
N.H.	18	18
N.J.	18	18
N.Mex.	18	18
N.Y.	18	16
N.C.	18	16
N.Dak.	18	18
Ohio	18	18
Okla.	18	18
Ore.	18	18
Pa.	21[b]	18
R.I.	18	18
S.C.	18	17
S.Dak.	18	18
Tenn.	18	18
Tex.	18	17
Utah	18	18
Vt.	18	16 (delinquency) 18 (supervision)
Va.	18	18
Wash.	18	18
W.Va.	18	18
Wis.	18	18
Wyo.	19	19

[a] 18 to sign contracts of personal property.
[b] 18 for many activities.

APPENDIX C

Legal Age for Sale of Beer, Wine, or Liquors to Minors

	Beer	Wine	Liquor
Ala.	19	19	19
Alaska	19	19	19
Ariz.	19	19	19
Ark.	21	21	21
Calif.	21	21	21
Colo.	21	21	21
Conn.	19	19	19
Del.	20	20	20
D.C.	18	18	21
Fl.	19	19	19
Ga.	19	19	19
Hawaii	18	18	18
Idaho	19	19	19
Ill.	21	21	21
Ind.	21	21	21
Iowa	19	19	19
Kans.	18	18	18
Ky.	21	21	21
La.	18	18	18
Maine	20	20	20
Md.	21[a]	21	21
Mass.	20	20	20
Mich.	21	21	21
Minn.	19	19	19
Miss.	21	21	21
Mo.	21	21	21
Mont.	19	19	19
Nebr.	20	20	20
Nev.	21	21	21
N.H.	20	20	20

N.J.	21	21	21
N. Mex.	18	18	18
N.Y.	19	19	19
N.C.	18	18	21
N.D.	21	21	21
Ohio	19	21	21
Okla.	18 (if not over 3.2%)	21	21
Oreg.	21	21	21
Pa.	21	21	21
R.I.	20	20	20
S.C.	18	18	21
S. Dak.[b]	18 (if not over 3.2%)	21	21
Tenn.	18	18	18
Tex.	19	19	19
Utah	21	21	21
Vt.	18	18	18
Va.	18 (on premises) 19 (off premises)	21	21
Wash.	21	21	21
W. Va.	18	18	18
Wis.[c]	18	18	18
Wyo.	19	19	19

---

[a] If born after July 1, 1964.
[b] Unless in presence of parents, guardian, or spouse.
[c] Any age if accompanied by parent or guardian.

APPENDIX D

Age of Consent for Medical and Sex-Related Health Care

Ages at which state legislation or court decisions have specifically affirmed the right of individuals to give consent for their own medical treatment as of January 1983[a]

State	May Consent for Medical Care in General			May Consent for:		
	No Limitation	If married, emancipated or parent	In Emergency	Contraception	Pregnancy-connected care	VD care
Ala.	14	E,[i] M	X	14	X	X
Alaska	18	E,[e] M	X	X	X	X
Ariz.	18	E, M	X[j]	E, M	E, M	X
Ark.	X[b, d]	E, M	X	X[b, 1]	X[m]	X
Cal.	18	15 E,[f] M	X	X	X	12
Colo.	18	15 E,[f] M	18	X	E, M	X
Conn.	18	E, M	18	E	E, M	X[q]
Del.	18	E, M	18	12	12	12
D.C.	18	E, M	X	X[c]	X[c]	X

Ga.	18	M	X	XF	X	X
Hawaii	18	18	18	14	14	14
Idaho	18	18	18	X[d]	18	14
Ill.	18	M[f]	X	X[h]	X	12
Ind.	18	E, M	X	18	18	X
Iowa	18	E, M	X	18[l]	18	X
Kansas	18	18	16	16	X	X
Ky.	18	M, E, P	X	X	X	X
La.	18[s]	M	X	F	X	X
Maine	18[r]	E	X	X[r]	18	X
Md.	18	M, P	X	X	X	X
Mass.	18	M, E, P	X	X[d]	X	X
Mich.	18	18	18	18[l]	18	X
Minn.	18	M, E, P[e]	X	X	X	X
Miss.	X[d]	M, E, P	X	X[o]	X	X
Mo.	18	M, E, P	X	X[f]	X	X
Mont.	E, 18[i]	M, E, P	X	F[h]	X	X
Nebr.	19	M		19[k]	19	X
Nev.	X[e, r]	E, M, P	18	X[d]	X[d]	X

N.H.	18	E, M	X	18	18	14
N.J.	18	E, M	18	18	X	X
N.Mex.	18	E, M	X[j]	18[l]	X[p]	X
N.Y.	18	E, M, P	X	X	X[d]	X
N.C.	18	E, M	X	X	X	X
N.D.	18	E, M	18	18	18	14
Ohio	X[d]	18	X[d]	X[d, l]	X[d]	X
Okla.	18	E, M	X	M, P, E[e]	X	X
Oreg.	15	M	X	X[m]	15[m]	X
Pa.	18	E,[i] M	X	X[r]	X	X
R.I.	16	M	16, M	18	18	X
S.C.	16[t]	E, M	X	X[g]	X[g]	X[g]
S.D.	18	E, M	18	18[k]	18	X
Tenn.	18	18	18	X[o]	18	X
Tex.	18	16 E, M	X	16	X[m]	X
Utah	18	M	X	18	X	X
Vt.	18	E, M	18	18	18	X
Va.	18	E, M	14	X[c]	X	X
Wash.	18	E	18	18	18	14

W.Va.	18	16 E	X		18[l]	18	X
Wis.	18	E, M	18		18	18	X
Wyo.	19	19	19		19[l]	19	X

Note: X = any age; M = married; F = female; E = emancipated

a. The fact that no affirmative legislation, court decision, or attorney general's opinion has been found in a particular state does not mean that some or even all categories of minors below the ages shown in the table do not have the right to obtain some or all medical services on their own consent.
b. Excluding voluntary sterilization if under 18 and unmarried.
c. Excluding voluntary sterilization.
d. If mature enough to understand the nature and consequences of the treatment.
e. Emancipated defined as living apart from parents and managing own financial affairs.
f. And/or pregnant.
g. Whenever such services are deemed "necessary" by the physician.
h. If "professes" to be pregnant.
i. Emancipated defined as a high school graduate, a parent, or pregnant.
j. If no parent available, others may consent *in loco parentis*.
k. Only for treatment of venereal disease.
l. Comprehensive family planning law permits (or does not exclude) services to minors without parental consent.
m. Excluding abortion.
n. If referred by clergyman, physician, or Planned Parenthood or if "failure to provide such services would create a serious health hazard."
o. If referred by clergyman, physician, family planning clinic, school or institution of higher learning, or any state or local government agency.
p. Examination only.
q. In public health agencies, public or private hospitals, or clinics.
r. If married or pregnant or "may suffer, in the opinion of the physician, probable health hazards if such services are not provided." Surgical services excluded.
s. If minor "is or believes himself to be afflicted with an illness or disease."
t. Except for operation essential to health or life.

APPENDIX E

Age at Which Young People May Marry

	Without Parent Consent		Court Permission Required	
	Male	Female	Male	Female
Ala.	18	18		
Alaska	18	18		
Ariz.	18	18	Under 16	Under 16
Ark.	18	18		
Calif.	18	18		
Colo.	18	18	Under 16	Under 16
Conn.	18	18	Under 16	Under 16
Del.	18	16		
D.C.	18	18		
Fla.	18	18		
Ga.	18	18		
Hawaii	16	16	15–16	15–16
Idaho	18	18	Under 16	Under 16
Ill.	18	18		
Ind.	18	18		
Iowa	18	18	16–18	16–18
Kansas	18	18	Under 18	Under 18
Ky.	18	18		
La.	18	18		
Maine	18	18	Under 16	Under 16
Md.	18	18		
Mass.	18	18		
Mich.	18	18		
Minn.	18	18	16–18	16–18
Miss.	17	15	Under 17	Under 15
Mo.	18	18	Under 15	Under 15
Mont.	18	18	16–18	16–18
Nebr.	19	19		

Nev.	18	18	Under 16	Under 16
N.H.	18	18	Under 18	Under 18
N.J.	18	18	Under 16	Under 16
N.Mex.	18	18	Under 16	Under 16
N.Y.	18	18		14–16
N.C.	18	18		
N.Dak.	18	18		
Ohio	18	18		If pregnant
Okla.	18	18		If pregnant
Oreg.	18	18		
Pa.	18	18	Under 16	Under 16
R.I.	18	16	Under 18	Under 16
S.C.	18	18		
S.Dak.	18	18		
Tenn.	18	18		
Tex.	18	18	Under 14	Under 14
Utah	18	18		
Vt.	18	18	Under 16	Under 16
Va.	18	18		
Wash.	18	18	Under 17	Under 17
W.Va.	18	18	Under 16	Under 16
Wis.	18	18		
Wyo.	19	19	Under 16	Under 16

APPENDIX F

Age Under Which Tobacco Products Are Permitted

	Age	Action Prohibited
Ala.	Minor	Sale, barter, exchange, or gift
Alaska	16	Give, sell or exchange
Ariz.	Minor	Furnish
Ark.	18	Give, barter or furnish
Calif.	18	Sell, give or furnish
Colo.	(No applicable law)	
Conn.	16	Sell, give or deliver
Del.	17	Sell, give or purchase
D.C.	16	Sell, give, furnish
Fla.	Minor	Sell, barter, furnish, give
Ga.	(No applicable law)	
Hawaii	15	Sell or furnish
Idaho	18	Sell, give or furnish
Ill.	18	Sell, buy or furnish
Ind.	13	Sell
Iowa	18	Sell, barter or give
Kans.	18	Sell
Ky.	(No applicable law)	
La.	(No applicable law)	
Maine	16	Sell, furnish, give away
Md.	15	Sell, barter, give (unless authorized by parent)
Mass.	18	Sell cigarettes
	16	Sell or give snuff or tobacco
Mich.	18	Sells, gives to or furnishes
Minn.	18	Furnishes
Miss.	18	Sell, barter, deliver or give
Mo.	(No applicable law)	
Mont.	18	Sell
Nebr.	18	Sells, gives or furnishes
Nev.	18	Sell, give or offer

N.H.	(No applicable law)	
N.J.	16	Sells, gives or furnishes
N.Mex.	(No applicable law)	
N.Y.	18	Sell
N.C.	(No applicable law)	
N.Dak.	Minor	Sell, furnish or procure
Ohio	(No applicable law)	
Okla.	18	Furnish, sell or give
Oreg.	18	Sell
Pa.	16	Purchase or furnish
R.I.	16	Sell, give or deliver
S.C.	18	Supply, sell, furnish, give or supply
S.Dak.	18	Sell or give
Tenn.	18	Sell, give, furnish or procure
Tex.	16	Sell, give or barter
Utah	19	Sell, give or furnish
Vt.	17	Sell or give
Va.	(No applicable law)	
Wash.	18	Sell or give
W.Va.	18	Sell, give or furnish
Wis.	(No applicable law)	
Wyo.	(No applicable law)	

APPENDIX G

Age at Which Females May Consent to Sexual Intercourse

	Age	Qualification & Exceptions
Ala.	16	If female is over 12, male may not be 2 years older than female
Alaska	16	When male is 16 or older
Ariz.	18	
Ark.	16	If female is over 14, male may not be over 18
Calif.	18	
Colo.	15	
Conn.	No law	
Del.	16	
D.C.	16	
Fla.	18	Male or female, if chaste
Ga.	14	
Hawaii	14	
Idaho	18	
Ill.	18	Male or female, other partner must be 14 or older
Ind.	16	
Iowa	16	If 14 or 15, partner may not be 16 or older
Kan.	16	
Ky.	16	
La.	17	If female is 12-16, male may not be over 17 or greater than 2 years older
Maine	14	Male may not be 5 years older if female is 14–16
Md.	14	Other partner may not be 4 years older
Mass.	16	
Mich.	16	
Minn.	16	If female 13–16 male may not be more than 2 years older

Miss.	12	But no female under 18 of previously chaste character can consent if male over 18
Mo.	16	But cannot consent at 16 if male 17 or over
Mont.	14	But if 14–16, cannot consent if other person is 3 or more years older
Nebr.	16	Male may not be 19 or over if female under 16
Nev.	16	Male may not be 18 or over if female under 16
N.H.	13	
N.J.	16	If female is 13–16, male may not be 4 years older
N.Mex.	13	If 13–16, can't consent to person in position of authority over child
N.Y.	17	
N.C.	12	Male may not be 4 or more years older
N.Dak.	15	
Ohio	15	Male may not be 18 or older
Okla.	16	If female is over 14, male may not be over 18
Oreg.	18	If 16–17, male may not be 3 years older than female
Pa.	16	Male must be 16 or older
R.I.	13	
S.C.	14	
S.Dak.	15	
Tenn.	18	But 14, if female is bawd, lewd, or kept
Tex.	17	But 14, if not a virgin
Utah	14	
Vt.	16	
Va.	13	
Wash.	16	If female is under 11, male may not be over 13; if female is 11–14, male may not be over 16; if female is 14–16, male may not be over 18
W.Va.	16	Male may not be over 16; unless both consent and female is over 11 and male is less than 16
Wis.	15	
Wyo.	16	

APPENDIX H

Age at Which Young People May Vote in State Elections & Serve on State Juries

	Vote	Juries
Ala.	19	19
Alaska	19	19
Ariz.	18	18
Ark.	18	18
Calif.	18	18
Colo.	18	18
Conn.	18	18
Del.	18	18
D.C.	18	18
Fla.	18	21
Ga.	18	21
Hawaii	18	18
Idaho	18	18
Ill.	18	18
Ind.	18	18
Iowa	18	18
Kan.	18	18
Ky.	18	18
La.	18	18
Maine	18	18
Md.	18	18
Mass.	18	18
Mich.	18	18
Minn.	18	18
Miss.	18	21
Mo.	18	21
Mont.	18	18
Nebr.	18	19

Nev.	18	18
N.H.	18	18
N.J.	18	18
N.Mex.	18	18
N.Y.	18	18
N.C.	18	18
N.Dak.	18	18
Ohio	18	18
Okla.	18	18
Oreg.	18	18
Pa.	18	18
R.I.	18	21
S.C.	18	18
S.Dak.	18	18
Tenn.	18	18
Tex.	18	18
Utah	21	21
Vt.	18	18
Va.	18	18
Wash.	18	18
W.Va.	18	18
Wis.	18	18
Wyo.	18	"Adult"

APPENDIX I

Age Under Which School Is Compulsory

Ala.	16	
Alaska	16	
Ariz.	16	(14 if employed)
Ark.	16	
Calif.	16	
Colo.	16	
Conn.	16	(14 if employed)
Del.	16	
D.C.	16	(14 if completed eighth grade and is regularly employed)
Fla.	16	
Ga.	16	
Hawaii		(school year during which one becomes 18 on or before Dec. 31) (15 if employed and legally excused)
Idaho	16	
Ill.	16	(except persons necessarily employed with permission of school board and superintendent; in some districts employed students must also attend school 8 hours each week)
Ind.	16	
Iowa	16	(14 if employed)
Kans.	16	
Ky.	16	
La.	16	
Maine	17	
Md.	16	
Mass.	16	
Mich.	16	
Minn.	16	
Miss.	13	
Mo.	16	

Mont.	16	(or completion of eighth grade)
Nebr.	16	
Nev.	17	
N.H.	16	
N.J.	16	
N.Mex.	18	(or graduation or 16 and excused by local school board)
N.Y.	16	(except 17 in New York City) (15 if student cannot profit from further education and is working full-time)
N.C.	16	
N.Dak.	16	
Ohio	18	(or graduation)
Okla.	18	(or graduation)
Oreg.	18	[or graduation (16 if employed)]
Pa.	17	(or graduation)
R.I.	16	
S.C.	16	[or graduation (unless married or pregnant or completed eighth grade and employed with court determination that employment is necessary)]
S.Dak.	16	
Tenn.	16	
Tex.	17	
Utah	18	[or graduation (or completion of eighth grade when employment is necessary to support family)]
Vt.	16	[or graduation (or completion of tenth grade)]
Va.	16	
Wash.	18	(15 if employed or determination by superintendent of proficiency in grades 1–9)
W.Va.	16	(or graduation)
Wis.	16	(18 if vocational school)
Wyo.	16	(or completion of eighth grade)

APPENDIX J

Age Under Which Sale or Distribution of Pornographic Materials is Prohibited

Ala.	18
Alaska	No provision for minors
Ariz.	Minors
Ark.	17
Calif.	Minors
Colo.	18
Conn.	17
Del.	17
D.C.	17
Fla.	17
Ga.	18
Hawaii	Minors
Idaho	18
Ill.	18
Ind.	18
Iowa	Minors
Kans.	18
Ky.	Minors
La.	17
Maine	Minors
Md.	18
Mass.	18
Mich.	18
Minn.	18
Miss.	18
Mo.	18
Mont.	18
Nebr.	19
Nev.	18
N.H.	18
N.J.	18

N.Mex.	18
N.Y.	17
N.D.	18
N.Dak.	Minors
Ohio	No provision for minors
Okla.	No provision for minors
Oreg.	18
Pa.	17
R.I.	18
S.C.	16
S.Dak.	18
Tenn.	18
Tex.	17
Utah	18
Vt.	18
Va.	18
Wash.	18
W.Va.	18
Wis.	18
Wyo.	No provision for minors

APPENDIX K

Ages at Which Driver's License and/or Training Leading to License are Permitted

	Operator's License Available at Age:	Learner's Permit or Junior License	Driver's Education Necessary if Under:	Parental Permission Necessary if Under:
Ala.	16	15		16
Alaska	16	14		18
Ariz.	16	15		18
Ark.	16	14		18
Calif.	16	15	18	18
Colo.	16	15½	16	18
Conn.	18	16	18	18
Del.	15	15 and 10 months	18	
D.C.	16			
Fla.	16	15		18
Ga.	16	15		18
Hawaii	17	15		20
Idaho	16	14	16	18
Ill.	16	15	18	18
Ind.	16 and one month	15	16½	18
Iowa	16	14	18	18
Kans.	16	14		16
Ky.	16			18
La.	15		17	18
Maine	15	15	17	18
Md.	16	15	18	18
Mass.	18	16½	17	18
Mich.	16	14	17	18
Minn.	16	15	18	18
Miss.	15	14		17

Mo.	16	15	16	
Mont.	15	14½	16	18
Nebr.	16	15		19
Nev.	16	15½		18
N.H.	16	15	18	18
N.J.	17	16	17	
N.Mex.	16	14	15	18
N.Y.	17	16	18	17
N.C.	16	15	18	18
N.Dak.	16	14	16	18
Ohio	18	16		18
Okla.	16	14	16	16
Oreg.	16	15		18
Pa.	17	16	17	18
R.I.	16	16	18	18
S.C.	16	15		18
S.Dak.	16	14		18
Tenn.	16			
Tex.	16	15	18	18
Utah	16	16	18	18
Vt.	18	15	18	18
Va.	16	15 and 8 months	18	18
Wash.	16	15½	18	18
W.Va.	18	16		18
Wis.	16	14	18	18
Wyo.	16	15		18

Selected Bibliography

Davis, S., *Rights of Juveniles: The Juvenile Justice System* (Clark Boardman, New York, 1983).

Fox, S., *Juvenile Courts in a Nutshell*. 3d ed. (West Pub. Co., St. Paul, 1983).

Harvard Law Review, "Developments in the Law—The Constitution and the Family." vol. 93, no. 6. (Harvard Law Review Association, Cambridge, 1980), pp. 1157-1383.

The Legal Status of Adolescents 1980 (Department of Health and Human Services, Washington, 1981).

Piersma, P. et al., *Law and Tactics in Juvenile Cases*. 3d ed. (American Law Institute, Philadelphia, 1977).

Sussman, A., and Guggenheim, M., *The Rights of Parents* (Avon, New York, 1980).